SPIES
AND
COMMISSARS

SPIES

and

COMMISSARS

THE EARLY YEARS OF THE RUSSIAN REVOLUTION

Robert Service

PUBLICAFFAIRS
New York

Published in 2012 in the United States by PublicAffairs™, a Member of the
Perseus Books Group
Published in 2011 in Great Britain by Macmillan

PublicAffairs books are available at special discounts for bulk purchases in the
U.S. by corporations, institutions, and other organizations. For more information, please contact the Special Markets Department at the Perseus Books
Group, 2300 Chestnut Street, Suite 200, Philadelphia, PA 19103, call (800)
810-4145, ext. 5000, or e-mail special.markets@perseusbooks.com.

Designed by Timm Bryson
Text set in 11.25 point Arno Pro by the Perseus Books Group

Cataloging-in-Publication data for this book is available from the Library
of Congress.
LCCN 2012932280
ISBN 978-1-61039-140-5 (hardcover)
ISBN 978-1-61039-141-2 (e-book)
First Edition
10 9 8 7 6 5 4 3 2 1

To Adele, with love and thanks

CONTENTS

Three: Probings

Four: Stalemate

LIST OF ILLUSTRATIONS

Illustrations can be found after page 218

1. Lenin in deep thought. (© *Getty Images*)
2. Trotsky in his Red Army uniform. (© *Getty Images*)
3. An encounter between German and Russian troops in the neutral zone. (*Hoover Institution Archives*)
4. Living quarters of the peace talks delegations at Brest-Litovsk. (*Hoover Institution Archives*)
5. The peace talks at Brest-Litovsk before Trotsky joined them. (*Topfoto*)
6. Sir George Buchanan. (*National Portrait Gallery*)
7. David Francis. (*St Louis Public Library*)
8. Joseph Noulens. (*Roger-Viollet*)
9. Cheka leaders Felix Dzerzhinski and Yakov Peters. (© *Getty Images*)
10. Leaders of the People's Commissariat of Foreign Affairs abroad in Berlin in 1922. (*Roger-Viollet/Rex*)
11. Bukharin. (*By kind permission of Harry Shukman*)
12. John Reed. (© *Getty Images*)
13. Louise Bryant. (© *Getty Images*)
14. Sylvia Pankhurst. (*By kind permission of Harry Shukman*)
15. A 1919 anti-Spartacist and anti-Bolshevik German poster depicting a Spartacist murdering a family. (© *Getty Images*)
16. A poster offering 10,000 marks for the arrest of Karl Radek. (*By kind permission of Harry Shukman*)
17. The Spartacists get themselves organized in January 1919. (*Hoover Institution Archives*)
18. André Marty. (*By kind permission of Harry Shukman*)

RUSSIA AT WAR AND PEACE, 1917–1918

International frontier

December 1917 demarcation line

Treaty of Brest-Litovsk frontier agreed by Sovnarkom, March 1918

500 kilometres
300 miles

NORWAY

Barents Sea

Murmansk

White Sea

Archangel

Haparanda Tornio

SWEDEN

Dvina

FINLAND

Vologda

Helsinki

Petrograd

Stockholm

Tallinn (Reval)

Yaroslavl

Volga

Baltic Sea

Riga

Moscow

Dvinsk

GERMANY

Vistula

Brest-Litovsk

Don

Oder

Warsaw

Kharkov

Kiev

Dnieper

UKRAINE

Rostov-on-Don

Vienna

Danube

Dniester

Budapest

Odessa

AUSTRIA-HUNGARY

Black Sea

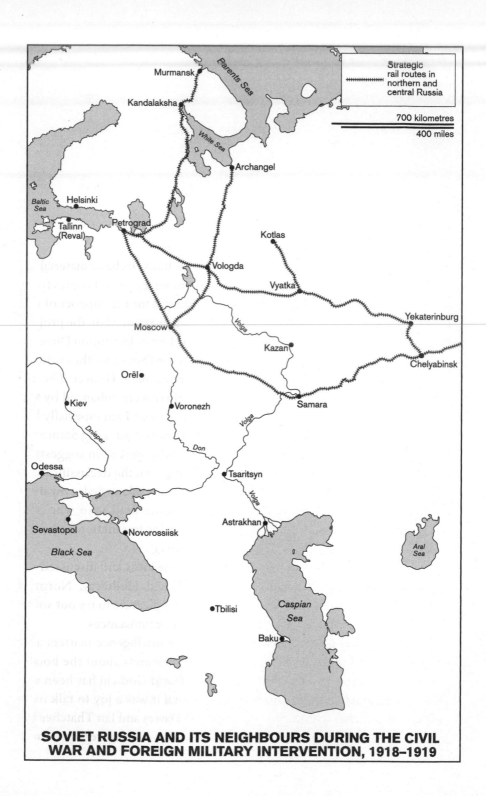

**SOVIET RUSSIA AND ITS NEIGHBOURS DURING THE CIVIL
WAR AND FOREIGN MILITARY INTERVENTION, 1918–1919**

PREFACE

Many people have given generous help with this book. Its basic material on all aspects of Russia and the West in the revolutionary period comes from the Hoover Institution Archives, and I am grateful for the support of the Sarah Scaife Foundation in enabling me to work in Stanford on the project over two whole summers. My thanks also go to Hoover Institution Director John Raisian and Senior Associate Director Richard Sousa for the enthusiasm they have shown for the investigations carried out at Hoover. The exceptional conditions for research and writing there were enhanced by the active co-operation of all the staff in the Archives, and I am especially beholden to Linda Bernard, Carol Leadenham, Lora Soroka, Zbig Stanczyk, Brad Bauer and Lisa Miller. Their efficiency and expertise in suggesting boxes and folders unknown to me and in helping with the declassification of valuable files are appreciated. In that respect I must acknowledge my debt to Julian Evans, UK Consul-General in San Francisco until 2010, who persuaded the UK Foreign and Commonwealth Office to sanction access to some of Robert Bruce Lockhart's papers at Hoover.

Scholars in the San Francisco Bay area gave me ideas and discussed aspects of the research: Robert Conquest, David Holloway, Norman Naimark, Yuri Slezkine and Amir Weiner. It was a pleasure to try out some of the ideas for the book with them in convivial circumstances.

In Britain, Roy Giles shared his expertise on intelligence matters and Simon Sebag Montefiore helped to steady my instincts about the book's argument and orientation. My literary agent David Godwin has been unfailingly supportive about this project. As usual it was a joy to talk over ideas with him. My thanks go, too, to Norman Davies and Ian Thatcher for answering specific questions. Andrew Cook kindly shared several products of his sleuthing in the UK archives about British intelligence in 1918; Harry Shukman did the same with his copies of British official papers on Georgi Chicherin. I am grateful to both Andrew and Harry as well as to Michael Smith for answering questions on various research topics—and to Angelina Gibson for assistance with the Bulgarian language. Thanks are due to John Murphy of the British Broadcasting Corporation, who alerted me to material in Oxford on Allied politics and intelligence while we worked together on a radio programme about the British plot of 1918. Richard Ramage, Administrator and Librarian of the Centre of Russian and Eurasian Studies, was patient and helpful with my frequent enquiries about our library holdings at St Antony's College.

Harry Shukman cheerfully agreed to examine the entire first draft, and his expertise in Moscow and London history are much appreciated. Likewise Katya Andreyev, at short notice, went through the chapters; I had talked with her about several themes and am grateful for her agreeing to look over what I did with the advice. Roland Quinault generously read the draft while on his travels in the US and gave advice on British political history. Georgina Morley, my editor at Macmillan, went through the draft with imaginative care and prompted many amendments of style and content; and I have yet again been very fortunate in working with Peter James as copy-editor. My wife Adele Biagi, above all, looked at the draft not once but twice. Like me, she caught the contagion of interest in British politics and intelligence in the early Soviet period. Her deft, insightful touch with the chapters saved me from innumerable misjudgements and infelicities.

Some last technical points. I have been flexible about transliteration, using a simplified variant of the US Library of Congress scheme. But the conventional renderings of Trotsky, Zinoviev, Benckendorf and others are retained. So too are the 'Anglo-Russian' variants of certain Polish and Latvian names such as Felix Dzerzhinsky and Yakov Peters whenever the individuals were notably Russified in their culture. The names of certain institutions, too, are simplified. For example, the People's Commissariat for Army and Navy Affairs appears as the People's Commissariat for Military Affairs. The book uniformly uses the Gregorian calendar even though the Russians in Russia officially used the older Julian one until January 1918. I recognize that this makes for one big oddity inasmuch as the Bolshevik seizure of power in November 1917 is universally known as the October Revolution, but it would surely be perverse after all these years to start calling it the November Revolution. For purposes of concision, the US is referred to as one of the Allies even though it formally called itself an Associated Power.

ROBERT SERVICE

March 2011

INTRODUCTION

The story of the Bolshevik Revolution of October 1917 has been told a thousand times and usually the focus is on Russian events to the exclusion of the global situation. There is nothing wrong with examining 'October' and its consequences in such a fashion. But this book is an attempt to see things in a different light. The early years of Bolshevik rule were marked by dynamic interaction between Russia and the West. These were years of civil war in Russia, years when the West strove to understand the new communist regime while also seeking to undermine it; and all through that period the Bolsheviks tried to spread their revolution across Europe without ceasing to pursue trade agreements that might revive their collapsing economy. Looking at this interaction in detail reveals that revolutionary Russia—and its dealings with the world outside—was shaped not only by Lenin and Trotsky, but by an extraordinary miscellany of people: spies and commissars certainly, but also diplomats, reporters and unofficial intermediaries, as well as intellectuals, opportunistic businessmen and casual travellers. This is their story as much as it is the story of 'October'.

The communist leaders believed that their revolution would expire if it stayed trapped in one country alone; they were gambling on their hope that countries elsewhere in Europe would soon follow the path they had marked out in Russia. The October Revolution happened in Petrograd—as the Russian capital St Petersburg had been renamed to do away with its Germanic resonance—while the Great War between the Allies and the Central Powers raged across Europe, and until November 1918 the world's powers gave little thought to revolutionary Russia except when examining how its situation could be exploited to their advantage. The Germans had signed a separate peace with Lenin's government at Brest-Litovsk in March that year in order to redeploy their army divisions in the east to serve on the western front against France, Britain and the US; the French and British meanwhile increased their efforts to bring Russia back into the fight against Germany even if this meant bringing down the communist government. When peace came to Europe after the German surrender, the 'Russian question' was transformed in content as Western politicians at last gave priority to preventing the contagion of communism from spreading beyond the Russian borders into the heart of Europe. Sporadic revolutionary outbreaks in Germany, Hungary and Italy occurred but, to the frustration of the Russian communist leadership, petered out in failure. The Western Allies meanwhile undertook direct military intervention in Russia as well as the subsidizing of the anti-communist Russian armed forces. But in late 1919, when these enterprises ran into difficulty, they withdrew their expeditionary forces. Communist Russia had survived its first international trial of strength.

At the same time the Russian communists were engaged in efforts to export their revolution. In 1918 they sent emissaries, including some of their most prominent leaders, to subvert Germany. In the following year they also founded the Communist International (Comintern) in Moscow which aimed to create communist parties abroad and destroy global capitalism. In 1920 they sent the Red Army itself into Poland. And although Lenin and Trotsky were disappointed when 'the European revolution' did not take place as they had expected, they remained convinced that their original gamble would end in triumph.

I stumbled upon the idea for the book when looking at personal papers of the British intelligence agent Paul Dukes. His memoirs are an outstanding eyewitness account of conditions under early communist rule. Dukes on one of his spying missions enlisted with the Red Army and reported what he saw with the mind of an outsider. This led me to investigate other examples of reportage by foreigners, ranging from lively pro-Soviet cheerleaders like the newspaper correspondents John Reed and Arthur Ransome to the sombre attack on communism by Bertrand Russell in 1920. Then I found that the diplomats, too, had recorded many important things in their telegrams and autobiographies. This, I freely admit, was something of a surprise since I had shared the widespread idea that they were a rather slow-witted and incompetent bunch. From there it was only a short hop to investigating the entrepreneurs who lined up to restart the Russian trade in 1920–1. Such sources provide opportunity for a fresh insight into the history of communist Russia and supplement the abundant documentation that has become available in Moscow in recent years. Russian history cannot be written satisfactorily on the basis of Russian archives alone.

Other discoveries came to hand as this material was brought under scrutiny. I had taken it for granted that the Reds and the White Russians— and for that matter the Allies—knew rather little about each other. As Ethel Snowden first put it in 1920 on her visit to Petrograd and Moscow, an 'iron curtain' appeared to have been built along the frontiers of Russia. In fact the telegraphists, decoders and spies on every side did an effective job for their masters. Their activity filled large gaps in information by providing timely, accurate reports in the absence of conventional diplomacy after 1917. The Red Army was well informed about the White armies and vice versa. And although the White armies were separated from each other by huge distances, they could usually make contact through wireless messages. They were also helped by access to Soviet telegraph traffic which was intercepted by the British, French and Americans. The Reds lost a lot of Russia's experts in communication and decryption who fled into obscurity or abroad soon after the October Revolution, but they increasingly made up for this failing. This was consequently a period when each side found out enough about the others to be able to formulate plans and policy on the basis of genuine knowledge—and the spies, telegraphists and decoders were as important in this process as the diplomats.

No realistic calculus of military power in Europe favoured the Bolsheviks after the October Revolution. Their weak and ill-equipped Red Army would have stood no chance against the Germans if they had invaded Russia in 1918. Russia would have been equally vulnerable if the Western Allies had concerted an all-out invasion in the years that immediately followed. The communists were fortunate that external factors inhibited foreign great powers from marching into east-central Europe and overthrowing the revolutionary state. They were equally lucky that states abroad increasingly found it advantageous to end Russia's economic isolation: trade treaties were signed first with Estonia and Scandinavia in 1920 and then with the United Kingdom in the following year.

When the communists led by Lenin and Trotsky took power in Petrograd, they could not be certain that their government would last more than a few days. But this did not dent their optimism. If the Russians could so easily cast down capitalism, it would surely not be long before others did the same. The communists declared that imperialism, nationalism and militarism were about to be liquidated everywhere. Bolsheviks outlined their project in global terms. The working classes of the world were about to achieve liberation from every kind of oppression. Industrial societies would start to pay, feed, clothe and educate properly those who had suffered down the generations. Governments would tumble. The market economy would be eliminated. An end would be put to war and people would administer their affairs without hindrance from kings, commanders, priests and policemen. Communism was on the point of spreading itself worldwide. Soon there would be no government, no army, no bureaucracy on the face of the earth.

But even while aiming at world revolution, the communist leaders saw the sense in hedging their bets. They knew that the great powers, if they wanted, could conquer Russia without much difficulty. The Kremlin went on talking to its foreign enemies for fear of an international crusade being organized against it. Its fear was not misplaced. In 1918 the communists knew full well that the Western Allies in the Great War—France, Britain and America—were supplying finance and advice to the anti-communist Russian forces. In the August of that year they discovered an outright conspiracy by the British—later known as the Lockhart Plot—to disrupt and possibly even to overturn Soviet rule in Moscow. Yet the Kremlin never broke off attempts to negotiate with the West. All the Allied diplomats had left the country before the end of the first full year after the October Revolution when the communist leadership put British, French and American officials on trial. (Robert Bruce Lockhart, architect of the conspiracy, was by then in London and safe from Lenin's clutches.) Yet the Russian economy had been destroyed by war and revolution and the Bolshevik government needed foreign trade for its survival—and communist emissaries continued to make overtures for the resumption of commercial and diplomatic links with the advanced industrial countries, which culminated in the Anglo-Soviet trade treaty of March 1921.

The political rupture between Soviet Russia and the West in autumn 1918 made it difficult for both the communists and the Allies to gather information and explain their purposes. At first after the October Revolution, Western ambassadors had used unofficial intermediaries while refusing official recognition to Lenin's government. In this way the Allies had continued to negotiate with the communists in Petrograd and Moscow, and the governments in London and Washington also liaised discreetly with the designated representatives of the Soviet authorities.

But just as Soviet Russia played its double game of diplomacy and revolution, so the Western Allies persisted with their schemes to bring down Lenin and Trotsky. A lot of this has been kept a secret for almost a century. Western diplomats were deeply involved in subversive activity but full disclosure would have embarrassed subsequent governments in the West, governments which wanted to appear as clean as the driven snow in the way they conducted their political and military rivalry with the USSR. They preferred to suggest that all the skulduggery took place on the Soviet side. Yet the British conspiracy in 1918, even though it was bungled, was a serious project to undermine communist rule—and it is hard to see why so much of the documentation should remain officially classified. In any event, Allied espionage and subversion did not end with the exodus of the diplomatic corps when the plot was exposed. Intelligence operations were quickly resumed both to finance the anti-Bolshevik White Russians and to gather information; and although these failed to dislodge the communist government, they certainly provided data of value to Western governments.

The British, French, Japanese and Americans had sent military expeditions after the Brest-Litovsk treaty in March 1918, but they never moved out from the periphery of the old empire and were anyway much too small to overthrow Lenin and Trotsky. The battles on the western front constrained what could be done until the end of the war in November that year. Subsequently, none of the Allies was willing to organize an invasion of Russia. Both economic and political considerations held them back. Even Winston Churchill, the arch-advocate of the White cause, had no idea how to do more in Russia than the Allied powers actually did. Yet Russia continued to attract attention. Attempts were made to restore the links of international trade outside the Soviet-occupied zones. The French had their plans for southern Ukraine. American entrepreneurs, especially those on the west coast, were eager to do business in Siberia. British intelligence agent Sidney Reilly characteristically planned to pull off big commercial deals in post-communist Russia, and others in Britain wanted to do the same. Food supplies to Russia were another instrument which the American government contemplated using against the communists. In 1919 initiatives were taken both to offer grain to Lenin on political conditions and to send it to feed the regions of Russia that came into White hands.

Lenin and Trotsky after the Russian Civil War successfully tempted several foreign countries into trading with Russia. But the conventional idea that this marked the end, for a while, to Soviet expansionist schemes is utterly wrong. Comintern, on orders from Moscow, tried in March 1921 to overthrow the German government. The communist action in Germany was undertaken despite the knowledge that this would bring British and French armies on to German soil to restore their continental dominance. Although the Party Politburo spoke the rhetoric of peace for Europe, its members had mentally prepared themselves for another European war.

Yet there was no German communist revolution in the inter-war period despite Comintern's intensive efforts. The Soviet leadership underestimated the resilience of anti-communist groups and feelings across Germany—just as they had overlooked Polish nationalism when marching on Warsaw in 1920. No matter how good the information that was available to politicians, it was only as useful as they allowed it to be. Lenin and Trotsky had already fixed their view on the world and its future. They were convinced that Europe was on the threshold of communist revolution and that it needed only a slight nudge from them to make all this happen. The 'masses' in the communist imagination would break off their chains and rise in revolt. Bolshevik leaders filtered the contents of reports they received from the West. Their informants themselves, being communists, pre-filtered a lot of it before sending material on to Russia. Political ideology was involved, but Lenin and Trotsky anyhow had little time for basic reflection. And although they adjusted policy to changing circumstances, they still did this within the setting of their general preconceptions. They led a party which objected whenever they abandoned established doctrine. They themselves were ardent believers in the communist cause. They had given their lives to it and, despite being agile in their political manoeuvres, kept any practical compromises to a minimum.

The Allied leaders too had their own prior assumptions. Wilson, Clemenceau and Lloyd George were in receipt of plentiful information from diplomats, reporters and agents—far more informants operated for them in Russia than the Soviet leaders could yet deploy in the West; but it was one thing for governments to obtain reports and an entirely different one to know what to do next. While being grateful for the fast flow of material, every Western leader had to contend with witnesses contradicting each other. Understandably, leaders who were already dealing with horrendous difficulties in their own countries and throughout central Europe worked as much by instinct and preconception as by steady analysis of the reports placed on their desks. Lloyd George in particular went his own way in his pursuit of Britain's post-war economic recovery, stealing a march on France and America by authorizing the 1921 trade agreement with Soviet Russia. He had an exaggerated belief in the erosion of communism that would result in Russia. As a result he donated a breathing space to Lenin for his New Economic Policy, decisively enabling the Soviet state to restore its economy and stabilize its control over society.

This book takes up an international vantage point on Soviet Russia and the West. The foreigners who reported, denounced, eulogized, negotiated, spied on, subverted or attacked Russia in 1917–21 rest in their graves. The Russians—Reds and Whites—who fought over Russia's future in their Civil War are long gone. Lenin's mausoleum still stands on Red Square in Moscow, a monument to an October Revolution that shook the world's politics to its foundations. His corpse remains there because Russian public opinion is not ready for its removal. What happened in Petrograd in late 1917 transfigured global politics in the inter-war period. Out of the maelstrom of revolutionary Russia came a powerful state—the USSR—which defeated Nazi Germany in the Second World War and for decades after 1945 was locked in the contest of the Cold War against the US and its allies. The October Revolution gave rise to questions which remain important today, questions that find expression in the polarities of democracy and dictatorship, justice and terror, social fairness and class struggle, ideological absolutism and cultural pluralism, national sovereignty and armed international intervention. This is a cardinal reason why the history of Soviet Russia and the West continues to command attention.

PART ONE

•

REVOLUTION

1. TROUBLING JOURNEYS

In March 1917, while Europe was convulsed by the Great War, news of a revolution in Russia began to spread abroad. It started in Petrograd, the capital, with an outburst of industrial conflict. Strikes had taken place in the two previous winters and the army and political police had dealt with them efficiently. Workers determined to bring down the Imperial monarchy walked out of the factories and joined demonstrations. Emperor Nicholas II was at GHQ in Mogilëv, five hundred miles away, and saw no reason for concern. This time, however, the strikers did not simply go home, but massed on the streets and goaded the militants of clandestine revolutionary parties into joining them. When the army garrisons were mobilized to restore order, the troops went over to the side of the workers. The popular mood was fiercely radical. Workers and soldiers elected their own Petrograd Soviet (or Council) to press for their cause. Suddenly the Russian capital became ungovernable. Alert at last to the magnitude of the emergency, the emperor sought to abdicate in favour of his haemophiliac young son Alexei. When counselled against this, he suggested that his brother Mikhail should take the throne, but this compromise was angrily rejected by those demonstrating on the streets. They would be satisfied only by the removal of the Romanov dynasty, and they had Petrograd at their mercy.

The end for the Romanovs, when it came, was abrupt. It was also unexpectedly peaceful. On 15 March Nicholas II's nerve suddenly cracked and he stood down, allowing a Provisional Government to take power. It was led by the liberal Georgi Lvov with Pavel Milyukov as Foreign Affairs Minister and Alexander Guchkov as Minister for Military Affairs. Most of the cabinet's members were liberals, with Guchkov as the sole representative of moderate conservative opinion. There was but one minister on the political

left. This was the Socialist-Revolutionary Alexander Kerenski, a young lawyer who became Minister of Justice.

The Petrograd Soviet, led by Mensheviks and Socialist-Revolutionaries,
gave its blessing to this arrangement. The Mensheviks were a Marxist faction
dedicated to the ultimate objective of socialist revolution; but they believed
that the country had not yet reached the level of modernization necessary
to socialism, and they shuddered at the thought of burdening themselves
with responsibility for governance in wartime. The Socialist-Revolutionaries looked for support more to the peasants than to the workers. But they
too were influenced by Marxism and they shared the judgement of the
Mensheviks. Together these two socialist organizations could easily have
taken power in the Russian capital. Instead they gave approval to Lvov's
cabinet on condition that he agreed to renounce Nicholas II's expansionist
aims and fight only a defensive war. They also demanded the realization of
a full range of civic reforms. Lvov agreed. He understood that, without the
Petrograd Soviet's consent, the Provisional Government would be still-
born. So began an uneasy system of rule known as dual power.

The press in Paris and London initially held back from reporting what
was going on. The war against the Central Powers—Germany, Austria-
Hungary, the Ottoman Empire and Bulgaria—was poised on a knife edge,
and France and the United Kingdom wanted nothing done that might damage Russia's fighting capacity. The Russians had joined the French and the
British in the Triple Entente that had taken Serbia's side in its dispute with
Austria-Hungary in mid-1914. The Entente powers, usually known as the
Allies, were joined by Japan, Italy and others. Two great military fronts, the
western and the eastern, stretched across Europe. The early successes fell
to Germany as its armies pressed into northern France and Russian-ruled
Poland. But quickly the Great War became a conflict fought from trenches
as the fronts were stabilized and neither the Central Powers nor the Allies
appeared able to devise methods to break the stalemate until December
1916 when the flexible offensive of General Alexei Brusilov resulted in a
Russian advance. The French and the British, worn down on the western
front, acclaimed Russia's military achievement at the time; and when
telegrams arrived reporting the political disturbances in Petrograd, the governments in Paris and London avoided any semblance of interference. Not
until 19 March 1917, when the Provisional Government was already in office, did the press report that Nicholas II had abdicated.[1]

What happened in Russia had been predicted for years but few revolutionary emigrants had expected the final moments to be so orderly. Ivan Maiski, a left-wing Menshevik resident in London, raced around calling on fellow emigrants and 'congratulating' startled English passers-by. The cry went up among the comrades: 'To Russia!'[2] Another of the émigrés was Maxim Litvinov, who phoned his wife Ivy at a nursing home in Golders Green after the birth of their son Misha. Litvinov belonged to the Bolshevik faction of Russian Marxists, led by Lenin, which regarded the Mensheviks as disgraceful moderates; and he was no armchair revolutionary, having helped to launder the money stolen by Bolsheviks in the sensational Tiflis bank robbery in 1907. Ivy shared Maxim's delight: 'Darling it means we're not refugees any more.'[3] Litvinov was so elated that he tried to shave with his toothpaste and got into the bath without having turned on the water. He had waited for revolution all his adult life. Now it had happened, and his hands trembled with excitement as he read the newspapers.[4] 'The colony' of Russian Marxists assembled to confer about the situation: '[They] began to feel the compulsion to meet every day in each other's rooms, talking, exclaiming, surmising, looking from face to face, and their wives, unwilling to miss a word, popped the dishes into the cold oven, too impatient even to take them out to the scullery.'[5] The small world of Russian political emigrants bubbled with exhilaration.

Litvinov felt he had to do something, almost anything, for the revolutionary cause in Russia. His mind was bursting with frustration. While Petrograd was in political ferment, he was stuck hundreds of miles away in London. As a Bolshevik, he regarded the war as an 'imperialist' conflict between two coalitions of greedy capitalists. Most Mensheviks and Socialist-Revolutionaries thought the same. But no socialist organization in Russia, not even the Bolsheviks, had yet fixed its policy on how to end the war—it would take months before some degree of clarity emerged on this matter.

In a burst of zeal, Litvinov met up with British socialists who opposed the Allied war effort. The Labour anti-war MP Ramsay MacDonald received them in the House of Commons. MacDonald naturally did not share the British government's hope that the fall of the Romanovs would increase Russian combativeness on the eastern front. In fact he was predicting the opposite.[6] But although he was courteous enough, he disappointed Litvinov by providing no notion about what 'he was going to do about the Revolution'.[7] Litvinov called next day at the Russian embassy in Chesham

House and was received by the chargé d'affaires Konstantin Nabokov. He asked why the staff had not yet taken down the portraits of the Imperial family.[8] He enjoyed rubbing up the old regime's officials the wrong way. Nabokov stood his ground and behaved with dignity. He had never disguised his sympathy with the Russian liberals and was hoping to receive the trust of Lvov and his cabinet. Instead the Provisional Government gave the London embassy to former Foreign Affairs Minister Sergei Sazonov.[9] But as Sazonov failed to arrive, Nabokov continued to head the embassy.

On 31 March the Labour Party held a celebration of the revolutionary events at the Albert Hall. Ten thousand people attended and Ramsay Mac-Donald was the main speaker. Others on the platform included Israel Zangwill, who spoke on behalf of the Russian Jewish refugees in London's East End. The audience adopted Russian custom and bared their heads before observing a silence in honour of 'the countless sacrifices which the Russian people have made to win their freedom'.[10] It was an occasion that nobody present would forget. The Romanovs were gone and freedom had arrived in Russia. There was talk of a brotherhood of the Russians and the British no longer poisoned by the existence of tsarist despotism.

Most of the revolutionary emigrants in central and western Europe were impatient to return to Russia. The only routes available to them were across the North Sea, either directly to Archangel and onward by rail to any number of Russian cities or to Scandinavia and then by a longer railway journey looping over northern Sweden and Finland south to Petrograd.[11] Britain's Royal Navy had penned Germany's large fleet in Kiel and Wilhelmshaven for the duration of the war. The result was that transport to Sweden or Norway from the rest of Europe became a British prerogative, and even the French government had to seek authority to send ships eastwards. The big Russian revolutionary colonies in Paris, Geneva and Zurich therefore had to cross the English Channel if they aimed to go home. London was turned for the first time into the largest centre for Russian political emigrants.[12] Excitement grew about the chance of a trip to Scandinavia, and the passenger ferries from the French ports to Dover were kept busy with Slavic passengers. The editorial board of *Nashe slovo*, a Russian Marxist anti-war newspaper based in Paris, was stripped bare by the exodus; the same happened to the émigré revolutionary press in Switzerland. The place to shape opinion was Petrograd. Nowhere else mattered, and the emotional tug on the minds of émigrés was seldom resistible.

They knew the physical risks. Although the Royal Navy kept the German battleships trapped and inactive, the U-boats were a constant menace. Sneaking out from their ports, they had a licence to sink all Allied military and civilian shipping. In 1916 a submarine laid a mine that sank the ship carrying Lord Kitchener, the British Secretary of State for War, on a trip to Russia. There were grievous losses of ships and supplies throughout the year.

Yet the hastily invented convoy system protected a lot of commercial traffic across the Atlantic. The Americans were giving political and financial assistance to the Allies short of going to war. The German high command successfully pressed for a change of policy to allow its forces to attack US shipping. The rationale was simple. Germany's economy was being suffocated by the British naval blockade. Urban consumers had endured a 'turnip winter' when coffee, sugar and even potatoes ran out. Raw materials for military production were no longer plentiful. Meanwhile Britain and France were obtaining what they needed from their American friends. The Germans gave notice of unrestricted submarine warfare from 1 February 1917 and US merchant vessels began to be sunk in March. British intelligence sources discovered that Germany had promised to restore Texas, New Mexico and Arizona to Mexico if the Mexican government would agree to fight America. Washington fell into uproar. Until that point it had been impossible for President Woodrow Wilson to gain the support of his Congress to enter the fighting. These isolationist obstacles crumbled when news of the U-boat campaign was printed. On 6 April the US announced that it would join the Allied as an Associated Power in the struggle against Imperial Germany. Wilson intended it to be a 'war to end war'.

In New York the fall of the Romanovs had been greeted with wild enthusiasm. The American press, being free from the British and French constraints of wartime censorship, had reported quickly and extensively on the revolution.[13] News of the abdication appeared in the newspapers two days earlier than in London and Paris. Jewish refugees from the Russian Empire were ecstatic.[14] The tyrant had been overthrown; equality of religion and nationality was being proclaimed. Then came the complication of American entry into the war. The Jewish *Forward* newspaper approved of President Wilson's decision, whereas the anti-war left was furious with him. Lev Trotsky and Nikolai Bukharin were prominent critics of US 'militarism'. Trotsky had been deported from France for his agitation against the war;

he was, at that time, a far-left Marxist who was neither a Bolshevik nor a Menshevik but demanded the installation of a 'workers' government'. Bukharin was a young Bolshevik who was not shy of challenging Lenin's writings on the Marxist doctrines. Trotsky and Bukharin called on socialists in the US to oppose America's military involvement. Noisy public meetings took place in the cities of the east coast where anti-war and pro-war activists confronted each other about whether the old government in Washington and the new one in Petrograd merited support.

Nearly all the Russian political refugees in America, regardless of this dispute, were as keen as their comrades in Europe to get back home without delay. In the United Kingdom, the ultimate permission to travel across the North Sea rested with the cabinet. The Prime Minister David Lloyd George dallied for some weeks before allowing the anarchist Pëtr Kropotkin and the Marxists Georgi Plekhanov and Grigori Alexinski to make the trip. Kropotkin, Plekhanov and Alexinski were picked for having advocated the cause of the Allies.[15] Anti-war militants denounced this as favouritism, and the Mensheviks Ivan Maiski and Georgi Chicherin formed a repatriation committee with themselves as chairman and secretary. They visited the Foreign Office, the War Office and the Home Office to argue the case for a passage to Russia. After a month of frustration they called on Nabokov at Chesham House, where they were pleased to discover that he was under instructions from Petrograd to assist with all requests by emigrants to leave Britain. Nabokov duly issued the visas but, because of the risk of German U-boat attack, only to the men. Loud protests ensued from the female revolutionaries living in Whitechapel. (Nabokov later shuddered at the memory: 'God knows they *can* make a noise.') The chargé's job was not made any easier by the political emigrants' habit of using false passports. Nabokov complained that Litvinov alone had four or five aliases. So even when the embassy tried to be helpful it was not an easy process to issue visas.[16]

The first large group of applicants obtained tickets to sail from Aberdeen to Bergen on HMS *Jupiter*.[17] Having taken the train from King's Cross Station in high spirits, they then had to sit around in Aberdeen for four days. The ship's captain announced that this was normal procedure. He was waiting for a storm to brew up and curtail the German submarine patrols. He was also a little too optimistic. Halfway across the North Sea the *Jupiter* had to lurch to port to evade a German submarine.[18] Some later convoys were even less fortunate and one of the ships went down with all on board—it was the same vessel that Litvinov had hoped to take. Only the recent birth of his son had dissuaded him from buying a ticket.[19]

The anti-war activists did not thank the British for helping them. One of them, Georgi Chicherin, went around saying that Lloyd George was discriminating against them in the issuance of travel documents.[20] This was untrue, at least for those setting out from the United Kingdom. Nabokov as chargé had indeed co-operated with Chicherin, although nobody would have known this from Chicherin's journalism—and his tirades against the Allies could only aggravate the difficulties of British diplomacy in Petrograd. What is more, Chicherin was unusual in being in no hurry to depart for Russia. His presence in London became an annoyance, and the British cabinet was to lose patience with him in August on learning how he had written articles in *Pravda* that virulently condemned the Allied war effort— he was also suspected of favouring the German side. Without further ado he was taken to Brixton prison under a Defence of the Realm order.[21] Pëtr Petrov was already in custody for agitating among British workers against the war.[22] Chicherin and Petrov were recalcitrant prisoners. They interpreted their treatment as yet further proof that the Allied powers would stop at nothing to fight their 'imperialist' war. They declined to make a special plea to the Lloyd George cabinet for their release.

Nearly all other male political emigrants in the British, French and Swiss revolutionary colonies got back to Russia if they wanted to make the journey. Many of the travellers, moreover, had it in mind to throw out the Provisional Government; and some were determined to stop Russia from continuing in the war.

The shortest route to Russia from France or Switzerland, of course, would have been by rail across Europe. But this was impossible at a time when two military fronts with their millions of troops and artillery were stretched out from north to south down the middle of the continent. Revolutionaries based in Swiss cities had the theoretical option of travelling across Germany to Scandinavia and entering Russia via Finland. The snag was that Russian citizens on German territory were enemy aliens in wartime. Most Russians had fled Germany and Austria at the outbreak of hostilities rather than face possible arrest by police or a beating up on the streets. But the German government had always seen the advantage of subsidizing Russian and Ukrainian revolutionary groups that aimed to bring down the Romanov monarchy; and when Nicholas II abdicated, the German Foreign

Office expressed interest in schemes to infiltrate anti-war revolutionaries back into Russia. Diplomats in Switzerland began negotiations for the transit of Russian revolutionaries by rail across Germany to the Baltic coast. Lenin and his Bolsheviks were courted through intermediaries. Since Lenin not only wanted an end to Russian involvement in the war but actively advocated Russia's defeat, the German high command could not wish for a better helpmate.

Together with the Menshevik leader Yuli Martov, Lenin explored the opportunities, but Martov worried about the absence of sanction by the Provisional Government. He hated the liberals and thought of them as warmongers and imperialists. But he was loath to risk going back without an official imprimatur. Lenin was made of tougher mettle. He had taken too long to return from Switzerland in the 1905 revolutionary crisis and paid the price of diminished political influence. He was not going to repeat that mistake in 1917.

But he had to be circumspect. If the Provisional Government could in any way accuse him of collaborating with Germany he would be in jeopardy on arrival. He might even be shot for treason. He therefore struck a deal with the German ambassador Gisbert von Romberg that he and his supporters would travel over German territory without contact with Germans. Not even the driver or guard of the locomotive was to approach them. This would call for a 'sealed' train. German ministers readily agreed to Lenin's terms.[23] For his part Lenin sought to entice other anti-war emigrants like Karl Radek into putting their names down for the trip. Radek, a bright and witty Polish Jew with a record of criticizing Lenin in past years, belonged simultaneously to the German Social-Democratic Party and a far-left Polish Marxist organization. If he and Martov joined the train, the initiative would look less like an exclusively Bolshevik scheme. Radek consented but Martov continued to refuse. Although Martov was on the far left of Menshevism and deplored the Russian war effort, he continued to worry about being tainted by association with Imperial Germany. Nothing Lenin said would make him budge. Nevertheless thirty-two assorted political emigrants, mainly Bolsheviks, turned up in the cold on 9 April at the railway station in Zurich. Lenin was accompanied by his wife Nadezhda and his principal adjutant Grigori Zinoviev. His ex-lover Inessa Armand was also in the group—and Radek, renowned for his scabrous wit, was cracking jokes from the moment the train departed.[24]

Nearly everyone felt pleasantly entertained except Lenin, who took exception to the noise coming from the next-door compartment where Radek, Inessa, Olga Ravich and Varvara Safarova spent the entire time larking about. Olga Ravich had a shrieking voice when she laughed, and Lenin gruffly hauled her out into the corridor until her companions rescued her; but he then told them again to keep the noise down. Throughout the trip he was a killjoy: he was determined to get on with his writing as the train chugged its way through Stuttgart, Frankfurt-on-Main and Berlin on its route to the ferry port at Sassnitz. He reprimanded anyone who smoked. When he saw a queue building up for the toilets, he introduced a ticketed waiting system—this calmed his mood until he discovered that Radek was using his time in the closet to light up his pipe. Another scolding followed.

Once they had arrived in Denmark, Lenin and his fellow travellers made their way to Sweden where a reception committee awaited them in Stockholm. He himself adopted yet another assumed name. For a while this foxed the sympathizers who wanted to escort him on his way. An overture also arrived from Alexander Parvus-Helphand. Parvus was a Marxist from Odessa and a millionaire merchant who conducted political errands for the German government; and he wished to make an arrangement whereby the Germans could subsidize Bolshevik activity in Russia. Although Lenin wanted the money, he could not risk being reported as having met with Parvus. Instead he let subordinates negotiate on his behalf. Not everything went as he wanted. He lacked the strength to resist Radek's admonishments about his sartorial appearance. Radek explained that he simply did not look the part of a revolutionary leader while walking round in hobnailed mountain boots. As Radek got his own back for being told off on the sealed train, Lenin reluctantly agreed to buy new shoes and trousers. But he would go no further than that. He told his tormentor that he was not going back to Russia in order to establish himself in the clothing business. He might have added that someone with Radek's eccentricities of dress had little right to tell him what to wear.[25]

All this time Lenin was clarifying his thoughts about overthrowing the Provisional Government and introducing a socialist dictatorship. En route to Russia he wrote them up as his 'April Theses'. After the Swedish socialists had made their fuss of him, it was on to the border with Finland at Haparanda. This was a neat little riverside town where Swedish gendarmes kept order as the baggage was unloaded. Over the bridge was the village of

Tornio that already bore signs of the recent revolution. Russian soldiers were slovenly and unhelpful. The gendarmes had disappeared and the rail timetable had lost any semblance of reality.[26] For the travelling party from Switzerland it was an emotional moment as they began to experience the sights and smells of a proper revolution. On 13 April they boarded the train at Tornio, taking copies of the Bolshevik newspaper *Pravda* to their compartments with them. At Beloostrov they crossed the Russo-Finnish border, where they were greeted by Bolshevik Central Committee member Lev Kamenev. Shortly before midnight on 16 April they pulled into Petrograd's Finland Station where a huge crowd was waiting to welcome the returning revolutionary hero. Lenin was less than gracious to the Mensheviks and Socialist-Revolutionaries present; he snubbed their ideas about unity among socialists and brusquely called for 'worldwide socialist revolution'.[27]

Martov paid dearly for his scruples. He sat it out in Switzerland until he received formal permission from the Russian Ministry of Foreign Affairs to do what Lenin had done, not arriving in Petrograd until 22 May.[28] By then his Mensheviks had fallen decisively under the sway of comrades like Irakli Tsereteli and Nikolai Chkheidze who had persuaded the Petrograd Soviet to support the Provisional Government. Pavel Milyukov, the new Russian Foreign Affairs Minister, was the piggy in the middle of the negotiations about travel permits. He had not sanctioned Lenin's trip and consented to Martov returning solely because the Petrograd Soviet had stipulated that every single revolutionary emigrant should have the right to a visa. The Provisional Government could not lightly contradict the will of the soviets.

Martov was slow enough but Trotsky was even slower. It was little consolation for him that Lenin, his old opponent on matters of revolutionary strategy, was edging close to his ideas. Lenin's 'April Theses' were proof of this, but years of dispute between the two had to be surmounted before they could actively co-operate. And anyway Trotsky was stuck in New York. As soon as the Russian consulate had issued a visa for him, he booked a passage for himself and his family on the SS *Kristianiafjord*. The Trotskys left New York on 27 March. The ocean crossing was as perilous as any taken over the North Sea, and indeed that summer a German U-boat sank the *Kristianiafjord* on an Atlantic crossing. Trotsky gave no thought to the dangers. Any risk was worth taking when revolutionary Petrograd was the destination. In fact things went well until the steamship pulled in at Halifax, Nova Scotia. Canada was a dominion of the British Empire and the authorities were vetting the passenger lists of transatlantic ferries between Canada and Europe. The British control officers based in Halifax had been alerted to Trotsky's presence on board and were unhappy about facilitating the journey of a well-known anti-war militant to Scandinavia and Russia. He was arrested and, kicking and shouting, bundled off the vessel to a detention camp. He conducted propaganda among German prisoners-of-war while daily demanding the right to rejoin his family.

Word of what had befallen Trotsky quickly reached Russia, where both the Mensheviks and Bolsheviks in the Petrograd Soviet clamoured for his release as an honourable fighter against the hated monarchy. At first Milyukov had favoured this step. But then he pressed Sir George Buchanan, the United Kingdom's ambassador in Petrograd, to get the British to keep Trotsky in detention. This they duly did. But when the political left in Petrograd started a press campaign for Trotsky to be freed, Buchanan sensed a danger to the physical security of Britain's many businessmen in Russia. He leant on Milyukov to stress that the British were not responsible for the situation in Halifax. On 21 April the Provisional Government made clear its lack of objection to Trotsky's release, and he was reunited with his family and they were allowed to take the next scheduled boat—the *Helig Olaf*—across the Atlantic.[29] They reached Christiania (Oslo) without mishap and made for Haparanda before the last stage across Finland to Petrograd. Like others before him, he was greeted warmly at the Finland Station a month after Lenin's arrival. His close comrade Moisei Uritski and the Bolshevik Central Committee member G. F. Fëdorov had gone out to accompany him and help acclimatize him to Russian revolutionary politics.

He never forgave the British for his experience in Halifax. His Marxist doctrines and analysis should have told him that the leading capitalist powers were hardly any different from each other and that the French would have done the same in similar circumstances; indeed, from his own doctrinal viewpoint, it was little short of incredible that the American authorities had allowed him out of New York City harbour in the first instance. But Trotsky moaned that the British authorities had had the impertinence to strip-search him; he noted that even the Imperial Russian government had never subjected him to this degrading treatment. It was as if the compulsion to take off his clothes for inspection by a medical doctor was the ultimate barbarity. For a man who was about to introduce a harsh dictatorship this was remarkably over-sensitive.

With Trotsky's arrival in Petrograd, the Provisional Government was faced by not one but two exceptional troublemakers. He and Lenin set

about exploiting the political situation. Even before returning, both had denounced the cabinet as being militarist and imperialist; and they had dismissed those Menshevik and Socialist-Revolutionary leaders in the
Petrograd Soviet who supported Georgi Lvov and fellow ministers and
passed up the opportunity to take power in the name of socialist revolution.
Russia after the fall of the Romanovs was like no other great power in the
world. Restrictions on freedom had vanished. Lenin, the lifelong enemy of
the Imperial government and its oppressiveness, was impressed by the reforms undertaken by the Provisional Government. Famously he declared
before his return that Russia was the freest country in the world at that time.
He and Trotsky could write fluently and get their pieces quickly published.
Lenin had a ready-made faction of followers which he could turn into a
mass party. He was as yet a nervous speaker, but Trotsky—along with
Kerenski—was a talented orator who could stir vast audiences whenever
he appeared. And though Trotsky did not immediately join the Bolsheviks,
he and Lenin knew they had to bury their past disputes. They wanted the
same thing: supreme power in revolutionary Russia.

2. RUSSIA ON ITS KNEES

The returning emigrants came upon a disorientating mixture of the old and the new in Petrograd. The statue of Catherine the Great had a red flag flying from her sceptre. At noon every day without fail the bells of the Peter-Paul Fortress rang out the Glinka melody of 'God Save the Tsar'. Much also remained unchanged in Moscow and it was still possible to catch sight of the younger grand dukes near the Spasski Gates on Red Square going out for the evening. The brilliant ballerina Tamara Karsavina gave performances in both cities. The world-famous bass Fëdor Shalyapin sang in Verdi's *Don Carlos* at Petrograd's Bolshoi Opera; he had never been a supporter of the old regime and was enjoying his acclaim as a champion of the people. Despite the wartime evacuation of the Hermitage art collection from Petrograd to Moscow, there were weekly exhibitions of paintings as well as public lectures on painting and literature in the capital. Plays were put on which had long been banned. At the Alexandrinski Theatre there was a revival of Alexei Tolstoy's *The Death of Ivan the Terrible*. The censorship office ceased to function. The Salvation Army, which had been prohibited on Imperial soil by Nicholas II's government, plastered announcements of its gospel meetings on the walls. A vegetarian restaurant was doing a lot of business by enticing customers with a huge poster of the writer and Christian anarchist Lev Tolstoy and a sign that stated: 'I Eat Nobody'.[1]

The conventions of society were being turned inside out. Domestic servants became less likely to obey when their masters or mistresses made demands on them. Many waiters refused to accept gratuities because the practice offended their dignity: 'Just because a man has to make his living waiting on table is no reason to insult him by offering him a tip!' Social deference was disappearing. Tram conductors addressed passengers as

'comrades' regardless of social status—an innovation that middle-class passengers often found unnerving.[2]

The most remarkable phenomenon was the influence wielded by organized labour. Workers elected their own soviets in the factory yards. Many
cities acquired their own Red Guards to fill the gap left by the gendarmes
who had fled. The entire labour movement wanted both order and better
conditions for working people as they expanded their network of trade
unions and set up factory-workshop committees. And when one body failed
to satisfy their demands they either replaced its leadership or turned to
some other body to act on their behalf.[3] Although the industrial labour
force led the way, the enthusiasm for participation spread to every corner
of society—with the exception of the aristocracy and the landed gentry
whose members lay low after the monarchy's downfall. Peasants in most
Russian regions already had their own bodies, the village communes, to
run their affairs. The communes had traditionally engaged in rural self-
policing and they now extended their authority over all aspects of life in
the agricultural areas. Popular administration was a slogan of the day. Even
the Trans-Siberian railway was affected. Foreign passengers trying to make
their exodus from Russia found themselves being asked to choose a council
for their carriage. The motive was more practical than political as the train
had to pick up food and drink on the journey and there had to be effective
bargaining at each big station. Citizenship in 1917 required everyone to become something of a politician.

Workers wanted higher wages, improved living conditions and secure
employment. Increasingly they feared being conscripted if the Provisional
Government were to resume active operations on the eastern front. Garrison soldiers felt menaced by the same prospect. At any time they might be
ordered to the trenches, and everyone knew how poorly the Russian Army
was beginning to perform against the Germans. Peasant households were
also restless. They resented having to pay land rents and looked enviously
upon the woods and pastures of absentee gentry landlords. It seemed only
a matter of time before the villages became ungovernable.

The administrative disintegration picked up pace and the forces of order
broke down almost entirely. The gendarmerie in the Russian Empire had
never operated with the consent of society. As soon as the monarchy fell,
gendarmes pulled off their uniforms and hid themselves from the enraged
populace. The old political police—the Okhrana—was disbanded. The
commanders of army and navy garrisons could no longer enforce military

discipline. The Petrograd Soviet on 14 March issued Order No. 1 stipulating its right to overturn commands issued by military officers. This left the Provisional Government with few instruments to impose its will. Ministers were dependent on favours dispensed by the Mensheviks and Socialist-Revolutionaries in the great network of soviets elected by workforces and garrisons in the cities. Prince Lvov could hardly drink a cup of tea without checking whether he had permission. The cabinet kept itself busy and funnelled its policies down through the ministries. The old bureaucrats remained in place; many of them were eager to serve their new masters and implement instructions. But orders formulated in the capital were frequently slow to be obeyed in the provinces. The Provisional Government encountered difficulties from the very start of its rule.

Lvov's hand of cards held no trumps even before the first post-Romanov crisis occurred in early May. Pavel Milyukov, Minister of Foreign Affairs, shared the deposed emperor's war aims and expected to acquire the Straits of the Dardanelles for Russia once the Central Powers were defeated, something he made very clear in telegrams to Paris and London. Unfortunately this was in contradiction to the understanding between the Petrograd Soviet and the Provisional Government that Russia would fight only a defensive war. Workers in the telegraph offices informed the Menshevik and Socialist-Revolutionary leaders about Milyukov's telegrams. A protest demonstration was organized. The Lvov cabinet met in a panic, and Milyukov felt compelled to resign along with the Minister for Military Affairs Alexander Guchkov. Lvov also brought Mensheviks and Socialist-Revolutionaries into his reconstructed cabinet, hoping that a coalition of liberals and socialists could pull the country together. The Allied diplomats in Petrograd felt relieved. It seemed to them that the new government stood a realistic chance of restoring order to Russia and keeping its armed forces active on the eastern front.

The Bolsheviks had joined in the protest but they had also called for the overthrow of the Provisional Government and inception of a socialist order. Until Lenin's return to Russia there had been confusion among them. The Bolshevik leaders in the capital who had survived the arrests in the previous winter favoured the kind of radical extremism that Lenin advocated from far-off Switzerland. The Russian Bureau of the Bolsheviks took seriously its old factional doctrine about the desirability of a socialist dictatorship. The Bureau was headed by Vyacheslav Molotov, then only twenty-seven years old. Molotov called for unconditional struggle against the Provisional

Government. The moment for Bolsheviks to prevent the liberals from achieving power had already passed, but Molotov believed that Bolshevism required that he and his comrades should seek to reverse the outcome. This remained the official policy of the Russian Bureau until the arrival of senior figures such as Lev Kamenev and Joseph Stalin from Siberian exile. The Bolshevik Central Committee fell into their hands as they insisted on a policy of conditional support for the Provisional Government. But there were many Bolsheviks in Petrograd and the provinces who thought Molotov had been right, and it was not difficult for Lenin to persuade the faction to sanction the revolutionary course he had proposed in his 'April Theses'.[4]

Bolshevik militants stood against Mensheviks and Socialist-Revolutionaries, whom Lenin denounced as 'social-traitors', in elections to the soviets, trade unions and factory-workshop committees. Their party newspaper, *Pravda*, predicted that conditions for working people would not improve until a socialist revolution had occurred. They adopted slogans of Peace, Bread and Land and promised national self-determination to the non-Russians. They demanded the installation of a government based on the soviets, and declared that the era of socialism was at hand throughout Europe. Lenin and his comrades contended that Lvov's cabinet was a capitalist government motivated by militarist and imperialist objectives. Only a minority of workers and soldiers as yet accepted this, and hardly any peasants had heard of Bolshevism; but the drip-drip effect of Bolshevik propaganda was noticeable. Covertly helped by funds from the German government, which was willing to finance any organization that would pull Russia out of the war, the party expanded its printing facilities and grew in size as tens of thousands of people signed up for membership. Lenin himself attracted massive attention as the champion of the anti-governmental cause and Trotsky and other left-wing Marxists joined the Bolsheviks as the likeliest instrument of revolutionary socialism in Russia. The Provisional Government was put on notice that it could take nothing for granted.

Lvov now presided over a divided cabinet. Socialist ministers undertook reforms in industrial relations; they also permitted peasants to cultivate land left unsown by gentry landlords. The liberals in the cabinet, led by the Constitutional-Democrats (usually known as Kadets), worried that socialism was being installed by stealth. They wanted to resume military operations on the eastern front, which was in fact agreed by Alexander Kerenski in his new post as Minister for Military Affairs. Inside the cabinet, however, the debate continued. The Mensheviks and Socialist-Revolutionaries were pushing for a more active search for peace, and ministers duly sanctioned Russian involvement in an international socialist conference in Stockholm where this would be the core of the agenda. But at the same time Kerenski was laying plans for an offensive against the Austro-Hungarian forces on the southern sector of the front.

This display of commitment delighted the Allies. It did not displease Lenin and Trotsky, who said it proved that the coalition was as aggressive as they had always contended. The Bolsheviks exploited the popular unease by calling for an armed demonstration in Petrograd against government policy. This was set to coincide with the First All-Russia Congress of Soviets in mid-June. Suspecting that the Bolsheviks were plotting to overthrow the Lvov cabinet, the Mensheviks and Socialist-Revolutionaries decided to organize their own unarmed demonstration through the centre of the city. They dominated the Congress of Soviets; but when they asserted that no single party wished to take power in Russia, Lenin shouted from the floor: 'There is such a party!' The Bolshevik Central Committee, confident that its fortunes were improving, organized a yet further demonstration. The Kronstadt naval garrison—a hotbed of anti-cabinet feelings—promised to sail over to the capital and bring their rifles. Lenin chose this moment to take a few days' holiday in the countryside. This was an artificial display of nonchalance. Anatoli Lunacharski, one of Trotsky's sympathizers and someone who would soon join the Bolshevik party, later admitted that the demonstration was intended to 'probe' the scope for a socialist insurrection.

The Provisional Government was crippled by internal dispute. Menshevik and Socialist-Revolutionary ministers were insisting on granting regional autonomy to Ukraine; they wanted to recognize its Central Rada—the as yet unofficial elected body that combined a broad range of Ukrainian organizations—as the legal holder of administrative authority in Kiev. The Kadets objected to this as the first step to breaking up the entire multinational state. They resigned from the cabinet when Lvov sided with the socialists. Yet the rump of the cabinet held firm. Loyal troops in Petrograd were sent out to break up the Bolshevik-led demonstration. Dozens of civilians were killed. The Ministry of Internal Affairs seized the opportunity to suppress the Bolshevik party in the capital and manipulate public opinion by the release of documents pointing to the secret German subsidy. A warrant was issued for Lenin's arrest. Lenin fled to sanctuary in Finland; Trotsky flaunted his sympathy with the Bolsheviks and was taken into custody. The rest of the Bolshevik leadership in Petrograd went underground and waited for the political storm to blow over.

Lvov had run out of energy in the emergency; he could see no future for his premiership and handed over power to Kerenski, who spent weeks putting together a fresh cabinet. The June military offensive was a disaster and the Central Powers marched deep into Ukraine. War-weariness spread to garrisons and trenches. Food supplies to Russian cities dipped. Industrial conflict intensified in factories and mines as owners faced down the demands for higher wages. Inflation racked the financial system. Law enforcement was pitiful while garrison troops showed allegiance exclusively to the nearby soviets. Peasants began to use the gentry's pastures and woods without compensation, and it was obvious that a vast land grab was in the offing. The outlying regions of the old Russian Empire grew restless; and as the economic crisis sharpened, local administrations took to ignoring Petrograd and engaging in self-rule. The socialist ministers who had served under Lvov resigned in order to devote themselves to shoring up the Mensheviks and Socialist-Revolutionaries in the Petrograd Soviet. Kerenski held supreme power but was politically isolated. His oratory was losing its impact. His capacity to impose the decrees of the Provisional Government was diminishing.

Few options were available to him as he sought to widen his base of support. On 25 August he opened a State Conference that brought together every anti-Bolshevik group from the Kadets through to the Mensheviks and Socialist-Revolutionaries. His idea was to demonstrate that Russian politicians were still capable of responding to the country's needs in times of war. He spoke with something like his earlier panache and was fêted by female admirers as he left the proceedings.

But it escaped nobody's attention that the Commander-in-Chief Lavr Kornilov was greeted rapturously by the liberals and right-of-centre groupings. Kerenski assured Kornilov that he still desired to reinforce the eastern front and bring the city soviets to heel. Kornilov consented to send reliable troops from the front to quell the Petrograd disorder. As the trains started to move them to the capital, Kerenski changed his mind for fear that Kornilov might be scheming against him. He gave orders for Kornilov to pull back his contingent. This exasperated Kornilov, who concluded that Kerenski now lacked the nerve to act for the good of the country. The situation was not helped by the confusing reports received by Kerenski from his own military adviser Boris Savinkov. The advance on Petrograd continued and developed into an outright mutiny. Kerenski in panic turned to the Mensheviks and Socialist-Revolutionaries, asking them to go out and cajole Kornilov's force into disobeying his commands. Bolsheviks joined in the effort and the mutiny collapsed. Kornilov was put under arrest. Kerenski drew a sombre lesson. Noting that the Kadets had cheered on Kornilov as the hope of Russia, he called a Democratic Conference at the end of September that excluded all those liberals who had failed to stand by the Provisional Government. Kerenski saw this as the only way to obtain broad popular approval.

Hatred for the Romanovs remained strong among workers, and Kerenski worried that things might run out of control. His first thought was to arraign the former emperor before a proper court and, if he was found not guilty, send him off to England and his cousin George V. But the Provisional Government, with all its pressing difficulties, formulated no decisive policy. A commission was appointed to investigate Nicholas, his wife Alexandra and the rest of the Romanov family. The public agitation against the Romanovs induced the Provisional Government to enquire whether the British would give asylum to the Romanovs. Kerenski, when Minister of Justice in the first cabinet, had gone to see the former Emperor Nicholas at Tsarskoe Selo and pass on best wishes from his Windsor cousins, but the family was deprived of liberty for its own protection. But now, although Lloyd George had no objection, George V worried that the ex-tsar's arrival in Britain would make the house of Windsor unpopular.[5] The British authorities replied in the negative. The Provisional Government held an unminuted discussion and decided to deposit the Imperial family in Tobolsk in Siberia. Its distance from the main centres was a primary advantage and the old governor's residence was chosen for them. Nicholas told Kerenski: 'I'm not worried. We trust you.' The planned destination was kept secret; and although monarchist militants tried to reach him in Tobolsk there was no serious attempt at a rescue.[6]

Other policies of the Provisional Government were less effective. Manufacturers despaired of order being restored to the factories; many closed down their businesses and moved their accounts abroad. Few landowners dared to stay on their estates. Bankers focused their endeavours on preserving their assets and cut off financial credits to industry. The urban economy was crashing to the ground and conditions worsened for all social strata. Shopkeepers were pulling down their shutters. Mass unemployment rose steadily in the cities. Whereas the industrial workforces had once struck for higher pay and better conditions, the priority became to keep enterprises open and save jobs. Kerenski raised the prices paid for agricultural produce so as to entice the peasantry into selling to government procurers. The result was disappointing. Peasants complained about receiving rubles that were useless for purchasing farm equipment that was unavailable. Armed units had to be put at the ready to march into the countryside in order to feed the cities and the front. At the same time there were disturbing reports from the trenches that troops were deserting in an ever swelling stream. Discipline was falling apart in the Russian Army. The entire state was ceasing to exist and Russia fell to its knees.

The Bolshevik party benefited from this collapse. Increasingly its militants were again operating in the open; indeed they had never disappeared from view outside Petrograd and Moscow. Trotsky was released from prison and returned to public platforms to heap the blame for Russia's misfortunes on the Provisional Government. Lenin in his Helsinki refuge declared that the Kornilov affair proved that there were only two alternatives: military dictatorship or socialist revolution. The Bolsheviks attended the Democratic Conference only to state their case against Kerenski and walk out.

Far from being delighted by this, Lenin thought the Bolsheviks were allowing themselves to become distracted from the organizing of an insurrection. He got articles couriered to Petrograd from his places of hiding. He nagged his comrades about the urgent need to overthrow the cabinet— and it was becoming clear that he could count on Trotsky, the newly recruited Bolshevik, to support his strategy. Although the Central Committee did not always accede to Lenin's ideas, it never wholly ignored them. The anti-Bolshevik press went on building up his importance, representing him as a demonic figure with a mesmeric power over the Bolsheviks and Trotsky was depicted as his political twin. In the Petrograd Soviet there was anxiety among Mensheviks and Socialist-Revolutionaries whenever Trotsky appeared. He replaced Kerenski as the great orator of the Revolution. From early September he was Chairman of the Petrograd Soviet, and other city soviets throughout Russia quickly began to go over to the Bolsheviks. The mood in the party grew confident that some new kind of coalition would eventually be formed with willing Menshevik and Socialist-Revolutionary leaders. Kerenski and his cabinet appeared about to be consigned to oblivion, and opinion grew among workers and soldiers in favour of a government composed exclusively of dedicated socialists.

Lenin's thoughts were fixed on an uprising; he denied that 'Kerenski's clique' could be removed without violence. He returned incognito to Petrograd to put his case at the Bolshevik Central Committee. A nocturnal meeting was held on 23–24 October when he harangued fellow leaders as only he could do. Lev Kamenev and Grigori Zinoviev opposed him. They doubted that the working class was firmly in favour of an uprising. They questioned whether Europe was on the point of experiencing socialist revolutions; they feared that any premature move by the Bolsheviks would expose them to an irresistible counter-strike. But Lenin beat them back and the vote went ten to four in his favour. The Central Committee met again six days later with Bolshevik leaders from the rest of Russia. For the second time Lenin faced down his opponents after a blistering dispute. Official Bolshevik policy was set definitively in the direction of seizing power.[7]

The principle of insurrection but not the practicalities were debated. As Lenin went back into hiding on the outskirts of the capital, it was Trotsky who devised tactics and strategy. The Petrograd Soviet had recently established a Military-Revolutionary Committee to oversee the garrisons. Trotsky saw that he could use this body to rally support among troops and co ordinate armed action against the Provisional Government. This would have the advantage of making the coup appear less as a Bolshevik party *coup d'état* than as a step towards installing rule by soviets. What happened in Petrograd could then be copied in other cities. And once Kerenski had been arrested or expelled from the Winter Palace, power could be presented to the Second Congress of Soviets that was scheduled to meet in the next few days. Lenin was not pleased: he wanted instant action. Kamenev and Zinoviev broke ranks by divulging their trepidation about the Central Committee decisions. Everyone in Petrograd now knew that the Bolsheviks were about to embark on drastic measures. Kerenski and his ministers did not intend to go down without a fight. They made efforts to rally support from garrison commanders as the moment of armed collision grew closer. They felt certain that Russia's woes would increase a thousandfold if it fell under Bolshevik rule.

The situation was deeply unpromising for the Provisional Government. Germany's army marched into Riga on 3 September and the Russian Army was scattered into retreat. The railway network was disrupted as troops piled on to any train moving towards their home regions. The economy was disintegrating. In the cities a winter of unemployment and food shortages was the prospect for all but the wealthy in the cities. In the villages of Russia and Ukraine agitation for the transfer of all arable land to the peasantry grew. Whole regions ignored government decrees. A French propaganda film of model guns and planes was shown in Petrograd to encourage Russian patriotic enthusiasm. This was never going to be popular since Russia's war was all but over.[8]

By October the mood on Petrograd streets was flagging. Outwardly there was normality. The trams were running. The post and telegraph system was working. But people were talking about what the Germans might do next; they wondered whether zeppelins and aeroplanes might be used to drop bombs on the capital. The authorities took the necessary precautions. Air-raid sirens were given frequent tests. There were rehearsals for the measures to be taken in case of an attack, and firemen doubled the number of practice exercises. Street gas lamps were banned. Crime and disorder had been bad enough since March when the gendarmes fled. Now they were worse.[9] These were weeks of sombre news as the war went in favour of the Central Powers. German forces seized the two islands at the extreme northern edge of the Gulf of Riga in mid-month. Russian armed forces were pushed eastwards. Although they held on to Estonian territory, they had to withdraw their strategic defence to the Gulf of Finland for the first time.[10] Supplies in the capital's shops dwindled. There was no tobacco on sale and anyone wanting chocolate had to queue for it with a ration book.[11]

Kerenski seldom left the Winter Palace. His courage and commitment remained high but there were days when his morale dipped low. The Bolsheviks no longer troubled to debate with other socialists. They sped round Petrograd making final preparations for a decisive violent clash. Kerenski was visibly losing his earlier confidence. He was no longer waving to his crowds: he was drowning.

3. THE ALLIED AGENDA

As the Russian Army fell apart on the eastern front, the Western Allies ceased to pay much attention to the opinions of Alexander Kerenski. They came reluctantly to this position. Sharing a dislike of the Romanov monarchy, they had hoped to co-operate well with democratic Russia. There was no rush among them to ditch the Provisional Government. But the news from Petrograd was constantly depressing, and leaders in Paris, London and Washington concluded that it was no longer sensible to fund and supply the Russian armed forces.

The French President Georges Poincaré was prominent among the small group of politicians who revised the agenda of the Allied powers. An intensely ambitious lawyer who had once acted for the writer Jules Verne, he had been elected President in 1913, and held the post through to 1920. Poincaré was a political conservative and had served regularly in cabinets before the Great War, constantly pushing for the firm pursuit of France's national interest. The turnover in ministerial postings enabled him to increase his influence. There were four premiers—Aristide Briand, Alexandre Ribot, Paul Painlevé and Georges Clemenceau—in 1917 alone. Not until Clemenceau, a fierce Radical who had made a name for himself by speaking against anti-Semitism during the Dreyfus Affair, became premier in November that year was there a rival to Poincaré's dominance and the President would find himself sidelined. The two men anyway agreed about national military and foreign policy. German armies occupied departments in northern France. No leading politician in France proposed the slightest appeasement of the Central Powers. The war had to be fought to a victorious end. Germany had to be made to pay for the devastation it had caused—and subjected to a peace settlement that would disable it from threatening the French again.

David Lloyd George, the British Prime Minister, was usually less strident in his rhetoric but agreed that the Germans had to be totally defeated. He had acceded to supreme office in December 1916 to lead a governing coalition of Conservatives and Liberals and so straddled the political right and centre-left. He was a Welshman whose accent had not entirely left him, and he was a Nonconformist. Becoming MP for Caernarfon Boroughs, he supported social reforms with a panache which brought him to attention inside and outside the House of Commons. His private life was a mess. He kept his secretary Frances Stevenson as a mistress; he shamelessly sold peerages for political favours. But he proved himself as a war leader, and helped to lessen the U-boat threat by imposing the convoy system on the Royal Navy. He spoke with equal impressiveness to aristocrats at house parties and to factory workers and shop girls at the hustings. A man of abundant self-belief, he was acknowledged alongside Winston Churchill as one of the great orators in the House of Commons.

As the war dragged on, Lloyd George concentrated on military questions to the exclusion of post-war planning. But President Woodrow Wilson had no intention of letting the topic disappear from the Allied agenda. He was determined to see that victory over the Central Powers would be followed by a peace which offered a better future to the peoples of the world. Wilson had occupied the White House since 1913. Patrician in appearance and austerely intellectual, he was the most academic of the leaders of the world's great powers, having headed Princeton University before becoming Governor of New Jersey. He wrote a Ph.D. thesis on congressional government. He detested militarism, and, like other American politicians, he also hated empires. He had won a second presidential term in 1916 by promising to keep his country out of the Great War. He was resolute in his principles but open to correcting them in the light of examined reality. He could not directly explore the currents of European politics since constitutionally he was prevented from travelling abroad on long trips. For that purpose he employed his confidant Edward House, who despite having no military experience was always known as Colonel House. No one talked directly with so many leading politicians of the Allies and the Central Powers, and President Wilson received the very best and latest information about war and politics in Europe.

The Allied leaders knew that the great cities in Germany and Austria were experiencing a growth in discontent. Allied intelligence agencies and embassies reported regularly on the situation in Germany. British and French diplomats in Sweden were well placed to gather information simply by speaking to ferry passengers arriving from Hamburg. The Swedish newspapers were anyway discussing the same material.[1] The government in Berlin got wind of this and sometimes produced a false edition of some German newspaper containing misinformation. But although Stockholm experienced a swirling fog of claims and counter-claims, there was no denying that Germany faced growing difficulties.[2]

German politics was entering a volatile period. The extreme left had been rounded up and imprisoned in mid-1916, including leading revolutionaries such as Karl Liebknecht and Rosa Luxemburg. Their Spartakusbund, named after the gladiator who headed the slave revolt against Rome in 73–71 BC, continued clandestine activity. Liebknecht and Luxemburg smuggled articles out of prison which argued that the war was being fought for the exclusive purposes of the rich and powerful. More and more German socialists were attracted to their message. By 1917 the Social-Democratic Party of Germany was splitting apart as its radical members, led by Hugo Haase in the Reichstag, refused to obey the party line. By then it had become plain not only that the General Staff under Paul von Hindenburg and Erich Ludendorff dominated both Kaiser and government but that they were pushing for policies of naked territorial expansion. Haase and his comrades would no longer tolerate the mildness of their party's critique of the government and the high command. As a result, they established the Independent Social-Democratic Party of Germany—and they brought the old party's great theorist Karl Kautsky along with them and communicated with the imprisoned Spartacists.

Ludendorff and Hindenburg resolved to take an all-or-nothing gamble on the western front—indeed this was why unrestricted submarine warfare had been introduced. Every last resource was to be dedicated to an offensive strategy. They insisted that the Kaiser should replace the vacillating Theobald Bethmann Hollweg, Chancellor since 1909, with their protégé Georg Michaelis. If they were to beat the Allies on the western front it was essential to win battles decisively before the American armies reached France and acquired the necessary training. The industrial capacity of Germany had reached its limit. The adherence of the US to the Allied cause was bound to aggravate the problems in the economy. Time was not on the German side; and the fact that Austria-Hungary was known to be searching for a way of obtaining an honourable withdrawal from the war was an additional complication. Yet Ludendorff and Hindenburg also knew that morale was slipping in the French Army and that Marshal Pétain was having to deal with mutinies by the most severe means. The Germans would never have a better chance to swarm over the Anglo-French defences and finish the war in the west.

The Western Allied leaders were sensitive to this possibility. While reinforcing their troops and equipment in northern France, they continued to look to the Russians to make their contribution in the east. Financial credits were still forthcoming. Military supplies came across the Pacific and the North Sea. Russian armed forces in the winter of 1916–17 had registered success with an offensive planned by General Alexei Brusilov. London, Paris and Washington had no illusions about where Germany had to be defeated. The western front would be their priority. But for this to happen it was essential for Russia to remain a threat in the east. The millions of peasants in uniform had to stay at the eastern front and tie down hundreds of German divisions.

Throughout the war the Western Allies had frequently sent official visitors to Russia to gather information and consolidate support for the war effort. A group of French and British socialist parliamentarians arrived at the Finland Station on 14 April 1917. They included Marcel Cachin, Ernest Lafont and Marius Moutet—two professors of philosophy and a lawyer. The British sent cabinet-maker James O'Grady and plumber Will Thorne.[3] Although they received a warm welcome from the Provisional Government and the Petrograd Soviet, their impact on popular opinion was negligible. The French resolved to improve on this in midsummer by sending no less a personage than their Minister of Munitions Albert Thomas. He too was a socialist and the idea was that he would find it easy to talk to leaders of the Russian labour movement. But Thomas overdid his performance as a man of the people. At a banquet in his honour he ate his meat off the end of his knife; Russians detected a degree of condescension.[4] The British suffragette Emmeline Pankhurst arrived around the same time. She lost no time in criticizing opponents of the Allied military endeavour. She denounced the anti-war MP Ramsay MacDonald on the grounds that he was simply copying what Lloyd George had done in the Boer War in order to gain cheap popularity.[5] MacDonald would have liked to visit Russia but the patriotic Seamen's Union made it impossible for him to set off.[6] The Provisional Government anyway did not want people like him in the country. As for Pankhurst, she got on well with Kerenski and his wife but attracted little wider attention. The political situation was no longer influenced by the thoughts of strangers.

President Wilson's special representative Elihu Root arrived in the same weeks and stayed in the Winter Palace.[7] The Americans had offered a loan of a hundred million dollars to the Provisional Government on condition that it was used to buy products and supplies from American companies.[8] That had been in May. The other requirement was for Russia to prove its military capacity to benefit from such assistance. Root, a former secretary of state, had a direct manner. His mission was 'to devise, in accordance with the Russian government, effective means to aid Russia in her efforts to defeat the universal enemy'.[9] He warned ministers that American aid would depend on the Russians continuing to keep up the fight on the eastern front.[10] On returning to the US, he praised Kerenski to the skies and denounced American protesters against the war: 'There are men here who should be shot at sunrise.' He claimed that German agents were at work everywhere; he attacked Trotsky and other political emigrants who had returned to Russia and now vilified the country that had given them asylum.[11] His advice to Wilson was to release funds to the Provisional Government. He insisted that the Russians, with American help, could still make an important contribution to victory over Germany.[12]

The information reaching London and Paris was of good quality throughout the war; and the American diplomats quickly matched this effort. In March 1917, just before the United States entered the war, the American consul-general in Petrograd, North Winship, had found himself surrounded at the entrance to his office in the Singer Building by a crowd suspicious that he was pro-German. Singer seemed a Teutonic name; and as for the American bald-headed eagle, perhaps it was really a German symbol. Winship courageously held his nerve and set about supplying Washington with a detailed, daily summary of Petrograd politics. He followed the proceedings in the Petrograd Soviet. He explained the doctrines and policies of the 'Maximalists' under Lenin. He reported on every big newspaper's reaction to President Wilson's declaration of war. He described the poor showing of Russia's armed forces and the decline in popular support for the war.[13] His expertise was invaluable to David R. Francis, who had been appointed to the US embassy at the age of sixty-five in March 1916.

The dean of the Petrograd diplomatic corps was the United Kingdom's Sir George Buchanan. Tall and always dressed to perfection, Buchanan had not troubled to learn Russian despite having been ambassador since 1910. When about to be honoured with the freedom of the city of Moscow he had to spend an hour learning the word for 'thank you' (*spasibo*). But as the mayor hung a gold chain round his neck, Buchanan instead said *pivo*, which is the Russian for 'beer'.[14] Moscow's dignitaries showed their magnanimity by pretending they had not heard the plea for alcoholic refreshment, and Buchanan survived his faux pas in serene ignorance. For the rest of his time in Russia he remained unapologetically monoglot except for when he spoke French (in which he was fluent but with a British lack of enthusiasm). Buchanan kept to the steady manners of the British ruling class abroad. He was thought the quintessential Englishman, although in fact he was Scottish. He was respected but not liked. Joseph Noulens, the French ambassador, described him as 'dry, cold and disdainful'. High society in the Russian capital retained a lot of its old liveliness, but an evening at the Buchanans' was unlikely to be a jolly occasion.[15]

Buchanan was never going to make a close friend of the American ambassador. When visiting the US residence with Noulens, Buchanan seldom forbore to comment on what he saw as the vulgarity of the Americans. He scorned the large photograph of himself that Francis had hung outside his reception room: 'Don't you find this in bad taste?' If asked to dine, he would turn to Noulens and say something like: 'Ah, we're going to have a bad supper . . . cooked by a Negro.'[16]

Ambassador Francis sensed this contempt but continued to think well of Buchanan.[17] Evidently he had a generous side to his nature; he had kindly Southern manners and rarely lost his temper. Nor did he disguise his own feeling that he was not the right man for the Russian posting. His qualifications were slim indeed. Like Buchanan, he spoke no Russian; but, unusually for a diplomat in those days, Francis's French was primitive. This was hardly his fault. Although he had served in the cabinet of President Grover Cleveland as Secretary of the Interior in 1896–7, he had made his name not in international affairs but as a St Louis banker.[18] While his staff busied themselves with liaising with the Russians, he maintained a high level of fitness. He was a big man who played a lot of golf. He was also an enthusiastic dancer at Petrograd balls. He practised a set of physical exercises each morning and arranged that no day passed without his devoting several hours to his pastimes. Among them were a partiality for comely young secretaries and a fondness for whisky, which he claimed he was drinking only to please his doctors.[19]

The other leading Allied diplomats were Joseph Noulens and the Marchese della Torretta. Ambassador Noulens, who arrived in Petrograd in July 1917, was younger than Francis but temperamentally rigid despite his criticism of Buchanan for the same quality. As France's ex-Minister of War, he hated the revolutionary turbulence in Russia under the Provisional Government.[20] Della Torretta, the Italian chargé d'affaires, was still more settled in his ways. It was said that his preference would be to go to sleep and wake up with the Romanovs still in power. Russia's traumas after the February Revolution left him dumb with incomprehension.

The British and French embassies had built up military missions and intelligence agencies to look after their national interests in wartime. The Americans, coming late into the war, were slow to do the same. But once they were in it, they were determined to win it. By early autumn they were assembling an Information Service which covertly gathered data for Washington's attention. But there remained a reluctance, felt keenly by Woodrow Wilson, to meddle in Russian internal affairs; and he overruled Senator Root's advice to grant $5 million for the purposes of propaganda in Russia.[21] Wilson was at any rate less disengaged than he appeared to be. Sir William Wiseman, head of the New York station of Britain's Secret Intelligence Service, put the case for an Anglo-American joint intelligence effort to support Russia and its military commitment. He had already made a positive impression on Colonel House.[22] Since the US as yet had no serious network of agents it was easy for Wiseman to persuade House and the Secretary of State Robert Lansing to let the British take the lead—and the President on 15 June 1917 sanctioned funds to the value of $75,000. The Foreign Office in London was to supply the same amount.[23] The Western Allies were increasingly concerned about Russia's capacity to go on fighting. They used their missions and agencies to discover whether alternative arrangements might be possible without the Provisional Government.

For their chief covert agent in Petrograd the British picked the distinguished writer W. Somerset Maugham.[24] This broke a rudimentary rule of intelligence. Maugham's renown meant he could never be inconspicuous in the Russian capital. One of his plays was currently in performance there. What is more, Maugham was ignorant about Russian politics and was acquainted with no Russian public figures. He knew no Russian; he had not even mastered the Cyrillic alphabet. In other ways, though, he was a sensible choice. Maugham had wartime experience as an operative working for Mansfield Cumming of the Secret Intelligence Service. He had demonstrated steely qualities on missions to France and Switzerland; he summed up individuals and situations and could keep a cool head. He was quietly pleased that the authorities thought him the best man for Russia, and he took the chance to regularize his employment. Until then he had given his services as a patriot, receiving only expenses but no pay. Now he insisted on being remunerated as a professional. He adopted no cover but lived openly in the Russian capital, contacting his former mistress Sasha Kropotkina to gain an entrée into high society. Through her he met Alexander Kerenski and took him out for meals at the fashionable Bear restaurant.

Maugham thought he was picking up gems of information but in truth he discovered nothing closed to Sir George Buchanan. His main contribution was in cheering up Kerenski. But he preferred the company of Boris Savinkov, who was no longer on speaking terms with Kerenski after the Kornilov affair. Savinkov, a former deputy leader of the Socialist-Revolutionary Combat Organization that had assassinated Imperial officials before the war, was a fervent militant to the core of his being and now made proposals to crush anti-war agitation at the front and to shelve Kerenski's plans for the Constituent Assembly election. Victory in the war should be the supreme goal. Maugham liked Savinkov's idea of forming a strong centre party of Mensheviks and Socialist-Revolutionaries standing clear of the Kadets and the Bolsheviks. Savinkov proposed recruiting a Czech Corps to reinforce the Allied effort.[25] Maugham rushed to get to know the Czechs. Most of them were ex-POWs captured by the Russians earlier in the war. They offered their services to the Allies in the hope of forming an independent state for Czechs and Slovaks after defeating the Central Powers. Maugham came up with an offer of money and supplies. He was not the first to do so. The British and French military missions were touring the Czech and Slovak camps trying to recruit volunteers to fight either in northern France or in the Balkans, establishing their own national contingents under the joint command of the Allies.[26]

Allied personnel scurried to every public occasion to get a sense of what was going on. Colonels William B. Thompson and Raymond Robins of the

American Red Cross went to the Democratic Conference.[27] Thompson lavishly subsidized pro-war newspapers in Petrograd, often dipping into his own pockets—he had made his wealth as a businessman before the war.[28] And although the Red Cross was meant to be a charitable, non-combatant and apolitical agency, Robins secretly employed informers in the Petrograd garrison; what they told him was not confined to the supply of medicine and the dressing of wounds.[29] Robins concluded that the war was dead 'in the heart of the Russian soldier'.[30]

Sir George Buchanan could see how badly things were going for the Provisional Government. His own health was frail but, despite withering to a skeletal thinness, he had not lost the forthrightness that once led him to tell Nicholas II that reforms were urgently necessary.[31] On 9 October it fell to Buchanan to go with Noulens and Della Torretta and tell Kerenski that he was losing the confidence of Russia's Western Allies. They disliked interfering in the affairs of a troubled, friendly power, but the Provisional Government had to understand their worries. The Russian Army was falling apart; it no longer constituted any serious threat to the Germans or even to the Austrians. The Allies were reluctant to divert precious resources to Russia at a time when their own forces in northern France were fighting hard. Buchanan delivered the message with firm solemnity. Kerenski, exhausted by all the woes of his rule, bridled at what he heard. He replied in Russian as Foreign Affairs Minister Tereshchenko interpreted for him. For once he was concise, demanding that the stream of aid should be restored. It was Kerenski's last attempt to persuade the Allies that the eastern front was not a lost cause.[32]

Colonel Thompson called a meeting of Allied military representatives in his rooms in the Hotel Europe on 3 November 1917. Present were Colonel Alfred Knox, General Henri Niessel and General William V. Judson as well as General Neslukhovski and David Soskice from Kerenski's office. Thompson also invited his Red Cross colleague Raymond Robins. It was not a pleasant occasion. Knox and Niessel were scathing about the failings of the Provisional Government. Tempers were lost when Niessel called Russia's soldiers 'yellow cowardly dogs' and the Russians soon walked out.[33] Knox was usually as forthright as Niessel. He thought Robins should have supported Kornilov's campaign for a military dictatorship. He highlighted the danger from Lenin and Trotsky: 'I tell you what we do with such people. We shoot them.'[34] Robins retorted: 'You do if you catch them. But you will have to do some catching. But you are up against several million. General,

I am not a military man. But you are not up against a military situation. You are up against a folks' situation.'[35] Suitably translated into Marxist jargon and shorn of its colloquialism, this could have been Lenin speaking. The angry exchange between Knox and Robins was about to be repeated in Western capitals as governments debated their policy on Russia. Should Russians be left to decide their own future or could the Allies pressurize them to continue the war on the eastern front?

4. CHEERING FOR THE SOVIETS

Most newspapers in the Allied countries supported the effort to keep Russia in the war. But there were always dissenters, especially among the reporters based in Petrograd. They had diverse reasons for opposing conventional opinion. But one thing united them: their appreciation that the Provisional Government stood no chance of sustaining the military effort. They thought Kerenski was, politically, a dead man walking. They shared a feeling of moral outrage at the sufferings of Russian soldiers who were compelled to confront the German armies without hope of operational effectiveness. And they turned sympathetically to the single big party—the Bolsheviks—that promised to take drastic action to pull Russia out of the war. The Western dissenters became cheerleaders for Bolshevism.

Nobody was more ardent than Arthur Ransome. His early social contacts in London had been in the book trade and he had not shown socialist leanings before leaving for Russia as a freelance author in 1913. From working in publishers' offices he had started to write books of his own. His *Bohemia in London* achieved a decent success but then his biography of Oscar Wilde got him entangled with the courts when Wilde's former lover Lord Alfred Douglas sued him for libel. The court case was a draining experience for Ransome even though he emerged the victor. He had achieved only moderate success before the time of his marriage to Ivy Walker and the birth of their daughter Tabitha. He and Ivy got on badly from the start, and the journey to Russia offered him an escape from her evening rages. He industriously picked up the language and wrote a book that stayed permanently in print. This was *Old Peter's Russian Tales*, a retelling of folk stories meant for children but read with equal pleasure by adults. With the onset of war Ransome's facility in Russian and his zest for adventure permitted a change of tack, and he became a correspondent for the *Daily News* and the *Manchester Guardian*. Steadily his interest in the socialist movement in both Britain and Russia grew. He showed an exceptional talent for listening carefully to his interviewees and relaying their thought in crystal-clear prose.[1]

Ransome sought out the Menshevik and Socialist-Revolutionary leaders after the fall of the Romanovs. His sympathy with socialism loosened their tongues and they spoke to him in a way they did not dare in public. By late summer 1917 they knew that the Russian Army would not stay in the trenches much longer. When the Constituent Assembly eventually met, there would be huge pressure for the signing of a separate peace if some kind of negotiations with the Central Powers had not already begun.[2] Ransome thought this over. He did not question the urgent need for the Allies to defeat Germany. He was a British patriot and his own brother had died in the fighting, but he could see no good in trying to compel Russia to keep its troops on the eastern front since they were already exhausted and defeated. His conclusion was anathema to official circles in London; and British intelligence kept its eyes on him as a dangerous free-thinker and opened the letters he wrote to his wife Ivy in England.[3] But just as he was starting to annoy the authorities, he announced his desire for a period of English leave. The daily tasks of following the fast-moving political drama in Petrograd had worn him out. When granted permission for a holiday, he took the dangerous ferry journey back across the North Sea and reached Aberdeen on 17 October.[4]

Ransome told everyone in London willing to listen that Kerenski was doomed. Within days his prophecy had been realized in Petrograd. He kicked himself for having missed the greatest newspaper scoop of his lifetime, and pestered his editors to sanction another assignment in Russia. His enthusiasm was reciprocated: few journalists were better qualified to report on Russian affairs.

Less extravagant in his dismissal of the Provisional Government was the British consul-general in Moscow. Robert Bruce Lockhart had proved himself a sharp-eyed observer of the Russian political stage and, like Ransome, had gone native in Moscow. His Russian contacts gave him a Russian Christian name and patronymic and knew him as Roman Romanovich Lokkart.[5] Perhaps his full name in English, Robert Hamilton Bruce Lockhart, was too much of a mouthful for them. Lockhart had arrived in Russia in 1912. No Scot was prouder in saying, as he often did: 'There is no drop of English blood in my veins.' He claimed descent from the noble families of Bruce,

Hamilton, Wallace and Douglas—and he boasted of a genealogical connection with Boswell of Auchinleck. He was as restless as Ransome, having
tried to make a career as a rubber planter in Malaya, where an amorous dalliance with a local princess got him into hot water. He loved writing poems
and stories and could easily have become a journalist but instead applied
for the Foreign Office and scraped through the entrance exam. He married
Jean Turner and brought her out with him on his Russian posting. Ambassador Buchanan took him under his wing as a bright diplomatic prospect
even though Lockhart's politics were to the left of centre in Britain.[6]

Unhinged by her husband's philandering, Jean went back to Britain. He
treated her departure as a licence to indulge himself. He spent many a night
out on the tiles after carousing in the Gypsy encampment on the city outskirts at Strelnaya. He dabbled in the occult with his friend Aleister Crowley.[7] But he was not entirely feckless. He read Tolstoy's *War and Peace* in
the original. He steeped himself in Russian poetry and was a regular visitor
to the theatre. He was young and fit; on first arriving in Moscow he had
played a good game of football for a Russian team. He had plenty of self-
confidence and determination. And throughout this time he made himself
acquainted with all shades of public opinion in wartime Russia.

By autumn 1917 neither Buchanan nor Lockhart would have bet on the
Provisional Government's survival or the Russian Army's continuation in
the war. But Lockhart was no longer in Moscow when the Bolsheviks seized
power. His reason for absence was more dubious than Ransome's. All his
life Lockhart had an attraction for neurotic upper-class women who wanted
to throw off convention. Russian high society had plenty of such examples,
and it had not been long before the young Scot was conducting an illicit affair with a lady from one of Moscow's prominent families. Ambassador
Buchanan, on being informed, told Lockhart that the embassy could not
afford such a scandal in the country of a wartime ally. The discreet solution
was to send him back to London on medical grounds. Lockhart went to a
Russian doctor who signed an affidavit that he was suffering from anaemic
exhaustion.[8] Buchanan, it must be said, was no expert in dissembling. Instead of sticking to the agreed story, he told his fellow ambassador Joseph
Noulens mysteriously that Lockhart had left against his advice.[9]

One Briton remained in Russia who was willing to welcome a left-of-
centre alternative to Kerenski. This was the *Manchester Guardian*'s Morgan
Philips Price. Throughout the war he had criticized the motives of all the
belligerent powers even at the risk of his public standing. Philips Price was

a wealthy man from the west country. Educated at Harrow School and Trinity College, Cambridge, he had inherited an estate of 2,000 acres near Gloucester and came from a political family. His father was a Liberal MP and he himself was adopted as prospective candidate for the same party, but he was dropped for his strident opposition to the war. Philips Price then joined the Union of Democratic Control. He also wrote *The Diplomatic History of the War* at manic speed and got it published within weeks of the outbreak of hostilities. He lamented the tragedy of diplomatic failure: 'But for the outbreak of war there was a reasonable hope that the liberal political elements in Austria and Russia would have gained the day.'[10] Soon he came to the attention of C. P. Scott at the *Manchester Guardian* and he was sent out to Russia as its reporter. He was one of the earliest to warn about the sorry condition of Kerenski's armed forces and to argue that other Russian political elements should be given consideration by the Allies.

Philips Price quickly became friends with American journalists who thought along the same lines. Quite a number of them had gathered in Petrograd, including John Reed, Louise Bryant, Bessie Beatty and Albert Rhys Williams. Unlike Philips Price and Ransome, they worked for newspapers with a predominantly local base and had yet to make an impact in the US public debate on the war. None of them wrote for a Washington or New York daily. But they made up for this in their energy and initiative. They were determined to challenge the Wilson administration's liaison with the Provisional Government.

John Reed and Louise Bryant, who married in 1916, were well known in US radical circles. Reed had never enjoyed good health, and had known poverty as a child. He lived on his nerves and by his wits. His father was a Progressive Party militant who together with Lincoln Steffens had smashed the Oregon Land Fraud Ring. As the family's fortunes improved, Reed went to boarding school and on to Harvard. After college he became a journalist and covered the war in Europe before America's entry.[11] He was bitterly hostile to President Wilson's decision to bring the US into the fighting, and together with his father's friend Steffens he appeared as witness for the defence in a New York trial in July against the two anarchist anti-war protesters and Russian-Jewish immigrants Emma Goldman and her husband Alexander Berkman.[12] Reed criticized a bill going through the US Congress making it a felony to speak or write in such a way as to foster disaffection in the American armed forces.[13] The US State Department was understandably edgy about his decision to work in Russia since he could obviously cause trouble for it and for the Kerenski administration there. Before receiving their travel documents, Mr and Mrs Reed had to promise that they would conduct no propaganda in Russia.[14]

This was not enough to calm the worries of the British Imperial authorities. In August, the ship carrying Reed and Bryant was detained in Halifax, Nova Scotia just as Trotsky's had been. It took a week before permission was granted for the resumption of the sailing. A similar delay was experienced at Haparanda on the border with 'Russian' Finland. Reed and Bryant were furious at their treatment. Only later did Bryant comfort herself with the thought that one of her fellow passengers from New York took five months longer to arrive in Russia.[15]

The couple reached their destination in September 1917 and had their first experience of Russian revolutionary politics. It was the time of the Kornilov mutiny.[16] Whereas Reed had never set foot on Russian soil, it was Bryant's second visit.[17] She too was a fiery critic of the political status quo in the US. Her father was a Pennsylvanian miner who had moved out west for work. Although she made it to the University of Oregon and embarked on a career in journalism, financial circumstances compelled her to seek employment as a teacher of Hispanic children in Salinas, California. Her undergraduate thesis had been on the war against the Indian tribes in Oregon, and in California she took up the cause of the indigenous people. She was also a suffragette who mingled with anarchist militants. Her first marriage quickly fizzled out and, after meeting Reed in Oregon, she followed him to the east coast. By 1917 she was working simultaneously for *Metropolitan Magazine* and the *Philadelphia Public Ledger*.[18] Bryant had less knowledge than her husband about the war and international relations, but she was no less critical of Woodrow Wilson and wanted to do her bit to change US policy back to one of non-involvement in the Great War. Like her husband, she wrote muscular prose and hit her deadlines.

Others in the American group were Albert Rhys Williams and Bessie Beatty. Rhys Williams, who belonged to the Socialist Party, worked in Russia for the *New York Evening Post*. Born in Ohio, he was also a former Congregational minister who had obtained leave of absence from his duties so as to go off and report on the war in Europe.[19] His Welsh parentage brought him under suspicion as a British spy in Belgium, and he was detained for a while by the German occupation forces. Out of this experience came the book *In the Claws of the German Eagle*, published in 1917. By then he was working in Petrograd and was instantly attracted to Russian far-left socialists who sought Kerenski's downfall. Bessie Beatty took to him immediately: 'He was a decidedly American type, tall, with a pleasant frank face and a delightfully inclusive smile.'[20] Beatty herself was a daredevil and a radical. She went to Occidental College in Los Angeles but left without completing her degree; and taking up journalism, she covered the 1912 Nevada miners' strike and wrote searing articles on prostitution. Events in Russia after the monarchy's collapse excited her. Throwing up her job as editor of *McCall's Magazine*, she left San Francisco in April on her trip to Petrograd by the Pacific route. She arrived in early June.[21]

The last of the Western dissenters based in Russia was the French military attaché Jacques Sadoul, who arrived in the Russian capital on 1 October 1917. He came on the recommendation of Munitions Minister Albert Thomas, and his assignment was to act as a political observer. Someone who saw him three years later described him as having 'a "Chaplin" moustache, Norman head, alert yet reposeful eyes, and [being] dressed like a very respectable shop assistant'.[22] But in 1917 he wore military uniform. He quickly concluded that most Russians were determined to avoid further involvement in the war and would sooner or later sign a separate peace with the Central Powers. He let Ambassador Noulens know of his radical socialist opinions and stuck out like a sore thumb among most other diplomats.[23] Sadoul was a man of some eccentricity. After studying to become a lawyer, he had written a doctoral thesis on tax legislation.[24] He also worked for an American businessman who owned a Montana ranch and a Wyoming gold mine. In his free time he rode in the Rocky Mountains. Subsequently he returned to Paris as an Appeal Court advocate. He was brash and ambitious, and gained renown for obtaining lengthy interviews with President Theodore Roosevelt.[25] The war shifted him away from the French establishment. He believed there was no end in sight to the military conflict on the western front. Sadoul was a soul looking for its resting place and he began to find it in Russia and in Bolshevism.

What distinguished this group of temporary residents of Russia was their determination to seek sources of information independent of the Provisional Government and its supporters. They quickly made contact with the Bolsheviks. Trotsky gave an hour-long interview to John Reed on 17 October 1917 about the projected dictatorship of the proletariat. This consisted mainly of a description of the evils of the Russian bourgeoisie. According to Trotsky, the Provisional Government was powerless and the Kadets headed the 'militant counter-revolution' while the Mensheviks and

Socialist-Revolutionaries were fools to think that they had any kind of 'alliance' with the middle classes. He called for a 'Federated Republic of Europe'. He refrained from saying what the proletarian dictatorship would be like. One of his supporters, though, was a certain V. Volodarski, who suggested that the dictatorship would be 'a loose government, sensitive to popular will, giving local forces full play'.[26]

The American correspondents raced around Petrograd, often in each other's company, to get their stories. Reed and Bryant hooked up with Bessie Beatty as they strove to understand the exciting developments taking place. None of them spoke any Russian; they made up for this by taking Alexander Gumberg around everywhere with them. Gumberg was a 'Russian product of New York's East Side' who had returned to Russia after the collapse of the Imperial monarchy.[27] Beatty admitted to continued difficulties with the Cyrillic alphabet; and when she published her account *The Red Heart of Russia* in the following year it was full of misspellings— Zenoviev for Zinoviev, Dydenko for Dybenko and so on.[28] Reed wrote *podporuchik* (second lieutenant) as 'dodparouchik'.[29] Bryant was more punctilious but even she depended heavily on what the communist informants chose to tell her. She was to claim that by the time she left Russia in January 1918 she could read Russian 'slowly'.[30] Beatty was modest about her own progress.[31] But she too found Bolsheviks willing to help her. Among them was Georgi Melnichanski, who had been known as George Melcher in New Jersey but now led the metalworkers' union in Moscow. (Reed had encountered him when covering the Standard Oil strike in 1915.)[32] The Latvian Bolshevik Yakov Peters also made himself available. As a member of the London Russian Marxist colony, he had a working knowledge of English; and Bessie Beatty made his acquaintance through Albert Rhys Williams, who was so close to the Bolsheviks as to seem to be on the point of becoming one himself.[33]

The problem for Rhys Williams as an advocate was his poor Russian. Lenin himself, as Rhys Williams recalled in his memoirs, was aware of this: "'Ah!" he said with sudden animation . . . "and how goes the Russian language? Can you understand all these speeches now?" "There are so many words in Russian," I replied evasively. "That's it," he retorted: "You must go at it systematically. You must break the backbone of the language at the outset. I'll tell you my method of going at it.'"[34] Williams thought he was about to be let into an extraordinary secret. But Lenin simply counselled him to learn—in sequential order—all the nouns, all the verbs, all the adverbs and adjectives, then the grammar and the rules of syntax. He adjured him to practise 'everywhere and upon everybody'.[35] The worst thing of all, he said, was to go on talking only to Americans. Lenin advised him to put an advertisement in the newspaper for exchange lessons with a native speaker of Russian. He expected immediate improvement: 'Next time I see you I'll give you an examination.'[36] Rhys Williams was dispirited by this kind of guidance. He felt he had been listening to Lenin's 'system of the conquest of the bourgeoisie applied to the conquest of a language, a merciless application to the job'.[37]

Within a few years the foreign anti-war writers in Russia would acquire the name of 'fellow-travellers'. They were not yet Bolsheviks—and most of them never became one. None had studied Lenin's doctrines with any closeness. They had not read Marx. But they increasingly sympathized to a greater or lesser extent with Lenin, Trotsky and their practical purposes. They strongly disapproved of what the Allied governments were doing with Russia. They were caught up in the revolutionary swirl. The old romance of exotic Russia entered their minds and gave their lives a new meaning. They wanted to be the people who explained the complexities and traumas of Russian affairs to readers who barely knew where the country was. In their euphoria they intended to pass on their impressions in whatever way was available. They did not yet know that this would lead them down the road of raising the cheers for a bloody revolutionary dictatorship.

5. REVOLUTION AND
THE WORLD

Lenin had obtained sanction for insurrection from the Bolshevik Central Committee at its October meetings but he could not stop worrying. Lodged in a safe apartment on Petrograd's outskirts, he wrote frantic notes to leading comrades. His suspicion was that they were losing their nerve. If the chance to get rid of Kerenski were to be lost, he believed, there might not be another one soon. With the Ministry of Internal Affairs still searching for him as a German agent, he nonetheless decided to run the risk of taking a tram to the Smolny Institute, where the Petrograd Soviet as well as all the main socialist parties were based, intending to cajole the Bolshevik leadership into an immediate insurrection. Lenin's only precaution against being recognized was to wrap a bandage round his face. His wild urge to make revolution rubbed out any fear of arrest, and he made for the city centre in an angry mood.

He underestimated quite how much had been done by the night of 6–7 November 1917. Left undisturbed, Trotsky had worked on his plan to ensure that the insurrection coincided with the opening of the Second Congress of Soviets. Kamenev and Zinoviev, whom Lenin had branded as strike-breakers for their exposure of the Central Committee's decisions, returned to help the leadership. As delegates arrived from the provinces, it was clear that the Bolsheviks by themselves would fail to obtain an absolute majority at the Congress. But they would definitely have the largest delegation and could count on approval from many other delegates. Trotsky acted with panache through the Military-Revolutionary Committee of the

Petrograd Soviet; he did everything but announce the times, date and places of the planned action. Kerenski saw what was coming and gave orders to close the bridges over the River Neva and to suppress the Bolshevik newspapers in the capital. This allowed Trotsky to depict his own actions as being of a defensive nature. In the Smolny Institute, where the Congress was scheduled to take place, sat the Menshevik and Socialist-Revolutionary leaders. Too late they were at last considering how they might replace Kerenski. Unlike Trotsky, they had no idea how to accomplish this. The morning of 7 November was full of action. The insurgents seized strategic points around the city on orders from the Military-Revolutionary Committee. Railway stations and the telegraph offices were occupied. Garrisons were placed under supervision.

The Petrograd Soviet met in emergency session that afternoon in the Smolny Institute. Trotsky led for the Bolsheviks by announcing the downfall of the Provisional Government. He then introduced Lenin, who until that point had kept out of sight on the Bolshevik corridor. Lenin, recognizable even though he had shaved off his beard, received a huge ovation and spoke as if the insurrection was complete. Fighting was in fact continuing, but Kerenski was a spent force. When the Congress of Soviets opened in the evening, it was obvious that the other parties could put up no obstacles to the seizure of power. The Bolsheviks accrued support from the floor, including from many Mensheviks and Socialist-Revolutionaries. After yet another defiant statement by Trotsky, Martov got up to demand negotiations among all the socialist parties. The Congress fell into uproar as Bolshevik responsibility for the street violence was criticized. The Menshevik and Socialist-Revolutionary leaders walked out, taking scores of their followers with them. Only the Left Socialist-Revolutionaries stayed in their places, but even they refused to join the Bolsheviks in a coalition.

This did not fluster Lenin or Trotsky. Instead they focused on spreading the news that the Provisional Government had been overthrown and that the Council of People's Commissars—Sovnarkom—had taken power. The Bolshevik leadership had a quick, informal discussion about who should fill the posts. Lenin was to be Sovnarkom's Chairman. He was the party's veteran leader and nobody contemplated having anyone else in the supreme office. But Lenin, appreciating Trotsky's talent and seeing the need to appear gracious, made the gesture of offering the post to him. Lenin must have been relieved when Trotsky refused; and indeed the only problem was that Trotsky at first expressed to reluctance to take over any big political job. He took some persuading before agreeing to become People's Commissar of Foreign Affairs. He and Lenin worked closely in tandem. Sovnarkom rapidly issued revolutionary decrees that signalled the new direction of policy being taken after Kerenski's removal.

The Decree on Land transferred the cultivation of estates owned by monarchy, gentry and Church to the peasantry. The Decree on Press sanctioned the closure of anti-Sovnarkom newspapers. The Decree on Peace called for an end to the Great War. Lenin claimed that 'the peoples' of the belligerent powers had a direct interest in this objective. In making an appeal in Sovnarkom's name, he avoided Marxist jargon. If he wanted to achieve his ends, he needed to win over organizations and groups which as yet had no affiliation with Marxism. Lenin was no close student of Allied diplomacy, but he sensed that the Americans might be more responsive than the French or British to his decree. Consequently he used language reflecting some of President Wilson's public statements on the kind of peace that was desirable. As Soviet Chairman he aimed to convince opinion in the US that Russia under communist leadership wished the nations of Europe to secure their freedom. He was hoping to edge President Wilson away from his Allied colleagues in Paris and London. He also wanted workers and soldiers to feel that the Soviet government recognized peace as the imperative priority. Most of them were not Marxists. Communist discourse had to take their ways of thinking into account.[1]

Sovnarkom's future was uncertain for several days as negotiations began among the Bolsheviks, Mensheviks and Socialist-Revolutionaries. Lenin and Trotsky had never described their preferences with precision, which proved to have been brilliantly devious. Workers and soldiers voting Bolshevik in soviet elections had assumed that this would lead to the formation of a socialist government coalition. Most Bolsheviks felt the same, and it was a basic requirement of several Bolshevik Central Committee members who had taken Lenin's side at the October meetings.[2]

Kamenev was eager to bring such a coalition to birth. The Central Committee deputed him to conduct discussions with the Menshevik and Socialist-Revolutionary leaders—and Lenin and Trotsky were impotent to prevent this. The Menshevik-led Railwaymen's Union went on strike to destroy any chance of the Bolsheviks ruling alone. Menshevik and Socialist-Revolutionary leaders felt strong enough to stipulate that they would join a coalition only on condition that it excluded Lenin and Trotsky. Politics were caught in a storm as Kerenski unexpectedly returned to the outskirts of Petrograd with a Cossack cavalry unit. Garrison troops and the Red Guard were sent out to confront them. A brief conflict followed before the Cossacks were routed and Kerenski fled. This steeled Lenin and his supporters in the Central Committee in standing firm against the demands being made upon them. Their confidence grew when the strike on the railways faded away. The Central Committee resolved to drop the talks with the Mensheviks and Socialist Revolutionaries; and although overtures continued to be made to the Left Socialist-Revolutionaries, the Bolsheviks were willing to rule by themselves in the interim. Even Kamenev and his sympathizers became willing to cast their lots in with a strategy that excluded those socialists who had co-operated with the Provisional Government.

The Bolsheviks were desperate to spread the news around Russia. The party published newspapers in all the main cities and its local committees could issue proclamations and put up posters. Sovnarkom's occupation of the telegraph offices enabled it to relay the exact text of decrees.

In city after city in Russia there was a declaration of the transfer of power to the soviets. Workers took control of factories and mines. Peasants were stimulated by the Decree on Land to occupy the landed estates. Sovnarkom and the Bolshevik Central Committee sent out messages explaining that it was up to the 'localities' to make their own revolutions. Non-Russians, who made up half the population of the old empire, were promised national self-determination. Central power remained weak and patchy, and experienced personnel were needed too badly in Petrograd and Moscow for many militants to be spared for work in the provinces. Lenin and his leading comrades felt that history was on their side. The Bolsheviks hoped that their revolution would proceed as much from below as from on high. Difficulties were unavoidable. The parties to the right of the Bolsheviks were not reconciled to being deposited in the wastepaper basket of politics. The middle and upper classes detested the Bolshevik seizure of power. The Orthodox Church was appalled by it. Kerenski's armed sally would not be the last attempt at counter-revolution. But Lenin and Trotsky trusted that events would validate their strategy. Russia would undergo a socialist transformation and seizures of power by far-left socialists would soon follow all over Europe. A whole new epoch was in the making.

Neither the Allies nor the Central Powers had any interest in helping a regime that was calling for their downfall and an immediate end to the war. Few foreign newspapers greeted the rise of Bolshevism with enthusiasm. What is more, Sovnarkom had no diplomatic service and the Provisional Government's ambassadors lobbied Allied governments to refuse recognition to the Bolsheviks.

The Western cheerleaders in Petrograd came into their own at this juncture. As John Reed, Louise Bryant, Bessie Beatty and Albert Rhys Williams roamed around the city, they understood that events of historic importance were taking place. They had the luck to be on the spot. Within minutes of the fall of the Winter Palace they had entered the building to inspect the scene.[3] The Bolsheviks welcomed assistance from the little American group in propagating the news in a positive spirit to foreign countries. Reed and his friends were given passes to enter virtually any public building they wanted.[4] They were given privileged use of the international telegraph system, and on 15 November the Military-Revolutionary Committee allowed Reed to send the very first international cable from Petrograd—he could also travel free on the railway network.[5] The Americans avidly wrote dispatches telling the story as they saw it. They tried to dispel the impression given in most of the Western press that the Bolsheviks were insincere, bloodthirsty or incompetent. They reported on the ease with which power had been seized. They recapitulated the decrees and endorsed objectives of peace, bread and land. They were acting as Sovnarkom's window on the world.

Trotsky entranced them, especially Bryant and Beatty. He was an elegant man who was punctilious in his manners and fastidious about his appearance. For years he had denounced Lenin for his divisive tendencies; he was known for his efforts to bring the Bolsheviks and Mensheviks back together before the Great War. In the revolutionary crisis of 1905 he had shown his exceptional qualities. No one spoke more vividly, and he had no need for anything more than a short set of notes before he occupied the platform. Trotsky was a master of Russian prose. He had gone to the Balkan war in 1912–13 as a special correspondent for a Kiev newspaper. His autobiographical fragments sold well. But in writing them he exposed his vanity. Despite his efforts to bring the Mensheviks and Bolsheviks back together in the Russian Social-Democratic Workers' Party before the Great War, many critics suspected him of being just as egocentric as Lenin. But what surprised everybody in 1917 was how literally he believed in the need for a ruthless proletarian dictatorship. Plenty of Russian Marxists had talked about revolutionary violence without genuinely meaning it. Trotsky meant it—and he found a like-minded comrade in Lenin.

When Beatty met Trotsky in the Smolny Institute on 7 November, she enjoyed feeling 'his lean hand grasping mine in a strong, characteristic handshake'.[6] Louise Bryant left an equally adoring picture:

> During the first days of the Bolshevik revolt I used to go to Smolny to get the latest news. Trotsky and his pretty little wife, who hardly spoke anything but French, lived in one room on the top floor. The room was partitioned off like a poor artist's attic studio. In one end were two cots and a cheap little dresser and in the other a desk and two or three wooden chairs. There were no pictures, no comfort any-where. Trotsky occupied this office all the time he was Minister of Foreign Affairs and many dignitaries found it necessary to call upon him there.[7]

Two Red Guards stood on constant duty, but Bryant noted how little he had changed his work habits and availability for interviews.[8] Of all Bolsheviks he best understood the importance of talking to foreigners who could take the revolutionary gospel to the world. Bryant recorded: 'He is the easiest official to interview in Russia and entirely the most satisfactory.'[9]

Jacques Sadoul of the French military mission agreed with this assessment.[10] On 7–8 November he spent hours in the Smolny Institute, and he wrote to his patron Albert Thomas in Paris commending Lenin and Trotsky.[11] The Bolsheviks soon treated him as a 'comrade'. Sadoul bemoaned the lack of information reaching France. He criticized Ambassador Noulens for not being abreast of events; he argued too that the French press was failing in its duty to keep its country in touch with the situation—he thought it disgraceful that he came across only one correspondent from Paris at the Smolny Institute. Not working for a newspaper, Sadoul strove to exert an influence through Albert Thomas. He reported on Trotsky's belief that the Decree on Peace would induce deep political stirrings in Europe. Even if revolutions did not instantly occur, popular pressure to end the war would grow. Although Sadoul did not expect the Germans to agree to the truce

on the eastern front that the Bolsheviks were proposing, his admiration for
Lenin and Trotsky was wholehearted: 'Today Bolshevism is a fact of life.
This is my contention. Bolshevism is a force which in my opinion cannot
be damaged by any other Russian force.'[12]

As yet he did not approve of the Bolsheviks ruling by themselves, as he
explained on 15 November: 'What preoccupies me is the urgent need for
a Menshevik–Bolshevik concentration in power in the interests of the Allies, Russia and the Revolution: I repeat this daily to Trotsky and to all the
Bolsheviks I've had contact with.' Sadoul gave the benefit of the doubt to
Bolsheviks and blamed the Mensheviks for rejecting their overtures.[13]

Trotsky and Lenin were seen to have an equal influence on events. But
Lenin concentrated on his work in Sovnarkom and the Central Committee
and did not speak to foreign correspondents. Until his beard grew back, he
did not look like the Lenin known to us from so many later posters; and
few people outside the centre of Petrograd knew what he looked like because Russian newspapers carried no photographs of him.[14] To party comrades, though, he was immediately familiar. He had founded the Bolshevik
faction of the Russian Social-Democratic Workers' Party in 1903. Although
he had sometimes co-operated with the Menshevik faction, he did this only
for tactical reasons. He wrote on every big question of Marxist theory: industrial capitalism, land, imperialism and epistemology. His co-factionalists
followed him into extremism, and there were times when they themselves
objected to his insistence on temporary compromises. Whenever he was
thwarted he formed his own sub-faction. He was the most notorious schis-
matic in the European socialist movement before the Great War. At the beginning of 1917 his band of close supporters was tiny. Russia's political and
economic disintegration as well as its military defeat gave him an opening
that was not his own handiwork. He now intended to make the most of the
situation.

Lenin was shortish, pedantic and impatient. With his thumbs tucked
into his waistcoat, he seemed at times like an angry Sunday preacher. He
gave the impression that there was only one answer—his answer—to any
complicated question. He was a gambler who trusted his intuitions. He
lived for the cause. He was a stickler for party discipline when his ideas were
official policy, but he broke all the rules as soon as he was in a minority.
Power for himself and the Bolsheviks was important to him but still dearer
to his mind was the achievement of a revolutionary dictatorship to cast

down capitalism and imperialism worldwide. He and Trotsky formed a
bond of trust in the early weeks of Soviet rule.

Trotsky organized the People's Commissariat of Foreign Affairs from a
distance and seldom entered its premises. The priority for him and Lenin
was to secure authority in Petrograd. Trotsky liked the anecdote told about
him that he intended simply to publish the secret wartime treaties of the
Allies and then 'shut up shop'.[15] On the first occasion he had tried to accomplish this, he failed. The officials who had worked for the Provisional
Government barred the doors of the old ministry to him. As soon as his
entourage forced the locks, there was a mass exodus of personnel and Trotsky discovered that former Deputy Foreign Minister Neratov had made off
with the treaties.[16] This only temporarily foiled Sovnarkom. Texts of the
treaties were discovered and verified, and Trotsky immediately released them
for publication on 21 November 1917.[17] They confirmed what the Bolsheviks had been saying all year—and indeed the Mensheviks and Socialist-
Revolutionaries had said the same thing. Now it was proved beyond fear of
contradiction: the Allies had entered the war with ambitions of territorial
aggrandizement.

Every Allied power was assured of benefit if and when the Central Powers were defeated. In March 1915 it had been agreed that Russia would
annex Constantinople and northern Persia while Britain and France would
acquire spheres of influence in what subsequently became Iraq, Jordan and
Syria. The following month Italy was promised the Trentino as well as territory in Anatolia in return for joining the Allied side. In May 1916 the
British and French agreed between themselves how to divide up the Middle
East. In August that year France, Britain and Russia offered Transylvania
and Dobruja to Romania to secure its adherence to the Alliance. Further
deals were done in 1917 satisfying demands by the Japanese, British, French
and Russians for the post-war settlement. Soviet newspapers were the first
to print the treaties. The content was so sensational that the Western press
followed suit—and it was Trotsky's expectation that workers and soldiers
throughout Europe would conclude that the war should be stopped at once.
And whereas British and French public opinion had been easy to stir up in
favour of war in 1914, the American entry into the conflict was always con-
troversial in the US and President Wilson repudiated expansionist aims.
Lenin and Trotsky hoped to prise Washington out of the Anglo-French embrace. Wilson had already insisted on being informed about the Allied

treaties. His abhorrence of them was instantaneous; and on a visit to Washington the British Foreign Secretary A. J. Balfour had to express regret at the spectacle of European states striving to distribute countries among themselves as the spoils of war. Wilson refused to be bound by treaties made by others before America had joined the war.[18]

The question meanwhile arose about what was going to happen in Russia. The decrees streamed thick and fast from Sovnarkom. Workers' control was approved for industrial enterprises. Universal free education was introduced for children. Church and state were separated. The official calendar was changed from Julian to Gregorian—and many Orthodox Christian believers thought this proved that Lenin or Trotsky was the Antichrist. Religious processions were banned or discouraged. Economic nationalizations were announced. The banks were expropriated. Large industrial concerns were taken into the hands of the revolutionary state—and a further programme of seizures was projected. The entire export and import trade was turned into a state monopoly. Wherever local soviets found the peasantry withholding grain from sale, they dispatched armed workers' units to take it by force. The People's Commissariats replaced the old ministries. An entirely new security apparatus, the Extraordinary Commission (Cheka, in its Russian acronym), was established under Felix Dzerzhinski to combat sabotage and counter-revolutionary activity. Lenin deliberately arranged for the Cheka's operations to lie outside Sovnarkom's control. Annihilation of resistance to Sovnarkom was the cardinal aim. As they consolidated their power, the Bolsheviks repeated their offer to share power with the Left Socialist-Revolutionaries and a concordat was agreed on 20 December 1917.

All this happened under the grim shadow of war. Sovnarkom had sued for peace on 22 November and dismissed General Dukhonin for refusing to transmit the request to the Germans. The Bolshevik ensign Nikolai Krylenko temporarily took over command. Ludendorff asked General Hoffmann, at the headquarters of the German forces on the eastern front, whether it was possible to negotiate with 'these people'. Hoffmann said yes. If Ludendorff needed additional troops in northern France, this was the way to get them.[19] On 15 December an armistice was agreed along the entire eastern front from the Baltic Sea to the Black Sea. Both sides prepared for talks to be held a week later.

The Bolsheviks at the same time encouraged Russian front-line troops to fraternize with Germans. While urgently seeking to reduce the likelihood of Germany renewing its offensive, Sovnarkom was eager to expand revolutionary activity. Propaganda was distributed across the trenches to German and Austrian soldiers who were urged to stop fighting and overthrow their governments. Sovnarkom also tried to gain control of Ukraine by sending forces to Kiev against the Central Rada, which had started acting like the government of an independent state after Kerenski's downfall. Conflict raged between Bolsheviks and the Ukrainian administration throughout the winter. The Bolsheviks saw no absolute distinction between internal and external policy. In December 1917 Lenin summoned Finnish ministers to Petrograd and granted independence to their country. The Finns were less than enthusiastic since they worried that any collusion with Sovnarkom would be held against them by the Western Allies. But they acceded to the Soviet offer and returned to Helsinki to celebrate. The Bolsheviks calculated that if the Finns became independent they would cease to mistrust the Russians—and eventually they would acquire a far-left government that would align itself with Sovnarkom. Finland would come back to Russia.

The Soviet leadership tried to make light of its difficulties. The Constituent Assembly election took place in late November and resulted in defeat for the Bolsheviks, who gained less than a quarter of the votes. Lenin had wanted to call off the election rather than risk this outcome, but his advice was rejected because he and his comrades had made great play of being the only party that would convoke the Assembly. The Bolsheviks would have done better if the electoral lists had been drawn up after the Left Socialist-Revolutionaries split organizationally from the rest of their party and entered Sovnarkom. In fact no single party achieved an absolute majority. But the rump of the Party of Socialist-Revolutionaries emerged with easily the biggest number of seats. When the Constituent Assembly met on 18 January 1918, the Socialist-Revolutionaries took control. Sovnarkom reacted by ordering closure of the proceedings a day later, and Red Guards enforced Lenin's orders. Lacking the troops to resist, the Socialist-Revolutionary leaders moved off to their political stronghold in the Volga region. In the provincial capital Samara they established the government they had wanted to create in Petrograd. Its name was the Committee of Members of the Constituent Assembly, or Komuch in its Russian acronym. Komuch resolved to take power back from Sovnarkom by armed force.

The Bolsheviks remained calm about this state of affairs even though it was bound to lead to civil war. They had made their revolution. They could not know how long they would last in power. They and their families were aware that danger could be in store for them in Petrograd. Bolshevik leaders joked that they kept their suitcases packed for fear that they might suddenly have to flee. But they were determined to fight to the end for the revolutionary power they had established.

6. IN THE LIGHT OF THE FIRE

The Bolshevik leaders saw themselves instead as the advance guard of Marxist science and revolutionary progress—they hated being thought of as mere politicians. Abroad, in the months before their propaganda reached foreign far-left socialists, they remained something of a mystery; and unsympathetic newspapers—as the vast majority were in the West—depicted them as a gang of vandals who had exploited the unusual circumstances of Russia's wartime travail. The Russian adversaries of Bolshevism generally offered the same analysis. The few among them who accepted that Lenin and Trotsky were bright and intelligent nonetheless insisted that they had taken leave of their senses. The general prediction was that Bolshevik rule would be ephemeral. No one thought they stood much chance of holding on to power. Although the Bolsheviks themselves shared the suspicion that their days in government might be numbered, they still believed that their example would be followed elsewhere even if they went down to defeat. They were willing to lay down their lives in the revolutionary cause, convinced that history was on their side—and it was about to be shown that only those observers who took account of the communist mental universe could properly plan ways to counteract it.

Nikolai Bukharin, Bolshevik Central Committee member and young philosopher of communism, offered an ecstatic hymn to the glorious communist future:

> The human race is not broken up into warring camps: it is united here by common work and the common struggle with the external forces of nature. Border posts are dug out. Individual fatherlands are

eliminated. All humanity without national distinctions is bound together in all its parts and organized into one single whole. Here all
the peoples are one great friendly working family.[1]

Like the Old Testament prophet Isaiah who had rhapsodized about the wolf
dwelling with the lamb and the leopard lying down with the kid, Bukharin
clearly felt that a great and perfect epoch lay ahead for humankind.

Communist thinkers swaddled their ideas in global clothing. They believed that the Great War was no accident of dynastic rivalries or personal
misjudgements. The slaughterhouse of 1914 was the result of economic development reaching a level where profits were insecure without conquest
of new foreign markets. European states had scrambled to colonize Africa
and Asia in the last years of the nineteenth century. Rising powers like Germany had arrived too late to seize what they thought they deserved, and
their governments were under pressure by banks and industries to adopt a
belligerent policy towards the established empires. Capitalist economic development required the taking of gambles with assets and elbowing com-
petitors aside. Cabinets had to satisfy the demands of their most powerful
businessmen. 'Finance capitalism' was the dominant force in the world
economy, a case powerfully made by the Austrian Marxist Rudolf Hilferding in his 1910 book *Finance Capital*. Bolsheviks had welcomed the book
as scientific proof that capitalism had reached its highest possible stage of
development. Economic crises and world wars would occur until such time
as socialism took control. It did not matter to the communists in Russia
that Hilferding did not share their ideas on violent revolution and dictatorship. They praised his economics while rejecting his politics.

They spat out contemporary European socialism in disgust. They honoured Karl Marx and Friedrich Engels and continued to subscribe to the
usefulness of earlier writings by Georgi Plekhanov and Karl Kautsky. But
they believed that Plekhanov and Kautsky had turned traitors to Europe's
labour movement by their actions since 1914. Plekhanov had supported
the Russian military effort and Kautsky had failed to call for Germany's defeat. Unconditional opposition to the war was shared by the entire Bolshevik leadership.

Bolsheviks marked out their position by calling themselves communists
and denouncing most other socialists as 'social-traitors' while claiming
that they were the only true socialists. Which were they? Communists or

socialists? Lenin tried to clear up the confusion in *The State and Revolution*, which he wrote in 1917 and published the following year. He had no time for any kind of socialism other than Marxism. He also insisted that Marxists for decades had misinterpreted Karl Marx and Friedrich Engels and allowed their essential ideas to fall into abeyance. Genuine Marxism according to Lenin was founded on the need for violent revolution and a 'dictatorship of the proletariat' so that capitalism might be supplanted. The dictatorial structure would only be temporary. It would establish a socialist order enshrining the principle of 'an equal amount of products for an equal amount of labour'. As support grew throughout society, the reliance on force would steadily decrease. A second stage would then begin that would be the ultimate stage in human history: communism. No compulsion at all would be required in communist society. There would be no army, no bureaucracy and no state. Social classes would disappear. Life would proceed on lines set by the people of the entire world with the common good in mind. Although Lenin was not someone who often displayed his poetic side, he looked forward keenly to a time when the universal principle would be 'from each according to his ability, to each according to his needs'.

Lenin pinned his arguments to the coat-tails of Marx and Engels. If he could prove to his own satisfaction that his was the correct interpretation of Marxist doctrine, that was quite enough for him. Trotsky and Bukharin were uncomfortable about this. Bukharin felt it important to subject the recent technological and social changes in contemporary capitalism to close scrutiny. Witnessing the latest profusion of inventions, he insisted that well-being and stability would remain out of reach for most people until after a socialist revolution. Trotsky too disdained to hark back endlessly to the founders of Marxism. His forte was to highlight the unfettered profiteering and bottomless human misery brought about by the war.

Bolsheviks agreed that they were living in an era when the downtrodden of the earth would become its rulers. Ivan Zalkind, Trotsky's deputy in the People's Commissariat of Foreign Affairs, put it like this:

> Our revolution is a revolution belonging completely to the workers. Go to Petrograd and see the district soviets, go and see the Red Guards and you'll notice that it's above all a workers' revolution. The peasants and soldiers come only in second place. The bourgeoisie

doesn't exist in this second revolution. The intellectuals who played the primordial role in 1905 today are only supernumeraries. Lenin and Trotsky are merely the spokesmen of the workers. We are currently carrying out a great experiment of the dictatorship of the proletariat. It's no longer a revolution of the *sans culottes* [as in the French Revolution] but of the penniless.[2]

Bukharin, too, felt sure that the communists had the world at their feet:

People in [the] communist order don't sit on one another's neck. Here there are no rich or parvenus, there are no bosses and subordinates; here society is not divided into classes, one of which lords it over another. But once there are no classes, this means that there are no different sorts of people (poor and rich) with one sort sharpening its teeth against another—the oppressors against the oppressed or the oppressed against the oppressors.[3]

Lenin admitted that Russia's factory workers were only a small part of society. Sensing that this infringed his theory of 'the dictatorship of the proletariat', he sometimes brandished slogans such as putting power into the hands of 'the workers and poorest peasants'. Bolshevik writers anyway made clear that the urban 'proletariat' did not consist only of the factory workforce. A booklet was issued about domestic servants, who were to be attracted into the revolutionary movement. So too were the unemployed. Communists announced that the days of the privileged few enjoying the ministrations of the poor were coming to an end.[4]

Trotsky thought that events had validated the revolutionary strategy he had advocated since 1905. In his booklet *What Next?* he declared:

Throwing off the manacles of capitalist power, the revolution would become *permanent*, i.e. uninterrupted; it would apply state power not so as to consolidate a regime of capitalist exploitation materially but on the contrary so as to surmount it. Its definitive success along these lines would depend on the successes of the proletarian revolution in Europe. On the other hand, the Russian revolution has been capable of delivering the more powerful thrust to the revolutionary movement in the West the more decisively and bravely it

breaks the resistance of its own bourgeoisie. Such was and remains
the *only real* prospect for the further development of the revolution.[5]

Was this utopian? Trotsky answered no. The true idiocy in his eyes had been
the doctrines of rivals like the Mensheviks and Socialist-Revolutionaries
who went into coalition with 'capitalist ministers'. They lacked spirit and
clear-sightedness; they were double-dealers. The Bolsheviks were not carrying out a 'national' or a 'bourgeois' revolution but had started an international socialist one. He declared: 'And the twentieth century is "our
fatherland in time".'[6] Trotsky gave out the slogan: 'Permanent revolution
against permanent carnage!'[7]

   Communism would soon change everything, and communists assumed
that Europe was where they stood their best chance of political advance.
The continent was the cockpit of world war. Surely the deaths and material
privations since 1914 had perfected the conditions for the Marxist case to
attract popular support. 'European revolution' tripped easily off Bolshevik
tongues.

   Russian communist ideas about Europe in the party were not those of
conventional geography. The school textbooks said it stretched from Por-
tugal to the Urals. This was not what Bolsheviks had in mind when they
talked of 'going' to Europe despite the fact that Russia had its own large European zone. Bolshevik leader I. I. Kutuzov was to write an account of his
westward journey by train from Moscow in the early 1920s. The first stage
took him to Latvia. He commented that people started calling him mister
rather than comrade when he crossed the frontier. He noticed how clean
Riga appeared after his experience of Russian cities. Latvia was impressive
enough, but when at last he reached German territory at Eidkunen, Kutuzov's eye was caught by the almost complete absence of dirt and litter. Even
the countryside of Germany was remarkable to his eyes—and all this was
before he got to Berlin, a city that surpassed his every expectation in its
modernity. To Kutuzov it seemed self-evident: 'This was the beginning of
Europe.'[8] And Europe in the Bolshevik imagination was one half of 'the
West' whose other half lay across the Atlantic in North America.

   Bolsheviks took it for granted that socialist revolution in Germany was
the key to their survival and success in Russia. Former emigrants like Lenin,
Trotsky and Bukharin admired the cultural and organizational achievements
of the German labour movement. Marx and Engels, the originators of Marxism, had been German. The left wing of the German Social-Democratic

Party had broken away to form the Spartakusbund and, as Lenin saw it, proved that the labour movement in Germany retained the potential to effect a seizure of power and a revolutionary transformation. German workers were the flower of the European socialist movement. They were the most educated, skilled labour force in the entire continent. Their discipline at work was legendary. Their commitment to self-improvement at home and at leisure was remarkable. Most of them voted for the social-democrats, and the party had 633,000 members in 1909. Bolsheviks were angry when the German Social-Democratic Party's caucus in the Reichstag voted financial credits for the war effort in mid-1914; but Lenin and his friends put the blame for this 'betrayal' on the party leadership. They refused to believe that Germany's workers would tolerate this situation for ever. The Spartacists, when they obtained their opportunity, would surely prove able to pull them back to the line of revolution—and the great potential of the German proletariat would be fulfilled.

What is more, Bolsheviks were impressed by the steps taken in Germany towards centralized state regulation. Capitalists had never been more closely integrated into planning mechanisms. Trotsky in particular was intrigued by the government's measures for bringing official order and purpose to the economy. He proposed to use this approach in order to further his revolutionary aims: 'For the introduction of control over production and distribution the proletariat has had extremely valuable models in the West, above all in the form of Germany's so-called "war socialism".' In Russia this would require the carrying out of 'an agrarian revolution'. If state economic co-ordination was going to be introduced it would have to be done in a steady fashion.[9]

Yuri Larin, a left-wing Marxist who joined the Bolsheviks in 1917, was equally inspired by what he read about the German situation. He noted how the state had taken food supplies into its hands and compelled agricultural producers to form unions so as to make them easier to control. Each German region and district was strictly supervised. Transport of goods beyond local borders was forbidden except with official permission. Prices were set for basic products. The entire economy was operated according to a central plan. According to Larin, Germany's government found itself unable to avoid conceding to demands by urban and rural workers.[10] Even so, the war had disrupted and lowered output. Most German people were worse off than before the fighting had started, and the effect of this was registered on socialist leaders who began to demand the forcible expropriation of agricultural land for the benefit of consumption in the cities. It was Larin's belief that the drift of thinking towards the needs of urban residents would soon be seen in Russia too.[11] As he pointed out, Germany's workers had called for a universal compulsory system of food rationing at the outset of war. Fairness had fallen by the wayside as the propertied classes secured greater supplies than the average. The way forward in Russia as in Germany was to introduce a regime corresponding to the requirements of the people as a whole.[12]

Larin argued that the best outcome for the workers and everybody else would be the 'urbanization' of agriculture. Farms should be set up on the outskirts of cities. The principle should be adopted that 'agricultural enterprises must be subordinated to direct supervision and administration by the *consumers* of grain'. The industrial proletariat ought to have a dominant influence.[13] Larin pointed out that no warring country was without its economic problems. He predicted high cereal prices for a long period after the war. He could not see how Europe could cope with its problems unless power was being exercised by the workers to ensure a swift expansion of farm output.[14] Nikolai Bukharin spelled out how this could be done. Rather than allow peasants to grab and divide up the landed estates he recommended the establishment of large collective farms.[15] The peasantry should not be left to decide how to plough, sow and reap—and the same prescription should be applied in every European country. The entire property order in Russia was going to be toppled and Bolsheviks wanted to ensure that the precedent would be followed elsewhere. The purpose was to persuade everybody that material possessions were always withheld from the poor in the most unfair fashion. A Bolshevik called Kii argued that the mystique of private ownership had to be exposed as the deceit that it was. Revolutions were not as difficult to undertake as 'bourgeois' social science contended.[16]

The fundamental ideas of the Bolsheviks were never less than grandiose. They loved cities, industry, the proletariat and central state planning. They believed in the imposition of expertise. They praised order and control. Their priority was to provide what they thought were the basic requirements of civilization: work, health care, social insurance, food, shelter and education. They thought they knew better than the people they intended to serve. In the end—and they thought that the end would come soon— the people would understand and accept their wisdom.

They rejected all counter-ideals as reactionary, pernicious nonsense. They disliked agriculture, handicrafts, the 'chaos' of markets, religion, private income and individual freedom. They detested banks—when Ivy Litvinov went into the Hampstead branch of Lloyds to cash a cheque she was treated by Maxim's comrades as if she had done something immoral. She was not well off. She could not understand why revolutionary militants should be so grim towards her when they themselves aspired to a bourgeois lifestyle.[17] But Bolsheviks liked to think they saw through the hypocrisies of middle-class prejudices. They thought marriage to be one of these. When Lenin wed Nadezhda Krupskaya it was only so that the police would allow them to stay together in Siberian exile. Trotsky and Alexandra Sokolovskaya went through a marriage ceremony for the same reason. Bolsheviks dropped and acquired partners with more than average frequency at that time. Their loyalty was to the Revolution. Family took second place to the Revolution in the lives of the militants. The cause was everything.

It was all very well to study the history of Russia and to appreciate the difficulties ahead, but 'science' could take the movement for liberation only so far (although it was true that some Bolsheviks had written extensively on the Russian past). The party had to show daring and take risks. An exemplary opportunity was being offered to the political far left in Petrograd. Where Russians went, others would soon follow. There was no time for intellectual doubt.

One big distinction of the Bolshevik leadership lay in their readiness to use massive force to achieve their ends. Ivan Maiski offered a shrewd estimate of Lenin. His leader reminded him of a sentence in the Book of Revelation: 'So then because thou art lukewarm, and neither cold nor hot, I will spue thee out of my mouth.'[18] Lenin had always been notorious for his fondness for dictatorship and terror. Trotsky had been rather enigmatic. While proposing extreme schemes such as a 'workers' government', he had kept comradely relations with the Mensheviks and criticized the Bolsheviks. In 1917 he revealed that he accepted that a government of workers would indeed need to use severe methods. For once he called on Marx as an authority. It was Marx who had lauded the Jacobin terror with its frequent use of the guillotine in the French Revolution and called it 'the plebeian method' of crushing resistance. Trotsky admired the Jacobins for their 'iron repression'.[19] Not all Bolshevik leaders were yet of the same ferocity. Kamenev and Bukharin often questioned the need for severe repressive measures and occasionally did something to moderate them. But they in no way forswore such methods in principle. As time went on, the entire leadership came over to the idea that there could be no revolutionary consolidation without harsh dictatorship and widespread state terror.

Communists cared little for detailed prognostication. They dealt in visions and slogans, in promises and threats and commitments. They talked about 'class struggle', 'class war' and even 'civil war'. They paid no attention to details of governance. Adolf Ioffe, one of Trotsky's close associates, was unusual in writing a booklet about local administration.[20] Action took precedence over forethought. Lenin used to quote Goethe to the effect that theory is grey whereas the tree of life is green. (Not that this stopped him being doctrinaire and bookish when explaining his own theoretical vision.) He and others stated endlessly that they were encouraging a 'revolution from below'. They saw themselves as liberators of the working class. Soon there would be proletarian self-administration. But how this would be combined with the party's objective of a highly centralized state was never elaborated—there was no serious attempt to ask the question. The Bolsheviks cheerfully smashed institutions to smithereens at the same time as insisting on internal organizational discipline as a permanent requirement. They had no concern about the disruption they were bound to cause. Their refrain was that revolutions were messy. They detested what they called politicking. They were repelled by compromise; they preferred open decisions to a public life of fudges and corruption.

They felt that they were the true Reds of revolutionary Russia. Conservatives and liberals called every Menshevik and Socialist-Revolutionary a Red. But the Bolsheviks were undeniably more radical than their rivals, and so they monopolized political ownership of the colour. But although they displayed an expansive confidence, their doctrines were far from being comprehensive: there were not just marginal gaps in these doctrines but huge, hazardous holes. Like utopians of earlier centuries, they scoffed when this was pointed out to them. They called on their followers to show belief and confidence. They took pride in their willingness to experiment. They regarded themselves as open-minded scientists and humanitarians. When others predicted disaster they shrugged and claimed that advanced capitalism had already brought the world to catastrophe. Something entirely different was due to be tested. It was the dawn of a new epoch.

Bolsheviks liked to think that they were unique in the Russia of 1917. This was not wholly true. In every modern profession there were many practitioners who partook of all or some of the Bolshevik ideals and had the same negative prejudices. Among the other revolutionary parties too there were leaders and militants whose mental world shared territory with Bolshevism. Indeed the communists borrowed much of their thinking from others. The professions had many members who wanted to take control of their sector of public life and set policy in the direction of rapid change. Left-of-centre economists favoured increasing governmental regulation of industry and finance.[21] Teachers, scientists, artists and commanders were eager for a chance to transform their occupations by the introduction of new techniques; and they were aware that they needed a strong central government to achieve modernization. There was a welcome for any government that looked as if it would subsidize their activity. What is more, several features of thought in rival parties corresponded to what was intended by the Bolsheviks. The need for the state to play a big part in the running of the economy was widely felt by all socialists and even by liberals. Mensheviks and Socialist-Revolutionaries continued to regard most Bolsheviks as comrades. The communist determination to turn Russia upside down was shared far beyond the confines of the party.

Much though Bolshevik doctrine pretended to scientific status, it was in fact rooted in blind faith and the Russian revolutionary tradition. Lenin and Trotsky never seriously took account of the dire warnings about the likely result of their project. The Mensheviks and Socialist-Revolutionaries may have shared a lot of their social and economic assumptions but they also issued clear predictions that the horrors of civil war would be the inevitable result if the Bolshevik party somehow managed to hold on to power. They doubted that Europe was on the brink of revolution. They ridiculed Lenin's promise to regenerate the Russian economy swiftly or at all. They were talking to the deaf. Bolsheviks had made their choice. If there was going to be civil war, it would be of short duration and easily won. There would surely be European socialist revolution and, when Germany acquired its revolutionary government, economic exchange between the Russians and the Germans would guarantee rapid recovery from wartime devastation. It was in this frame of mind that Bolshevik leaders had seized power in Petrograd. Foreigners saw only chaos and weakness in Russia. The Bolsheviks asked them to look through different spectacles and observe the fire being lit for a brilliant new world order.

7. DIPLOMATIC IMPASSE

Lenin's Decree on Peace set out fresh basic principles for the kind of peace he wanted in the world. Both the Allies and the Central Powers tried to ignore him. The exception was Woodrow Wilson, who was fired by the urge to achieve a lasting peace and saw the defeat of the Central Powers as a prerequisite. Coming before a joint session of the US Congress on 8 January 1918, he declared that the Allies should impose a universal peace involving democracy, free trade, open treaties and national self-determination. He depended on advice and assistance from his confidant Colonel Edward House, who had returned from a tour of the European capitals, and a group of key advisers, known as 'The Inquiry'; but the impetus came from Wilson himself. Wilson was aiming to prescribe the shape of the post-war world order. His Congress speech was delivered with panache and gained instant fame as the 'Fourteen Points'. The American press endorsed the President's words as offering the first great contribution to ending the carnage brought about by the rivalries of ancient European states. Wilson was enabling the US to stand tall among the nations. Many Americans had disliked his decision to enter the war against Germany, but many took pride in his vision of a global framework for peace and freedom.

Wilson's advocacy of national self-determination disturbed the Western Allies. Lloyd George had his hands full with the consequences of the Easter 1916 rising in Dublin against Great Britain, not to mention growing demands for independence among Indians and other peoples in the British Empire. Clemenceau and Italy's Prime Minister Vittorio Orlando felt disquiet, too. But they feared annoying a US President who was sending indispensable finance, munitions and troops across the Atlantic. They had always stressed that their war against Germany and Austria-Hungary was a just and moral one. They could hardly speak out against democracy or free trade, and it was difficult to deny the right of nations to determine their own futures. The Western press reported Wilson's Fourteen Points in detail, and the American embassy gave away many thousands of free copies of a translation on the streets of Petrograd—altogether 5.5 million copies were printed for distribution in the territories of the former Russian Empire.[1] This contrasted with the Allied treatment of Lenin's Decree on Peace which appeared abroad in full only in far-left booklets after being translated in Petrograd. The Allied powers had no interest in facilitating its distribution.

The Bolsheviks had to improvise their publicity. Trotsky, with his instinct for propaganda, was frustrated at being unable to write for the foreign press or get his speeches carried by newsreels. In desperation he asked his People's Commissariat to call in Claude Anet of the *Petit Parisien* newspaper and offer exclusive stories.[2] Nothing came of this. Trotsky had to make do by relying on his existing group of cheerleaders to write whatever they liked for their editors.

The pattern of work became smoother after he took on the young Bolshevik Yevgenia Shelepina as his secretarial assistant. Born in 1894 and educated at grammar school, she was working in the Ministry of Trade and Industry and disapproved of those civil servants who went on strike against the October Revolution. She was seconded to the People's Commissariat of Labour before being recruited for work with Trotsky in room 67 of the Smolny Institute:

> I found [him] in that same room where I used to see him, at the end of the corridor on the third floor. It was differently furnished then. There was just one table in the corner by the two windows. In the little room partitioned off was some dreadful furniture, particularly a green divan with a terrible pillow on it. You see it had been the room of the resident mistress on that floor of the Institute when it was still an Institute for girls. Trotsky sat on one side of the table and I sat on the other. I did not hide from him that I was quite unfit for the work, but that I wanted to do anything I could.[3]

Shelepina started by calling him 'comrade Trotsky' but this only made him laugh, so they addressed each other with conventional politeness as 'Yevgenia Petrovna' and 'Lev Davidovich'. She smartened up Trotsky's room and requisitioned a functioning typewriter to replace the antique machine on his desk.[4]

He was still in the habit of writing all his letters in longhand,[5] and she wanted to relieve him of this. Since she had not been trained in shorthand, he arranged to dictate on to a phonograph; but he could not get on with this contraption and they reverted to amateurish methods. Shelepina was thrilled at being involved in the work.[6]

Trotsky wrote frequently to the Petrograd embassies stressing that Sovnarkom was the real power in Russia and deserved official recognition. This was vital if the Bolsheviks were to break down the obstacles to international communication. He had to admit that any diplomatic relations would be of an unusual kind since the Bolsheviks remained open enemies of every state in the world. He insisted that he aimed to have such relations not only with governments but also with 'socialist-revolutionary parties that are thrusting themselves at overthrowing the existing governments'.[7] At the same time he was determined to prevent Allied diplomats from interfering in Russian politics. When he thought that the British embassy was helping the anti-Soviet efforts of Boris Savinkov, he threatened to arrest Sir George Buchanan—if only in conversation with Sadoul.[8] He refused to see a contradiction between demanding official recognition and encouraging worldwide subversion.[9] Only the Spanish embassy would parley with Trotsky, and its chargé d'affaires Garrido Cisneros welcomed the Soviet proposal for an armistice and peace negotiations. The rest of the diplomatic corps expressed outrage. But Spain was taking no part in the war and, although Cisneros had blotted his copybook in Allied eyes, nothing of practical consequence resulted.[10]

Routine work at the People's Commissariat—in the old Ministry of Foreign Affairs building—was done by Trotsky's deputy Ivan Zalkind. Zalkind's professional qualifications were no better than Trotsky's, but his science doctorate from Algiers University meant that he had fluent French.[11] He was even brusquer than the average Bolshevik. France's diplomats thought that he had a particular dislike for them,[12] but he was just as aggressive to every other nationality and seemed to make trouble just for the sake of it. Skinny, myopic, with long silvery hair, he was puny in appearance; British agent George Hill, with no attempt at impartiality, described him as 'a most unpleasant hunchback with the viciousness of a rat'.[13] Zalkind compensated by adopting a quasi-military uniform and contriving to look bold and combative.[14] (The sporting of military apparel was a growing trend among Bolsheviks: Party Central Committee Secretary Yakov Sverdlov had a black leather jacket and trousers tailored for him and bought a pair of long black boots and a black leather cap.)

Trotsky and Zalkind set up a Bureau of International Revolutionary Propaganda for the Commissariat under Boris Reinstein, one of the revolutionaries who had returned from America; and John Reed and Albert Rhys Williams were taken on to the staff to bring 'American advertising psychology' to the publications directed at the troops of the Central Powers. There was also a Department of Prisoners-of-War, led by Radek, as well as a Department of the Press. These bodies produced material in German, Hungarian and Romanian.[15] Reed, Rhys Williams and others were paid about $50–$60 a month.[16] The Propaganda Bureau printed tons of material for dispatch across the trenches of the eastern front. Half a million copies of the German daily newspaper *Die Fackel* (later called *Der Völkfried*) were printed. The Hungarian print run was the same, while there were a quarter of a million copies each of the Czech, Romanian and Turkish versions.[17] Even Rhys Williams helped out with *Die Fackel* despite his primitive grasp of German. He and Reed had little Russian but they possessed all the skills needed to sub-edit English translations of Soviet announcements.[18] The Decree on Peace was hurriedly translated into German, French and English. Yakov Peters, the Latvian who oversaw the work, admitted that his own fluency in English and even Russian was inadequate—and Reinstein, Reed and Rhys Williams became as active in the Bolshevik cause as it was possible to be without joining the Bolshevik party.[19]

Allied diplomats tried to make sense of all this for their governments. On 19 November 1917 the American ambassador David Francis issued an appeal to 'the People of Russia': 'I address you because there is no official in the Foreign Office with whom I can communicate, and all of the members of the government or ministry with which I had official relations are inaccessible, being in flight or in prison, according to my best information.'[20] He emphasized that the US had signed no secret treaties and he repeated President Wilson's hope of preserving good relations with Russia.[21] On 27 November Sir George Buchanan fired off a telegram saying that it was unrealistic to expect the beaten and exhausted Russians to stay in the war. He proposed a change of policy. Russia should be released from its contractual obligations to keep up the fight on the eastern front. Buchanan argued that this would make a rapprochement between Russia and Germany less likely and might even induce the Russians to continue other kinds of resistance to the Germans.[22] He did not recommend recognition for Sovnarkom. The Bolsheviks were not to be allowed privileges until their policies changed. But talks had to be held with them. Buchanan advocated using informal intermediaries for this purpose, and the Foreign Secretary A. J. Balfour agreed.[23]

The Petrograd ambassadors have a reputation for being stupid old fogeys who lacked the intellectual and cultural depth to understand Soviet communism. Although some were indeed fogeyish and a couple were elderly, none was unintelligent. They thought seriously about Bolshevism as they witnessed it. Italy's Marchese della Torretta knew about the breakdown of order from direct experience after being robbed late at night on his way back to the Hôtel de l'Europe.[24] Leading diplomats, whether they represented the Allies or neutral countries, expressed revulsion at the end to civilities they had thought they could take for granted in Russia. They understood what Lenin and Trotsky wanted to do in the world. They saw from the start that religion, nationhood, civil peace, legality and civic freedoms were under threat. They observed for themselves how 'the dictatorship of the proletariat' brought about state terror. They came from a different world, and they preferred their world, warts and all.

Sovnarkom, however, had kept hold of some bargaining chips. On 28 November Trotsky sent a note to Buchanan saying that if the United Kingdom continued to imprison Chicherin and Petrov, British citizens conducting counter-revolutionary propaganda in Russia would not go unpunished. In gaol, Chicherin had cut his ties with the Mensheviks and become a Bolshevik. He announced that he would return to Russia only 'as a free man'. He hired a lawyer. He demanded that he should be allowed visits by Joseph King MP; he intimated that he had personal friends including Consul-General Onou in the Russian embassy. He sent demands for the Mensheviks to repay the money he had lent them in the past—and he expressed the wish that his associates should buy him marmalade and golden syrup to supplement the poor prison diet.[25] Consul-General Onou flatly refused to help. He thought there were 'already enough dangerous madmen in Russia' and did not want to add to the number.[26] Chicherin hated having to rise early in the morning. He complained often about the injustice being done to him; but as the weeks passed he repeated that he would strenuously object to being released if the plan was to deport him straight away. When he left Brixton prison, he intended put his affairs in order before moving on to Russia.[27]

The cabinet in London at first refused to yield to Trotsky's intimidation even though there seemed no national interest in holding on to Chicherin or bringing him to trial.[28] When Buchanan made no reply to Trotsky, the People's Commissariat indicated that exit visas from Russia would no longer be issued to British subjects, including diplomats; Trotsky also threatened to take 'counter-revolutionaries' from Britain into custody.[29] When in mid-December Trotsky demanded an interview with Noulens it was difficult to refuse him after he threatened that otherwise he would expel the military mission.[30] Trotsky complained that France had sent agents to talk to the Central Rada in Kiev. Noulens replied that the French initiative was simply a reaction to Ukrainian national independence and that the Bolsheviks themselves had decreed the right of non-Russians to secede from the old multinational state. That the current governments in Petrograd and Kiev were enemies was not the fault of the French. Noulens added that the military mission had been instructed to avoid interference in Ukrainian politics and to stay out of the Russo-Ukrainian conflict.[31]

Lloyd George and Balfour soon yielded on the treatment of Chicherin and Petrov, and Buchanan relayed the news to the Soviet authorities. Trotsky exulted: 'Sir Buchanan [*sic*] is a practical man with whom one can come to an understanding.'[32] By the end of the month Buchanan had also conceded Sovnarkom's freedom to send its couriers without hindrance to London.[33] The British government edged towards putting Anglo-Russian relations on a fresh footing.

On 21 December the War Cabinet approved a memorandum on the Russian question for consultation with the French. Buchanan's request for sick leave for his vertigo was to be granted, and Sir Francis Lindley would become chargé d'affaires in Petrograd.[34] The ambassador's departure was desirable on political as well as medical grounds: he was too closely associated in the Bolshevik mind with the Kadets to be able to liaise with Sovnarkom. 'Unofficial agents' would be used to conduct relations. British diplomacy should emphasize that the United Kingdom would not meddle in Russia's internal politics or favour a counter-revolution. The Foreign Office would not even highlight its displeasure at Russia opening negotiations with the Central Powers. But the British reserved the right to stay in contact with Ukraine and other parts of the former empire not ruled by the Bolsheviks. Balfour's idea was for France to take care of Ukraine while Britain busied itself with the other borderlands. He stressed the priority of facilitating the transport of Ukrainian supplies to Romania, and he wanted the

Bolsheviks to accept the need to prevent foodstuffs and munitions reaching Germany from its territory.[35] The French welcomed the memorandum two days later.[36]

Every Allied embassy made use of unofficial agents. David Francis turned to Raymond Robins of the Red Cross as his intermediary with the Soviet leadership. Robins had friendly links with the Smolny Institute. He thought it was in the American interest to come to some kind of accommodation with Lenin and Trotsky—and he hoped to make an impact in Washington by influencing what went into Francis's reports.[37] Trotsky felt that he could exploit Robins and encouraged him to get himself appointed to the American Railway Mission to Russia. The restoration of the rail network to a normal working pattern was a priority for the Bolsheviks. If the Americans assisted in this, Trotsky promised to enable the transit of Allied military stocks currently held in Russian warehouses; he told Robins he would make him Assistant Superintendent of Russian Ways and Communications.[38] Truly the People's Commissar would do whatever it took to get the results he wanted. He let Red Cross trains run down to Iasi inside the Romanian sector of the eastern front. He also issued a prohibition on the growing export of Russia's copper and other goods to Germany via Finland.[39]

Sovnarkom was being devious. While seeking to keep the Allies sweet, it was anxious to avoid any trouble with the Germans. In the night of 28–29 December, something extraordinary happened, something which had barely seemed possible a few weeks earlier: the German and Austrian diplomatic contingent arrived in Petrograd.

> There were two delegations—one stopped at the Hotel Bristol on the Moika and was headed by Rear-Admiral Count Kaiserling and Count von Mirbach . . . This committee was known as the Naval Delegation and their mission was to discuss means of stopping the naval war in accordance with the armistice treaty. The second delegation was headed by Count Berchtold, German Red Cross representative, and met to consider the exchange of war prisoners. They established themselves at the Grand and the Angleterre. British and French officers were stopping at both these places, which was obviously embarrassing.[40]

The contingent was sixty strong; the Central Powers meant serious business in Petrograd.[41]

This turnabout was the product of the recent military truce and the opening of peace negotiations at Brest-Litovsk near the eastern front. The Soviet authorities knew about it in advance but everyone else in Petrograd was taken by surprise; and every attempt by the Bolsheviks to lessen the impact was ineffective. The Germans ignored their request that they should remain in their residences. They enjoyed causing embarrassment and openly walked the streets of the capital, renewing old contacts in high banking and industrial circles.[42]

Mirbach's previous posting was as Germany's ambassador in Rome. After obtaining a degree at Heidelberg, he had proceeded to a study course in Oxford. Generations of his family had served the Hohenzollerns.[43] Mirbach wore formal attire when presenting himself at the People's Commissariat of Foreign Affairs:

> 'Hello!' [Zalkind] said, 'what are you doing here?' The count was abashed. 'Why, I am just returning your call,' he said stiffly. Zalkind was amused. 'Excuse me, Count,' he said, 'we are revolutionists and we don't recognise ceremony. You might have saved yourself the trouble if you had remembered that you are in New Russia.' He thought a minute. 'But you can come in,' he added, 'and have a glass of tea.' Von Mirbach did not accept the invitation. He looked down at Zalkind's rough clothes, his rumpled grey hair and his inspired face. Very awkwardly he got himself out of the alien atmosphere of the [People's Commissariat].[44]

The German delegation obdurately affirmed the ways of traditional diplomacy; and when Karl Radek tried to complain about the treatment of far-left socialists in Germany, Mirbach cut him short: German politics was none of Radek's business.[45]

The Allied embassies refused to have anything to do with the German diplomats. Ambassador Francis became dean of the corps with Buchanan's departure on 7 January 1918.[46] Early that same month a group of anarchists arrived from Helsinki to speak with him. They protested about the imprisonment of their American comrades Alexander Berkman and Emma Goldman and about the projected execution of a San Francisco bomb-thrower. The anarchists threatened to hold Francis personally responsible if any harm came to these comrades. Francis urged Washington to take no notice.[47] (He suspected that John Reed had provided the information about

Berkman and Goldman.)[48] A few days later Zalkind, while passing on a similar threat on behalf of Petrograd anarchists, declined to offer protection for the embassy. Francis asked Robins to intercede with Lenin. Although Zalkind refused to apologize, the contretemps was ended by his replacement by Chicherin, who had just arrived from England.[49]

Sovnarkom still needed to neutralize the threat of a German invasion while avoiding causing undue offence to the Western Allies. But the communist leaders also aimed to make revolution. They were not always prudent in how they went about this. Russia still had a large number of troops stationed on Romanian territory, and Lenin and Trotsky saw the opportunity to get its agitators to spread the Russian anti-war spirit to the Romanian troops. They hoped that this might lead to revolutionary stirrings. Romania's Prime Minister Ionel Bratianu had no intention of letting the Bolsheviks dissolve his army from within. Pushed by Germany's continuing military operations, he was determined to preserve what little power remained to his government in its rump independent territory around Iasi. Lenin and Trotsky saw things from an opposite viewpoint. They were angered by the encroachment of Bratianu's Romanian Army into Russian-ruled but Romanian-inhabited Bessarabia to form a new Moldavian state.[50] Sporadic violence broke out between Russian and Romanian units, and Romania's beleaguered authorities responded by arresting five thousand Russians on service near Botosani.

The Soviet government was in no mood to tread carefully. Every untoward event near the borders could be the beginning of an invasion. Sovnarkom always suspected the worst—and it was often proved right in these years. Soviet retaliation in this instance was an act unprecedented in modern diplomacy. On 13 January Red troops were ordered into the Romanian embassy in Petrograd to arrest the ambassador Constantin Diamandy and his staff.[51]

Diamandy's detention outraged the Petrograd diplomatic corps. When a Russian mob had looted the German embassy at the start of the war, Nicholas II's government had restored order and shielded the ambassador from harm.[52] The Romanian imbroglio was of a different order. If an accredited diplomat could be thrown into prison, was any foreigner safe in Russia under the Bolsheviks? Were not Lenin and Trotsky the barbarians of global politics? Diplomats in Russia aimed to make them appreciate the importance of centuries-old international convention and law while Sovnarkom met to discuss what to do next.[53] Francis made the arrangements by phone and the corps went en masse to see Lenin, who was accompanied by Zalkind. Lenin and Zalkind concentrated on the rights and wrongs of the incident in Botosani.[54] Francis strenuously objected: 'No discussion on the subject whatever.' He pointed out that every diplomat's person was inviolable. Noulens pitched in and prolonged the discussion, which went on for an hour and a half. Or at least this was how Francis recalled the event. Noulens remembered it differently and said that it was previously agreed that his own superior legal understanding as well as his native fluency in French made it sensible for him to give a lengthy exposition of the scandal that would fall upon the heads of the Bolsheviks if they refused to back down.

When the Belgian minister Désirée tried to join in, Zalkind told him to be quiet. Lenin agreed to put the matter to Sovnarkom, but this failed to stop Serbia's Ambassador Spalajkovic pointing his finger a yard from Lenin's face and shouting: 'You are bandits; you dishonour the Slav race and I spit in your face!'[55] Noulens sprang up to calm things down but Zalkind said: 'Forget it, forget it, Mr Ambassador, we like this brutality of expression better than diplomatic language!' Negotiations were resumed that evening and Noulens visited Diamandy next day in his underground cell in the Peter-Paul Fortress. The food was foul and Diamandy had not been allowed a knife to cut it. But the final result was positive and Diamandy was released on condition that he speedily left the country.[56] Zalkind made mischief by publicly implying that Francis had consented to Diamandy's incarceration.[57] The fragility of dealings between the Bolsheviks and the Western Allies was revealed all too clearly. Each side wanted more than the other was willing to concede. And the communist authorities were willing to risk rupturing relations with the Allied powers. They were pushing their luck while simultaneously dreading the prospect that one side or another in the Great War might somehow contrive to organize an invasion. Sovnarkom was minded to bite before being bitten even though its own teeth were worn down to the gums.

8. THE OTHER WEST

In embassies around the world, the diplomats appointed by the Provisional Government denounced the October Revolution. Ambassador Vasili Maklakov, freshly arrived in Paris from Petrograd, led the way and alerted his colleague Boris Bakhmetev in Washington to the danger that America might recognize the territories breaking away from Petrograd's control. Maklakov was a prominent Kadet and Bakhmetev had been a Marxist as a young man before withdrawing from party politics. The common nightmare of the ambassadors was the dismemberment of 'Russia'. Maklakov spoke out against the secession of Ukraine; he argued that the Baltic littoral would always be essential to Russian military security—he demanded the retention of naval bases in Helsinki and Tallinn.[1]

The Western Allies, angered by the Soviet regime's withdrawal from the fighting on the eastern front, withdrew their financial credits to Russia while allowing the Provisional Government's accredited diplomats to continue occupying their embassies and enjoying the immunities of their status.[2] Yet they no longer represented a functioning administration and the British cabinet, needing somehow to communicate with Sovnarkom, decided to talk to Maxim Litvinov and Theodore Rothstein, who were among the few Bolsheviks who had stayed behind in Britain.[3] A little Bolshevik colony survived in Switzerland, and Vatslav Vorovski informally handled Sovnarkom's interests in Stockholm;[4] but London was the only Western capital to host a leading Bolshevik such as Litvinov, and he now became Sovnarkom's principal spokesman outside Russia.[5] He had begun to attract notice just before the October Revolution and was lionized when he took Ivy out to the theatre in London. The liberal journalist Salvador de Madariaga, an acquaintance, spotted him from a few rows away and moved to sit near him. In the interval he shouted over: 'Litvinoff, the very man I wanted to meet! What's going on in Russia?' Others joined in the conversation and Litvinov told them to look out for the name of Lenin. When the Bolsheviks seized power the next day in Petrograd, Litvinov's reputation spread across London as the seer of Russian politics.[6]

In January 1918 Trotsky cabled Litvinov to announce his appointment as Sovnarkom's very first 'plenipotentiary' in a foreign country. Just as they did not like the word 'minister', the communists forbore to call Litvinov an ambassador: revolutionary times called for fresh terminology. Litvinov was pleased to have a job that genuinely aided the party's cause. Exactly what the job should involve, however, was unclear because Trotsky had to be cautious about what he wrote in open telegrams and anyway knew little about British high politics; and Litvinov was imaginative and willing to take initiatives: his time had come at last.

The British War Cabinet discussed Russia on 17 January 1918 and confirmed what Foreign Secretary Balfour had been telling the House of Commons. The Bolsheviks had repudiated their obligations under the treaties of alliance. They had aggravated the jeopardy to Britain and France on the western front by closing down the eastern one. They were stirring up revolutions in the West. The Italians pressed for the Western Allies to sever all relations with them; but Lloyd George and Balfour wished to maintain their para-diplomatic links through Litvinov in Britain and British intermediaries in Russia.[7] Balfour expressed the hope that the Bolsheviks might yet cause trouble for the Germans.[8] This was not an entirely fantastical consideration. Soviet official policy as yet ruled out signing a separate peace with the Germans, and if the Russo-German negotiations broke down the assumption was that Russia would go back to war with them. Rumours spread around the world. If the British were talking to Litvinov, perhaps the same kind of arrangement might be made in France where Trotsky was said to be planning to appoint another plenipotentiary.[9] The British denied that they were granting *de facto* recognition to Sovnarkom, and Balfour stressed that he would never speak directly with Litvinov or allow him on to Foreign Office premises.[10] Litvinov would be used only as a convenient conduit for urgent discussions.[11]

This, however, was progress for Sovnarkom; the same was true of Chicherin's release from prison and the permission given for him to return

to Russia.[12] Litvinov made the most of the situation. He wrote to Konstantin Nabokov demanding that he vacate Chesham House and hand over the
official ciphers. Nabokov replied that it was he and not Litvinov who enjoyed official recognition.[13] Litvinov did better for himself when he inau-
gurated contact with the Foreign Office through an official called Rex
Leeper, who conferred regularly with him on matters of politics and war.
Meanwhile he scrambled together a working office. In fact he had no offices
except the rented rooms he lived in, no designated couriers and no code-
book.[14] But he cheered himself up by producing headed notepaper in Sovnarkom's name and asserting a claim of appointment to London's
diplomatic corps.[15] He did the rounds of public meetings in February 1918,
asking how it could be fair for the British government to prefer Nicholas
II's reactionary government to be in power rather than a democratically
elected government.[16] He was silent about the violent suppression of the
Constituent Assembly. He relied on ignorance or undemanding sympathy
among his British listeners, and he saw his task as being to turn sympathizers into enthusiasts.

Litvinov also spoke at the Labour Party annual conference and called
on the British to 'speed up your peace'.[17] On Chicherin's instructions, he
wrote to the anti-war socialist John Maclean appointing him Soviet consul
in Glasgow:

> Dear Comrade Maclean,
>   I am writing to the Russian Consul in Glasgow (I am not sure that
> there exists such a person) informing him of your appointment and
> ordering him to hand over to you the Consulate. He may refuse to
> do so, in which case you will open a new Consulate and make it pub-
> lic through the press. Your position may be difficult somehow, but
> you will have my full support. It is most important to keep me in-
> formed (and through me the Russian Soviets) of the Labour Move-
> ment in N. B. [North Britain].[18]

He thought that the revolution he had missed in Russia was in the offing in
the United Kingdom. As Special Branch reported, he actively fomented
anti-war feelings among resident or visiting Russians—this included making contact with ship crews in British ports.[19]

Conservative MPs began to ask questions in the House of Commons
about his activities:

Major Hunt asked the Prime Minister whether, in view of the fact that M. Litvinoff is advocating a revolutionary movement in this country, he can now say whether he will be prosecuted or interned?

LORD R. CECIL [Under-Secretary of State for Foreign Affairs]: My right hon. Friend asks me to answer this question. I have nothing to add to the reply given by the Home Secretary on the 14th instant to the hon. Member for Hertford, and to the reply given yesterday to the hon. Member.

MAJOR HUNT: Is it the fact that M. Litvinoff has sent round a document, signed by himself, to the trade unions, advocating revolution, and stating that a social revolution is absolutely necessary if a lasting peace is to be secured, and is that sort of thing to be allowed in the case of an alien when it is not allowed in the case of any of our own people?

LORD R. CECIL: I am afraid I can only repeat the answer I have given. I really have nothing to add to what I have already said on the subject, that the matter is being considered.[20]

This remained the government's position over the next few months.

Maxim and Ivy Litvinov were enjoying themselves. At New Year 1918 it was their turn to throw the annual party for the colony. Fifteen sat down to celebrate. In characteristic Russian fashion the guests came with contributions to the feast. Ivy wrote:

> They brought whisky (lamenting vodka) and zakuski from the Jewish shops in Soho—short, rotund salted cucumbers, smoked salmon, *voblya* [which is] a strange fish cured hard as a board which I had difficulty in cutting into strips and which I thought more suitable for a clown to slap another in the face with than for human consumption.[21]

The cry went up: 'There's no caviar, there's no caviar!' It might be wartime in a foreign country but the colony expected to dine in the manner to which they were accustomed. Relying on Maxim's advice and the labour of their red-faced charlady Mrs Bristow, Ivy produced a satisfactory *borshch* (beetroot soup) followed by roast beef and an immense apple pie.[22] The Russians would normally have asked the servants to sit and eat with them but decided that Mrs Bristow would be unable to understand any word that was spoken. She was invited just for the toasts to the New Year and to the Revolution. More toasts followed, including one to Maxim as 'the First People's Ambassador of the First Socialist Republic'.[23]

Soon, along with Ivy, Maxim was attending luncheon and dinner parties in Westminster and Mayfair. On one occasion they were received at Downing Street; unfortunately there is no record as to whether it was at Number 10 or Number 11, but the guest list included Ramsay MacDonald and Bertrand Russell. A fellow guest ventured the question: 'Wasn't it a bolt from the blue, Mrs Litvinoff, living quietly in West Hampstead with your husband and baby, suddenly to be plunged into the whirlpool of public events? We immediately imagined you handing your husband his cup of tea at breakfast and him looking up from *The Times* and through the newspaper.' Ivy refused to be patronized. 'It was', she said firmly but implausibly, 'what we expected.'[24]

Intellectuals of the political left courted the Litvinovs. As Ivy recalled, Sidney and Beatrice Webb and Charles Roden Buxton as well as Russell made social overtures to Maxim:

> It was a pity they felt obliged to invite me too. I was such a chatterbox and Maxim by nature so taciturn and glad to have others do the talking for him. Whatever the subject under discussion I generally managed to get round to psychoanalysis, and people who sincerely wished to discover what the structure of the Soviets was, found themselves diverted into acrimonious wrangles about Freud and even obliged to listen to the relation of my childhood complexes.[25]

While Ivy had an altercation with Russell her husband 'was glad to be able to enjoy his lunch in peace'.[26] (His calm temperament proved an asset when he served under Stalin in the 1930s as People's Commissar of Foreign Affairs.) Maxim was anyway more confident with pen in hand. His pamphlet *The Bolshevik Revolution: Its Rise and Meaning* derided the Mensheviks and Socialist-Revolutionaries, praising the Bolsheviks as the only party that had the support of the 'masses'. He defended the dispersal of the Constituent Assembly on the grounds that only Sovnarkom could guarantee that the 'bourgeois parties' would not come back to power.[27]

On 23 January the *Manchester Guardian* ran an article by an unnamed correspondent, possibly Theodore Rothstein, denying that communism stood for 'class war'. This alleged mistake was said to result from a mistranslation of the German *Klassenkampf,* which was better rendered as 'class struggle' and was widely used by European socialists without connection with Bolshevism.[28] This was an inaccurate presentation of Lenin's ideas. Since 1914 he had called for the 'imperialist war' to be turned into a 'European civil war', and by war he meant war and not just struggle.

There was no Bolshevik of Litvinov's stature in America because all the resident leaders of the Russian far left had departed for Petrograd. The most active advocate of Bolshevism in the US was not a Russian but a Finn, Santeri Nuorteva, who headed the Finnish Information Bureau in New York. The Bureau was an agency of the Provisional Revolutionary Government established by the Red Finns in January 1918 as civil war broke out between the Reds and the Whites in Finland. Bolsheviks kept close ties with the Bureau, which operated as an unofficial embassy for the Reds in Russia as well as Finland. The US Secretary of State Robert Lansing would have nothing to do with Nuorteva, who then reached out to sympathetic officials in the State Department such as William Bullitt, William Irwin and Felix Frankfurter (political discipline under Lansing was much more lax than in Balfour's Foreign Office). Nuorteva also approached likely journalists such as Walter Duranty of the *New York Times.* Although he was later to operate as a cheerleader for Joseph Stalin, at this time Duranty was still wary of associating himself with the Russian communist cause. The Finnish Information Bureau's Harold Kellock derided him in a letter to Frankfurter: 'Walter reminds me a bit of a sort of orthodox Virgin Mary who is always fully conscious of being Queen of Heaven. Perhaps he's a direct descendant "son of the Jewish Revolution".'[29]

The weakness of the Soviet propaganda effort in the US induced John Reed and Louise Bryant to volunteer to return to America on Sovnarkom's behalf. This would undoubtedly involve a certain risk. A Federal Grand Jury had indicted Reed in November 1917 for violating the Espionage Act with his article 'Knit a Straitjacket for your Soldier Boy' in the *Masses.* But Reed did not flinch and on 29 January 1918 the People's Commissariat of Foreign Affairs appointed him New York consul.[30] The State Department retorted that Lenin's government lacked even *de facto* recognition.[31] Trotsky at this point saw that he was annoying Washington for no good purpose, and he withdrew Reed's name from his list of appointees. The most important thing was to facilitate Reed's arrival in the US.[32] Reed and Bryant disembarked on 28 April.[33] Although the indictment was quietly forgotten, in late May he was arrested in Philadelphia on a charge of inciting a riot.[34] Yet again the authorities stepped back from providing him with the publicity of a trial. On release he delivered speeches against the war, sharing platforms with Nuorteva and *Masses* editor Max Eastman.[35] Reed's articles and pamphlets were disseminated widely in the American labour movement. He thought he had seen the world's future in Russia, and he recommended it.

The community of foreign sympathizers in Petrograd continued to promote the Soviet cause. The most eccentric was *Daily News* and *Manchester Guardian* correspondent Arthur Ransome. Caught in the United Kingdom at the time of the October Revolution, he had returned to Russia on Christmas Day 1917.[36] Ransome inspired great affection: every one of his acquaintances, even those who detested Bolshevism, was fond of him. Moura Benckendorff, Lockhart's mistress, noticed 'his Bolshevik appearance' but still felt sorry for him. Thinking that he was not eating well, she 'stuck a piece of veal in his mouth ... and a few radishes in his pocket'.[37] Ransome might have preferred something sugary: he loved his 'sweets'.[38]

The British intelligence officer George Hill was another who warmed to him: 'He was a tall, lanky, bony individual with a shock of sandy hair, usually unkempt, and the eyes of a small, inquisitive and rather mischievous boy. He was a lovable personality when you came to know him.'[39] Hill and Ransome lived on the same hotel corridor. Only Hill had a bathroom, which he allowed Ransome to use each morning:

> Our profoundest discussions and most heated arguments took place when Ransome was sitting in the bath and I wandering up and down my room dressing. Sometimes, when I had the better of an argument and his feelings were more than usually outraged, he would jump out of the water and beat himself dry like an angry gorilla. After that he would not come for his bath for two or three days, then we would meet and grin at each other, I would ask after the pet snake which lived in a large cigar box in his room, and the following day he would come in as usual and we would begin arguing again, the best of friends.[40]

The species and provenance of the snake remain unknown.

Ransome, an unhappily married man, had fallen in love with a Bolshevik—and British intelligence wondered whether he had become one too.[41] The object of his affections was none other than Trotsky's secretary Yevgenia Shelepina. Hill asked her out to dinner but she refused, claiming she had to work at her desk till late.[42] The true reason may well have been her growing fancy for Ransome, and the two were soon conducting an affair. A bit of politics was involved, too. Ransome was sympathetic to the Bolsheviks as well as convinced, from a patriotic viewpoint, that it was in the British interest to have good relations with them and not to bully or subvert Sovnarkom. And Shelepina was anyway a useful source of material for his dispatches home. Her close knowledge of Trotsky's planning and activity was a priceless asset.

C. P. Scott, Ransome's editor in Manchester, was not keen on the Soviet revolutionary experiment. While appreciating his reporter's extraordinary access to the Bolshevik elite, Scott used the old device of muffling a correspondent's enthusiasms by judicious editing and occasional spiking of reports. At least Ransome kept his job. Louise Bryant lost her contract of employment with the *Philadelphia Public Ledger* and was in no doubt about the reason. As soon as a reporter tried to tell the news honestly, she claimed, the editor at home disowned him or her.[43] Morgan Philips Price complained that his telegrams were being suppressed or emasculated.[44] But the cheerleaders kept up their work. Determined to write as they pleased, Bryant and Ransome published booklets on Russia after the October Revolution. Ransome's *Letter to America* so pleased Karl Radek at the People's Commissariat of Foreign Affairs that he helped to get it published in the US and supplied his own introduction. Ransome denied that the Allies had any right to compel Russia to do what they wanted. While allowing that the Revolution might fail, he applauded the Soviet order and its appropriateness for Russia; he dismissed the anti-Bolshevik majority in the Constituent Assembly as an 'indifferent mass' of people incapable of achieving the decisiveness and popularity of the Bolsheviks.[45]

Jacques Sadoul and Raymond Robins went on pressing the case for gentle handling of Sovnarkom by their governments. At the beginning of 1918 their chorus was swelled by Robert Bruce Lockhart, who had caught the eye of Lloyd George as someone with an open mind about the Bolsheviks. The Prime Minister decided to send him back to Russia as 'Agent' or 'Head of the British Mission'.[46] Before departing, Lockhart spoke to Viscount Milner (Secretary of State for War), Sir Edward Carson (First Lord of the Admiralty), Earl Curzon (Lord President of the Council and soon to become Foreign Secretary), Lord Hardinge (Under-Secretary at the Foreign Office) and Sir George Clerk (private secretary to the Acting Foreign Secretary).

Lockhart emerged well briefed on the general problems of the British war effort. He also learned that Lloyd George had a low opinion of A. J. Balfour and the Foreign Office, which gave Lockhart an opening for writing reports without inhibition.[47] Lockhart's linguistic competence and political contacts as well as his self-confidence were undeniable. Lloyd George got no sense of Lockhart's recklessness. Perhaps his own personality and unconventional lifestyle—he took his mistress Frances Stevenson along with him nearly everywhere—blinded him to the risks of sending the Scot back into a post of political responsibility without a senior diplomat like Buchanan to keep an eye on him. Lockhart was like quicksilver, a man who loved the thrills of adventure.

He left for Russia on 14 January 1918 with a letter of recommendation from none other than Maxim Litvinov.[48] Only one person in Whitehall poured cold water on his mission. General Sir Nevil Macready, who on learning that Lockhart's assignment was to help to restore the Russians to the eastern front, said: 'Don't the boys in the Foreign Office read history? Don't you know that when an army of seven million runs away in disorder, it needs a generation before it can fight again?'[49] But Lloyd George believed that Raymond Robins was carrying out useful work for the Americans and wanted Lockhart to do the same for the British. He told him simply: 'Go to it.'[50] With Lockhart went his personally chosen team of Captain William Hicks, Edward Phelan and Edward Birse. Hicks had recently worked in Russia as an expert on poison gas; Phelan was scooped from the Ministry of Labour, presumably on the premise that he knew how to talk to far-left socialists. Birse was a Moscow businessman.[51] They took the normal wartime route across the North Sea and made for Finland, only to discover that the direct rail line down to Petrograd was broken. Instead they made for Helsinki, where they encountered fighting in the streets between the Red and White Finns. The travellers set off quickly to Russia, reaching the capital on 30 January.[52] Lockhart wrote in his diary: 'Streets in a dreadful state, snow had not been swept away for weeks. Everyone looks depressed and unhappy.'

Among his first steps was to arrange a meeting with Trotsky. He lunched beforehand with Raymond Robins, who told him: 'Trotsky [is a] poor kind [of] son of a bitch but the greatest Jew since Christ.' Trotsky tried to convince Lockhart that the Bolsheviks would engage in partisan warfare if the Germans mounted an invasion. Lockhart recorded in his diary: 'Loud in his blame of the French and said the Allies had only helped Germany by their intrigues in Russia.'[53] Robins took a liking to Lockhart and offered him a deal:

> Let us assume that I am here to capture Russia for Wall Street and American business men. Let us assume that you are a British wolf and I am an American wolf, and that when this war is over we are going to eat each other up for the Russian market; let us do so in perfectly frank, man fashion, but let us assume at the same time that we are fairly intelligent wolves, and that we know that if we do not hunt together in this hour the German wolf will eat us both up, and then let us go to work.[54]

From that day onwards they took breakfast together.[55]

Lockhart slotted himself back into old routines, getting official accreditation as Roman Romanovich Lokkart from the People's Commissariat of Foreign Affairs even though Britain was withholding recognition from Sovnarkom.[56] He was enjoying himself. He saw Trotsky regularly and put the case for Russian military co-operation with the Allies. Sadoul too maintained amicable ties with Trotsky. Ambassador Noulens was later to declare that Sadoul favoured communist Russia over France. Ambassador Francis, he thought, was coming to the same conclusion about Robins. And soon Lockhart's oddities too were remarked upon.[57] Colonel Alfred Knox put things with succinct brutality: '[Robins] is a fanatic with the temperament of a hero-worshipping schoolgirl, and while without the mental equipment or the experience to enable him to advise on policy, he is a dangerous companion for anyone as impressionable as Lockhart.'[58] General Henry Wilson on behalf of the Imperial General Staff urged the War Cabinet either to stop Lockhart commenting on military questions or, failing that, to recall him from Moscow.[59] But Lockhart, Robins and Sadoul were excellent conduits for contact with the Soviet leadership and were still too useful to be dropped.[60] The Western Allies needed to make the best of a bad situation. There was a war to be won and it was important to go on cajoling the Russians to stay in the war.

PART TWO

◆

SURVIVAL

9. TALKS AT BREST-LITOVSK

The Bolshevik leaders were optimists. Believing that only a little time was needed for their revolutionary example to be followed abroad, they had agreed to a truce on the eastern front on 15 December 1917. Sovnarkom demobilized the Russian Army—when the formal order went out by wireless on 7 December, the slim chance of having any forces available to repel the Germans disappeared;[1] Russia was rendered indefensible as peasant soldiers, rifles over their shoulders, jumped on trains and went back to the villages. Lenin and Trotsky were counting on 'European socialist revolution' and felt that the October Revolution depended on their gamble. The Allied powers looked on anxiously. The consequences for their armies on the western front would be deeply damaging if a deal was struck between Germany and Russia. The Germans stood to gain from being able to transfer army divisions from the east as their manpower ran low in northern France. They had already sent experienced troops there while the Russian Army had been falling apart. There could also be economic benefit because Germany wanted access to goods and markets in Russia, Ukraine and the south Caucasus so as to circumvent the British naval blockade of German ports.

Russia and Germany continued to negotiate at the little German-held town of Brest-Litovsk close to the eastern front. The German high command was getting anxious. It badly needed its armies to crush the Western Allies before the Americans could be fully deployed there.[2] Each side in Brest-Litovsk expected to achieve its purposes to the detriment of the other. The Germans wanted a separate peace with Russia, the Russians a German communist revolution. Berlin was confident that the talks would be of brief duration since the communists had empty trenches and no soldiers. German commanders and diplomats felt no need for preparations beyond allocating a set of two-storeyed dwellings to house the delegations in the snow-laden town.[3]

The Germans and their allies—Austrians, Hungarians, Bulgarians and Turks—sat down with the Russians in the Officers' Building on 22 December. Trotsky was needed in Petrograd and so it was his friend Adolf Ioffe who headed the Soviet delegation that departed by rail via Vilnius and Białystok. Ioffe was from a rich Jewish family from Simferopol in Crimea. His father had a reputation as Minister of Finances Sergei Witte's 'favourite Jew' in the 1890s, and Adolf's choice of a revolutionary career aroused parental consternation. He had also married young, gaining family consent solely because the girl was Jewish—Ioffe senior had feared that his atheist son might marry outside the ancestral faith. Adolf received a regular financial allowance that enabled him to enrol as a student in the Berlin University medical faculty. Although he worked hard at his studies, the police objected to his activities on behalf of the Russian Social-Democratic Workers' Party and expelled him from Germany. He decamped to Vienna where he became a pupil of the psychologist Alfred Adler and made the acquaintance of Trotsky. In 1917 he wrote prolifically and served on the Military-Revolutionary Committee. Although he had no expertise in international affairs, his command of German and familiarity with central Europe were thought an asset for dealing with Germany and Austria-Hungary.[4]

Travelling with Ioffe in the delegation were Lev Kamenev and a handful of lesser Bolsheviks including the rising official of the People's Commissariat of Foreign Affairs, Lev Karakhan. Radek joined them later. Some military officers attended as special advisers; their morale was so low that it was said that they went 'like lambs to the slaughter', believing that the Bolsheviks were bent on signing terms that were tantamount to treason. Admiral Altvater was apparently an exception: Trotsky sardonically reported that he 'was touched by grace and has returned from Brest-Litovsk more Bolshevik than the Bolsheviks on this peace question'.[5]

Ioffe had a preliminary conversation with the Austrian Foreign Minister Count Ottokar von Czernin and politely rejected his entire worldview. When Czernin commented sceptically on Soviet political expectations, Ioffe leant across and said: 'I still hope we'll succeed in calling forth a revolution in your country.'[6] Such was the atmosphere when Prince Leopold of Bavaria opened the formal talks on behalf of Germany, Austria-Hungary, Bulgaria and Turkey. Ioffe spoke for the Russian side and insisted, in the face of Turkish objections, on full publicity for the proceedings in Russia and among the Central Powers. He exploited the occasion by giving an explanation of the purposes behind Lenin's Decree on Peace. Over the next few days Ioffe and Kamenev completely ignored the big topic at the centre of everyone's attention: the German demand for Russia to sign a comprehensive peace on the eastern front. The Bolsheviks had vowed to start a 'revolutionary war' rather than make a separate settlement with the Germans, so they needed to keep the Central Powers talking and talking. Ioffe expatiated on the complications likely to arise from Soviet economic nationalizations as yet to be announced. He also drew attention to the problems arising from a separate delegation from the Ukrainian Central Rada, which had declared Ukraine's independence in January but had yet to be recognized by Sovnarkom. Ioffe explained all the niceties with elegance and courtesy.[7]

The Germans tried to hurry things along but were under instructions to observe diplomatic proprieties. They soon saw that Ioffe, liaising regularly with Trotsky, was hoping to gain time for revolutionary upheavals to occur in Berlin and Vienna. Indicating that their patience was not inexhaustible, they threatened that unless the Soviet leaders submitted quickly to their terms they would face the might of their forces.

Trotsky decided that his presence in Brest-Litovsk had become essential and he joined the talks on 27 December 1917. Smartly attired as usual, he stepped off the train with a bright scarf tucked into a dark fur coat; his shoes were polished as if for an evening ball. He was a virtuoso performer. He spoke in his fluent German whenever he wanted to get his meaning across quickly to the military monoglots. He picked holes in the draft documents produced by the Germans. Why on earth could the translators not see the difference between words like 'nation', 'people' and 'state'?[8] Over the table from him sat men who had acted haughtily towards Ioffe. Trotsky presented them with a different personality. He appeared indifferent to their threats; and although he was invariably polite he left more than a suspicion that he was treating them condescendingly. They had assumed that he would be embarrassed by the inclusion of the Ukrainian delegates who turned up on the same day as him. Not a bit of it. He accepted their participation, mentioning only that he expected that the territorial allegiance of the Black Sea region would be decided by a plebiscite of its residents.[9] Trotsky gave an actor's display of calm confidence. It was hard to believe that he spoke for a state that was utterly incapable of repelling any German invasion.

His stay in Brest-Litovsk coincided with Lenin's decision to leave Petrograd for a few days' holiday in Finland, which provoked the sardonic comment from Jacques Sadoul: 'And so here we are without a dictator.'[10] As soon as Georgi Chicherin arrived from England he deputized for Trotsky at the People's Commissariat, so that Soviet foreign affairs were entrusted to steadier hands than Zalkind could supply.

Yevgenia Shelepina became Trotsky's 'courier extraordinary'. She had grown bored when Trotsky left, and asked Lenin and Stalin for a job that would bring some excitement. Shelepina was depressed by what she saw in Brest-Litovsk:

> The town was a dead town. All the houses were broken in some way or other, some with their roofs blown off, others with their walls blown in. Nothing had been done to mend the houses, but the streets had been tidied up, so that there was an oppressive orderliness even in the disorder of the broken town. There were only two or three little shops open, selling necessary things, tobacco and thread, and such things, and then there was a bookstore, over which, of course, Radek spent more time than over all the rest. When he was buying cigarettes, I told him to buy some for me. He told me the permission given him by the Commandant did not allow him to buy any more.[11]

The signs of distress near the front line surprised her. Time and again she caught sight of ill-kempt Russian POWs being marched around by their captors. Shelepina felt like pulling a gun on the Germans—having run out of cigarettes, she was agitated by the absence of nicotine in her bloodstream. Radek, by contrast, was never without a well-stocked tobacco pouch and called out to the same POWs: he never missed a chance to spread the message of revolutionary socialism.[12]

Trotsky brought order to the Soviet delegation and raised its morale. He put an end to the growing practice of taking meals with the negotiators of the Central Powers. He saw that if he wanted to maintain a firm bargaining stance, it would not help if his team became too friendly with the Germans. He told his comrades to take greater care with their appearance. The Germans had to feel that Bolsheviks were more than just a rabble from the street.

He had seen enough of conditions near Brest-Litovsk to know how difficult it would be to restore the Russian armed forces. Lenin agreed. Although
he went nowhere near the eastern front, he drew the same conclusion from
a survey among the armed forces.[13] The only hope lay in dragging out the
talks and using them as an instrument of propaganda abroad. Trotsky's slogan for the Bolshevik Committee was 'neither war nor peace'. The German
high command refused to accept this affront to military and diplomatic
convention. Annoyed by the Soviet tactics, the Central Powers on 6 February signed a separate peace with the Ukrainian Rada. Whether Trotsky
liked it or not, Ukraine could no longer be brought under Soviet rule. The
Germans then issued an ultimatum: either the communist leaders accepted
the terms on offer or they would face an immediate invasion of Russia. This
was intended to bring Trotsky to heel, but he had a surprise of his own for
them. When the talks resumed on 10 February, instead of responding to
the ultimatum, he declared the state of war between Russia and the Central
Powers to be 'terminated'. The eastern front was no more. The Russians
were withdrawing from the armed conflict regardless of the threats being
made by the Germans.[14]

Trotsky's statement was more than Richard von Kühlmann, Germany's
Secretary of State for Foreign Affairs, could bear. A government facing invasion had sent a plenipotentiary to Brest-Litovsk who refused to indicate
his response to the threat of military attack. This was still an age when empires and nations declared war on others before waging it. The Blitzkrieg
was invented by Hitler: no diplomat in 1918 felt comfortable about initiat-
ing armed conflict in Europe without having completed the formalities of
mutual communication. The rest of the world was a different matter, and
European powers had marched into Africa and Asia in their pell-mell scram-
ble for colonial conquests in the late nineteenth century. It therefore took
some minutes for Kühlmann to collect his thoughts and point out that wars
could not end without agreements on borders, trade and a host of other
practical matters. Trotsky's rhetoric would not be allowed to remove the
current question on the agenda for Sovnarkom. Was it going to be war or
peace? But Trotsky was unbending and curtly announced that his delegation had exhausted the powers invested in it. Then he and his comrades
picked up their papers and left the room.[15]

Since Trotsky's démarche had not been prearranged with the Party Central Committee or Sovnarkom, he had to return to Petrograd fast so as to

argue his case. He knew that he could expect grave criticism from Lenin in the Central Committee. Lenin was no less impatient than Kühlmann about the need to make a clear choice between war and peace. Having disbanded the old Russian Army in December, Sovnarkom set about forming a Workers' and Peasants' Red Army two months later; but the first small, ill-trained units were undeniably in no condition to withstand attack by German military divisions. In Lenin's view Trotsky was putting the October Revolution in peril. By 14 February the Soviet leadership was noting that the German missions in Petrograd were getting ready to leave the city. This was interpreted as a sign that invasion was imminent. Lenin snarled that a peace treaty had to be signed before all was lost.

The Bolshevik Central Committee met on 17 February and conducted a congested sequence of votes. Lenin made steady but excruciatingly slow progress. Everyone conceded in principle that, under certain conditions, a peace could be signed with Germany. The conditions were not specified; but even Bukharin was recorded as acknowledging that the signing of a separate treaty with the Central Powers should not be entirely dismissed in principle as an acceptable manoeuvre. Nobody any longer held out unconditionally for a policy of revolutionary war. Indeed three out of eleven voters at the Central Committee—Bukharin, Ioffe and Georgi Lomov—abstained from registering their opinion on the matter on the grounds that Lenin had put the question in an incorrect fashion.[16] But if they objected to his blunt wording, it is hard to see how else he could have phrased things. The Germans had made clear that the Bolshevik party had to agree to a separate peace treaty or else endure a military offensive. What would Bukharin and his sympathizers do if the Germans were to attack? They answered with their silence, and it became obvious that they at last saw that the idea of revolutionary war throughout Europe was unrealizable.

Trotsky's hope was that something might be done to elicit practical support from the Western Allies since Russia could no longer defend itself without external assistance. He and the British diplomat Robert Bruce Lockhart met frequently, and Trotsky railed against the United Kingdom's schemes to assist the enemies of Sovnarkom. His passion seemed sincere to Lockhart, who implored London to ignore the wildness of Bolshevik policies and consider help for the Soviet military effort. Trotsky talked to him ceaselessly about resuming the war against Germany—and Lockhart was persuaded that this would happen sooner or later.[17] When Trotsky requested help from the French, Lockhart saw this as 'sufficient proof' of his good intentions on the eastern front. Lockhart also passed on Trotsky's promise to aid the Allied cause by fomenting revolution in Berlin.[18]

Earlier in the month, Kamenev had been sent off to France on a diplomatic assignment to win favour among the Western Allies. Kamenev was the first leading Bolshevik to leave Russia since the October Revolution. A French reporter left this account of his appearance:

> An elongated oval head, myopic blue eyes which are generally soft under a gold-mounted pince-nez and become wilful and penetrative when the discussion is animated. A little goatee, a blazingly blond and strong moustache falling over a mouth which they half cover, long, bulky, straw-coloured eyebrows, light brown hair. From a distance, a surly air but, from close by, a man who is always amiable and smiling.[19]

Kamenev left Petrograd accompanied by Zalkind, who was designated Soviet plenipotentiary to Switzerland. Balfour, the British Foreign Secretary, confirmed in the House of Commons that they could come to London on their way to Paris.[20] But, on setting foot in England, Kamenev immediately met with obstacles as the Foreign Office refused point-blank to talk to him and he was ignored by *The Times* in an attempt to deny him the oxygen of publicity. The *Manchester Guardian* interviewed him, however, and Kamenev displayed his ebullience by stating that if the Germans marched on Russia the workers would fight them in the streets of Petrograd. He claimed that, even if a separate peace was signed, the cause of the Western Allies would not suffer damage since it would take many months to send back POWs to Germany. He also predicted that Ukraine would never deliver grain to Germany unless promised industrial products in return.[21]

Kamenev was talking nonsense but received support from the anti-war Labour MP Ramsay MacDonald, who protested against the way that customs officers in Aberdeen had treated him. The sum of £5,000 was removed from his possession until such time as he left British shores and there was a rumour that he was relieved of an Orthodox Russian Bible and a box of matches. Supposedly he was bringing the Bible for Litvinov.[22] (This was unlikely since Kamenev and Litvinov were atheists by doctrine and Jews by birth, although possibly the Bible was going to be used for the purpose of encrypting messages to and from Russia.) MacDonald spoke up in the House of Commons for Sovnarkom's democratic credentials and claimed that the Soviet form of government was the only form of authority with a chance of survival in Russia. Lord Robert Cecil, Under-Secretary of State at the Foreign Office, replied that a personal search of Sovnarkom's envoy was entirely appropriate in the current situation. MacDonald kept up his line of questioning. Why were police detectives hanging around Kamenev in London? Why did the authorities allow the allegation to go unchallenged that Litvinov had been mixed up in the 1907 Tiflis bank robbery? In all innocence MacDonald called this a 'vile slander'. Kamenev wrote a letter to the *Manchester Guardian* denying that the Bolsheviks were apathetic about losing Ukraine. In due course, he asserted, the old multinational state and its peoples would be brought back together.

The French gave a dusty reply to Kamenev's and Zalkind's request to cross the English Channel. The two Bolsheviks had no choice but to return to Russia. Yet nothing dampened their mood. Paul Vaucher, correspondent for *L'Illustration* magazine, travelled on the same boat and noted their complete confidence that the German workers were about to overthrow their rulers.[23]

Lenin was still some way from victory in the Central Committee—and Kamenev's absence did not help since he was one of the sturdiest advocates of a separate peace along with Stalin, Zinoviev and Sverdlov. The resistance led by Trotsky and Bukharin remained strong. On 18 February, albeit by the slim margin of seven against six, the Central Committee voted against resuming talks with the Germans.[24] By the evening, news was coming through that the Germans had carried out their ultimatum and had advanced to occupy Dvinsk. Trotsky wanted to cable Berlin and Vienna and ask about the further intentions of the Central Powers. Sverdlov and Stalin objected that time was too short for the Bolsheviks to wait for an answer and that the Brest-Litovsk talks had to be resumed immediately.[25] The Central Committee, after yet another discussion, overturned its entire previous policy and voted by seven to five for signing an immediate peace with Germany. The decision was to be cabled to the enemy without delay. Lenin and Trotsky were instructed to draft the text. The Left Socialist-Revolutionaries were to be informed of what the Bolshevik leaders were now planning.[26] All this time the menace to Petrograd was growing as German forces moved onward unopposed. The cables received on 19 February were grim. Minsk, Polotsk, Lutsk, Dubno and Rovno fell to the Germans without resistance. Pskov had to be evacuated. The Austrians organized an offensive and took Kamenets-Podolsk; and Romanian armed forces crossed the River Dniester and cut into Ukraine. A Turkish army marched on Trebizond, which had been occupied by the Russians since 1916. Lenin's dark predictions seemed about to be fulfilled. The Germans, now occupying Mogilëv where the Russians had kept their GHQ in 1917, were poised to seize Petrograd.

Despite this, the Western Allies did not stop hoping to keep Russia in the war. They closely monitored the internal debate of Bolshevik leaders and knew who the main advocates of separate peace with Germany were. Stalin had always been sceptical about the prospects of imminent revolution in the West; and when Lenin began to argue for signing a treaty, Stalin put the case more unconditionally than Lenin felt comfortable with. Zinoviev, Sverdlov and Kamenev too favoured the signature of a separate peace. But it was Stalin who pushed the hardest and there is some evidence that officers of the British Secret Intelligence Service decided that something should be done to get rid of him. One of their number, Stephen Alley, later claimed that he had been asked to find a pretext for an interview with Stalin. Once inside Stalin's office, Alley was to assassinate him. Alley was a brave patriot but saw that any such exploit would end in his own death even if he succeeded in killing Stalin. He therefore rejected the proposal.[27] (Only in retrospect was it possible for him to appreciate how much he would have benefited the world if he had snuffed out the life of one of the twentieth century's greatest mass murderers.)

Only Trotsky among Bolshevik leaders gave any heart to the Western Allies, and the French ambassador phoned him to say: 'In your resistance against Germany you can count on France's military and financial support.'[28] Noulens was acting on information from Sadoul. Trotsky, though, was not so foolish as to expect a lot from the French. He knew that they could do next to nothing from the other end of Europe to prevent Russia from being overrun by the Germans. He pointedly asked Noulens what scale of support the French had in mind.[29]

Lloyd George, ever resourceful, tried out a British initiative by striving to entice Sovnarkom with the offer to ship potatoes to Archangel. Lenin was minded to say yes, but for his own reasons. He always wanted to play off one 'imperialist' coalition against another. Even a slight rapprochement with the Allies might perhaps strengthen the Soviet bargaining hand at Brest-Litovsk. The 'Left Communists' in the Central Committee were appalled. They got their name from opposing the compromises that Lenin had advocated since taking power—and they criticized what they saw as his right-wing policies. It was bad enough for them that he wanted to sign a separate peace, and now he showed he also wished to wheel and deal with the British. For Lenin's opponents, this was proof that he could no longer be trusted. They demanded the calling of a Central Committee meeting. Lenin used the excuse that only Yakov Sverdlov as Central Committee Secretary could convoke such a meeting and he was nowhere to be found. Sverdlov's elusiveness was probably a contrived one. Lenin too made himself unavailable. This meant that when the leftists assembled they could not designate it as a meeting of any authoritativeness.[30] It was the kind of behaviour that would have thrown Lenin into a rage if anyone had tried it on him.

Although no one now remained under any illusions about German power and aggressiveness, on 22 February Trotsky told the Central Committee that France and Britain were offering military assistance. Trotsky can hardly have pressed his case hard in the light of his earlier sarcasm towards Noulens. Lenin was not present but sent a memorandum in favour of taking 'potatoes and weapons from the robbers of Anglo-French imperialism'. His words seem to have been ignored since the Central Committee rejected the French military mission's note without debate. Bukharin said that France's behaviour merely showed that the Western Allies hoped to turn Russia into one of their colonies. The discussion was mainly between Trotsky and Bukharin. Trotsky won the vote with his suggestion that Russia should not fight a revolutionary war until such time as it had built a decent new army.[31] What happened to Lloyd George's potatoes is lost to history. But Lenin and his supporters had already done what was needed to break up and destroy Bukharin's opposition; and on 23 February Lenin returned and got the Central Committee to reconfirm its commitment to signing the peace treaty on Germany's terms.[32]

The disruption in the Bolshevik party was enormous. Bukharin resigned as editor of *Pravda*; Trotsky stepped down from the People's Commissariat of Foreign Affairs. The Left Socialist-Revolutionaries abandoned the Sovnarkom coalition and became the main opposition to the Bolsheviks in the soviets. Every political party in Russia denounced Lenin as a traitor. And even among Bolshevik leaders there was a natural reluctance to volunteer to go out to Brest-Litovsk and sign the treaty on the government's behalf. Lenin, the driving force behind the capitulation to Germany, refused to go. Instead Central Committee member Grigori Sokolnikov agreed to carry out the task.

The signing ceremony was scheduled for 3 March 1918. On 28 February the American embassy took the precaution of sending its personnel by train to Vologda, 370 miles to the east in the direction of Vyatka on the Trans-Siberian line, and the Japanese did the same. Robins and Ransome went with them. Ambassador Francis told everyone he had no intention of getting caught 'like a rat in a trap'; he planned to move further eastwards if conditions got worse. Vologda, a quiet town with little industry and a scrappy agricultural hinterland, was known mainly as a site of religious pilgrimage; it was far enough away from the big centres of population for the Imperial authorities to have used it as a dumping ground for convicted revolutionaries. European diplomats declined to join Francis there. Instead they took a train north to Finland, reaching Helsinki three days later. All the Allied embassies cut down their staff to a minimum and sent most of their people home.[33] Yet Trotsky was still not entirely beaten. On 1 March, as the German high command continued to order its troops eastwards, he instructed the Murmansk Soviet to be ready to take any help from the Allies to halt the advance.[34] But then the Germans abruptly halted and the treaty was signed on the day appointed. The Bolsheviks held a Party Congress from 6 March to discuss what had happened. The debates were angry. Despite this, Lenin knew he had internal party victory in his grasp.

Known to the Russians as the 'obscene peace', this was a drastic defeat because it meant that the Bolsheviks were giving up the claim to Ukraine and most of the Baltic region. Abundant resources of coal, iron and wheat were handed to the Germans in return for peace, and a quarter of the Russian Empire's population came under Germany's sway. It was the most humiliating end to a war for Russians since the Mongol invasion in the thirteenth century. The Bolsheviks had made the October Revolution with the expectation of expanding into Europe. Four months later they found themselves penned in a territory little bigger than old Muscovy.

10. BREATHING DANGEROUSLY

On 21 March 1918 Germany started its great military offensive on the western front after weeks of troop transfers from the east. The French and British were forced back to within forty miles of Paris; it looked as if Ludendorff and Hindenburg might pull off a decisive victory and finish the war.[1] Lenin boasted of the 'breathing space' achieved by his policy at Brest-Litovsk, but he knew he could not trust the German high command. Soviet leaders understood that if Paris fell to the Germans, it would not be long before they invaded Russia. And were the Germans to tear up the treaty and march on Petrograd, the newly created Red Army could not stop them. Sovnarkom would have to evacuate to the Urals and appeal to the Western Allies for aid. The Bolsheviks could not therefore afford to break ties with Allied representatives in Russia. This meant that Lenin and Trotsky were by no means as hostile to each other as most people thought at the time. Ioffe got other party leaders to support his suggestion that Trotsky be made People's Commissar for Military Affairs,[2] and Lenin followed this up with a personal plea to Trotsky, who made a brief show of demurral before accepting the appointment—and Chicherin took his place at the People's Commissariat of Foreign Affairs, at first on a provisional basis.[3]

Lenin and Trotsky now headed a one-party government. The Left Socialist-Revolutionaries had walked out of Sovnarkom in protest at the Brest-Litovsk treaty. They kept their seats in the soviets, and many of them continued to work in official capacities, even for the Cheka. But the tension between the two parties was acute.

On 5 March, two days after the ink had dried on the treaty, Raymond Robins asked Trotsky about the consequences for Russia at home and abroad. Despite having handed over his post to Chicherin, Trotsky was happy to give him answers. He himself hoped for American assistance for the Red Army. But Robins asked why the communist leaders had signed the treaty unless they aimed to cease fighting. Trotsky explained that no treaty could involve a permanent commitment, and he did not discount the possibility of moving into active military co-operation with the Allies. Robins believed him but was reluctant to accept that Lenin shared this way of thinking. Trotsky escorted him to the Sovnarkom meeting chamber so that he could ask Lenin for himself, with Alexander Gumberg tagging along as interpreter. Lenin confirmed Trotsky's words; he said he had an open mind about entering into a 'military agreement with one of the imperialist coalitions against the other' since he had no fundamental preference for the Central Powers or the Allies. The cardinal criterion for him was what benefited the Revolution in Russia.[4] Lenin had questions of his own for the American authorities. What would the Western Allies do if the Bolsheviks ripped up the treaty? Would the US give military aid? Would Washington help Russia if the Japanese invaded Siberia? Would the United Kingdom send help to Murmansk and Archangel if Russia got into difficulties with Germany?[5]

Robins asked Ambassador Francis to accept that Lenin and Trotsky were genuinely open to restarting hostilities against Germany. He discussed the matter with Lockhart, who enthusiastically wired London:

> Empower me to inform Lenin that the question of Japanese intervention has been shelved; that we will persuade the Chinese to remove the embargo on foodstuffs; that we are prepared to support the Bolsheviks in so far as they will oppose Germany, and that we will invite [Lenin's] suggestions as to the best way in which this help can be given. In return for this there is every chance that war will be declared between the Bolsheviks and Germany.[6]

Oliver Wardrop, the UK consul-general in Petrograd, was of similar mind and advised London that the Bolsheviks embodied the only hope that Russia might return to fighting Germany.[7] Ambassador Francis too displayed flexibility by cabling the American Railway Mission across the Russo-Chinese frontier in Harbin to get a hundred experts ready for sending into Russia with a view to restoring the rail network—and he kept Washington informed of his action. Even the *Times* correspondent Harold Williams, a fierce critic of Bolshevism, rushed to alert Lloyd George to the opportunity for a diplomatic initiative on Russia and the Bolsheviks.[8]

The Bolsheviks maintained a healthy distrust of Germany and decided to shift the Russian capital into the interior, to Moscow. Lenin and most of the other People's Commissars left Petrograd on 10 March. On arrival, they found that the great clock on the Spasski Gate overlooking Red Square still played 'God Save the Tsar' on the hour.[9] And if the Germans did invade, the monarchy's restoration might not be wholly improbable.

Power to ratify or reject the treaty lay with the Fourth Congress of Soviets, which opened in Moscow on 15 March. It was no longer feasible to wait for messages from Washington or London. Lenin grimly told Robins: 'I shall now speak for the peace. It will be ratified.'[10] He had arranged for the foreign missions to attend and hear his speech. In it he mentioned nothing of his recent approaches to the Western Allies and, seeking to keep his party's spirits up, he asserted: 'We know that [the German revolutionary] Liebknecht will be victorious one way or another; this is inevitable in the development of the workers' movement.'[11] But on 29 April he had to admit: 'Yes, the peace we have arrived at is unstable to the highest degree; the breathing space obtained by us can be broken off any day both from the west and from the east.'[12] He still could not afford to let the Germans conclude that he intended to challenge the terms of the treaty, but, provoked by criticisms in Russia, he came before the Central Committee to urge that the priority of Soviet diplomacy ought to be 'to manoeuvre, retreat and wait'.[13] This was as far as he could go without alarming Berlin. Many Russians thought that he was more interested in power for himself and his party than in spreading revolution westwards. But Lenin meant what he said: he remained committed to revolutionary expansion whenever the opportunity appeared.

The People's Commissariat of Foreign Affairs lost much of its earlier influence. It was obvious that Chicherin would never dominate policy. Lenin and Trotsky wanted him to operate as an expert executant of their wishes, and generally he was willing to comply. Chicherin in any case had his hands full coping with 'subordinates' who showed him no deference. The People's Commissariat seethed with its own disputes. Radek was an unrepentant advocate of 'revolutionary war' whereas Karakhan favoured compromise with the Allies. Radek put it about that Karakhan—'a donkey of classical beauty'—was not up to the job. Karakhan thought Radek a hothead who was too sharp-tongued by half. The rivalry suited Lenin, who could play them off against each other—or at least this was how Lockhart assessed the situation.[14]

Trotsky at any rate was again seeing eye to eye with Lenin; and when the new People's Commissar for Military Affairs finally left for Moscow on 16 March, he took Lockhart on the same train.[15] Sadoul dismissed the Scot as 'un bon bourgeois' and regretted that the Allies had sent out no genuine socialist among their diplomats.[16] But Lockhart at least counted for more with the Bolsheviks than Robins did. Trotsky disliked Robins for his lack of enthusiasm for the October Revolution and his past association with 'imperialists' like President Theodore Roosevelt.[17] Lenin felt the same, and when Albert Rhys Williams put in a good word for Robins, Lenin exclaimed: 'Yes, but Robins represents the liberal bourgeoisie of America. They do not decide the policy of America. Finance-capital does. And finance-capital wants control of America. And it will send American soldiers.'[18]

Lenin and Trotsky were also sceptical about Lockhart but thought he might come in useful while the Bolsheviks were looking for chances to play off the Allies and Germany against each other. Trotsky was hoping to get assistance as he built up the Red Army. Lockhart was a willing helpmate, assuring London that the Bolsheviks had been 'wonderfully patient'.[19] The Allies could perhaps be persuaded to lend a hand if they judged that the Russians might one day soon break with the Germans. But his words increasingly fell on deaf ears. Foreign Secretary Balfour, while encouraging him to be frank in his reports, complained that he had supplied no evidence of genuine anti-German purposes among the Bolshevik leaders.[20] General Alfred Knox, the British military liaison officer in Siberia, was blunt about those Allied representatives who continued to press the case for accommodation with the Kremlin. In a report to London he wrote that Lockhart's bland commentaries on Soviet politics were 'criminally misleading'.[21]

Anti-Bolshevik Russians were angry about liaison between the Allies and the Reds. E. D. Trubetskoi and fellow monarchists warned the French consul-general Fernand Grenard in Moscow that Allied policy was wrong in every way. They stressed that Lenin had not the slightest intention of fighting Germany. If France and Britain continued to indulge Sovnarkom, the result might be to push Russian patriots into seeking help from the Germans. Trubetskoi's words were ignored and the Allies went on probing the possibilities of co-operation with the Soviet leadership.[22]

Lenin's manoeuvres annoyed the German high command. Rudolf Bauer, head of Germany's military intelligence in Russia, threatened a German occupation of Petrograd unless Sovnarkom showed full compliance.[23] But generally there was satisfaction in Germany at the closure of the eastern front. On 7 March the Germans signed a treaty with the White Finnish government and helped General Mannerheim to crush the remnants of the Finnish Reds and eliminate the prospect of socialist revolution in Helsinki. In April they tore up their treaty with the Central Rada in Kiev and installed Pavlo Skoropadskyi as a client ruler. Ukraine became a colony in all but name. The German military campaign stretched from the Baltic to the Black Sea and was accomplished with ease, enabling the high command to divert men and equipment to the western front. Not only the Allies but also the Bolsheviks hoped that Germany's onslaught in northern France would prove ineffective. The fate of the October Revolution rested on the resilience of the French and British armies in their cold, wet trenches. If the Germans overwhelmed the Allies, they would rip up the Brest-Litovsk treaty and turn their power against Sovnarkom.

The Western Allies were exasperated by a treaty that allowed the Germans to concentrate their forces against them in northern France. But Soviet leaders were pleased at least that London, Paris and Washington left their diplomats in Russia. President Wilson declined to do anything further to assist Sovnarkom. He replied politely but blandly to overtures from Lenin and Trotsky.[24] He was simply being diplomatic. Things did not need to be made worse by an offensive telegram from the White House. Wilson disliked the British and French proposal for the Japanese to intervene in Russia from Siberia. He refused to contemplate a similar expedition by the Americans—and he insisted that in any case the outcome of the Great War was about to be decided on the western front.[25]

The staff of the European embassies returned from Finland to Russia and joined the Americans and Japanese in Vologda. They all absolutely refused to transfer to Moscow even though they maintained consuls or other representatives there. Bruce Lockhart watched all this from afar: 'It was as if three foreign Ambassadors were trying to advise their governments on an English cabinet crisis from a village in the Hebrides.'[26] He thought no Allied ambassador was up to the task. Francis in his eyes was 'a charming old gentleman of nearly eighty' and he recorded that Trotsky dubbed Noulens 'the Hermit of Vologda'. Noulens supposedly shaped his attitude according to 'the prevailing policy of his own party in the French Chamber', whereas Della Torretta spoke Russian but allowed himself to be bullied by Noulens. Rumours proliferated in Vologda's fetid diplomatic atmosphere; and Lockhart had to chuckle when Noulens, who had heard that the Germans had installed one of Nicholas II's ministers in power in Petrograd, nervously asked whether the story was true.[27] Moves were afoot behind the scenes to send expeditionary forces to protect Allied interests. The British were gathering troops for a landing in the Russian north at Murmansk and the Japanese were planning the same for eastern Siberia. Sovnarkom would receive no prior notice. The idea was to do the deed before anyone noticed, but the Bolsheviks got wind of Japan's intentions and sought to pre-empt them by making pleas to the other Allies.

In April, the United Kingdom landed a force of 2,500 men in Murmansk, mainly British but also including some French and Serbs.[28] Their stated purpose was to protect Allied military supplies from falling into German hands. Trotsky retorted: 'This is what the wolf said to the hare whose leg it had just snapped.'[29] But there was nothing he could do to get rid of the British, and anyway he wanted their help in enhancing Soviet security. The operation in northern Russia had been kept strictly secret out of concern for British popular opinion and also in order to avoid letting Berlin know what was afoot. The troops led by Brigadier General Finlayson had been trained in seclusion in the Tower of London. The force was kept in the dark about its destination when it boarded the train at King's Cross Station in London; and the officers were informed only when their ship, *City of Marseilles*, was already at sea. Things went awry early on when Spanish influenza afflicted the crew and the troops. Indian Muslim stokers succumbed first. As it was the month of Ramadan, they had had to fast daily until dusk. Soldiers and then even officers had to shovel coal before the ship docked in Murmansk.[30]

Lenin and Trotsky were shocked by the British action, but they soon surmounted this. Increasingly the Allied landings appeared a helpful counterweight to Germany's rapacity. The Bolsheviks had assumed that they would keep control of Crimea; but this did not stop the Germans from invading and imposing their control over the northern coast of the Black Sea. Rostov-on-Don, Yekaterinodar, Voronezh and Kursk too fell under German occupation.[31] The treaty in March had drawn a line from the Baltic Sea only as far south as Brest-Litovsk. Trotsky, while concentrating on his ploy of 'neither war nor peace', had overlooked the need for agreement on Russia's new frontiers. This was an elementary blunder, and the Russian and Ukrainian governments were still negotiating over the line to be drawn between Russia and Ukraine until well into the autumn.[32] No one in the Central Committee, least of all Lenin, had foreseen the consequences as Russian-inhabited cities continued to fall to the Germans. Nevertheless even the German high command held back from a total invasion. It assisted the Cossack leader General Krasnov in building up an army that one day might be deployable against the Reds. Yet already on 2 April 1918 Stalin was questioning the point of the treaty and mooted the idea of forming an anti-German military coalition with the Ukrainian Central Rada when the Germans seized Kharkov.[33] Stalin's change of stance was a sign of the panic in Sovnarkom. Rather than a breathing space, Brest-Litovsk appeared to have produced an opportunity for suffocation.

The Central Committee met in emergency session on 10 May. Six members were in Moscow and available, and it was the most tumultuous gathering since the discussions of January and February. Sokolnikov, the very man whose hand had signed the treaty, argued that Germany's recent military actions had breached the terms of the Soviet–German agreements. What lay behind this, according to Sokolnikov, was a confluence of interests between the Russian bourgeoisie and German imperialism. He urged the pursuit of 'a military agreement with the Anglo-French coalition with the objective of military co-operation on certain conditions'.[34] Lenin rebutted this proposal and persuaded the Central Committee to stick by its peace policy. Sokolnikov did not give up. On 24 May he wrote in *Pravda*: 'Should Germany break the Brest peace treaty, the Soviet government will have to ask itself whether it should not try and obtain military help from one imperialist power against another. The communists are in no way opposed to such methods as would cause the imperialists to break each other's heads.'[35] This was no more than Trotsky had been thinking since November 1917; it had also been in Lenin's mind at the time when the treaty was signed. But no one had previously made such a suggestion on the pages of the central party newspaper.

Trotsky appealed for five hundred French officers to assist with the Red Army.[36] France's diplomats and military attachés, with the exception of Sadoul, were sceptical. Georges Petit said: 'All this sterile and hypocritical blustering ought not to be taken seriously.' Henri-Albert Niessel of the French military mission went further. After hearing Trotsky blame the Allies for the Brest-Litovsk treaty, Niessel lost his temper and addressed him 'in a way that no general would dare to speak to a subordinate officer'.[37] Niessel's comrade Jean Lavergne sent officers into Ukraine to cause trouble for the 'Austro-Germans'. Despite telling Lenin he would assist in training the Red Army, Lavergne doubted that Sovnarkom would meet the French condition that the Reds should demonstrably prepare to fight Germany.[38]

Trotsky had greater success with the United Kingdom. For advice on a Soviet air force he enlisted the British intelligence officer George Hill and appointed him inspector of aviation, and two or three times a week he laid
aside half an hour for Hill to instruct him in aeronautics. Hill relished the
queerness of being asked to teach the arts of war to a man who was famous
for having opposed militarism throughout Europe. His task was to enable
the communists to build up an air force that could take on Germany's
fighter and reconnaissance planes in the event of war.[39] Ambassador Francis
tried to appear helpful, cabling Robins on 3 May 1918: 'You are aware of
my action in bringing about the aid of the military missions towards organizing an army.'[40]

This support pleased Trotsky, who asked Lockhart on 5 May to request
the help of the British government in building the Red Army and for the
dispatch of the Royal Navy to 'save the Black Sea fleet'. In exchange he
promised to allow the large contingent of Czech ex-POWs to proceed to
Murmansk and Archangel for shipment across the North Sea to the western
front against the Central Powers.[41] Serb volunteers had already done this
with Soviet consent. Negotiations about the Czechs, based mainly in Penza,
had gone on since shortly after the Brest-Litovsk treaty. The Bolsheviks
sniffed the danger that the British in the north might treacherously deploy
them against the Red Army; they also worried about how the Germans
might react to such a deployment of the Czechs.[42] Trotsky therefore tried
to persuade Czech units to join the Red forces. But the Western Allies had
to be appeased if he wanted anything from them, so he sanctioned an
arrangement for the Czechs to make their way out of Russia via Vladivostok
for onward transportation to Europe.[43] Trotsky ignored the taboo against
assisting one of the two military coalitions in 'the imperialist war'. He assured Lockhart that the British force could keep its stores undisturbed in
northern Russia.[44] The British pushed for more. Rumours grew that the
Germans were about to march on Petrograd and there was a danger that
the entire Baltic Sea would fall under their control. The Admiralty in
Whitehall instructed Francis Cromie, the naval attaché in Petrograd, to explore ways of scuttling the ships as a precaution. On 11 May Cromie set off
for Moscow to see whether Trotsky would make trouble; he also spoke to
Lockhart and the Red Army General Staff.[45]

The United Kingdom continued to strengthen its presence at Murmansk
in the Russian north, raising its force steadily from the initial strength of
450 officers and men.[46] The French took responsibility for the Allies in the

south, sending a flotilla to Odessa on the Black Sea and depositing a force there. The Murmansk landings provoked protests but no action from Sovnarkom. Soviet leaders lacked the military strength to remove the British expedition; they also quietly welcomed the arrival of a counterbalance to the Germans. France's force in Odessa received critical comment but it was far from being at the top of *Pravda's* agenda since the Bolsheviks had lost their toehold across Ukraine.

The military position was tricky enough, but Sovnarkom also faced an ever worsening economic situation. Until the Brest-Litovsk treaty it had been possible for old contracts to be fulfilled and new ones drawn up with foreign businesses. Sovnarkom had valuable goods for sale or rent. Lenin had consistently said that foreign capital was essential for industrial reconstruction; he wanted to offer 'concessions' in the Russian economy—and Sovnarkom resolved to draw up a plan on non-capitalist principles.[47] (Why capitalists should want to invest without any chance of making a profit was not given consideration.) The idea of inviting businesses abroad to invest in Russia had been debated in Soviet governing circles since the beginning of the year.[48] It was not widely popular among Bolshevik leaders but Lenin would not let go of it, believing that capitalist powers were inherently greedy. He hoped to inveigle the Americans into doing business in Russia and deflect the military threat from Japan. Lenin suggested that President Wilson might put pressure on Tokyo if Sovnarkom used Siberian concessions as an enticement to American big business.[49] The Allies, even if they were willing to prop up Sovnarkom, saw the Russian trade as a growing risk for governments as well as businesses. Platinum was held in large stocks in Russia, and the British government had been negotiating their purchase; but in May 1918 a prosecution was brought in London against a British firm that had sought to buy up Russian platinum through the businessman William Camber Higgs of Petrograd. An Allied economic blockade of the territory under Soviet rule commenced.[50]

Lenin turned instead to Germany and made an appeal to its industrialists and financiers. The Germans did not make this easy for him. Their ambassador, Count von Mirbach, was exigent and imperious. He was also a stickler for diplomatic propriety. He insisted on presenting his credentials in the time-honoured fashion of diplomacy. This he did to Sverdlov as Chairman of the All-Russia Central Executive Committee of the Congress of Soviets. His one concession to the Bolsheviks was to wear only a day suit and not a top hat and tails.[51]

Mirbach treated Chicherin at the People's Commissariat of Foreign Affairs as an underling. Whenever he wanted to speak to him, he barged into his rooms without ceremony and flung his hat, overcoat and cane on the table. He shot his mouth off in Radek's office for everybody to hear.[52] He intended that the Bolsheviks should feel that Moscow had become part of Germany's domains. It had taken until 26 April for Mirbach to set up his official residence at 5 Denezhny Pereulok (Money Lane). The German consulate was on the other side of the street at Number 18. The position could not have been more awkward since the French military mission worked and lived on the same street.[53] The chauffeurs of the two nations competed to get their limousines ahead of each other. On one occasion they screeched to a halt just three inches apart.[54] The efficiency and zest of the Germans impressed onlookers in comparison with the pomaded diplomats of several other embassies.[55] Setting the tone, Mirbach paid visits to leading monarchists, including a sister-in-law of Nicholas II.[56] He insisted that Sovnarkom should restore money and companies seized from German owners in the war or after the October Revolution.[57] Sovnarkom complied, committing itself to punish anyone who tried to obstruct the policy. Russia's subordination appeared complete.[58]

The Soviet leadership did not pretend to like the situation, as *Pravda* made clear: 'The German ambassador has arrived in the revolutionary capital not as a representative of the toiling classes of a friendly people but as the plenipotentiary of a military gang which with boundless insolence kills, rapes and pillages every country.'[59] But rhetoric was one thing, practical resistance entirely another.

Trying to make the best of a bad job, Sovnarkom appointed missions to central Europe on 4 April 1918. Lev Kamenev was the choice for Austria, Adolf Ioffe for Germany and Yan Berzin and Ivan Zalkind for Berne.[60] On his way back from the United Kingdom Kamenev had been apprehended on one of the Åland Islands by the White Finns and the announcement of his Viennese appointment seems to have been a ploy to get the Central Powers to exert their influence to release him. (In fact he was not freed until 17 June 1918 by means of a deal to swap him for half-a-dozen White Finnish officers.)[61] It anyway was Ioffe who had the key posting. Berlin was the capital of the power which had forced the 'obscene peace' on Russia; but, like Trotsky, Ioffe was willing to suppress his feelings about Brest-Litovsk. He could perhaps salve his conscience by doing what he could to promote the cause of revolutionary internationalism in Berlin. Leonid Krasin and

Vladimir Menzhinski went with him. Krasin had been a manager for Siemens-Schuckert in Germany and Russia before the Great War; he had also been involved in the Bolshevik robbery unit after the failure of the 1905–6 revolution. He was hardly a veteran of big business but he was the best qualified among the Bolsheviks. Menzhinski was a trusted Chekist who was assigned to undercover work.

No one could tell what would come out of this hazardous international situation. For nearly two months after the treaty of Brest-Litovsk had been signed, anything seemed possible—or at least this was the assumption underlying the activity of the politicians and the diplomats. The treaty had solved everything and nothing. Any slight shift in the fortunes of the Allies or the Germans could have immense consequences. The war was not over and any trembling of 'Soviet power' could result in the collapse of Bolshevism. The government in Moscow was far from secure and the economy was in free fall.

Even the German leadership was perplexed. The flotsam of many nations was swept around in the Russian tumult. Hundreds of thousands of prisoners had fallen into the hands of the Russians since 1914, and Lenin and Trotsky regarded them as excellent material for revolutionary indoctrination. Many POWs needed no new stimulus to turn against their old governments. The belligerent mood was especially remarkable among Czech and Hungarian captives who wished to return home and overthrow the Habsburg authorities.[62] Many had newly developed communist sympathies— this was true of Czechs, Hungarians, Bulgarians as well as Austrians and Germans. The Bolsheviks organized an All-Russia Congress of POW Internationalists in Moscow on 9 April 1918.[63] By freeing the military prisoners of Imperial Russia they intended to foster insurrections in Europe. It was the Central Powers which had reason to fear what was afoot. Within days of the Brest-Litovsk treaty, according to Sadoul, German and Austrian volunteers were being sent into Ukraine from Moscow to take up the struggle against the military occupation.[64] Prisoner-of-war associations were being formed all over the country—and predictably the Central Powers showed little eagerness to welcome them back across their frontiers.

Robert Vaucher left an account of the Germans freed from detention camps by Sovnarkom:

> In the streets of Petrograd the German ex-POWs walk around freely, dressed in new attire several days previously, belted in their blue,

green or white pre-war uniforms, fully ornamented with frogging, with braids and with insignia. They parade the length of Nevski Prospect in their flamboyant lion-tamer uniforms with the air of victors and look down on their Austrian allies who are still dressed in their old uniforms which are patched, faded and threadbare.[65]

Not everyone was eager to go back to Germany, for fear of being mobilized to the trenches of the western front. Nor was the German high command enthusiastic about using them as soldiers until all traces of Bolshevik influence had been removed. The Austrian commanders were still more worried about the contaminating effects of communism.[66] Lenin's peace needed careful handling. The outcome of the Great War was being decided in northern France, but the dismantled eastern front retained its capacity to affect the situation in the western trenches.

11. REVOLTS AND MURDERS

While the Allies were gathering intelligence and even plotting the downfall of the new Bolshevik regime, organized opposition—as yet clandestine—to the Bolsheviks was growing. In the early summer of 1918, an informal coalition took shape bringing together anti-Bolshevik politicians in Moscow and Petrograd from the Kadets to right-wing socialists; no effort was made to appeal to monarchists. Leading liberals such as Pëtr Struve joined the enterprise and the National Centre, as it became known, kept up links with the so-called Volunteer Army in Rostov-on-Don as well as with Allied officials across Russia.[1] The Volunteer Army was the first of the White forces to be formed and was initially led by Generals Kornilov and Alexeev. The Whites chose their colour to distinguish themselves from the Reds and to suggest that their cause was a pure and just one. The Allies quietly welcomed them as determined enemies of Bolshevism. They also preferred the National Centre to the Right Centre, which included figures like Pavel Milyukov who made overtures to the Germans for help to bring down the Bolsheviks.[2] The Allied embassies feared that the Volunteer Army might make the same choice. There was also a Left Centre. Based in Ufa in the Urals, it consisted of socialists and successfully set up a local administration.[3] Allied diplomats reported on these processes and kept a lookout for signs that the people of Russia were getting ready to overthrow Bolshevism and re-enter the embrace of the Allies.

In fact the deadliest threat to the Soviet regime as yet came not from Russians but from Czechs. It crystallized when the Czech former POWs journeying in armed batches from Penza to the Pacific coast turned violently against the Bolsheviks.[4] The trouble flared up in late May when the

Chelyabinsk Soviet tried to disarm the Czechs before allowing them to travel any further. Trotsky had issued an appeal for the Czech volunteers to join the Red Army; he had followed this up with an order that they could proceed to Vladivostok only if they handed over their weapons. Instead the Czechs seized control of Novonikolaevsk and then travelled back westwards as far as Penza to rescue their comrades.[5] Opinion was divided in the People's Commissariat of Foreign Affairs about Trotsky's management of the process. Radek tried to convince Robert Bruce Lockhart that Soviet leaders in Moscow had simply acted out of anxiety about letting the Germans think them indulgent to Allied interests.[6] Karakhan was less charitable, admitting that Trotsky could have handled things with greater understanding.[7] Whatever their views, the outcome was a disaster for Sovnarkom as 25,000 Czech troops assembled in the Volga region and put themselves at the disposal of the Komuch government in Samara. They no longer intended to fight on the western front but planned to stay and fight Bolsheviks. Komuch had always been militarily weak, but the Czechs could help to rectify this.

The Allies pretended to be mere spectators of this turnabout. This was less than convincing. The French had been subsidizing and liaising with the Czechs from March to May. The British too had been involved. In essence the Allied leaders wanted the Czech troops to cause trouble and undermine Soviet rule in Siberia—and the Germans, having negotiated Russia's withdrawal from the war, were annoyed by this.[8] The Bolsheviks reeled from blow after blow. Workers grumbled about conditions in factories and mines and demobbed soldiers returned to villages where anger at the state seizures of grain was acute. Peasants in many provinces were on the brink of revolt. Sovnarkom governed only the areas of Russia around Moscow and Petrograd plus the Urals. The Red Army was still a shambles. The Cheka could scarcely cope with the growing number of plots and protests. In the soviets there was unceasing criticism from the Left Socialist-Revolutionaries who hated the peace treaty and the turn in agrarian policy towards forcible seizures of grain. Food shortages in the cities worsened. Urban residents with any ties to the land fled to the countryside.

Ambassador Noulens in Vologda hoped that the Bolsheviks were on the brink of collapse. Wanting to make his own assessment, in early June 1918 he paid a return visit to Moscow where he held a meeting with what remained of the French colony. He knew he was under surveillance. At the

time he felt his trip was worthwhile since he learned about the various subversive actions being contemplated. But Noulens' interpreter and confidant
was the French reporter René Marchand. It soon became clear that Marchand's sympathy lay with the Bolsheviks—and indeed he later transmitted
everything he knew to the Cheka.[9]

The rapid westward advance of the Czech troops forced the Kremlin to
think again about the Romanovs. Until the winter of 1917–18 the former
emperor and his immediate family and retainers had been quarantined in
Tobolsk in western Siberia, where they had been dispatched by Kerenski—
and the emergencies in Russian affairs meant that few people wondered
what was happening to them. But, although they were out of sight, the Bolshevik leaders did not forget about them. On 11 February 1918 Sovnarkom
considered a proposal to bring the former emperor to Petrograd to be put
on trial;[10] but no action followed until 9 March, when Lenin and the government decided instead to move them to Yekaterinburg in the province
of Perm for fear that monarchists might try and liberate them in Tobolsk.[11]
Yekaterinburg was the Soviet administrative centre of the Urals region and
a stronghold of Bolshevism; it was also nearer than Tobolsk to Petrograd
and Moscow and on the Trans-Siberian railway. Moisei Uritski, head of the
Cheka in Petrograd, oversaw the transfer, and the precise place of confinement was left to the Yekaterinburg comrades.[12] They picked the large walled
mansion of the once-wealthy merchant, Nikolai Ipatev. The transfer and
the reasons for it were announced by Sovnarkom in early May.[13]

Nicholas II whiled away the time by reading novels by Turgenev as well
as anti-Semitic tracts. He and his wife behaved as normally as possible while
tending to the needs of their son Alexei and their daughters. The Bolsheviks
kept up the pressure by changing their guards frequently and making it difficult for the Romanovs to form any friendships with them. Each fresh shift
started by uttering obscenities and shunning overtures. At least the food
was adequate, but the uncertainty was demoralizing. Sensing that they
might be moved again in unpredictable circumstances, the former empress
Alexandra and her daughters sewed jewels into their underwear for use as
currency in an emergency.

By mid-July the Czechs were within days of reaching Yekaterinburg and
the Bolshevik leadership in the Urals were panicking. The fear was that
Nicholas Romanov might be freed and used as a rallying symbol of the anti-
Soviet cause. The order came from Moscow to liquidate the entire family.

Exactly who issued the instructions, and how and when, was deliberately kept unclear. No communist leader wanted to put his signature to a warrant that might later incriminate him. The deed was done early in the morning of 17 July when the Romanovs were ordered from their beds and marshalled in the cellar. Armed men, sodden with drink, stood them against the wall before gunning them down. The news was suppressed: the fear remained in Moscow about the likely reaction in Russia and abroad. Trotsky's diary records that the Kremlin leaders in Moscow had held a discussion about the plan for liquidation and given their instructions to the Yekaterinburg Bolsheviks. Lenin and Sverdlov were actively involved. Trotsky, tied up with his military duties on the Volga front, heard the story from Sverdlov and was disappointed. Although he had no objection in principle to the killings, he would have preferred to put the ex-emperor on show-trial to publicize the iniquities of the Imperial government. Trotsky never liked missing any propaganda trick.[14]

Sovnarkom met on the day of the killings to hear Sverdlov's confidential report.[15] Nothing was said in public for several months. It was understood that foreign monarchies, including the Hohenzollerns, would be enraged by what had been done. The Kaiser and the emperor were cousins, and even though their armies had fought each other in 1914–17 the ties of consanguinity still meant much to Wilhelm II. His anger would have been still fiercer if ever he learned that the communists had butchered Nicholas's wife and children along with him. Empress Alexandra had originally been Princess Alix of Hesse and, although it was impolitic for the Kaiser to enquire about the deposed Nicholas, he could very properly send an emissary to ask Ioffe about Alexandra as a native German and indeed a relative. One of her brothers made the same approach. Lenin hid the full truth from Adolf Ioffe in the German mission, telling Felix Dzerzhinski: 'Don't let Ioffe know anything. It will be easier for him to tell lies there in Berlin.'[16] Ioffe therefore simply repeated the official story he had heard from Moscow. He prised the facts out of Dzerzhinski only later in the year when the head of the Cheka made a trip incognito to Berlin and Ioffe gained the opportunity to question him directly.[17]

Even in Russia, most party leaders and militants were kept in the dark. As late as March 1919 Bolsheviks at their Eighth Party Congress were asking why Nicholas II was not being brought back to Moscow for a public trial.[18] But by then the Western Allies were able to make an informed guess about the fate of the Imperial family. The American army contingent in Siberia now followed the Czechs to Yekaterinburg and learned from anti-Bolshevik investigators about their preliminary enquiries. It was no longer reasonable to doubt that the Romanovs had been slaughtered. King George V in Britain expressed his acute concern for his cousin Nicky and the family in comments that must have been tinged with guilt since he had turned down Kerenski's request to grant them asylum in 1917.

The Bolsheviks felt steadily less secure in power, and Czech military actions were not the only cause. Humiliated at Brest-Litovsk, they were forced to give away further territory under German pressure in June. The Germans, worried by the British landings in the Russian north, demanded that Lenin should cede the western segment of the Murmansk area to the Finns. This would provide the contingent of German troops already stationed in Finland with a base to counteract the spread of Allied armed strength in Russia.[19] The Bolsheviks gave way: they had no choice short of going to war against Germany. But they were not totally acquiescent. Even some of the Left Socialist-Revolutionaries said that no party had done more than the Bolsheviks to assist Ukrainians willing to take up arms against the German occupation of Ukraine.[20] Uprisings took place in small towns and villages. (The British officer George Hill helped with this, even though his claim to have led the entire campaign of sabotage was a somewhat exaggerated one.)[21] But the Ukrainian forays by Bolsheviks were marginal to the Kremlin's general line of appeasing the Germans. However arrogantly their diplomats behaved in Moscow, the communist leadership continued to draw a deep breath and overlook any offence.

This was an attitude that infuriated the Allies. Although Bruce Lockhart continued to parley with Trotsky, he no longer believed that Sovnarkom would ever fight Germany. It now made sense for the British to strengthen contacts with the enemies of Bolshevism and lend them their support. Approaches were made to Lockhart by the Volunteer Army and others.[22] When a certain Fabrikantov asked him for help in enabling Kerenski to escape from Russia, he ignored protocol and issued him with travel documents under the alias of a Serbian soldier.[23] Lockhart also handed over £200,000 worth of Russian rubles to George Hill and Sidney Reilly for delivery to Patriarch Tikhon to help with the Orthodox Church's resistance to the Soviet government.[24] William Camber Higgs, who owned a small British firm in Moscow, facilitated such subventions by cashing cheques drawn on the British Treasury. (George Hill did the same thing as Lockhart but specified the War Office.)[25]

Lockhart passed on funds to Boris Savinkov for an uprising in Yaroslavl, 155 miles north east of Moscow; Ambassador Noulens, from Vologda, provided finance for Savinkov through Consul-General Grenard and the military attaché Jean Lavergne.[26] Savinkov had assembled a Union for the Defence of the Fatherland and Freedom to organize a chain of resistance to Bolshevism on the eastern side of Petrograd and Moscow. As Lockhart reported to London, the immediate objective was to establish a military dictatorship. Savinkov had himself in mind as Minister of the Interior and some well-known general—almost certainly Mikhail Alexeev—as head of a national government; he alerted both the Czech Corps and the Volunteer Army to his plan and co-ordinated his activity with them.[27] He also informed Sergei Sazonov, who by then was serving as the chief anti-Bolshevik diplomat attached to the Western Allies in Paris. Lockhart explained to London that Savinkov hoped to stir up a peasant revolt culminating in the execution of Bolshevik leaders. When Lord Curzon, as a member of Lloyd George's War Cabinet, received Lockhart's report he declared Savinkov's methods to be on the drastic side, but nonetheless wished him well. What Curzon avoided was any promise to augment the British forces of intervention even though Lockhart had spelled it out that Savinkov's scheme depended on such assistance from the Allies.[28] Ambassador Noulens was less straightforward. Wanting to multiply the attacks on Sovnarkom, he advised Savinkov that the Allies were on the very point of undertaking a full invasion; and, although the French had no expeditionary force in the north, Noulens told him that he could count on decisive reinforcement from that direction.[29]

Noulens achieved his purpose and the insurrection duly occurred on 6 July. As well as Yaroslavl, Savinkov occupied Vladimir, Rybinsk and Murom and proclaimed the overthrow of Soviet rule across Yaroslavl province.[30] He restored private trade, promising to regenerate the economy and feed the hungry. He announced that he was acting in concert with anti-Bolshevik governments in Siberia and by the Volga. Savinkov put himself forward as leader of the Northern Army of rebels against communism while affirming his subordination to the command of General Alexeev, who was striving to build up the Volunteer Army in southern Russia.[31] But when the Reds moved against the rebels no French or British assistance was made available to relieve Savinkov when he faced defeat. The Allies had never intended to invade—and indeed President Wilson would have opposed any such enterprise. Savinkov had been tricked.[32]

The timing was awful for the anti-Bolshevik cause in Moscow. The Fifth Congress of Soviets opened in the Bolshoi Theatre on 4 July, and the Bolsheviks gave every sign of determination to fight on and win. The foreign missions sat in the boxes and watched from above. On one side was Mirbach with his Austrian, Hungarian, Bulgarian and Turkish colleagues; the head of German intelligence, Rudolph Bauer, was also present. On the other side were the Allied representatives with Lockhart prominent among them; the French and the Americans had places in the upper tier. (Sadoul turned up in a silk hat, frock coat and kid gloves.)[33] Lenin spoke for the Brest-Litovsk peace, Trotsky for the Red Army's preparedness. All Bolsheviks contended that every official policy had merit. No sliver of disagreement appeared between one Bolshevik commissar and another. Maria Spiridonova who led the Left Socialist-Revolutionaries, still operating openly under the regime, denounced Sovnarkom at length; her comrade Boris Kamkov declared them to be inhuman scoundrels and, as he looked up at Mirbach's party, shouted: 'Down with the assassins!'[34] The Bolsheviks at the Congress did not try to silence the Left Socialist-Revolutionaries because they knew that Sovnarkom was guaranteed an absolute majority of votes. If the Germans were worried, they did not show it.

Foreseeing the results of the voting, the Left Socialist-Revolutionary Central Committee secretly sanctioned terrorist attacks in Russia. The idea was not to kill Lenin or Trotsky but to organize a 'provocation' that would wreck the Brest-Litovsk treaty and bring the Bolsheviks back to the path of 'revolutionary war'. Left Socialist-Revolutionaries thought that they would achieve this simply by assassinating Ambassador von Mirbach. If they were successful, Berlin would break with Moscow immediately.

On 6 July Yakov Blyumkin, an eighteen-year-old Left Socialist-Revolutionary working for the Cheka, entered the German embassy on a false pretext and shot Mirbach. Sovnarkom instantly proscribed the party and arrested several of its leaders. Dzerzhinski, embarrassed by the lapse in state security, sped off to their headquarters only to be taken captive by them. He was liberated thanks to resolute action by the Latvian Riflemen—a force which had gone over en masse to the Bolsheviks from the old Imperial army and quickly formed the effective core of the Red Army. Without their Latvians, the Bolsheviks would have been helpless. Lenin and Radek took a limousine to the German embassy at Denezhny Pereulok to express formal condolences. They were grovelling because they feared that unless they expressed outrage, however insincere, Germany might overrun Russia.[35] In Berlin, Ioffe's first thought was that German agents had killed Mirbach so as to sharpen the conflict between Russia and the Allies. He deduced this from the German Foreign Office's request for Lenin to put the blame on Allied agents. The Germans called for the killers and their 'ideological inspirers' to be caught and punished.[36] They also demanded the right to dispatch their own troops into Russia.[37] But things calmed down and the leading Bolshevik Anatoli Lunacharski spread the news among the foreign community in Moscow that the emergency was nearly over. This needed doing since the Bolsheviks were worried that the British and French would start a preventive war to save Russia from German occupation.[38]

Young Blyumkin was nowhere to be found. He had escaped to Ukraine, hoping to return when the Bolsheviks tore up the peace treaty. Frantic to oblige the Germans, the Soviet government ordered the execution of V. A. Alexandrovich, the Left Socialist-Revolutionary who had worked as Deputy Chairman of the Cheka. The German authorities let it be known that they were satisfied with the Bolshevik official reaction. Radek could be relied upon to make the best jokes about the emergency. He told acquaintances that a job could now be found for the generals of Nicholas II's armed forces: they could be formed into detachments and trained to shed crocodile tears in Mirbach's funeral cortège.[39]

The Bolsheviks badly needed a counterweight to German power. Chicherin, who was appointed People's Commissar of Foreign Affairs on a permanent basis at the end of May,[40] cabled Ambassador Francis to say that Vologda was unsafe and that the diplomatic corps should move to Moscow. He added: 'I am sending Radek to Vologda to execute the invitation.' The word 'execute' did not exactly reassure Francis after the Mirbach murder. He replied that he felt secure in the north 'because we do not fear the Russian people'. Radek, taking Ransome as his interpreter, turned up uninvited; he was sporting a jacket pulled tight with a belt from which hung a conspicuous revolver.[41] To Francis this was an attempt to look like a 'cowboy on the war path'. He told Noulens: 'Ah, the miserable little Jew! If he comes back to see me with his revolver in his holster, I'll get mine from out the drawer; I'll put it on the table and tell him: "Now let's talk!"'[42] Soviet leaders, not for the first or last time, were behaving incautiously. The French were picking up their wireless traffic passing through Petrograd and knew what Radek and

Chicherin wrote to each other seated at their Hughes apparatuses—this was the most up-to-date method of telegraph communication, which allowed people to type and exchange messages instantaneously. Radek ought to have avoided mentioning Francis's predilection for his embassy secretaries; Chicherin was unwise to refer to the false tone of deference he used with the American ambassador. Ambassador Noulens enjoyed passing both these titbits on to Francis.[43]

Noulens and Francis faced Radek down. The fact that he had tried to stir up the feelings of a 2,000-strong crowd of workers against the Allies did nothing to reassure them. They reasoned that they could too easily end up as Lenin's hostages if they moved to Moscow. Radek and Ransome returned to Moscow with their tails between their legs.[44]

After Francis had received cable intelligence that Chicherin had indeed ordered the local soviet to take them hostage, the Western diplomatic corps could see that Vologda was no longer a safe haven. This would have been the last straw for the ambassador even if he had not known that the British force in Murmansk was planning to overthrow the Archangel Soviet. The Bolsheviks had their own intelligence about this and had been executing known enemies in the region. Northern Russia became a theatre of war. Francis already had a secret agreement with the Vologda station master to keep a locomotive and carriages ready for his embassy to leave for Archangel at an hour's notice. On 29 July he decided that the time had come to flee but, wanting to avoid the appearance of colluding in British military aggression, he changed the destination to Kandalaksha, a few miles south of Murmansk.[45] Shortly before boarding he practised a little deceit by wiring Chicherin: 'We have determined to take your advice.' Chicherin heard what was really being planned and tried to prevent it: 'Archangel means leaving Russia.' He could hardly complain. His own deceit would have delivered Francis into Soviet custody. Chicherin had acted too late and soon all the Americans were sound asleep on a moving train.[46]

Whatever brittle trust had existed between the Kremlin and the White House now vanished. Raymond Robins had already left for America on 14 May, still convinced that the Western Allies should not attempt a military intervention in Russia unless given Sovnarkom's explicit sanction—by then his friend Lockhart had come round to recommending an Allied campaign regardless of the Kremlin's wishes.[47] But room for diplomacy through informal mediation had already disappeared. A bleak future of armed conflict loomed on the horizon. The Bolsheviks had dealt with the threat from Germany by signing the treaty of Brest-Litovsk. The Western Allies had yet to clarify their military intentions—and the communist leaders pondered their own options with heightened concern. They had hoped to crush their Russian enemies before meeting the challenges from abroad. Now they could no longer be confident that the Allied powers would allow them this freedom.

12. SUBVERTING THE ALLIES

The foreign military campaigns against Soviet rule ran the Cheka ragged across Russia and the borderlands of the old empire. The Germans held Poland, Ukraine and the Baltic region and maintained a force in Finland at its government's request. The British were in occupation of Murmansk and Archangel. The French presided in Odessa. The Turks were pushing into the south Caucasus. The Japanese and the Americans landed expeditionary forces in eastern Siberia. The 'intervention' was multi-angled and highly dangerous. Nor could Soviet security forces ignore the potential for trouble from armed foreigners like the Czech ex-POWs who had been in Russia. The disintegration of the Russian Empire gathered pace as Georgians, Armenians and Azeris rejected the authority of Sovnarkom. The Volga region in south-east Russia was governed by Komuch. Russian anti-Bolshevik armies—the Whites—were stiffening their efforts in south Russia and mid-Siberia. Each of these forces sought to make contact with supporters in the areas under Bolshevik control around Moscow and Petrograd. The Chekists had their hands full with the tasks of combating counter-revolutionary activity over this entire zone. There was little time or personnel to spare on espionage and subversion abroad.

The tasks of governing the Soviet-dominated zone were huge. The Bolsheviks accepted that they had to employ in the People's Commissariats 'specialists' who had worked in the ministries before the October Revolution. Some did this with much reluctance and zealously persecuted anyone they thought to be acting disloyally. Although Joseph Stalin was notoriously suspicious of 'bourgeois' experts, he was not alone among Bolsheviks. It was their preference to promote the working class to administrative authority in the 'proletarian state'. Lenin had said and written this throughout

1917.[1] Yet he recognized that years would be needed for workers to acquire confidence and training. While this was happening, the old personnel had to be kept in post under the watchful eye of communist commissars. Lenin and Trotsky were adamant that the Soviet state would collapse without qualified professionals; but they had a problem in securing acceptance for their pragmatism.

Even they, though, did not want to employ former Okhrana officials. Like other communists, they detested what the political police had done to revolutionaries under the Romanovs, and they felt they could not trust any of them. The Soviet Constitution stripped former policemen of civil rights. Since the Chekists refused to employ such people, they had to teach themselves from scratch how to organize intelligence and counter-intelligence— on this as on other practical matters, Marx and Engels had left no handbook of instruction behind. The sole asset that the Bolshevik party possessed was its long experience of struggle against the security police. Clandestine political work had required the Bolsheviks to take precautions against infiltration and provocation. Cool vigilance had been essential. In fact when the Okhrana's files were opened after the February Revolution, it was shown that police agents had penetrated the revolutionary parties more systematically than anyone had imagined. The Bolsheviks had prided themselves on their conspiratorial prowess. So Lenin was astounded to learn that one of his protégés in the Central Committee, Roman Malinovski, was a paid employee of the Okhrana. When Malinovski imprudently came to Petrograd and threw himself on Sovnarkom's mercy, Lenin had no compunction about having him executed.[2]

The Chekists learned some lessons better than others and were notably slow in acquiring technical expertise in code-breaking and encryption. This was something of an oddity. Before 1917 all of them—in the underground, Siberian exile or emigration—had used forms of secret writing for internal party correspondence. Often this involved little more than working with an agreed piece of printed text or list of specific words, and the chemicals they deployed for invisible script might sometimes be no more complex than the contents of a milk bottle. This experience taught them the importance of codes, but their political suspiciousness deprived them of a chance to increase their practical cleverness. Imperial Russia had brought on a brilliant group of cryptographers. None was more remarkable than Ernst Fetterlein, who fled across the Finnish frontier in June 1918. Fetterlein had decrypted the British diplomatic codes in the Great War, giving an invaluable tool to Russia's Ministry of Foreign Affairs and the War Ministry in their dealings with London.[3] The communist authorities were able to invent only rather primitive codes—and the art of decryption for a while was out of their reach.

They were aware that the security of their wireless communications left much to be desired. It took them years to recover from the loss of many of Russia's most expert telegraphists, who walked out on them after the October Revolution.[4] Bolsheviks could see that they were technically inferior to the Allies, the Germans and the Whites. One way round the problem was to send deceptive messages *en clair*. This is the only sensible way to interpret a particular conversation on the Hughes telegraph apparatus between Karl Radek in Moscow and Khristo Rakovski in Kiev. With theatrical extravagance, Radek claimed he could see no cloud in the Soviet sky. Lenin was recovering well from illness. The Red Army was conquering all the counter-revolutionary forces ranged against it and would definitely prevent the Czechs from linking up with the Allies. British and French prisoners were being held as hostages and would be summarily shot if trouble started up from Vologda. Radek boasted to Rakovski that things were entirely fine with the Germans.[5] Such nonsense can only have been meant to reassure German snoopers that the Bolsheviks were sticking firmly to the Brest-Litovsk treaty. Just possibly Radek was hoping to scare the Allies away from interfering in Soviet affairs—or perhaps he had both purposes in mind at the same time.

Chekist leaders were determined to rectify their lack of effectiveness. One thing they found easy was in recruiting officials. Plenty of Bolsheviks and their supporters had grievances against the middle and upper classes in the light of their personal experience under Romanov rule and were eager to join the security services and liquidate the plots against Sovnarkom.

Felix Dzerzhinski at first glance was not the most obvious man for Lenin to have wanted as head of the Cheka in December 1917. He had no recent acquaintance with underground activity. Born near Minsk, he was a Pole from a noble family and went to a grammar school before being expelled for 'revolutionary activity'. He was a poet and liked to sing. But political rebellion was his passion; and once he had discovered Marxism, he helped to found the Social Democracy of the Kingdom of Poland and Lithuania. He detested nationalism, being wary of fellow Poles who wanted their own independent state. He was allergic to internal party polemics—and, like his comrade Rosa Luxemburg, he had despised the shenanigans let loose by

Lenin and the Bolsheviks in the world of Marxism before the Great War. He was exiled to Siberia in 1897 and again in 1900, but both times he escaped. Shortly after he had married Zofia Muszkat, she was arrested and he was left alone with their baby son. Yet he kept up his revolutionary activities. He had a rough time in prison after his last arrest in 1912, suffering beatings and being held for long periods in manacles—his wrists bore permanent scars. When released at the fall of the monarchy, he was more austere and restrained than before—and he was plagued by bronchitis.

The fact that Dzerzhinski did not want the Cheka post was a recommendation in itself, and Lenin never doubted that he had made the right choice. Dzerzhinski applied a clinical judgement to any situation and had no qualms about ordering mass executions. Józef Piłsudski, who led the Poles to national independence in 1919, remembered him generously from their schooldays: 'Dzerzhinsky distinguished himself as a student with delicacy and modesty. He was rather tall, thin and demure, making the impression of an ascetic with the face of an icon . . . Tormented or not, this is an issue history will clarify; in any case this person did not know how to lie.'[6] The British sculptor Clare Sheridan, who did a bust of Dzerzhinski in 1920, was struck by his demeanour:

> His eyes certainly looked as if they were bathed in tears of eternal sorrow, but his mouth smiled an indulgent kindness. His face is narrow, high-cheek-boned and sunk in. Of all his features it is his nose which seems to have the most character. It is very refined, and the delicate bloodless nostrils suggest the sensitiveness of over-breeding.[7]

Dzerzhinski told her: 'One learns patience and calm in prison.'[8] Sheridan was unusual in coaxing such intimacies out of him since he did not welcome conversations of a personal nature. Dzerzhinski was nobody's acolyte but he agreed with Lenin about what needed to be done in Russia. Ascetic and dedicated to the case, he would run the Cheka just as Lenin wanted—and he would not be held back by the kind of moral scruples that would have bothered Luxemburg.

Dzerzhinski was not the only Chekist with a reputation for dispensing violence with a degree of distaste. Yakov Peters, his Deputy Chairman, impressed Louise Bryant in the same way: 'Peters told me at various times that the only people he believed in killing were traitors in his own ranks, people who were grafters and who tried to steal everything, people in a time like that who did not stick to the high moral principle of revolutionary discipline.'[9] If terror occurred under Soviet rule, she said, it was carried out by reluctant perpetrators like Peters who were harder on delinquent Bolsheviks than on 'enemies of the people'. Even George Hill, less friendly than Bryant to Sovnarkom, felt that Peters 'really hated what he was doing, but felt that it was necessary'.[10] But Peters had a darker personality than he revealed to sympathetic foreigners. When living in London he had been involved in the murder of policemen which led to the Sidney Street siege in 1910. Like Dzerzhinski, he would do anything for the Revolution. As time went on, Dzerzhinski and Peters became more enthusiastic about taking the bridle off the Cheka. Enemies of the Bolsheviks did not scruple to use conspiracy and insurrection—an attempt was made on Lenin's life in December 1917. Chekists wanted to meet fire with fire. They stopped at nothing to uphold the Soviet order while continuing to speak softly with foreigners.

Martyn Latsis, a member of the Cheka Board, called in the Cheka house journal for the class enemies of the Soviet order to be exterminated. He was advocating classocide. It was not enough to suppress capitalism; just as important for Latsis was the requirement to liquidate all living capitalists. But although the legislative framework was permissive in the extreme, Dzerzhinski at first trod carefully and consulted the central party leadership regularly. The coalition between Bolsheviks and Left Socialist-Revolutionaries was among the factors holding back the Cheka, but after July 1918 the Bolsheviks were running a one-party state. They faced enemies, foreign and Russian, who were becoming increasingly well organized and well financed. From then onwards the Chekists fired first and asked questions later, if they asked them at all.

The social groups they targeted were named in the Constitution adopted by the Congress of Soviets that July. In the clauses devoted to citizenship, several types of people were deprived of electoral and general civil rights. Aristocrats, priests and policemen were blacklisted, as were industrialists, bankers and landlords. The Constitution declared all the 'former people'—chilling phrase—to be suspect. Latsis wanted to victimize all of them. What he said openly, the Chekists quietly practised. When emergencies arose, the custom became to arrest people belonging to these categories and hold them as hostages. Such prisoners were executed whenever the Whites carried out terror against Bolsheviks. The gaols in Moscow and Petrograd were grim, filthy places of confinement and the work of rooting out counter-revolutionary groups brutalized the Chekists in attitude and practice. Their leaders at every level prominently included Jews, Latvians and other non-Russians whose animus against monarchy, Okhrana and Church was highly developed. They did not blanch at orders to terrorize people who had enjoyed privileges before 1917.

One of the great worries of communist leaders was that their enemies might find a way to disrupt the Brest-Litovsk treaty. The anarchists were always out to cause trouble. Four of their number had seized the car of Raymond Robins in April 1918. Robins drew his Browning pistol on them only to be confronted by their own four Brownings. The anarchists stole the vehicle, forcing the chauffeur to do the driving for them. Robins, stranded on the pavement, contacted the People's Commissariat of Foreign Affairs and demanded the return of his car as well as an apology. Chicherin met his indignation with the less than reassuring comment that 'he had had the same thing happen to himself only a week before'. This infuriated Robins, who said that no other foreign minister in the world would talk so complacently. Robins went next to the Cheka, which is what he should have done in the first place. Dzerzhinski's people promised that the American's property would be back with him within a week, and this is exactly what happened.[11] On the night of 11–12 April 1918 the Cheka and the Red Army moved decisively against the anarchist strongholds in Moscow. Twenty-six premises were attacked. Sovnarkom used the Latvian Riflemen to carry out a thorough suppression of resistance. By the end of the action they had killed forty anarchists and taken five hundred prisoners.[12]

Dzerzhinski, humiliated by having been captured in the Left Socialist-Revolutionary rising, resigned as Chairman of the Cheka on 8 July and agreed to resume his post only on 22 August. Eight days later Lenin was wounded in an assassination attempt that came very close to success. Dzerzhinski's morale again crumbled. In September he took himself off to Berlin. He travelled under the alias of a courier called Felix Damanski, leaving the Cheka in the care of Yakov Peters. Getting away from the scene of his embarrassment, he hoped to do something useful for the international communist cause. Adolf Ioffe refused to go easy on him and asked how the Chekists could mess things up so badly as to let Lenin be shot.[13] Another purpose of Dzerzhinski's trip was to retrieve the shreds of his private life. His wife Zofia had not seen him since before the Great War. After her release from Russian custody, she had moved to Switzerland with their son;

from 1918 she was employed in Berne by the Soviet mission. Dzerzhinski slipped over the border to visit his family. He took them to the zoo in Berne and on a boat trip on Lake Lugano. Zofia was later to write a less than reliable account, claiming that her husband unexpectedly came face to face with the British diplomat Robert Bruce Lockhart on the same pleasure steamer.[14] In fact Lockhart at that time was in London recuperating from the Spanish influenza.[15]

The Soviet authorities were not yet making much effort to infiltrate agents into foreign political establishments. If they had looked for a candidate as their master spy in the West it would surely have been Theodore Rothstein, who wrote for the *Manchester Guardian* in wartime and worked in the War Office press office as a translator.[16] Rothstein, an emigrant from the Russian Empire, was one of Lenin's old acquaintances in London and had taken his side in the original split between Bolshevism and Menshevism. He was also a veteran supporter of causes on the political far left in his country of refuge; no Russian Marxist had a better command of English. When the Bolsheviks took power in Petrograd he became a spirited advocate of their ideas. His journalism for the *Call* newspaper marked him out as a fanatical Bolshevik as he justified communist dictatorship and called for a Revolutionary World War.[17] This was never going to make Rothstein popular in the War Office after Sovnarkom had announced that Russia would not continue in the war,[18] and it was no surprise when his employment was terminated. According to Basil Thomson of Special Branch, Rothstein's duties had anyway never given him access to anything of use to an enemy power.[19] Rothstein expressed no regret about leaving the civil service. As a revolutionary he was reserving his energy for disseminating Soviet propaganda and money.

Although the Cheka had yet to set up a comprehensive operational network in Europe, there was another 'abroad' where Chekists were hard at work. When the Bolsheviks seized power in Petrograd in October 1917 it was not long before rival governments were established in those territories of the former Russian Empire where resistance to Bolshevism was strong. Sovnarkom took it for granted that such places should come under Moscow's authority. Chekists were trained to infiltrate with a view to subverting the current rulers and preparing a situation that would make the tasks of the Red Army easier to accomplish.

Activity in Europe was restricted to a few Cheka operatives, Vladimir Menzhinski in Berlin being one of them. Germany and Switzerland were easier places for communication than the Allied countries. Indeed, the breakdown of postal communication with the United Kingdom reduced Yakov Peters to asking friendly Allied intelligence officers to get a British diplomatic courier to carry letters to his wife in London.[20] Foreign intelligence operations were anyway not the monopoly of the Cheka. A confusion of agencies sprang up, involving the People's Commissariat of Foreign Affairs and sundry communists returning from Moscow to their native countries. The Russian Communist Party as well as Sovnarkom was plagued by overlaps in functional tasks. Soviet rulers wanted results. They were practical zealots, and as long as it looked as if something positive might come out of their plans they did not bother about institutional propriety. Dzerzhinski was pictured as the spider at the centre of a vast web of international intelligence. Nothing could be further from the truth. The Cheka, Sovnarkom and the Central Committee operated alongside each other in energetic activity and no single institution had a monopoly in the tasks of intelligence.

In fact Dzerzhinski and his comrades did not get round to setting up an illegal operations department for work abroad until June 1919: the emergencies in Russia were the priority to be dealt with. (On a point of detail, it must be remembered that none of the Cheka's operations in Soviet Russia were beyond the law for the simple reason that Sovnarkom had intentionally freed Chekists from legal restraints.)[21] But intelligence about foreign governments was vital for the formation of policy. Germany and the Allies constituted a dire threat to Sovnarkom's survival. Either of them might at any moment invade. Plots by Russians too had to be stamped out or prevented all over the territories under Soviet rule. White conspiracies sprouted up with Allied support. The communist leaders scrabbled around to improve their knowledge of what was going on in Washington, London and Paris. Litvinov and Rothstein ably discharged this task in the United Kingdom for the People's Commissariat of Foreign Affairs. In America, Nuorteva and Martens went around canvassing support for the Bolsheviks through the Finnish Information Bureau, and help continued to be made available by sympathizers like Felix Frankfurter.

Probably the best conduit of inside news, though, were informal diplomatic channels. Karakhan and Radek in the People's Commissariat of Foreign Affairs talked at length to influential foreigners in Moscow. Both were charming in their individual ways. Despite offending many people with his brashness and extreme opinions, Radek seemed decidedly winsome to

Arthur Ransome, who had his ear to the ground as he sought to track down Allied intentions. Ransome's pro-Bolshevism was an open secret and agents of the Allies had learned to be cautious in what they said in front of him; indeed his letters and movements were kept under close review even though he was simultaneously working for British intelligence.[22] Karakhan was anyhow always the more congenial acquaintance for Allied represen- tatives since he did not disguise his wish for some kind of deal between So- viet Russia, as it was starting to be called,[23] and the Western Allies. Lockhart claimed that his favourite commissar was known to like turning up 'be- gloved and armed with a box of coronas'.[24]

The gentlemanly pleasantries disguised the savagery of international re- lations. While Karakhan and Lockhart puffed on their cigars, they ex- changed opinions frankly about the situation. Karakhan rebuked the British for failing to assist the Bolsheviks; he claimed that the Red terror had ac- quired its wildness because the Allies had isolated and threatened Soviet Russia. Lockhart retorted that Sovnarkom had itself to blame after jeopar- dizing the Allies by closing down the eastern front. While Britain and France were fighting for national survival, Lenin had chosen to relieve the military pressure on Germany. If the Soviet intelligence effort abroad was frail in the year after the October Revolution, the Bolshevik leadership did not lack access to information about what the Allied powers thought of them. Radek and Karakhan were adept at picking up titbits useful for the formulation of foreign policy. They took what they discovered back to their comrades in the Kremlin. As yet it made little difference to Bolshevik ac- tions. Sovnarkom's room for manoeuvre between Germany and the Allies was minuscule; and Bolsheviks anyway saw the world around them through ideological spectacles: they assumed the worst in everything communicated to them by Allied diplomats about the intentions of foreign capitalist pow- ers. This was a prudent tactic in the circumstances of the time.

13. GERMANY ENTREATED

Archangel had acquired strategic importance early in the war when the German submarine fleet turned the Baltic Sea into the most dangerous waters for shipping in the northern hemisphere. The old timber quays on the east bank of the River Dvina became the main destination for cargoes to Russia from Britain; and in summer 1918, when German forces encroached on northern Russia from Finland, the War Department in London gave approval for the British expeditionary force to leave its station in Murmansk and seize Archangel. General Frederick Poole, who commanded the operation, saw it as the first step towards the overthrow of Sovnarkom.

The city was Russia's oldest port for international commerce. Since the sixteenth century, when England's Queen Elizabeth I ordered the creation of the Muscovy Company, it had supplied timber and furs to the rest of Europe. Its fortunes dipped in the early eighteenth century when Peter the Great privileged St Petersburg, his new capital, on the Gulf of Finland, and by the outbreak of the Great War Archangel's population had dwindled to 38,000. Its estuary was navigable for only half the year from May to the end of September. In the winter, temperatures could drop to minus 13° centigrade and wealthy local families put triple glazing in their windows. In the 'white nights' of the summer, when there were long hours of daylight, the mosquitoes were a torment for everyone. But Archangel remained a bustling entrepôt and its administration increased the number of quays to the physical limit in the interests of intensifying activity. Ships with draughts as deep as sixty feet could find a berth there. A road ran the length of the city—a whole five miles—parallel to the Dvina. Traders built their mansions and sawmills between the road and river, near enough to the quays to watch over their interests. The pavements were of timber and the industry was timber. Although other goods like tar, pitch, fish and flax were also traded, Archangel was well described as a 'wooden metropolis'.[1]

General Poole's plan was to use the entire province of Archangel as his base for an invasion. The plan was to send a force south up the Dvina to Kotlas which was the terminal of the rail line to Vyatka and the Trans-Siberian railway. His objective was to form an attacking semi-circle pointed at Petrograd and Moscow from the north and east.[2] After combining with the Czech Corps in the Urals and the Volunteer Army in southern Russia, he expected to tip the military balance against Sovnarkom.[3] The plan had French blessing; and although the Americans wanted no direct part in it, they discreetly indicated that they would not object to anything the British did.[4] Optimism was peaking. The Admiralty in London shared Poole's assumption that he could easily recruit and train an army of Russian volunteers to fight the unpopular and vulnerable regime in Moscow.[5]

On 26 July 1918 the Allied contingent sailed from Murmansk for Archangel. Poole issued an ultimatum and, more by bluff than anything else, the city fell to him on 2 August as the Red garrison and its political commissar Mikhail Kedrov made a hasty departure.[6] Nikolai Chaikovski, the septuagenarian revolutionary who had lived in London until the February Revolution, had agreed to head the Supreme Government of North Russia. (The word 'supreme' appeared obligatory for anti-Bolshevik enterprises.) Poole had taken little account of Russian geography and society and Chaikovski was already less than wholly confident. Peasants failed to greet the new administration with enthusiasm and the civil service was weak. The Allies attempted a little economic reform. It was agreed that the anti-Soviet authorities should have access to the funds in Western banks left behind by the Provisional Government and currently claimed by the Bolsheviks. John Maynard Keynes, then working as a Treasury consultant in London, submitted a memorandum explaining how to establish a stable currency in areas outside Soviet control; he recommended a fixed exchange rate between sterling or gold and Archangel rubles.[7]

The British press hardly mentioned northern Russia beyond noting that 'a considerable force' had been landed there.[8] When a Labour MP complained about the lack of public disclosure, the government simply refused to comment.[9] Months later, Douglas Young, Britain's consul in Archangel, was to go to the London press and denounce the subterfuge and the violence he had witnessed. While disliking Bolshevism, he contended that the way to deal with Soviet Russia was through diplomacy. Young denied that a few thousand troops seven hundred miles from Moscow could bring down Sovnarkom.[10] But at the time a curtain of mystery was drawn over the Archangel operation. The US embassy, having fled Vologda, made its base there as soon as Poole pronounced it safe for Allied personnel.[11] A degree of diplomatic fussiness was involved. The Americans still wanted the Soviet government to know that they had not taken part in the occupation of the city. They were merely going there after Poole had seized it. In this way the door was kept open for the US to negotiate with Sovnarkom if a suitable opportunity arose. These nuances had little influence on how the Bolsheviks reacted to Poole's military action. In their view, the Western Allies had committed a flagrant violation of Soviet Russia's sovereignty—and they feared that Poole would continue his advance.

Without being reinforced by fresh units, however, Poole could not expand his operations beyond Archangel province. The British government, before sanctioning the seizure of Archangel, had received advice from naval intelligence in Petrograd that at least two army divisions were necessary if the Bolsheviks were to be overthrown. Anything less than that would 'lead to the impression that operations were not being undertaken seriously'. By contrast, a truly substantial contingent would have an instant strategic impact since the Germans would no longer be able to transfer troops from east to west but would have to move them in the opposite direction, and this would be of benefit to the Allies on the western front.[12]

But it took the maximum of Allied human and material resources to repel the great German offensive that had begun in March. Poole had to sit tight and pray for victory in northern France. It had appeared that his hopes might be fulfilled on 18 July when the Germans, exhausted by months of attacking, had to fall back at Villers-Cotterêts. The French Army had shown that Germany was not invincible. Celebrations were in order and church bells rang throughout France that Sunday. But the German forces regrouped and the Allied commanders did not believe that two whole divisions could be spared at that crucial moment. Poole disappointedly dropped the idea of attempting a breakthrough to Vyatka. Instead he settled his men in Archangel until such time as the military situation should change either in Russia or in France. He had angered Sovnarkom without endangering its survival, and his force got used to enduring the insect bites in the long summer days.

For weeks, however, the German Foreign Office had been agitating for the communists to take back northern Russia and get rid of the British.

Ioffe reported from Berlin that the Germans had offered to undertake a joint military operation.[13] Germany's high command continued to worry that the Allies might succeed in restoring the eastern front—and a war on two fronts was the last thing that Ludendorff and Hindenburg could cope with. Sovnarkom resisted the German invitation until Archangel capitulated to Allied power. On 1 August Chicherin asked Karl Helfferich, who had headed the embassy since Mirbach's death, about collaborating in an attack on the British in Archangel and Murmansk. Concern about the potential threat from Poole intensified. On 13 August Chicherin put a request to the Germans to carry out an aerial bombardment of Archangel. Moisei Uritski, head of the Cheka in Petrograd, talked to German diplomats about the need to crush the British military platform in the north. Uritski's stipulation was that German troops should not go via Petrograd. He claimed to be nervous about Russian working-class opinion. More likely he did not entirely trust the Germans despite wanting help from them. If German troops were allowed into Petrograd there was no guarantee that they would leave Soviet rule intact.[14]

Germany's intentions were a source of constant worry to the Soviet leaders, and they were right to be concerned. Ruling circles in Berlin had never discounted the notion of invading Russia and throwing out the Bolsheviks. The war party was constantly tempted by this option. As late as June 1918 Ludendorff was saying: 'We can expect nothing from this Soviet government.' Enquiries were put in hand about practicalities.[15]

Ioffe and the Soviet mission in Berlin failed to penetrate such discussions. The German government had allocated to it the Russian embassy building on Unter den Linden. International etiquette required Ioffe to present his credentials in person to the Kaiser; but this was more than Ioffe, a severe opponent of the Brest-Litovsk treaty, would contemplate—and probably the Kaiser was not displeased. Although Ioffe always dressed smartly, in other ways he was far from the diplomatic stereotype. His office was chaotic. He had no idea how to keep financial accounts; he had no clue about the exchange rate and lacked the desire to find out.[16] Like other communist veterans, he regarded money with distaste. Nevertheless he continued to employ the German servants inherited from the old embassy.[17] Ioffe looked on servants through a Marxist prism of analysis. For him, they were 'proletarians' who were winnable to the revolutionary cause. The working atmosphere in the mission was nothing if not relaxed. The tone was set by

Ioffe's young Russian chauffeur who usually arrived in the mornings in his sports kit. This was not a problem until the day when Ioffe had to go to the German Foreign Office and told him to dress more demurely. The chauffeur's reaction was to don a pair of silk pyjamas.[18]

Ioffe's private life was equally chaotic. After the October Revolution, his wife and daughter Nadya lived in Baku until he brought them to Berlin. It was not a happy conjoining. What disconcerted Mrs Ioffe was the presence of the young woman operating as her husband's personal assistant. This was Maria Girshberg, who had joined the communist party in Petrograd in 1917. Everyone in the Soviet mission knew what was going on. Maria—or Musya as she was known—spent whole days with Ioffe and not always on revolutionary business. The Ioffes fell to arguing into the small hours and little Nadya could hear them through her bedroom wall. Her mother had red eyes every morning. Comrades in the Berlin mission thought he had fallen for a little schemer.[19] After the Ioffes took a short holiday in Sweden, the parents began sleeping apart. Musya had become the mistress in every sense.[20]

But Ioffe's true passion was revolution. As the man on the spot in Berlin, he thought he knew better than Chicherin. The People's Commissar liked to work through the night and felt free to contact Ioffe at four in the morning about trivial matters. He also used the telegraph facilities without adopting any security precautions despite the risk of the Germans taking advantage.[21] But the main question dividing them was about how to handle Germany. Ioffe thought Chicherin too timid, arguing that the Germans were fully exercised with occupying Poland and Ukraine and were unlikely to go for an open break with Russia. Although Ioffe was no longer hostile to doing deals with 'German imperialism', he was crude in the way he treated Germany's banks and businesses and had no intention of honouring contracts. Nikolai Krestinski, People's Commissar of Finances, objected that such trickery would find him out.[22] But others in the mission such as Lev Krasin and Vladimir Menzhinski took Ioffe's side when writing to Lenin.[23] Krasin was the Bolsheviks' expert on foreign trade;[24] Menzhinski was a Cheka officer marked out for a higher posting. Both denied that the German government would ever assist with Russia's economic recovery.[25] Lenin was so exasperated with Ioffe that for a while he rejected his request to make a trip to Moscow.[26] He accused him of trying to run the People's Commissariat of Foreign Affairs from Berlin and called for 'ambassador Ioffe' to cease querying Moscow's decisions.[27]

Ioffe told Lenin that 'you are ... very much mistaken if you suppose that Germany is sending its forces to the east with such pleasure'.[28] He got nowhere. Lenin had made up his mind and rebuked Ioffe for getting distracted and not writing enough German-language propaganda. Ioffe ignored him and ran the mission according to his own lights.[29]

In any case there was agreement about much else. Overt activity was only a part of the mission's duties and Ioffe's clandestine tasks included the reception of leaders, agents and couriers arriving from Moscow. Among his secret guests at various times were Nikolai Bukharin, Khristo Rakovski and Felix Dzerzhinski. Ioffe welcomed the help of these fellow Bolshevik leftists—all of them had originally objected to the Brest-Litovsk treaty.[30] Germany remained in the communist imagination the engine house of European revolutionary transformation. Lenin anyway shared the feeling that the separate peace and the weakness of the Soviet regime should not deter the Bolsheviks from promoting mass insurrection in Berlin. Ioffe helped to co-ordinate agents who dispensed communist literature and financial subsidies to likely supporters. He assisted the Moscow emissaries with their arrangements for onward travel to the rest of Europe.[31] The Berlin mission also became the base for propaganda directed at Allied countries. Receiving Moscow's proclamations on war and revolution, Ioffe sent them on to Britain, Switzerland and Scandinavia; and he obtained permission from the German government to print revolutionary material for dispatch across the lines of the western front to French, British and American troops.[32]

Many German public figures and organizations felt that it would not be prudent to treat Russia roughly. The liberal politician Gustav Stresemann told Ioffe that if only the Soviet leadership would agree to a proper alliance of some kind with Germany, he would look favourably on the idea of returning all but Poland and the former Baltic provinces to Sovnarkom. Ioffe and Stresemann also discussed how the two countries might help each other economically. But Stresemann was not in power. He could only promise to relay such ideas to Ludendorff and the high command.[33]

Ludendorff was not disposed to be gentle with the Russians. On 8 August his forces crumpled before a British surge at Amiens.[34] Steadily the war was being lost in northern France. There was panic in the German high command as the tactical ingenuity and superior resources of the Allies took their toll. Ludendorff called for a last great effort. With this in mind he resolved to force the Soviet government to yield up further territory and resources. A supplementary treaty was initialled on 10 August on terms that were even more onerous than those of the Brest-Litovsk peace. Sovnarkom was to renounce all claims to Estonia, Latvia and Lithuania, enabling a further tranche of German troops to be shipped to the western front. The Germans would receive access to the vessels of the Black Sea fleet. They could buy a quarter of Baku's oil output. The Soviet leaders agreed to pay an indemnity of six milliard marks from their gold reserves. They also undertook to try and expel the British from Archangel and Murmansk and to look kindly on any German military operation to that end. Lenin got almost nothing in exchange except a promise that the Germans would cease offering help to Sovnarkom's enemies in Russia. Signature of the treaty took place on 27 August.[35]

This was the apogee of Lenin's policy of appeasement. Already in June, as a sop to the Germans, he had ceded the western sliver of the Murmansk district to the Finns. This would help German troops in Finland to counteract the spread of Allied power.[36] The same readiness to help the Germans was evident in the south Caucasus. At German GHQ in Spa on 2 July it was reported that Ioffe had given 'a firm guarantee of oil from Baku'.[37] Germany expressed its readiness to stop its Turkish allies from invading the area. The Bolsheviks alone could not defend Baku. In return for Germany's diplomatic help they would sell fuel to Berlin.[38] On 29 July Lenin made clear to the Bolshevik leader Stepan Shaumyan in Baku that he was not to accept any military help from the British, who had offered to send troops. Disregard of this order would be treated as 'insurrection and treason'.[39] Lenin and his comrades put a brave face on all this. *Pravda* usually carried little news about the western front—the British naval attaché Captain Francis Cromie thought this was 'by Hun order, of course'.[40] But on 17 August the party newspaper suggested that the German setbacks at Villars-Cotterêts and Amiens made it unlikely that the Germans would now ever be able to invade Russia.[41] Even so, Lenin continued to predict trouble for the Allies. On 28 August he declared that the popularity of patriotic defence was in jeopardy in France and that the British working class was about to break with ideas about civil peace.[42]

His own preoccupation was with the Volga region of Russia. The adherence of the Czech Corps gave heart and strength to the Komuch armed forces in Samara. They pushed north and seized Kazan. This left them only 630 miles from Moscow by rail and river routes. Every available Red unit was rushed down to meet the challenge. Trotsky arrived in August to supervise the army high command and stiffen the morale of the troops. No one was in any doubt that, if the Red Army was forced out of the region, Komuch would pose an acute strategic menace to Moscow. Sovnarkom faced an existential challenge.

The Red Army regrouped at Sviyazhsk up the River Volga from Kazan. It suffered initially from chaotic organization. There were also mass desertions as troops and their commanders decided to have nothing to do with the war between Sovnarkom and Komuch. Military supplies to the Red Army were fragmentary. But the Reds held their line on the Volga and their morale and discipline began to grow. *Pravda* reported on this as if only Russian factors were in play. But as usual there was an international dimension. The Red Army's dispositions became possible only because of German consent. The Brest-Litovsk treaty had left the forces of Russia and Germany facing each other in the 'screens' arranged along the new Russo-Ukrainian frontier. Few doubted that the Germans could easily sweep aside the Red defences if they so desired. Sovnarkom could not risk leaving the borders unmanned unless it was confident that Germany would not take advantage. Ioffe explored the question with the German Foreign Office on 7 August, and he was gratified when the Secretary of State Paul von Hintze gave an official assurance that Germany would not exploit Soviet Russia's military difficulties.[43] If anything, the Germans were delighted by the Red Army's efforts. Indeed Chicherin was to claim, a few weeks later, that Germany was insisting that the Reds should liquidate the entire menace of the Czechs in the Volga region. German and Soviet strategic interests were conjoined.[44]

Lenin and Trotsky needed no pressure to prosecute war against Komuch. Far from fearing civil war in Russia, they actively sought it. They knew that their revolution would not be secure until they won a definitive trial of strength against the anti-communists. The last thing they wanted was some kind of compromise with their enemies. Trotsky sent the following confidential message to Lenin on 17 August 1918:

> I consider it unacceptable to let steamers sail [the Volga] under a Red Cross flag. The receipt of grain will be interpreted by charlatans and fools as showing the possibility that agreement can be made and that civil war is unnecessary. The military motives are unknown to me. Air pilots and artillerymen have been ordered to bomb and set fire to the bourgeois districts of Kazan and then Simbirsk and Samara. In these conditions a Red Cross caravan is inappropriate.[45]

He wanted nothing to intervene between the two combatant sides. Too bad if people in the Volga region were starving. Lenin and Trotsky both believed that the Soviet cause required an unflinching commitment to military practicalities. The Komuch government and its supporters had to be destroyed. Any other priority would be a mere sentimentality. The Bolsheviks were setting Russia on fire and, with German consent, planning to burn out any resistance before it could be consolidated.

14. SUBVERTING RUSSIA

Western espionage and subversion in Russia were conducted by some vivid individuals in 1918 and none was more colourful than Sidney Reilly, who arrived in the spring on a mission for British intelligence. Reilly throughout his life told contradictory stories about himself. It is likely—but not absolutely certain—that he came from Ukraine and was at least part Jewish. He was shortish, sallow complexioned and balding. Though his real surname was probably Rosenblum, he ran his commercial affairs under an alias borrowed from his estranged wife Margaret Reilly Callaghan.[1] He was attractive to women, and he sought them out with fervour.[2] His other passions were fashionable clothes, swanky hotels, good cigars and collecting Napoleonic memorabilia.[3] Reilly was a deeply manipulative man and in business was a greedy wheeler-dealer. Commercial partners came and went. They seldom stayed with him for long; many complained of sharp practices and indeed he treated everyone as fair game. No acquaintance ever suggested he had an excess of moral rectitude. Sidney Reilly was a compulsive conman.[4]

Mansfield Cumming at the Secret Intelligence Service trusted his instincts and took risks, and he was often proved right when choosing recruits whom others regarded as unqualified or unsuitable. He ignored the thick sheaf of warnings sent to him about Reilly.[5] The Bureau needed Russian-speakers with audacity and initiative, and Reilly fitted that bill. Cumming sent him to Russia via Archangel as agent ST1. Reilly started as he meant to go on, disembarking in Murmansk against orders and without explanation. The British expeditionary force there threw him into the lock-up of the merchant vessel that had brought him out from England. Admiral Kemp asked an intelligence officer, Stephen Alley, to interrogate him. Alley reported:

'His passport was very doubtful, and his name was spelled Reilli.' The peculiar spelling was possibly a deliberate one; it may well have been based on the calculation that a strange English version of the name would attract less suspicion since although Reilly claimed to be from Ireland and spoke with perfect grammar his accent was unmistakably from eastern Europe.[6] When challenged about his identity, he pulled out 'a microscopic message in code, which he had secreted under a cork of a bottle of aspirin tablets'. Alley recognized the message and instructed that Reilly be permitted to proceed south as he wished.[7]

On reaching Moscow in April 1918, Reilly avoided contact with British officials and threw protocol aside. Instead he made straight for the Kremlin where he claimed that he was researching a book on the achievements of the Soviet order. This got him an interview with Lenin's chief of staff Vladimir Bonch-Bruevich. The meeting was an amicable one and Reilly was given use of an official limousine as well as an invitation to attend the May Day celebrations at the Polytechnical Museum where Trotsky was to deliver a speech on the Red Army. The hall was already packed when Reilly and a friend arrived. With their privileged seats on the platform, only a piano separated them from Trotsky. Reilly whispered: 'This is just the moment to kill Trotsky and liquidate Bolshevism!'[8] But a sense of self-preservation intruded and Reilly stayed his hand. Although he had come to Russia with a rather gentle opinion of Bolshevism, a few days in Moscow changed his mind and he began to talk about the Soviet regime with venom.[9] It was only then that Lockhart heard that an unidentified Briton had visited the Kremlin to seek an interview with Lenin. He was furious at being bypassed and hauled Reilly in for a stiff lecture on lines of authority.

After clearing the air in this fashion, Lockhart felt he could take Reilly into his confidence about his current plans to bring down the Bolsheviks. Lockhart had gained greater liberty for himself after the British embassy decamped to Vologda—this was, as he liked to put it, his 'great luck'.[10] When he had moved to Moscow with Trotsky, he had specifically demanded authority from London to remain 'independent'; he insisted in particular that Oliver Wardrop, who served as consul-general, should render him every assistance without being set in authority over him.[11] He wanted to be free to pursue his tasks in diplomacy and intelligence without interference.

He also wanted freedom in his private life. Despite having previously been sent home to avoid scandal over an affair with a married woman, he lost no time in finding another lover in Moscow. He first met Maria Benckendorff (née Zakrevskaya) on 2 February 1918 over a game of bridge in Petrograd. On that occasion they only shook hands, but he was smitten by her glamour and vivacity.[12] Moura, as she liked to be known, still moved in the old high society that existed before the October Revolution. She was bored by her husband Ioann, who had retreated with their children to his large Estonian estate some weeks earlier.[13] Lockhart was looking for excitement and would confess: 'I fell desperately in love with her.'[14] Soon they were having an affair.[15] She fell pregnant by him and clearly expected that both she and Lockhart would soon divorce their respective spouses. But it is far from certain that Lockhart would have ended his marriage to Jean, and when Moura miscarried the baby in September, her happiness quickly started to sour.[16] Subsequently she came under suspicion of informing for Soviet intelligence—something she was certainly doing by the 1930s.[17] But there is no evidence that she already worked for the Chekists in mid-1918. At any rate Lockhart had taken a risk in having an affair with her and giving her the run of his apartment. If he was not spied upon, it was not because he took sensible precautions.

Lockhart and others in the British intelligence network in Moscow had an uninhibited lifestyle. But Sidney Reilly outdid them all. Among his many lovers was a young Russian actress, Yelizaveta Otten, who rented a well-appointed apartment in Sheremetev Lane a few hundred yards north of the Kremlin.[18] Yelizaveta's flatmate Dagmara Karozus was, according to George Hill, another of Reilly's conquests.[19] Dagmara was a German citizen who in 1915 had been investigated by the Ministry of Internal Affairs as a possible spy. She had sensibly responded by applying for Russian citizenship.[20] Then there was Olga Starzhevskaya, who fell head over heels in love with Reilly and foolishly believed they were about to be married. She knew him as a Russian called Konstantin Markovich Massino.[21] Starzhevskaya was a typist in the central administration of the All-Russia Executive Committee of the Congress of Soviets—no doubt her potential access to important material was her main attraction for him.[22] Reilly handed over the money for her to rent and decorate an apartment for them both on Malaya Bronnaya Street.[23]

Reilly was expert at running his amours in parallel and even employed several of the women as his operatives. Probably Maria Fride was the most useful of them. As a single woman in her early thirties, she had worked as a teacher and nurse.[24] Her prime asset was access to her brother Alexander, a lieutenant colonel employed in the communications office of the People's Commissariat for Military Affairs.[25]

There was no uniform pattern of work among the Allied intelligence agencies and the new US network was run noticeably more staidly than the British one. It was centred on the Information Service set up in Russia before the October Revolution and supposedly dedicated to 'educational and informational work'.[26] From March 1918, the head of the Service was the exotically named Xenophon Dmitrievich de Blumenthal Kalamatiano. Kalamatiano was born in the Russian Empire in 1882 and was of Greek and Russian extraction. As a boy he had emigrated with his mother and stepfather to America, where he took a degree in Chicago before returning to his native country for a job with an American tractor company in Odessa. He subsequently moved to Moscow where manufacturing contracts during the Great War made him a rich man. As his business fell off in 1917, he made himself useful to American diplomats trying to understand the situation in Russia.[27] The Information Service was the front for a network of thirty-two agents including Kalamatiano. After 1917, apart from gathering intelligence, their task was to make contact with Sovnarkom's military enemies.[28] Kalamatiano started by sending people to the bigger cities adjacent to the vast eastern front, cities stretching from Novgorod in the north to Rostov in the south. He then extended the coverage to Ukraine, Belorussia and the lands of the Baltic coast. When the Allied embassies left for Vologda he stayed behind and registered himself as a Russian citizen, which gave him the cover to continue his operations without going underground.[29] And although the American operation was late in getting started, it quickly became an effective one. Kalamatiano obtained material from informers in the Red Army and made contact with the Socialist-Revolutionaries.[30] He paid handsomely too—as did the other Allied agencies. Alexander Fride received up to 750 rubles a month from Kalamatiano for his reports.[31]

The intelligence agencies co-operated with each other, consulting regularly, sharing their findings and sometimes even running the same agents— Alexander and Maria Fride worked simultaneously for the British and the Americans.[32] The British and French secret services had plenty of practice in acting together without dropping their guard—each understood that the other might act independently for one reason or another in the national interest. When Noulens had stimulated Savinkov's ill-fated uprising in Yaroslavl in July he did not tell Lockhart what exactly he was promising to the rebels; and Lockhart was justifiably annoyed that the French had played fast and loose with the anti-Bolshevik resistance, risking and losing Russian lives in an irresponsible fashion.[33] The Americans would seem to have been more trusting than was good for them. In early 1918 British agents bought documents purportedly showing that Lenin and the Bolsheviks were the paid employees of the Germans. Reilly and Hill took a close look at them and found that most of the documents were produced on a single type-writer despite the claim of the sellers that they originated in places hundreds of miles from each other. The British, they concluded, had purchased expensive forgeries. So what did they do? They put the documents back on the market and let Edgar Sisson of the American Information Service buy them up—and in this way they recouped the financial loss. All was thought fair in wartime when budgets were tight.[34]

Sisson's 'revelations' failed to gain universal acceptance in the American press. The *New York Evening Post* made savage criticisms, and Santeri Nuorteva of the Finnish Information Bureau as well as John Reed had the opportunity to do the same in the *New York Times*.[35] The Committee on Public Information under George Creel investigated on the administration's behalf. Creel was already sympathetic to Sisson and, buoyed by support from Professor Samuel Harper and the National Board for Historical Science, pronounced most of the documents to be genuine. The threat to civilization in both Russia and America was said to come from a 'German–Bolshevik conspiracy'.[36]

Not everyone even among the British approved of such tomfoolery. Lockhart had never accepted that Lenin and Trotsky were agents of Germany or any other power. Denying that the Bolsheviks were 'pro-German', he reported that he 'had little faith in documents I have seen which over-prove the case for collusion';[37] he also pointed out that the French officials in Moscow shared his suspicions.[38] Sisson's 'discovery' interfered with his desire to convince the Allied governments that the Kremlin leadership were acting out of a sense of their own interests. He too wanted to overturn the Bolsheviks but argued that this would best be done in the light of a well-informed analysis.[39] The documents bought by Sisson in fact came from former officials of the Okhrana. They had made the forgeries either out of financial greed or because they frantically wanted to steer the Allies away from thinking that any kind of deal could be done with Sovnarkom after the Brest-Litovsk treaty. Lockhart had once been one of those who favoured collaboration, but he quickly abandoned that position. In any case the debate about Sisson's allegations wasted everyone's time and energy just when the Allies needed to be clear-headed about what was going on in Russia. All that could be said in favour of Sisson was that he helped to steel US public opinion against unnecessary compromises with the Soviet authorities.

While still pretending to be Trotsky's best Allied friend, Lockhart himself undertook a number of subversive activities after the Brest-Litovsk treaty—and although he had wide scope to use his initiative, he reported regularly to London and sought the permission of higher authority when he thought he needed it.[40] From inside the Bolshevik administration he had a frequent supply of information from Yevgenia Shelepina as well as from a 'Mr Pressman'.[41] He also secretly corresponded with the Volunteer Army in the south and met leaders of the National Centre in Moscow. He even attended an undercover National Centre conference in July and spoke with notable anti-Bolshevik politicians such as Pëtr Struve and with a colonel who represented General Alexeev and the Volunteer Army. Lockhart delivered ten million rubles to the Volunteers, whom he reported as making military progress. He noted that Alexeev was entirely opposed to Pavel Milyukov's overtures to the Germans. Lockhart now regarded the Volunteer Army as the best option for the Allies to back in Russia so long as the Whites could put aside old political quarrels and foster their political attractiveness to Russian workers. He reported that Struve was intending to travel north to consult General Poole; he also noted that Alexeev expected soon to be able to incorporate battalions of Czechs in his forces.[42]

The Allied occupation of Archangel worsened Lockhart's standing with the Bolsheviks, and on 5 August the British consulate in Moscow was raided and several officials were arrested. The French consulate and military mission suffered in the same way. Lockhart was left free; but he felt the need to destroy his ciphers, which made his further diplomatic work in Moscow impractical. (He had got rid of his written files when Mirbach was assassinated.) He also protested loudly to Karakhan, who apologized. Although the Allied officials were quickly released, they all were denied permission to leave Moscow.[43]

It was in this febrile atmosphere that Lockhart, being no longer able to communicate confidentially with London, resolved to undertake drastic measures of his own. He continued to have secret meetings with representatives of the National Centre and the Volunteer Army. This was dangerous enough for him after the Cheka's recent raid. But on 14 August he went further by confidentially hosting Colonel Eduard Berzin of the 1st Latvian

Heavy Artillery Division at his Moscow apartment. The two of them agreed a plot to dislodge the Latvians serving in the Red Army from supporting Sovnarkom.[44] In none of his later accounts did Lockhart explain how he came to approach Berzin. The reason for his reticence is fairly clear. He was to find it inconvenient to admit how deeply embedded he had been in British intelligence work in Russia. Privately, however, he gave a fuller account and acknowledged that Sidney Reilly initiated things by bringing representatives of the Latvians to him—and Lockhart then took over the planning and co-ordination.[45]

Whereas earlier Lockhart had provided money and encouragement for Russians to carry out subversion, now he was taking a British initiative without consulting any Russian organization. Lockhart arrived at an imaginative agreement with Berzin. The Latvian troops were known as the Soviet government's praetorian guard. Despite having crushed the Left Socialist-Revolutionaries and helped to recapture Kazan, the Latvians felt no debt of allegiance to Sovnarkom. George Hill recorded that they were fed up with being used as 'executioners' for the Bolsheviks.[46] They were the human flotsam of the Great War since it was impossible for them to return home while the Germans held Riga; but the Latvians were increasingly worried that fighting for the Soviet cause would irritate the Western Allies and cost them dearly if the Allied coalition won the war. In any case, why risk life and limb in the service of the Reds? Lockhart himself always denied that he had instigated anything. He claimed that it had been the Latvians who made the approach to him and not the other way round. He also maintained that his proposal had merely been to move the riflemen from Moscow to the side of the British in Murmansk.[47] The Cheka would bluntly reject this. The records of their investigation and interrogations indicated that Lockhart proposed to finance the Latvians to enable them to arrest the Soviet leadership and overthrow Bolshevism—and Lockhart in old age admitted to his son that the Soviet version of the episode was essentially correct.[48]

The scheme for a Latvian coup was not wholly outlandish. For a time, just tens of thousands of Czechs had tipped the balance in the war between Komuch and Sovnarkom. The Latvians occupied sensitive positions of power in Moscow, including the Kremlin itself. They could wreak havoc if they wanted. Of course, they would never get official permission to depart from Moscow. They would have to commandeer a train and probably use force. Soviet authorities would instruct stations on the Moscow–Murmansk line to obstruct their passage. The Red Army was unlikely to be allowed to stand still in the Volga region while the British expanded their influence. Lockhart had at the very least started a conspiracy to disrupt Soviet rule. There was bound to be fighting in Moscow—and he must have hoped that if things went well, his Anglo-Latvian initiative might somehow bring about the downfall of Sovnarkom. There was no other reason for causing mayhem in Moscow.

Lockhart met Berzin again on 15 August. This time Sidney Reilly and Fernand Grenard, the French consul-general, were present.[49] Two days later Lockhart gave an affidavit to Latvian rifleman Jan Buikis enabling him to talk to British intelligence officials in Petrograd.[50] The plot was thickening as Lockhart sought to lay the groundwork for the coming action. He was aware that the Soviet leadership's anger at the recent British occupation made his own situation in Moscow precarious. Thinking that the Foreign Office might recall him to London at any moment, he transferred the overseeing of the Latvian arrangement to Reilly. Berzin said that three or four million rubles would be needed to see things through to a successful conclusion. Reilly was given 700,000 rubles to hand over to the Latvians as a first instalment; Lockhart subsequently passed on another 700,000 rubles. Lockhart and Reilly saw each other as rarely as possibly. Both of them had complete trust in Berzin.[51]

Only at this juncture—according to both Lockhart's and Hill's memoirs—was the plot expanded to involve a *coup d'état*. Although they wrote admiringly about Reilly, they held him personally responsible for this changed objective; and Reilly was dead by the time their books appeared. They claimed that the new idea was for the Latvian military units guarding the Kremlin precinct to surprise the communist leaders at gunpoint in the course of a Sovnarkom session. Hill maintained that there was to have been no killing because Reilly sensed that the Russian people would object to a foreign force cutting down Russia's government. Reilly supposedly wanted to parade the communist leaders through the streets of Moscow with the aim of humiliating them and showing how vulnerable they were. Lenin and Trotsky would be stripped of their 'nether garments' and forced to appear in their shirts alone.[52] It is an entertaining but implausible story, and even Hill subsequently claimed to have thought the plan impractical. The idea that Reilly thought he would secure success by removing the underwear of the Soviet leadership is hard to believe. Hill, like Lockhart, knew he was breaking the rules by publishing a personal account of secret intelligence work and probably judged it wise to tenderize his account of British subversive activity in August 1918. Or maybe Hill and Lockhart simply wanted to clear their own names in connection with a conspiracy that went badly wrong.

At any rate a Cheka secret report, collated in 1920 by Yakov Peters from testimonies and interrogations two years earlier, told a very different story: Lenin and Trotsky were to be shot after capture.[53] Peters was not writing for general publication but for distribution inside the supreme communist leadership. And indeed even if the Cheka report was a fiction and the account given by Lockhart and Hill was true, there can be no doubt that the outcome of the conspiracy would inevitably have been a violent one. Lockhart had authored a scheme which, however it was activated, would soak Moscow in blood. The Western Allies sensed the coming of victory in northern France. The British Foreign Office and Secret Intelligence Service led the way in plotting to prepare a future for Russia free from Bolshevik rule. All Europe including its Russian extremity was to be transformed.

15. A VERY BRITISH PLOT

Robert Bruce Lockhart's fingers were still wrapped around the Latvian conspiracy on 25 August 1918 when he took Sidney Reilly to the US consulate to brief the Americans and French about his plans. The acting consul-general DeWitt Clinton Poole Jr and Xenophon Kalamatiano were present together with the French consul-general Fernand Grenard and the *Figaro* correspondent René Marchand.[1] Reilly later claimed to have felt doubts about whether he had been sensible in going to such a meeting.[2] The conversation covered progress with the Latvians and reportedly dwelt on the desirability of co-ordinating Allied undercover activities.[3] But Marchand, who had once regretted the fall of Kerenski and the Provisional Government, felt repelled by the conspiracy being set up by Lockhart and Reilly, and he took the silence of Poole and Grenard as proof that they condoned it. He wrote an angry letter to President Poincaré denouncing what agents of the Western Allies were getting up to—he rightly assumed that Poincaré was in the dark about the plot.[4] Of much greater importance was the fact that he also went to the communist authorities and told them what he had heard in the American consulate. Marchand became a turncoat.[5]

The Frenchman assumed that he was the first to inform the Chekists, but in fact they learned of the plot several days earlier. Colonel Berzin told Yakov Peters (another Latvian, as it happened) as soon as Lockhart had made his proposition. Peters consulted Dzerzhinski and the decision was taken to ask Berzin to play along with the British. They hoped that this would lead them to all the British, Russian and Latvian conspirators as well as supply a pile of compromising information on Allied diplomats.[6]

The Lockhart plot became an open secret at the top of the communist leadership. Ivy Litvinov would later recall:

Very interesting about Lockhart. They had Lockhart in—they arrested him, you know, and nobody here knew why. Oh, yes, being
implicated in a plot with White Russians to seize Lenin or something
like that. All true but it was all provocation. Yes, Maxime told me.
Our people employed, I mean the Soviet people—they were not
called Soviet people then—I forget . . . A certain agent provocateur—I am putting it very primitively, you know—said would you
like to take part in a plot . . . and he said 'Yes, with pleasure.' Then
they flung him into prison. That's never been written, you know.[7]

Allied officials in Russia had seriously underestimated the Bolshevik party's
hard-won expertise in methods of police infiltration and provocation. They
had also overrated their own cleverness. In reality they had set a trap
whereby they would ensnare themselves rather than the Bolsheviks.

Two events on 30 August induced the Cheka to abandon its stealthy approach. The first was the assassination of Petrograd's leading Chekist Moisei
Uritski by anti-Bolshevik socialist Leonid Kanegisser. Later in the day Lenin
gave a couple of stirring speeches to factory workers and was returning to
his limousine at the Mikhelson factory when shots were fired at him. Badly
wounded, he was hurried to the Kremlin for emergency treatment. For
some time it was uncertain whether he would survive. Dora Kaplan, a
woman loitering outside the factory for no good reason, was arrested as the
culprit and summarily executed. Since she was extremely myopic and mentally very confused, she had almost certainly not committed the crime. But
the Bolshevik leaders wanted to show that they meant business. Yakov
Sverdlov took command of both the party and the government. A Red terror was proclaimed.

The Cheka took hundreds of Allied officials and residents of Moscow
and Petrograd into custody. Chekist officials already had plenty of evidence
against prominent Britons, Frenchmen and Americans, and believed that
there could well be other intelligence operations they had yet to uncover.
Better to wait for more Allied spies and agents to come to light. Better, too,
to show the Allies that the Bolsheviks would not be pushed around and
were able to look after themselves. The Cheka behaved liked the vanguard
of the Soviet order when one of its units raided the apartment of Colonel
Henri de Verthamont, head of the French secret service. Verthamont escaped over the rooftops, leaving behind a cache of explosives and other
compromising material, but Chekists succeeded in capturing six of his

agents. As the news spread, the British broke contact with the French in the hope of being left alone.[8] This did not stop the Cheka. Lockhart, who had Moura Benckendorff with him, was arrested at his flat at 3.30 a.m. on 31 August. At first he refused to disclose his name. But the charade could not continue and he yielded to the Chekists. Moura and Major Hicks were also taken into custody.[9]

Lockhart was promised that there would be no harsh interrogation if he answered the accusations against him.[10] It was a gentle confinement by Soviet standards, and Lockhart and Hicks were released on 1 September.[11] Next day Lockhart returned to plead with Karakhan for the liberation of Moura and his own servants. Karakhan promised to do what he could. The following morning Lockhart was shocked to read Moscow newspapers 'full of the most fantastic accounts of Allied conspiracy of which I am said to be the head'. He stood accused of buying up the Latvian Riflemen and conspiring to murder Lenin and Trotsky and blow up bridges around the capital. A further charge was that the Allies aimed to appoint a compliant dictator.[12] The details may have erred on the fantastical side; but the truth was that Lockhart was genuinely distressed—both at being rumbled and at the possible public consequences that were likely to flow from this. Events quickened their pace. News came through that Maxim Litvinov had been imprisoned in London so as to ensure the safety of all Britons held in Soviet gaols.[13] Then, on 4 September, Lockhart was rearrested.[14] This time he was taken inside the precincts of the Kremlin: it was the only area of Moscow where security could be guaranteed, and the Soviet leaders were intent on holding on to their valuable British prize.

His captors yet again handled him with care. He was allowed visits by his lover Moura, now freed from imprisonment, who brought him food and tobacco. They were permitted to write to each other on condition that Peters could vet the letters.[15] Peters questioned Lockhart in a seemly fashion before handing him over to Karakhan. He too adopted a gentle approach. It was Karakhan who had issued Lockhart with diplomatic immunity and the two had often conversed. Now state interests and allegiances divided them.[16]

The two men had a fiery discussion lasting several days. Karakhan put the blame for the Red terror on the British. If the British had not interfered in Soviet affairs, he exclaimed, there would have been no need for the Bolsheviks to let loose the Cheka. He told Lockhart that Lenin had demanded: 'Stop the terror!'[17] Karakhan must have known that Lenin held exactly the opposite opinion at that very time. In a speech at the Cheka Club, no less, Lenin ridiculed the soft-bellied comrades who sought a gentler dictatorship.[18] As Lockhart knew, Karakhan was one of the more moderate Bolsheviks. What he said about Lenin was really an indication of the kind of communist regime he himself desired. Lockhart for his part upheld the official British line. By signing the Brest-Litovsk treaty, the Bolsheviks had reneged on Russia's contractual obligations as one of the Allies and had facilitated the massing of German military strength on the western front. Their foreign policy had put a dagger to the throats of Britain and France; they had only themselves to blame if they found themselves the object of Allied hostility. This, at least, is how Lockhart later described the discussion; the Cheka report suggested that he was less robust in putting his case. What is anyhow clear is that there was no meeting of minds.[19]

Lockhart attributed his easy treatment to the Soviet appreciation of the growing likelihood of an Allied victory over the Germans. If Germany was defeated, the Allied armies would have the military capacity to advance into Russia. Karakhan asked Lockhart courteously what it would take for Britain and Japan to end their intervention. He claimed that the communist leadership had no concern about the Americans, who were half-hearted about invading; and he judged that the French were too exhausted to be a serious threat. The Kremlin would offer commercial concessions to the United Kingdom, the US and Japan if they would agree to pull out their armed forces. It would even offer an honourable settlement to the Czech Corps and grant free exit from Russia. Conversations with Lockhart continued between 15 and 25 September, and Lockhart thought he was being sounded out as the conduit for a deal with the British. The Soviet leadership had gained a respite through Brest-Litovsk and now wanted some kind of equivalent so as to forestall an all-out British invasion.[20] A similar overture was made through Jacques Sadoul to the French government, no doubt without the disrespect that Karakhan had expressed to Lockhart for France's capacity to strengthen its force of intervention in Odessa.[21] This was a pretty desperate idea. Sadoul had long since lost the trust of French diplomats in Russia.

Dozens of Allied officials, including Grenard, the French consul-general, fled to sanctuary with DeWitt Poole in the American consulate. As an additional security measure, Poole ran up the Norwegian flag since Norway was a neutral country in the war and Poole rightly calculated that Soviet leaders would not like to offend the Norwegians.[22] Hill was still operating under cover and could not warn Reilly, who was on a trip to see Cromie in Moscow, about what had happened. Reilly's network of helpers and informants remained vulnerable. When Hill tried to alert them, one of his own 'girls' was arrested while visiting one of those working for Reilly.[23] Moreover, Marie Fride who also worked for the Americans turned up in the course of the raid. She panicked, inadvertently alerting the Cheka that she too was an Allied agent—and it was her arrest and interrogation that led to the rounding up of the American network.[24] Among those brought into custody was Lieutenant Colonel Alexander Fride—Maria's brother—from the People's Commissariat for Military Affairs. Another was former Major General Alexander Zagryazhski.[25] On 18 September Kalamatiano himself was caught coming back from a trip to liaise with the Czechs in the Volga region.[26]

Reilly escaped to London via Tallinn and Stockholm.[27] He has sometimes been accused of being a Cheka double agent—or alternatively of being tasked, as a British intelligence officer, with closing down the rival network of US agents. Reilly and Kalamatiano met and talked frequently in the office of British businessman William Camber Higgs.[28] The story goes that it was on a visit to Reilly that Colonel Berzin secretly found Kalamatiano's address. DeWitt Poole, on his departure from Russia later in September, told a British diplomat about circumstantial evidence pointing to the conclusion that Reilly had either compromised Lockhart or 'even betrayed him'.[29] Kalamatiano later noted that people connected exclusively with Reilly were released whereas all but one of his own associates were given prison terms. Such speculation is common in matters relating to the operation of intelligence agencies. But the case remains unproven in this instance. It was simply untrue that the French and American networks in Russia were wrecked beyond repair that September or that the British Secret Intelligence Service continued to work undisturbed.[30] Lockhart was in prison; Reilly and Hill were in hiding and their teams too had been broken up. The likelihood is that the Cheka had got its result by its own diligent efforts. It did not have or need help from Reilly.

Other Western prisoners in Moscow did not receive the courtesies accorded to Lockhart. And in Petrograd the treatment was still rougher. Captain Francis Cromie, left behind to protect the British embassy residence in Petrograd, barred the way to intruders on 31 August. He killed two of them before himself falling victim to the third.[31] The other British and French officials in the city were dragged off to the Peter-Paul Fortress. The cells were already crowded and the sanitary arrangements were abysmal. Rats scurried around the floors; the food was no better than when the Romanian ambassador had been held there. The prisoners suffered from diarrhoea and lack of medicines. The Petrograd Cheka expressed indifference to Allied complaints, but governments of neutral countries in the Great War were horrified by the murder of Russian citizens and soon indicated that they would expel all known Bolsheviks if the executions were not immediately halted.[32] The Swiss minister M. Odier became dean of the diplomatic corps after the Allied ambassadors' departure for Vologda. While asserting that he did not want to interfere in Russian politics, he protested to Zinoviev and Chicherin against the Red terror in Moscow and Petrograd; and he believed that only his vigorous intervention prevented Lockhart from being executed on 4 September.[33]

The German government was unconcerned about these events. When its Ukrainian puppet administration expressed outrage about the killings, Hintze blandly replied that he did not regard the repressive Soviet measures as terror and anyway did not wish to poke his nose into Russia's internal affairs:[34] the reality was that it suited the Germans that the Soviet leadership were at last turning on Allied officials.

The British government had at first reacted merely by increasing the surveillance over Litvinov in London. When he arrived at the tube station at Charing Cross, respectful policemen would ask: 'Going home, sir? Goodnight.' Then they queued for tickets and followed him home to Hampstead.[35] A few days later he was arrested and taken off to Brixton prison. The Defence of the Realm Act authorized the arrest without warrant of any person 'whose behaviour is of such a nature as to give reasonable grounds for suspecting that he has acted, or is acting, or is about to act in a manner prejudicial to the public safety or the defence of the realm'. Seized at the same time were his secretary Mr Wintin and his military adviser Captain Oshmyanski; Nikolai Klyshko, a party comrade and a draughtsman at Vickers Ltd's engineering business in Croydon, was also imprisoned.[36] They were effectively held as hostages to deter maltreatment of Lockhart. No decision was made about what to do if Lockhart was shot. Although Litvinov did not appear very disturbed, it was a truly shocking situation. European politics for centuries had regarded hostage-taking as behaviour only savages indulged in. The British in autumn 1918 felt they had no alternative if they were to keep their officials safe. Taking a diplomat captive was bad enough. But by implicitly threatening to retaliate physically against Litvinov if anything happened to Lockhart and his colleagues, Britain shattered the international consensus.

Lloyd George's tactic had a rapid impact as Chicherin announced a willingness to exchange Litvinov and others for the arrested Britons.[37] Karakhan and Peters made a last-minute attempt to secure Lockhart for the Soviet cause and asked him to consider staying on in Soviet Russia. Sadoul and Marchand were staying, and it would be a great success for Sovnarkom if an official of the British Foreign Office defected. They played on Lockhart's love affair with Moura. He saw what they were up to, as he was to confide to his notebooks over two decades later: 'Tempted. But this time heard the referee's whistle.'[38]

Lockhart was released from the Kremlin on 1 October. Karakhan and Peters amicably bade him goodbye, and Peters offered to replace the broken valuables in Lockhart's apartment.[39] Lockhart rejected the promise of monetary compensation. He had hardened his heart. Bolshevik Russia was no longer safe for him and he made arrangements to leave—without Moura. First, though, he had to secure the freedom of Major Hicks and get permission for him to marry 'the Russian lady of his heart'.[40] Lockhart's right-hand man had taken refuge in the American consulate and wanted to take Lyubov Malinina out of Russia with him. This could happen only if they were man and wife. Peters agreed, being 'highly entertained by the request';[41] he then made a request of his own: 'I have a favour to ask of you. When you reach London, will you give this letter to my English wife?' He handed over snapshots to help to identify her before second thoughts occurred to him: 'No, I shan't trouble you. As soon as you're out of here you'll blaspheme and curse me as your worst enemy.' Lockhart told him not to be a fool and took the letter, which he duly delivered to its addressee.[42]

Negotiations proceeded for the safe exit of all Western official personnel from Moscow. It was a tense situation. By then the British and French diplomats had taken refuge in the Norwegian legation. But even though the Bolsheviks were unlikely to attack the building, they held it under siege. The Allied diplomats stiffened their resolve: when water supplies were cut off, a Frenchman adroitly caught the rainwater, which enabled everyone to have a drink.[43]

Eventually an agreement was reached with the assistance of Swiss diplomats and the Swedish government;[44] and Arthur Ransome explained that it would be easier to promote the Soviet cause among British workers if Lenin showed mercy.[45] Lockhart and his party left the Russian capital by

train in the first week of October; Litvinov had already been released from
prison and was living at home with his wife and children. A policeman in
'a long rubber raincoat' was posted at their garden gate—he touched his
peaked hat on sight of Litvinov.[46] As Litvinov finalized his arrangements to
return to Russia, he bluntly told Ivy: 'You would just be a burden to me. I
would have to waste days trying to get you settled.' Ivy felt it hard to disagree
even though her uncle Sidney opined: 'I always said that fellow would abandon her.'[47] Having given birth to their second child just months earlier, she
was in no physical condition to travel, and Maxim and Ivy agreed that Russia in the middle of civil war and being subjected to foreign military intervention was not an appropriate place for a young family.

The bartering of Lockhart for Litvinov prefigured situations in the Cold
War when captured Soviet intelligence agents walked over the Glienicke
Bridge in Berlin as their Western counterparts proceeded simultaneously
from the other side. *The Times* in London reported that Litvinov and about
thirty of his compatriots departed for Scandinavia on 25 September 1918.
They were not to be allowed to reach Russia until Lockhart and the other
Allied officials crossed the Russian frontier.[48]

With Major Hicks and his new wife in the British party at the Finland
Station in Petrograd was George Hill, who appeared in uniform for the
first time in months; he needed to leave the country in order to arrange a
fresh source of funds for his work.[49] Lockhart stayed impassive as he bade
goodbye to Moura, perhaps so as to avoid transgressing public politesse,
and she left the platform an hour before departure.[50] When the full group
of thirty-one British and twenty-five French nationals crossed into Finland, preparations were made to convey Litvinov and his friends up to the
Swedish–Finnish frontier. The British and French arrived in groups. When
everyone was assembled the Allied representatives walked over the bridge
across the river from Tornio to Haparanda where they boarded a train to
Stockholm, arriving there on 9 October.[51] Others remained under guard in
Russia until Chicherin heard confirmation that Litvinov had reached neutral Norway, but soon the full exchange of officials was completed.

By then a new factor was being considered by the Bolshevik supreme
leadership. The Germans were unmistakably losing the war on the western
front. With the Western Allies nearing the point of victory, it might prove
unhelpful for the Soviet regime to have discriminated against French citizens. On 30 October the Bolsheviks dispatched Sadoul to interview Lu-

dovic Naudeau, a French journalist arrested in the summer. Sadoul's purpose became clear when he asked Naudeau for his opinion on the Allied military intervention in Russia. The journalist replied that he had supported the arrival of the Allies chiefly out of anti-German motives; but he stressed that he was now out of touch with events. Sadoul was blunt. If Naudeau wanted his freedom he would have to sign a denunciation of the intervention, allowing it to be printed in *Izvestiya* and *Pravda* and declaring his endorsement of Soviet principles. Peters of the Cheka had insisted on this as a condition. Naudeau sent Sadoul packing, but it was a sign of the uncertainties of the international situation that the Soviet leadership thought it worth while to try and do a deal with him just as they had sought to entice Lockhart to remain in Russia.[52]

The Bolsheviks soon reverted to a firmer line. Although Lockhart, Reilly and Verthamont had escaped their clutches, the Cheka had assembled a mass of evidence to put before the Russian public. It also had several prisoners; and although Kalamatiano was not half as culpable as the departed British and French, he was conveniently under lock and key and could serve as the main defendant in a show-trial. The Cheka referred to the 'Kalamatiano–Lockhart & Co. counter-revolutionary espionage organization'.[53] Until then the Americans in Russia had been treated gently. As late as 15 October 1918 a young US consul was released from Butyrki prison whereas his fellow prisoner, a Frenchman captured at Tsaritsyn on the Volga, was refused his freedom.[54] The implication was that Americans received softer treatment than the French—at least this was how Lockhart, safely back in Britain, interpreted the development.[55]

Soon after his return, he received a letter from a distressed Moura Benckendorf, writing from Moscow: 'I love you, Baby, past all balancing or cool reasoning. I love you more than all the world. If only you knew the longing for you. I lie awake repeating your name, visualising your surroundings, all you, my Baby.'[56] On 2 November Lockhart sent a flirtatious reply, saying she was naughty for thinking that his ship might go down in the North Sea. He also mentioned that his wife Jean had nursed him back to health after a bout of Spanish flu, adding: 'I cannot leave her.' He had told Jean about Moura—'she was very nice' about it.[57] Moura wrote back jealously about how Jean was monopolizing his medical recovery.[58] But by then Lockhart had put Moura at the back of his mind, ready to be fetched out only if ever the fancy and opportunity occurred. At the time such a prospect seemed permanently out of reach. Moura was both less sanguine and less fortunate. On 19 April 1919 she wrote to 'Locky' that 'some Esthonians out of revenge' had murdered her husband.[59]

The Lockhart Case opened before the Supreme Revolutionary Tribunal on 25 November 1918. Prosecutor-General Nikolai Krylenko outlined a plot against Soviet rule and a *Pravda* editorial announced: 'It is well known that the Allied missions in Russia have tried by means of conspiracies directly through their agents to overthrow the hated Workers' and Peasants' government.'[60] The art of the show-trial had yet to be refined in Soviet Russia. The authorities fumbled their hand by changing the charges between the original arraignment and the lengthy statement by Krylenko—and Angelika Balabanova, a fair-minded Bolshevik, drew attention to this.[61] At the heart of the case was the contention that there had been a violent conspiracy against Sovnarkom and that Lockhart and Reilly had led the plot. In their absence it was Kalamatiano who suffered along with his right-hand man Alexander Fride.[62] Altogether there were twenty defendants in court.[63] The majority were people who had worked for the Americans or the British. At the second sitting, on 28 November, the Cheka's deputy leader Peters recited the evidence that implicated Lockhart as the instigator of the plot. He recounted the activities of Reilly and Kalamatiano as well as the amount of foreknowledge in the possession of all the Allied diplomatic personnel.[64]

The defendant General Zagryazhski, a former military prosecutor and judge, did not deny his association with Kalamatiano but claimed he had acted as an 'economic informer' only. Krylenko pressed home his advantage and concentrated his fire on the absent Reilly. When he came to examine Reilly's lovers—especially Maria Fride and Olga Starzhevskaya—he represented them less as arch-conspirators than as foolish, deceived women.[65]

The trial ended on 3 December 1918. Kalamatiano and Lieutenant Colonel Fride were to be shot within twenty-four hours. Starzhevskaya received a three-month prison sentence. Zagryazhski, Maria Fride and others were sentenced to forced labour for five years. A captured Czech was also to stay in prison until such time as the Czech Corps ceased fighting against Soviet Russia. The absentees were not forgotten—this was, after all, officially the Lockhart Case. Lockhart, Grenard, Verthamont and Reilly were declared 'enemies of the working people' and sentenced to death if ever they were found on Soviet territory.[66] The authorities in Washington protested that Kalamatiano had had no involvement in spying activity, but did not retaliate or even apply much pressure on his behalf.[67] Kalamatiano was not executed but kept in prison. Possibly the protest had been enough to save him because the communist leadership did not want to freeze their already cool relations with the US. Perhaps, too, they hoped to use Kalamatiano in a future prisoner exchange. Whatever their intentions, the experience shattered Kalamatiano's nerves. While Reilly occupied a suite of rooms at the Savoy Hotel and Lockhart did the rounds of London's gentlemen's clubs, the American faced an indeterminate period in gaol.

The Bolsheviks had broken the British plot against them, but by the time the trial started the situation in the rest of Europe had been transformed. On 11 November 1918 Germany had surrendered on the western front and the Great War was suddenly over. The Soviet authorities had expunged the threat of Allied subversion only to face the still greater potential threat of an Allied invasion. France, Britain and America were masters of the continent. It was uncertain what use they would make of their power—and the rulers of the Kremlin looked nervously westwards as the New Year approached.

16. THE GERMAN CAPITULATION

On 11 November 1918 an armistice between Germany and the Allies was signed in a railway carriage in Compiègne forest, putting an end to the fighting on the western front. This was the start of a rolling thunder of events. Berlin was in turmoil. The Chancellor Max von Baden had resigned two days earlier, precipitating the Kaiser into abdicating. The German social-democrats seized the opportunity and proclaimed a new republican government with Friedrich Ebert as President and Philipp Scheidemann as Chancellor. In Moscow, the Bolsheviks had not sat idly by. Their first thoughts had been to work out how best to help the political far left in Germany. Indeed they had been making preparations for a sudden end to the Great War since late September when Sverdlov assembled Radek, Bukharin, Kamenev and others to plan an international communist congress in Russia. They decided to ask the Party Central Committee to issue guiding 'theses' for this event and make funds available to contact likely sympathizers abroad—and Bukharin and Rakovski meanwhile set out to join Ioffe in the German capital.[1]

The approach to European revolution, they thought, was quickening. Lenin had already ordered grain stocks to be laid aside for shipment to Germany when the revolutionary upsurge occurred. The Red Army undertook a massive additional recruitment so that Soviet forces could render military assistance for the same eventuality.[2] *Pravda* declared: 'The robber claws of the Prussian brute are too deeply embedded in the western front. The robber has been caught in a tight spring-trap.'[3] At the same time the Soviet leaders continued to play things cautiously and earned ridicule from the

German Independent Social-Democrats, passionate critics of Ludendorff and Hindenburg, for delivering the gold required by the Russo-German treaties of March and August. Lenin stopped shipments of bullion only when the Central Powers collapsed on the Bulgarian front and the Austrians surrendered to the Allies.[4] At that point the Bolsheviks felt free at last to render direct help to the German political far left. Civil war in Russia made it unfeasible to divert any forces into central Europe: the Red Army could not reach the Urals, far less Poland and Germany, at that time. But the Bolsheviks wanted to make an impact. Despite the food shortages in Russia, the Soviet authorities offered to deliver grain for the new German government to distribute;[5] and the scheme was finalized to establish the Communist International in Moscow.

The political climate in Germany had been fluid for some weeks before the armistice and the unconditional surrender. Wilhelm II discharged the cabinet installed in 1917, replacing it with ministers willing to work under Chancellor von Baden and negotiate for peace—and the Reichstag was no longer to be treated with public disdain. Even Ludendorff wanted the government to discover what terms might be on offer from the Allies. The last shred of hope among German ministers was that the Americans might moderate the French and British lust for a punitive settlement.

As a step towards conciliating socialists in the Reichstag, Baden released the Spartacist leader Karl Liebknecht from prison on 23 October. Pale from the lack of daylight, hair turned to the colours of pepper and salt, Liebknecht was, for Lenin and Trotsky, Germany's revolutionary hero.[6] He fervently believed that military defeat offered an opportunity to move the country by revolution to socialism. Two others headed the Spartakusbund with him: Rosa Luxemburg and Leo Jogiches. Only Liebknecht was German; Luxemburg was a Polish Jew and Jogiches a Lithuanian one. All three had spent time in prison for denouncing the war effort. Liebknecht now imposed himself upon them as a man of action. Before the Great War he had already been known for his capacity to inspire an audience:

> [Liebknecht], a dark man with lively gestures, shot words at us like darts, words which kindled anger and protest against governments which could drag their peoples into the bloody holocaust of war.
>
> [He] was a very good speaker. There was not only the art of the orator in what he said but a ring of truth and sincerity which won us over completely.[7]

He wanted to take the political struggle on to the streets. Nothing short of insurrection would satisfy him—and he scorned those in the German Social-Democratic Party who urged caution and compromise.

Germany's ally Austria-Hungary was falling apart, pressed heavily by the Italians from the south. Revolutions erupted in Vienna and Budapest on 31 October. Austria sued for an armistice, which was granted on 3 November; it took a further ten days for the Hungarians to achieve the same result.[8] The German high command had long since lost confidence in the benefits of the military coalition with the Habsburgs. Now Germany was on its own.

The Soviet mission in Berlin prepared a banquet for Liebknecht with a view to publicizing his revolutionary agenda. Bukharin was delighted to hear that he was 'in complete agreement with us'.[9] Urgent contact with Russia was needed after Ioffe heard that the Germans were about to sue for peace, and he called Moscow on the Hughes telegraph apparatus. Radek rebuked Ioffe for having failed to encode the message: 'Are you taking account of the seriousness of your communiqué and its possible consequences?' But when Ioffe simply repeated what he had said, Radek raced to the Sovnarkom offices, where the news made everyone feel suddenly 'liberated'.[10] The embassies that still remained in Moscow were anxious about the news that came through to them. For the moment the talk among diplomats was focused on what kind of territorial and political settlement might be imposed by the Western Allies; and when Radek told the elderly Austrian ambassador De Potere about Italy's pretensions in the southern Tyrol, he broke down in tears. Lenin and Sverdlov were ecstatic and asked Radek to draft an appeal to the Austrian working class. Since it was a Saturday evening, as Radek pointed out, the printworkers had gone home. The Hungarian communist leader Béla Kun, who was still in Moscow as an ex-POW, volunteered his fellow former prisoners to do the job if bread and sausages were made available. The atmosphere was euphoric. A crowd of Bolshevik supporters gathered next morning outside the Moscow Soviet on Tverskaya Street and, to their cheers, Lenin appeared on the balcony of the building. The celebrations lasted the entire day.[11]

Meanwhile in Berlin on 5 November the supporters of the October Revolution gathered outside the Soviet mission to chant their admiration for Lenin and Trotsky.[12] This was too much for German ministers, who knew exactly what the Bolshevik party thought of them after a crate being unloaded as part of the Soviet diplomatic 'pouch' was dropped at a railway station and insurrectionary propaganda spilled out.[13] Ioffe and his mission, including Bukharin and Rakovski, were given twenty-four hours to leave the country; diplomatic relations were severed.[14]

Their train left for the Polish frontier at six o'clock in the morning.[15] It had not yet reached Russia when the radio station at Khodynka north of Moscow intercepted a telegram from Kiel indicating that the German naval garrison had mutinied. Radek tried without success to establish contact with the rebel sailors. Then news was picked up from Allied stations of revolution in Germany as Ebert and Scheidemann took over from Baden. Ioffe's train had by this point pulled into Borisov, still in German-occupied territory. Using the Hughes apparatus, Radek instructed him to stay put while the Soviet authorities attempted to get his deportation revoked. Radek himself desperately tried to get through to the German Foreign Office:

> RADEK: Call the people's plenipotentiary, Mr [Georg] Haase, to the apparatus.
> CIVIL SERVANT: He's not in the ministry.
> RADEK: Who's deputizing for him?
> CIVIL SERVANT: There's nobody in the ministry. Everyone's run off.
> RADEK: I order you in the name of the All-Russia Central Executive Committee on your responsibility before the Berlin Soviet of Workers' and Soldiers' Deputies![16]

Silence followed. There was no such thing as a Berlin Soviet and Radek had no authority to tell anyone in Germany what to do. As usual he was trying his luck.

The German embassy in Moscow later left a message for Radek saying that Berlin had been calling him. Radek consulted Chicherin before sitting down at the Hughes apparatus to communicate with Haase. Unlike Liebknecht, Haase as a leader of the Independent Social-Democrats was no sympathizer with the October Revolution. But he sent courteous greetings and did not rule out the possibility of letting Ioffe back into Germany. Then he added: 'But knowing that there's famine in Russia, we ask you to direct the grain which you want to give up for the German revolution for the benefit of the starving in Russia. President of the American Republic Wilson has guaranteed Germany the receipt of grain and fats needed to feed the population in winter.' It seemed that American capitalist assistance was preferred to proletarian solidarity, which Radek took as a snub. He called Haase the Judas Iscariot of European socialism, and an exchange of insults followed.[17] Eventually Haase reverted to practicalities and asked for German embassy staff to be allowed to leave Russia. Radek replied that the German occupation of Ukraine and other territories made Russo-German armed conflict a distinct possibility—and he warned that official diplomatic communications needed to be maintained with Germany if this was going to be avoided.[18]

Hoping to guarantee that Ioffe's party came to no harm at Borisov, Sovnarkom detained Germany's consul-general Herbert Hauschild in Moscow.[19] Agreement was reached to swap diplomats on the Lockhart–Litvinov model. Two trains approached each other at Borisov station, and Ioffe was exchanged for Hauschild before proceeding in a second-class carriage to Orsha eighty miles east in Soviet-ruled Russia. His journey ended in Moscow on 24 November.[20]

The Kremlin leadership declared Friedrich Ebert and the new government in Berlin to be hand in glove with the Western Allies. Lenin suspected that German ministers aimed to secure better peace terms by offering to deploy German forces against Soviet Russia. Sovnarkom, in yet another breach of international law, allowed German and Austrian ex-POWs to occupy the embassy buildings of their countries. De Potere, already demoralized, felt grateful that the intruders left him his own office and bathroom. He did not mind if they brought girlfriends back at night, only drawing the line at their use of his suite as a thoroughfare, and even Radek warmed to him.[21] German diplomats were of a different mind, wanting nothing to do with leading Bolsheviks. The exception was the military attaché Schubert who asked for copies of The Communist Manifesto and read Lenin's State and Revolution from start to finish. At the same time, in Berlin the entire political system was being overhauled. These were strange times—and they were about to get stranger. Soviet leaders watched for any sign that the German situation might start moving their way. They had lost their direct source of information with Ioffe's expulsion and depended on patchy wireless traffic and on German newspapers brought by rail.

Liebknecht did not let them down as he pressed his arguments in the Spartakusbund in favour of an uprising. At first, Luxemburg and Jogiches took a lot of convincing. Berlin in the winter of 1918–19 was not like Petrograd in October 1917. Ebert and Scheidemann, unlike Kerenski, were not friendless on the political left. What is more, they could call upon the assistance of army regiments as well as of the unofficial armed squads known as the Freikorps. There was still no equivalent of the Russian soviets in Berlin.

Luxemburg had long objected to Lenin's authoritarian methods inside the labour movement, and she had never liked his penchant for bringing the peasantry into revolutionary politics. From her wartime prison cell she had quickly formed a severe opinion of the October Revolution. She was against the Brest-Litovsk treaty, thinking it damaged the prospects of revolution in Germany. She also objected to what she saw as Lenin's compromises on the land question and the national question. On dictatorship and terror she was horrified by the reports she received about the Bolsheviks in power. Liebknecht was less sensitive: 'One can't make revolution in white gloves. Whoever sincerely wants it must also want the means which guarantee it; there's no time to lose. Perhaps it will be necessary to pass through rivers of blood and mud to get to the destination. Anyway the German revolution won't require so many sacrifices.'[22] He believed that the Red terror in Russia would be of short duration,[23] and he wore down Luxemburg's doubts with his enthusiasm. She anyway considered Germany ready for its socialist transformation and had long advocated 'mass action' on the streets.

The Spartakusbund helped to form workers' councils in Berlin and announced the holding of a congress. The Bolsheviks received an open invitation and chose some of their leaders to attend, including Ioffe, Rakovski, Bukharin and Radek.[24] All of them had opposed Lenin throughout the Brest Litovsk controversy and were itching to foment revolution in Germany. Although all Bolsheviks agreed that Berlin would be the cockpit of 'European socialist revolution', Lenin worried that his ex-opponents would behave irresponsibly on their German trip. He had already written a warning note to Ioffe: 'Bukharin is loyal but has lunged into "left-wing idiocy" to a devilish extent . . . *Prenez garde!*'[25] Radek was another object of concern. Lenin had a firm word with him before departure and pointed out that if the Allied armies were to decide to march eastwards, the French commander Franchet d'Espèrey would have a clear route across Hungary and Romania into Ukraine and on to Russia. When Radek replied that French war-weariness would deter any such enterprise, Lenin interjected: 'They'll deploy coloured forces. How are you going to conduct agitation among them?' Radek replied by saying that he would use picture cards, though he added that he thought the Russian winter would prove intolerable for soldiers from Africa.[26]

Yet Lenin was still determined to assist in the making of a revolution in Germany—and Radek, who had belonged to the German Social-Democratic Party before 1914, was the Soviet leader with the closest acquaintance with the Berlin political scene before the Great War. Lenin told him to behave with caution and avoid forcing the pace.[27] Sverdlov handed over 200,000 German marks to cover the delegation's expenses. He gave little thought to their bodily requirements: they received only *kasha* (Russian porridge) and honey for the long trip through eastern Europe. Radek was cherished among the party leaders for his sense of humour; but when he said the Hebrews had got better conditions in their flight from the Pharaoh, Sverdlov just told him to stop complaining.[28]

The first stop for the delegation was an overnight one at Dvinsk where they fraternized with German soldiers from the local soviet and Radek fell asleep with his head resting on Khristo Rakovski's chest. When the German high command learned of their attempt to suborn its troops, it stopped them from continuing to travel further westwards by train.[29] By then the western borderlands of the old Russian Empire were in uproar, and the Bolsheviks were intent on establishing a Soviet republic in Ukraine. Pavlo Skoropadskyi, Germany's client ruler, was already under threat from nationalists led by Symon Petliura and was overthrown in December. The Soviet leadership in Moscow wanted to resume its revolutionary impetus and, as soon as possible, establish a Red administration in Kiev. Rakovski was chosen to head this attempt, and he abandoned his ambition to make for Berlin.[30] Radek, however, was determined to resume the German trip. Getting on a Hughes apparatus in Minsk, he secured permission from Sverdlov and Lenin to proceed in disguise to Berlin. A friend, German communist Felix Wolf, helped with the arrangements, and Radek continued alone on his westward journey by horse-drawn sleigh.[31] After crossing Poland he reached Königsberg and jumped on a direct train to Berlin.[32]

Arriving at the Schlesinger Bahnhof, he bought a copy of the Spartacist newspaper *Die Rote Fahne* and took a taxi to his hotel before meeting up with the leaders of the German political far left—not only Liebknecht and Luxemburg but also August Thalheimer and Paul Levi. He made contact, too, with his old mentor Leo Jogiches, with whom he had a warm discussion. Jogiches temptingly asked whether he wanted to remain an observer for the Soviet leadership or become an integral member of the Spartakus-bund,[33] but Radek stuck to his assignment as a Kremlin emissary. Obviously a lot of work had to be done before the Spartacists could lead an insurrec-tion. There had been only fifty of them at the Kaiser's abdication and they were also in a small minority at the Congress of Workers' Councils and had many internal disagreements on policy. Furthermore, Luxemburg contin-ued to attack the Bolsheviks for conducting a terror against their enemies. She asked Radek to relay her comments to Moscow and expressed shame that her former comrade Dzerzhinski had agreed to head the Cheka.[34]

Yet she went along with the other Spartacist leaders in their planning of an uprising in Berlin. A gathering was held with other far-left organizations from 30 December 1918 and the Communist Party of Germany was founded. Everyone present agreed with the Bolsheviks that a new era of human history was at hand. They had held this belief since before the Great War and their disgust at the immense loss of life since 1914 had convinced them that only revolution would prevent another such world war from oc-curring. Imperialism could not be curbed: it had to be eliminated. Capital-ism was at the root of the world's troubles and it too had to be swept away. No country was more advanced than Germany in industrial and educa-tional skills. Marxism taught that the 'proletariat' in the factories and the mines would inevitably lead society into a bright future where oppression and exploitation would be no more. What the Russian workers had done in Petrograd was about to be accomplished—and accomplished with greater success—in the German capital; indeed the Bolsheviks agreed with the Spartacists that Germany's working class was the readiest in the world for socialism. Conditions in the country were ripe for exploitation and the Spartakusbund intended to catch the new German government by surprise. Workers' councils would seize power before army or police could stop them, and the entire 'proletariat' would rally to the cause of revolution.

The leading Spartacists wanted Soviet comradeship, not tutelage, and felt that the sooner the insurrection was under way in Berlin, the easier it would be to avoid that outcome. Radek teased them that Lenin and Trotsky were revolutionaries of greater stature than anybody in the German Com-munist Party. As he no doubt intended, this only strengthened their resolve. They deputed a single comrade, Hugo Eberlein, to go Moscow for the in-ternational conference being organized by the Bolsheviks. Eberlein received strict instructions to prevent Lenin and his associates from taking control.

Meanwhile Liebknecht, Luxemburg and Jogiches set about planning how to seize the post and telegraph office, the garrisons, government buildings and big printing presses in Berlin.

The day chosen for a general strike and uprising was 5 January 1919. The proclamations had been written. The message went out early to militants in the metalworking factories to come out on to the streets. Liebknecht and his comrades got ready to talk to the crowds. Luxemburg already had a heavy heart, feeling that a serious revolution required more than high hopes. For their part, Ebert and Scheidemann reacted with vigour and called on the army garrisons, along with the Freikorps, to suppress the revolt. Many ex-soldiers of the western front saw the political far left as traitors to the national cause. The fact that several of them were Jewish intensified the hostility. In the eyes of many who had fought in the trenches, Germany had lost the war because people like Liebknecht and Luxemburg had undermined morale in the rear. Fighting was sporadic on the streets, but the rage to settle accounts was intense and it was quickly obvious that the combined action of army and Freikorps would overwhelm all resistance. The insurrection sputtered out almost before it began.

The Freikorps wreaked a terrible vengeance. Liebknecht, Luxemburg and Jogiches were hunted down and bludgeoned to death. The killers dumped Luxemburg's body outside the railings of the Zoological Gardens. The symbolism was intentional. The enemies of the Spartacists looked on them as being less than human. Dogs were being given a dog's death. The Spartacist leaders met their ends with courage and dignity. Of their leaders, only Thalheimer and Levi survived—and it was Levi who delivered the funeral oration for Luxemburg on 2 February.[35] Radek went into hiding. On the party's orders he had spent the year 1917 in Stockholm rather than Petrograd. For all his big talk he had no more experience of organizing a seizure of power than anyone else in Berlin. The German authorities, moreover, were aware of his illicit presence in the country. A search was begun for him, and he was captured on 12 February 1919 and thrown into Moabit prison.

While Ebert and Scheidemann resumed their attempts to bring about political stability and economic recovery, the newly formed German Communist Party sought to rebuild its organizations. It had lost the inspiring leaders who had founded it, but its revolutionary vision remained intact. Others filled the gap left by Liebknecht, Luxemburg and Jogiches. Their spirits stayed high. German communists continued to despise the new socialist government, a government that accepted responsibility for Germany's humiliation at the hands of the Allies. The communists foresaw abundant chances to undertake revolution. Like the Bolsheviks in Russia, they believed that Berlin was the city where the future of Europe would be settled. The German working class would surely soon see that Scheidemann and his ministers were collaborating with big business. The communist party offered an alternative vision of internal and foreign policy. Thalheimer and Levi preached the coming doom of capitalism—and they intended by political action to bring forward the date when this would occur.

PART THREE

◆

PROBINGS

17. REVOLVING THE RUSSIAN QUESTION

After their triumph on the western front, the Allies could no longer claim that they were intervening in Russia so as to bring its armed forces back into the fight against Germany. In the United Kingdom, Robert Cecil as Under-Secretary of State for Foreign Affairs circulated a memorandum to the King and the War Cabinet spelling out the constraints on British policy. Cecil suggested that a crusade against Bolshevism was impracticable. Allied measures, he argued, should be limited to offering assistance to 'our Russian friends' and the Czech Corps.[1]

But the survival of the Soviet government meant that the 'Russian question' was anything but a historical one. German commanders and diplomats who had cheerfully welcomed their government's use of the Bolsheviks to ease their tasks in the war now warned against the possibility that Bolshevism might move into the heart of Europe. Until November 1918 Allied politicians had looked on Russians mainly in terms of their potential to re store the eastern front. From being fitfully alarmed by pro-Soviet anti-war propaganda in their own countries, they began to appreciate that the Bolshevik revolutionary example might soon be followed abroad. Talk about the communist 'contagion' was growing. It was accentuated by the actions of the Bolsheviks themselves after the German surrender. The borderlands of the old empire underwent revolutions as Moscow supplied personnel to instigate seizures of power in Estonia, Latvia and Lithuania and proclaim Soviet republics. Fundamental economic and social reforms followed Russia's model. Once Tallinn, Riga and Vilnius had fallen under their influence, the Bolsheviks tried to extend the revolutionary order from the capitals to other towns and villages. Stalin drafted decrees in December recognizing the new Soviet republics and providing them with financial assistance.[2] If this could happen so quickly, who was to say that Poland or Germany would not soon fall to the communists? And what was to stop communist influence from spreading still further westwards?

In fact the German capitulation occurred just a little too soon for the Bolsheviks, who had not yet secured their hold on Russia. On 18 November 1918 in Omsk, a city in south-western Siberia, Admiral Alexander Kolchak pushed aside the regional administration led by Socialist-Revolutionaries and declared himself Supreme Ruler. Komuch by then was no more and the Red Army had seized control of the Volga towns. Kolchak, assisted by the remaining volunteers of the Czech Corps, despised the Socialist-Revolutionaries as much as he hated the Bolsheviks. His forces dealt savagely with the Reds and their sympathizers as he undertook his advance through the Urals. His was the first of the White armies to make serious progress and in December he occupied Perm, scattering the Bolsheviks to the winds. In the south, where another White force—the Volunteer Army—was still gathering under General Anton Denikin after the deaths of Generals Kornilov and Alexeev, the hope was that the Allied victory in the west would liberate resources to help against the Bolsheviks. Denikin welcomed the existence of the clandestine National Centre with its liberal and socialist members so that he could win friends in London and Paris.[3] The British quickly indicated approval and promised their help. The French made similar noises.[4] Action followed on 18 December when the French landed troops in Odessa while Britain's expedition remained in the Russian north. The situation was grim for Bolshevism and getting grimmer.

Although they temporarily gave up territory, the Bolsheviks tightened their grip on the areas under their rule. They had spent the year 1918 in internal disputes, nearly breaking apart as a party over the Brest-Litovsk treaty. There were also regular problems with indiscipline and lack of coordination between the various organizational levels. Bolshevik leaders in the provinces as well as in Moscow recognized that this situation had to change if Sovnarkom was going to win the Civil War against the Whites. Agreement was reached on the need for a properly functioning hierarchy. As personnel were drafted into the Red Army, fewer and fewer people were left to take the big decisions. The Party Central Committee established a system of internal sub-committees to facilitate rapid reactions to emergencies. The Political Bureau (or Politburo, as it was known) consisted of five members including Lenin and Trotsky; it quickly became the key agency of central party decision and command. The Bolsheviks were willing to militarize themselves if it helped against Kolchak and Denikin. They had always believed in centralism: now they set about practising it systematically. Gradually, the chaotic conditions in soviets, army, police and trade unions began to improve as the party imposed its institutional supremacy.

The Whites' strategic aim was simply to advance on Moscow and overrun the Bolsheviks. The Allies were more enigmatic. Lloyd George and Wilson still claimed they simply wanted to see Russia achieve internal peace. Clemenceau, who as French premier exerted authority at President Poincaré's expense, agreed. The difficulty remained that no Allied leaders recognized the legitimacy of Sovnarkom and the October Revolution—they commonly believed that the Russian people were oppressed by Bolshevik rule.

There were three basic options. The Western Allies—or one or two of them—could decide that Russia, by defecting from their side and relieving the military pressure on Germany, had forfeited the right to be left alone at the end of hostilities. The spectre of communism was haunting Europe. Lenin and his comrades had openly stated their wish to put global capitalism to the torch. They aimed to overturn the American, French and British governments. The Allied powers might reasonably conclude that the way to prevent the communist insurrections was to cauterize the 'contagion' by invading Russia. This would require a big army and a concentration of political will. A less demanding option would be to strengthen the Allied expeditions lodged on the periphery of 'Soviet power', supplying the Whites with money and arms but holding back from their own direct attack on Moscow and Petrograd. But political opposition and social exhaustion at home might rule out even this possibility. The Great War was over and few people in Britain, France or America had the appetite for yet another far-flung conflict and indeed many were fiercely opposed to the idea. In that case the ultimate option would be to conclude that Russia was a lost cause and to abandon the Russian people to their fate.

But even a policy of non-intervention left problems unresolved. Should Soviet Russia receive official recognition? Should normal trade links be resumed? Several business lobbies in the UK and the US called for a diplomatic and commercial rapprochement. The trade unions meanwhile campaigned against military action, and European socialist parties had leaders and militants who saw a lot of good in the social and economic reforms in Russia.

In the United Kingdom, too, a Hands Off Russia movement grew up, supplied with a rousing booklet by Arthur Ransome. In *The Truth about Russia* he lamented:

> I only know that, from the point of view of the Russian Revolution, England seems to be a vast nightmare of blind folly, by the sea, and beyond that by the trenches, and deprived, by some fairy godmother who was not invited to her christening, of the imagination to realise what is happening beyond. Shouting in daily telegrams across the wires from Russia I feel I am shouting at a drunken man asleep in the road in front of a steamroller . . . I think it possible that the revolution will fail. If so, then the failure will not mean that it loses its importance . . . No matter, if only in America, in England, in France, in Germany, men know what it was that failed, who betrayed it, who murdered it. Man does not live by his deeds so much as by the purposes of his deeds.[5]

A crusade against Soviet Russia was anathema to troops who longed for demobilization and shipment home. Powerful resistance grew to making war on communism.

This was certainly the line taken by Labour Party candidates at the hustings before the general election on 14 December 1918. Ramsay MacDonald thought that it had served the Allies right that Lenin had dragged Russia out of the war; he was also sympathetic to the Bolsheviks as fellow socialists, despite being regularly insulted by them in print.[6] The *New Statesman*, breaking its wartime silence about how to handle Russia, joined the *Daily Herald*, the *Manchester Guardian* and the *Daily Express* in putting pressure on Lloyd George and the government to halt the intervention. Even the *Daily Telegraph*, usually a supporter of the Coalition, objected to ministers refusing to ventilate their considerations on Bolshevism in parliament or the press. The Secretary of State for War, Lord Milner, was an exception; he openly contended that it would be 'an abominable betrayal, contrary to every British instinct of honour and humanity', if the country abandoned those Russians who had supported the Allied forces of intervention—and he confided to ex-chargé d'affaires Konstantin Nabokov that his personal preference was to reinforce the military intervention.[7] But generally the Coalition MPs avoided the Russian question save only for affirming that a vote for them would help defend the United Kingdom against Bolshevism. Their electoral tactic paid off. When the results were declared on 28 December the Coalition had triumphed.[8]

Robert Bruce Lockhart's line was more belligerent than Milner's. Newly returned from Moscow, he was acclaimed as a near-martyr who had done his patriotic duty. In the House of Commons only the Liberal MP Joseph King sounded a discordant note about him. King had got hold of the Soviet version of events and pointed out that Lockhart was no innocent but had tried to suborn the Latvian Riflemen into arresting Lenin and Trotsky.[9] This isolated clamour drew no response from Lockhart, who maintained his focus on seeking to influence governmental policy; with Germany defeated, he favoured an all-out invasion of Russia. On 7 November, the first anniversary of the October seizure of power in Petrograd, he forwarded a memorandum to the Foreign Office emphasizing the strength that accrued to the Soviet government from its repressive zeal as well as its popularity with workers and peasants. The Bolsheviks were easily the biggest party in Russia; the counter-revolutionary forces were hopelessly divided. Lockhart pointed out that the communist leadership was intent on expanding the revolution into central Europe. He mapped out the various options before recommending military force 'to intervene immediately on a proper scale'. He proposed sending British troops to Siberia and Archangel. But his idea was that the main offensive should be organized from the south; he called for 50,000 men to be dispatched to the Black Sea to link up with the Volunteer Army.[10]

Lockhart predicted success for an invasion at a time when the Red Army was weak and the Allies were not yet exhausted. No time was to be lost.[11] Balfour ignored him, and Lockhart sensed a general frostiness in Whitehall:

> After a week at home it is perfectly obvious that apart from the relief of having rescued me from the Bolsheviks the Foreign Office is not in the least interested in my account of things. They prefer the reactionaries who have never even seen Bolshevism. Tyrrell and Hardinge are frankly and avowedly hostile and I may even have difficulty in obtaining another job.[12]

W. G. T. Tyrrell served as head of the Political Intelligence Department at the Foreign Office; Charles Hardinge was Permanent Under-Secretary to Balfour. Behind them stood Lord Robert Cecil as Under-Secretary of State. They had disliked Lockhart since early 1918 when he was advising the government to give official recognition to the Bolsheviks. Now they rejected him as a whirligig. Lockhart learned that Tyrrell regarded him as 'a hysterical schoolboy who had intrigued with the Prime Minister behind the Foreign Office's back'. This was a reference to Lloyd George's dispatch of Lockhart to Russia as an antidote to the cautious policy pursued at the time by Balfour. Lockhart reasonably concluded of Tyrrell: 'Not much hope in this quarter.'[13]

Others, including the King, were more favourably disposed. Lockhart recorded his meeting with George V in his diary for 23 October 1918: 'The King was very nice and showed a surprising grasp of the situation; he however did most of the talking and during the forty minutes I was with him I didn't really get much in. He sees pretty well the need for reforms everywhere, and has a wholesome dread of Bolshevism.'[14] Lockhart, originally a proponent of accommodation with Lenin and Trotsky, stayed firmly anti-Bolshevik for the rest of his life.

Winston Churchill refrained from advocating an all-out Allied invasion, but he was the one politician to speak out more strongly than Milner against the Soviet order. In his electoral address to his Dundee constituents on 28 November 1918 he declared: 'Russia is being reduced by the Bolsheviks to an animal form of Barbarism . . . Civilisation is being extinguished over gigantic areas, while Bolsheviks hop and caper like troupes of ferocious baboons amid the ruins of their cities and the corpses of their victims.'[15] Even for Churchill this was pungent language. When referring to the Germans, mortal enemies of the United Kingdom until a few days previously, he called them 'barbarian'. But barbarians are human. Churchill's speech was aimed at dehumanizing the Soviet leaders and their followers as a way of persuading people that the October Revolution had somehow to be overthrown. On another occasion he wildly referred to Bolshevism as a baby that should be 'strangled in its cradle'. Churchill was fired up on the Russian question, but he usually liked to drop a phial of wit into his fulminations. About Russia he felt no such impulse.

Perhaps Churchill's monarchist sentiments had an influence. He had stood out against those who called for the hanging of the Kaiser, and anyway he was with Lloyd George in trying to prevent harsh peace terms being imposed on Germany. It was Churchill's habit to focus obsessively on chosen problems. His colleagues trembled when he was in one of his moods; and everyone remembered his pet military project in 1915–16 to land Allied troops at Gallipoli—people forgot that he thought that insufficient troops had been provided for the task. He was notorious for pushing forward with plans without having thought through how he would cope if things went wrong. When criticism was made, he grew obstinate and put himself beyond debate. Yet behind the frothing schemes and wild rhetoric there was his acuity of vision. His instincts told him that something deeply menacing—indeed evil—was in the making in the east. He knew no more than anyone else in the cabinet about the Soviet leadership and its intentions. But he had enough information to sense that they presented a fundamental threat. If the need arose, he was willing to stand alone and fight for his opinions.[16]

In France, the attention paid to revolutionary Russia was less intense for a while. The Great War was barely over and all thoughts were focused on the securing of Allied authority over central Europe. Germany had to be stabilized and peaceful economic recovery facilitated in several countries precariously poised on the brink of famine—and most French politicians sought to punish the Germans for the four years of carnage.

In America the State Department was fitful in its examination of Russian affairs. Ambassador Francis was no longer in northern Russia. By October 1918 his health had collapsed and he travelled to London for medical treatment.[17] Meanwhile Lansing was too busy with German questions to occupy himself with the situation further east in Europe. Inside the State Department, sympathizers with Soviet Russia were acquiring influence. Among them was the young William C. Bullitt, who headed the Far Eastern desk. Already in March 1918 he had held discussions with Santeri Nuorteva of the pro-Soviet Finnish Information Bureau in New York.[18] Bullitt and Nuorteva met and wrote to each other, and Nuorteva was pleased to have found a friend in high places.[19] Bullitt took the line that the October Revolution had a vast importance for world affairs and that American policy ought to be based on an informed acquaintance with Soviet intentions. Yet there was more to it than just that. Bullitt was one of the few Americans outside the labour movement and certain business lobbies who favoured some kind of accommodation with Sovnarkom. He detested the Anglo-French military intervention in Russia and Ukraine and hoped to lessen and reverse his own country's involvement in such ventures.

Bullitt's career had started in journalism. He had made a brilliant name for himself with interviews with politicians of the Central Powers that pointed to German complicity in Austria-Hungary's declaration of war on Serbia.[20] He came from a charmed background of well-to-do Philadelphia lawyers and had degrees from Yale University and the Harvard Law School. During the war he worked in Europe reporting for the *Philadelphia Public Ledger* and dabbled in writing novels. He married the aptly named socialite Aimee Ernesta Drinker and together they lived the high life until the call came for a posting at the State Department.[21]

Bullitt used his imagination in delving for information about the Russian communist leadership. Whereas others shunned contact with John Reed as a traitor, Bullitt saw him as a man on the spot who could be of use in liaising with Lenin and Trotsky. The 'awful diplomatic gulf' had to be closed up. Bullitt had encouragement from the distinguished lawyer Felix Frankfurter in this effort. Frankfurter nominally belonged to the War Department but was really President Wilson's special diplomatic aide and was keen to get a brief prepared on Russia. Using contacts such as Santeri Nuorteva, Frankfurter planned to send a cable directly to Trotsky. The State Department overruled him, sensing the need to restrain both Frankfurter and Bullitt in case they upset other US activities in Russia and co-operation with the Western Allies. The second-best step was an indirect one. Frankfurter received permission to approach the Red Finns with a view to using them as intermediaries with the Bolsheviks. Yrjö Sirola, their Foreign Minister until their defeat in mid-May 1918 in the Finnish Civil War, knew Lenin well and might be able to improve US–Soviet understanding on one of his trips to Petrograd. While normal diplomacy was failing, other methods had to be tried out.[22]

Bolshevism was widely seen as a menace to political stability in North America, although many politicians worried that Wilson's involvement in global affairs was distracting his administration from urgent domestic problems. Nonetheless, in early 1919 the Senate Committee on the Judiciary set up a sub-committee on Bolshevik propaganda under Senator Lee S. Overman. The stated purpose was to discover the extent of Russian subversion in America, but the proceedings were quickly fanned out to consider the situation in Russia itself. The sub-committee began meeting on 11 February 1919. The atmosphere was set by Attorney-General Alexander Mitchell Palmer who claimed that Russian Bolsheviks had used over a dozen 'German brewers of America' to buy up a great American newspaper with the intention of manipulating public opinion.[23] The names of Nuorteva, Reed, Bryant and Rhys Williams cropped up—and it was intimated that the Englishman Ransome had suspect connections with Imperial Germany.[24] Details were given of large quantities of Bolshevik material that had flooded into America since late 1917, and the smuggling methods were described.[25]

The large number of Jews among the pro-Soviet agitators was also a theme of the sub-committee proceedings. Rev. George A. Simons, until recently the superintendent of the Methodist Episcopal Church in Petrograd, recounted that Trotsky and other Jewish revolutionary refugees had set out for Russia from New York in 1917. Now, said Simons, admirers of the Soviet model were growing in number in America:

> In fact I am very impressed with this, that moving around here I find that certain Bolsheviki propagandists are nearly all Jews. I have been in the so-called People's House, at 7 East Fifteenth Street, New York, which calls itself also the Rand School of Social Science, and I have visited that at least six times during the last eleven weeks or so, buying their literature, and some of the most seditious stuff I have ever found against our own Government, and 19 out of 20 people I have seen there have been Jews.[26]

Although Simons denied being anti-Jewish, he stated that he had confidence in the authenticity of anti-Semitic forgeries such as *The Protocols of the Elders of Zion* that accused the Jews of a conspiracy to achieve global political dominion. He adjured the Senate to cease thinking of Bolshevism as a fad and treat it as a 'monstrous thing' with the capacity to undermine American society.[27]

His testimony agitated America's Jews. Lewis Marshall of the American Jewish Committee and Simon Wolf of the Union of American Hebrew Congregations sent in letters protesting against the slur that most Jews were Bolsheviks.[28] The journalist Herman Bernstein appeared before the sub-committee to point out that Reed, Bryant, Rhys Williams and Robins were Christians—or rather lapsed Christians. Thus the threat to American political stability consequently had nothing to do with religion.[29]

The Soviet sympathizers themselves were then called to testify. Louise Bryant was first. She defended her husband's work for the Bolsheviks in 1917–18 on the grounds that he was seeking to provoke revolution in Germany—and she claimed that this conformed to America's wartime interests.

But she had to admit to having acted as a Bolshevik international courier.[30] Her interrogation was lengthy and hostile and she complained of being treated worse than the earlier witnesses. John Reed received an equally severe questioning. Under pressure he acknowledged that he hoped for revolution in America. He added that he hoped for this to happen by peaceful due process and without the violence that had typically accompanied revolutions.[31] Next up was Albert Rhys Williams, who rebuked the critics of Bolshevism; he laid claim to an open mind about whether the Soviet order was 'a successful form of government', and he denied advocating it for the USA. He affected to believe that the communist leadership were considering the idea of convoking a Constituent Assembly again.[32] Raymond Robins was less enthusiastic about Soviet rule but continued to advocate trade with Soviet Russia.[33]

A few days later it was the Senate Committee on Public Information that called on Reed and Bryant to give an account of themselves. Reed admitted to having worked for the People's Commissariat of Foreign Affairs in publishing Soviet newspapers in multi-language editions. The Senators had done their homework and compelled him to admit to having promised the State Department in 1917 that he would not get involved in Russian politics. But Reed argued that he had not given his word under oath—and he lied that he had received no money from the Soviet government and was not in communication with it.[34]

When asked about atrocities under Bolshevik rule, he and Bryant cast doubt on the veracity of the reports. Bryant argued against America's right to intervene in Russia; but when pushed by the Committee, she refused to approve or disapprove of 'Bolshevist interference in American affairs'. She spoke up for the Cheka's Yakov Peters, calling him 'an aesthetic young man' and disclaiming any knowledge of his murky activities in London before 1914.[35] When Albert Rhys Williams took the stand, he too was open about the fact that he had been in the employ of the 'Trotzky–Lenine government'. He stated that, when leaving Russia in June 1918, he had an assignment to set up a propaganda bureau in New York but assured the Committee that this had not come to pass. By staying on in Russia five months after the Reeds had departed, moreover, he had seen more brutality than they had. But he rejected reports of the killing of innocents by the communists, whom he declared to have 'a sublime faith in the people'. He professed his abhorrence of violence and his feeling that if the communist experiment were to take place in the US, the means could and should be entirely peaceful.[36]

Politicians and reporters were deepening a debate that had begun with the October Revolution. Bolshevik rule and the consequences for Western policy were a divisive topic, and it was far from being the case that the advocates of conciliation with Soviet Russia were confined to the labour movement. Business interests too were beginning to make themselves felt.[37] On the other side of the debate, of course, there were political, commercial and ecclesiastical lobbies that wanted Russia and its communist rulers kept in strict quarantine. Dispute was often angry and seldom less than spirited. In Britain and France the press led the way in inviting public exchange; this also happened in the US, where the committees of the Senate gave additional propulsion to the process. Steadily the Russian question was rising up the public agenda. At a time when national governments had to concentrate their efforts on economic recovery, Russia and its communism could still not obtain priority of attention. But it was increasingly obvious that the revolutionary tide might at any moment surge across Russian frontiers into Europe, and many people in those countries as well as in North America doubted that their leaders had yet found sound measures to deal with this prospect—and the disarray of the Western powers on the Russian question at the Paris Peace Conference in the first half of 1919 was to do little to dispel these concerns.

18. THE PARIS PEACE
CONFERENCE

On 4 December 1918 President Wilson boarded the SS *George Washington* to cross the Atlantic and attend the Paris Peace Conference. He ignored advice from Robert Lansing, who said he would dilute his influence by going to France instead of dictating his wishes from a distance.[1] But Wilson held the Allied purse strings and controlled fresh military power, whereas Lansing was only his Secretary of State. He and not Lansing occupied the White House and he insisted on going to France. A terrible war had been brought to a close; a second one must be prevented.

Although Wilson was being lionized on the Paris boulevards, he cut an unimpressive figure in the closed proceedings of the conference. His 'Fourteen Points' had prescribed no practical policy, only a set of objectives. Even his ideas about Germany lacked exactitude and he made things worse by forbidding his delegation to carry out preparatory discussion and drafting.[2] He recognized his own lack of detailed knowledge about European controversies. His habit was to defer to Allied committees of experts, and Clemenceau and Lloyd George were adept at imposing their projects.[3] Wilson's ultimate passion was to gain approval for a League of Nations. The other delegations offered a flattering opinion of this project, and whenever they wished to obstruct one of his ideas they used the device of suggesting that only the League could resolve its complexities. The President forfeited advantage by never even raising his voice. His failing health was also finding him out and he simply lacked the energy for political disputes. He guarded his own counsel; even his confidant Colonel House had lost influence. French and British leaders saw that the President was a fading force and got used to agreeing the plans in advance of meeting him and gaining his imprimatur.

'Reparations' were on the lips of nearly every French politician except those few who sympathized with Lenin. Clemenceau aimed to make Germany incapable of striking France ever again. John Maynard Keynes offered this portrait:

> [Clemenceau] carried no papers and no portfolio, and was unattended by any personal secretary, though several French ministers and officials appropriate to the particular matter in hand would be present round him. His walk, his hand and his voice were not lacking in vigour, but he bore nevertheless, especially after the attempt upon [his life], the aspect of an old man conserving his strength for important occasions. He spoke seldom, leaving the initial statement of the French case to his ministers or officials; he closed his eyes often and sat back in his chair with an impassive face of parchment, his gray gloved hands clasped in front of him. A short sentence, decisive or cynical, was generally sufficient . . . [4]

Clemenceau behaved with elaborate courtesy, always asking Wilson for his opinion. But this was a feint: he wanted Germany punished.

In this environment there was little scope for the Western Allies to give careful consideration to Russia and its communist leadership. French, British, American and Italian forces were masters of the continent. They were determined to finish their business in central Europe first and foremost. The Allied Supreme War Council, founded on Lloyd George's initiative in November 1917 to oversee military strategy as well as plans for peace, did not entirely ignore the Russian question but quickly found it difficult to handle. There was no opportunity even to hear representations from Russia without offending one group or another. The Supreme Council (as it became known) began by keeping Sergei Sazonov, the tsar's Minister of Foreign Affairs till 1916 and now fulfilling the same role for the White Russians, at arm's length.[5]

On 16 January 1919, Lloyd George spoke in the Council of Ten—representing the main victor powers—at the Quai d'Orsay. While arguing that something had to be done about Russia, he depressingly stipulated:

- Firstly, the real facts are not known;
- Secondly, it is impossible to get the facts, the only way is to adjudicate the question; and
- Thirdly, conditions in Russia are very bad; there is general misgovernment and starvation. It is not known who is getting the upper hand, but the hope that the Bolshevik Government would collapse had not been realized.[6]

Intervention on an adequate scale would mean an occupation: 'The mere idea of crushing Bolshevism by a military force is pure madness.' And in any case it was almost inevitable that Allied troops would mutiny against any order to deploy them in yet another war, and a permanent blockade was objectionable since it would lead to mass starvation. The chances of the Whites overthrowing the Bolsheviks were therefore not the brightest. Lloyd George therefore felt it preferable to call the various sides in Russia's armed struggles to the negotiating table in Paris and get them to agree on a definitive settlement under the eyes of the victor powers.[7]

President Wilson agreed. In a memorandum of 19 January 1919, he urged the need to pull out the Allied expeditions as soon as possible: he had no intention of letting himself be 'led further into the Russian chaos'. This was the dominant opinion in the US delegation expressed by General Tasker Bliss and Herbert Hoover. When Bliss heard of Marshal Foch's proposal for a multinational army to invade Russia after the signing of the German peace treaty, he argued for American financial power to be brought to bear against it. Most countries in Europe, including France, were bankrupt. Even the United Kingdom would ruin its economy if it started a Russian crusade. Bliss argued that the US should use its economic strength to enforce the withdrawal of troops from Russia.[8] Hoover too opposed the idea of an American invasion, telling Wilson that 'our people at home' would look askance at US soldiers being assigned to assist the reactionary Whites. Kolchak and Denikin, he maintained, had a poor reputation in America and Wilson would be wise to take account of public opinion. Hoover added that the arrival of American soldiers in Russia would have the counter-productive result of uniting the Russians behind Lenin and Trotsky. His advice was to put aside the Russian question until such time as peace prevailed in the rest of the world. Diplomatic pressures were desirable; big armies were not.

But Allied officials who thought military intervention was the solution were still vociferous—and demanded to be heard. Joseph Noulens had left

Archangel in mid-December, and on 20 January 1919 he addressed the conference with a plea for the violent overthrow of Soviet tyranny and terror
since the communists were enemies of the Entente.[9] The Danish ambassador Harald Scavenius took the same line. As the latest of the foreign diplomats to leave Petrograd he was up to date with recent news and stressed
Moscow's intention to spread its revolution abroad by whatever means
came to hand.[10]

President Wilson would have none of this, however, and determined instead to send an emissary to Moscow to explore whether the Soviet leadership was willing to end the Civil War. William C. Bullitt came into the
reckoning. Impressed by his State Department reports on Europe, Wilson
had included him in the American delegation to Paris and made him head
of the Division of Current Intelligence Summaries.[11] The President thought
him just the person, despite his lack of diplomatic experience, to go and
talk directly to Lenin. Wilson and Bullitt agreed that peace could come to
Russia if the contending 'Russian factions' were put in a room together and
asked to settle their disputes. Lansing gave his assent to the dispatch of Bullitt even though he lacked any optimism about the outcome.[12] The Council
of Ten convened on 21 January to discuss Wilson's proposal. Lloyd George
gave his support, arguing that the Bolsheviks would lose influence if the
Russian people felt that they had received a fair hearing in Paris.
Clemenceau objected. Averse in principle to negotiating with Bolsheviks,
he warned that Bolshevism was already spreading westwards. But when
Wilson and Lloyd George combined against him he was forced to give
way.[13]

Wilson's spirits were rising. W. H. Buckler, an attaché at the US embassy
in London, discussed American peace proposals with Litvinov in Stockholm. Even though Litvinov had to leave for Russia—together with Vatslav
Vorovski and Arthur Ransome—when Sweden broke relations with Sovnarkom in January 1919, he had responded enthusiastically to Buckler, and
the President was excited by the report he received.[14] Litvinov now wrote
to Wilson indicating that American companies could do good business in
Russia. He urged Americans to hear the arguments of all the belligerents
in the Civil War. He promised that Soviet communists, in the event of a
peace being agreed, would desist from subversive propaganda in the West.
He warned that a White military victory would open the door to the Romanov dynasty's restoration. He expressed confidence in 'the good will of
the American Government'.[15] Litvinov's letter impressed Wilson and Lloyd

George, and the proposal for a conference of Russia's warring sides was prioritized. The Prime Minister had wanted to summon the Russians to Paris whereas the President preferred to assemble them on the largest of the so-called Princes Islands—Büyük Ada or Prinkipo—in the Sea of Marmara off the coast of Constantinople; Lloyd George gave way to him.[16]

The impetus for a Russian conference appeared unstoppable until Winston Churchill, the recently appointed Secretary of State for War, arrived in the French capital on 14 February. This happened to be the date when Wilson, who was constitutionally obliged to limit the duration of his foreign stays, was scheduled to leave for the US. Harold Nicolson, a member of the British delegation, recorded:

> Meet Winston Churchill in the hotel passage. 'Hello,' I say to him. 'Have you come over to hurry us up?' Things are very slow at the Paris Peace Conference.
> 'No,' Churchill answers. 'I have come to get myself an army.'[17]

Towards the end of that long day at the conference, Churchill caught sight of Wilson rising to leave for the Gare du Nord and asked: 'Could we not have some decision about Russia?'[18] Wilson rested his hand on Clemenceau's chair and said that he was putting his hopes in holding peace talks off the Turkish coast. He was willing to go there in person. Although his priority was to get out of Russia entirely, he commented that if his Russian initiative came to nothing he would 'do his share with the other Allies in any military measures that they considered necessary and practicable to help the Russian armies now in the field'.[19]

Even Churchill still stopped short of calling for an Allied crusade—the quips he made in conversation tended to disguise this. His preferred alternative was to give aid to the Whites while forming an alliance of the states on Russia's borders, and General Sir Henry Wilson, Chief of the Imperial General Staff, supported him on this. Wilson was strongly suspicious of Lloyd George, sometimes finding him 'pronouncedly Bolshevist'.[20] Careful husbandry of resources would be essential for Churchill's scheme and he suggested withdrawing British forces from the south Caucasus and assuring Turkey of London's friendly intentions. The United Kingdom's huge post-war surplus of munitions should be delivered to the Whites along with a contingent of British officers.[21]

Churchill aimed to get the Allies to establish a Council on Russian Affairs and ascertain what resources could be made available for action of every kind—military, political and economic—in Russia. Balfour liked the idea, and Churchill went back to Lloyd George to argue that, if the Prinkipo project fell apart, the Allies would be in a position 'to take a definite decision'.[22] Behind this measured statement lay Churchill's desire for action. If the Bolsheviks rejected the call for an armistice in their Civil War, he wanted the Allied powers to declare and increase military support for the Whites. Lloyd George wrote to his private secretary Philip Kerr expressing displeasure. Churchill was becoming a pest. The Prime Minister wanted to avoid political trouble and an unsustainable budget at home; he required proper evidence that the Russians wanted foreigners to interfere in matters relating to their governance. He probably also felt the need to guard against Churchill trying to increase the size of the Allied forces in Russia; and he knew his friend too well to believe that he would quietly abide by whatever policy emerged from the Allied Supreme Council.[23]

On 22 February 1919, Bullitt set off for Russia with his friend Lincoln Steffens. Both were pro-Soviet and had grandiose ideas about what they could achieve, even though Lansing's letter of assignation specified only 'the purpose of studying conditions, political and economic'—Wilson had characteristically left the drafting to the State Department.[24] Bullitt was anyway not of a mind or character to defer to Lansing. His ambition was to settle the Russian question on terms acceptable to the Soviet authorities, and he thought well of Lenin even before encountering him. In his pocket he had Colonel House's written assurance that if the Sovnarkom agreed to the American terms, the US would resume trade with Russia, institute a food-relief scheme and withdraw Allied troops. Bullitt had orders to avoid discussing the paying off of Russian state loans. The British were to be informed of the negotiating tactics but not the French. Wilson and Lansing knew that Clemenceau would make a fuss about the need to raise the grievances of French investors.[25] Bullitt consulted Philip Kerr before departing. In this way he felt satisfied that whatever he accomplished would enjoy endorsement from Lloyd George and Balfour.[26]

It was Bullitt's first trip to Russia; he spoke no Russian and his understanding of Russia's politics was less than deep. Yet he suffered no deficit of confidence in his talks with the Soviet leadership. With his flimsy acquaintance with Bolshevik history he was convinced that they were men of their word and open to peaceful compromise.[27] Lenin and Chicherin warned that if they were to sign an armistice, they needed 'a semi-official guarantee' that the Americans, British and French would enforce it on the White side as well.[28] The week of conversations was thrilling for Bullitt, who thought he had obtained a watertight deal he could take back to Wilson and Lloyd George in Paris. He and Steffens left Moscow on 15 March, escorted by Arthur Ransome and Bill Shatov.[29]

But back in Paris things did not turn out as Bullitt expected. George Hill was there on a Secret Intelligence Service assignment, under orders to put his special knowledge of Russia at the disposal of the British delegation.[30] When he discovered that Bullitt was pressing the case for recognizing the Soviet government, Hill contacted the anti-communist reporter Henry Wickham Steed—and the two of them conferred with Sidney Reilly, who was in France after a brief trip to Russia.[31] Steed had information that Lloyd George was close to approving Wilson's ideas on Russia. He was determined to thwart such an outcome. On 28 March 1919 the *Daily Mail* published an editorial by him fulminating against Lloyd George for betraying the White Russians and falling victim to a conspiracy by 'international Jewish financiers' and Germans to assist the communists in holding on to power in Moscow.[32] The tirade shook Lloyd George. When he breakfasted with Bullitt that morning, he said that the *Mail*'s editorial made it impossible for him to support the proposals he had brought back from Russia: 'As long as the British press is doing this kind of thing how can you expect me to be sensible about Russia?'[33] Bullitt had no greater success with his patron Woodrow Wilson. The Prinkipo project was scuppered before ever coming before the Allied Supreme Council.

Bullitt had overestimated his right to speak in the President's name. He was also credulous about Moscow. If Lenin was willing to call a truce in the Civil War and attend a conference, it was only because the Red military position was bad at the time. Sovnarkom would have benefited from another breathing space. Only a fool could believe that Lenin would not rip up an agreement when it suited him. It was equally unlikely that Kolchak would remain content with what he held in the Urals or that Denikin would stay put in southern Russia; and the National Centre leaders had no hesitation in rejecting 'artificial' attempts at peace-making.[34] They knew their Lenin and Trotsky better than Bullitt did.

Wilson was not without his devious side and was already giving consideration to Kolchak's request for military supplies. William Phillips, Assistant Secretary of State during Lansing's absence in Paris, wanted to take the side of the Whites and help them to victory. Wilson and Lansing asked for time to consult General William S. Graves who led the US expeditionary force that had landed in eastern Siberia in August 1918. When Graves answered positively about Kolchak, Wilson authorized financial credit to be provided to the White Army for 260,000 rifles on condition that Kolchak pledged to prevent a return to power of the Romanovs, hold free elections and honour Russian state debts. Kolchak gave his assent, and weapons, clothing and food were shipped to Siberia, albeit surreptitiously since Republican Congressmen were already criticizing the administration for interfering in the Civil War. The US administration hit on the device of using Boris Bakhmetev, the Provisional Government's ambassador to Washington. Bakhmetev retained the right of access to the bank accounts of the Provisional Government. Collaboration with him obviated the need to apply for funds and permission from the US Congress.[35]

Wilson at the same time remained adamantly opposed to an Allied invasion. Francis, after surgery in London, accompanied the President back to New York. He proposed sending 100,000 US troops to Petrograd to oversee fresh elections.[36] Francis was to recall how he explained the obstacles:

> The President replied that he had mentioned my recommendation to Lloyd George and that Lloyd George's expression was, if he should order any British soldiers to go to Russia they not only would object but refuse to go. The President furthermore stated that he had mentioned the same subject to Clemenceau, and he had met the reply that if Clemenceau should order French troops to go to Russia they would mutiny, but the President said he would give further consideration to my recommendation.[37]

Whether this was the real reason for American inactivity is doubtful. Wilson knew that so large a contingent would be practically an invasion force, and he wanted nothing to do with it. He preferred Hoover's idea of offering food aid to Soviet Russia on condition that Lenin promised to cease fomenting revolution across his borders.[38] There was no objection from

Britain and France, and Wilson invited the Norwegian polar explorer and philanthropist Fridtjof Nansen to head the relief mission to Russia. It was Nansen who radioed the proposal to Lenin in April 1919.

The Russians replied on 14 May, welcoming the offer of food supplies but refusing to cease fighting.[39] By then Kolchak was on the retreat. Lenin was not covetous of foreign grain at the expense of throwing away victory over a White army. Nor was Kolchak any more enthusiastic about Wilson's initiative. He judged that the difficulty of crushing communism would increase if food relief arrived under a communist administration. The White Russian ambassador Sergei Sazonov cabled from Paris advising him to be more tactful in his dealings with the Allies. Kolchak's response was to ask Sazonov to come to Omsk and see the Russian situation for himself.[40]

Churchill had so agitated Lloyd George that the Prime Minister asked him to provide a paper costing the military options for Russia. Churchill havered, arguing that the Allies needed to fix a clear political line before he could offer any financial accountancy.[41] This pleased Lloyd George, who felt he was denting Churchill's aggressive inclinations. The French leaders were as anti-Bolshevik as Churchill. In public, Clemenceau and Poincaré denounced the iniquities of Bolshevism—and they were eloquent about the Soviet expropriation of funds belonging to hundreds of thousands of French investors. But privately they admitted that a war against Soviet Russia would be as onerous for France as Lloyd George saw it would be for the United Kingdom. France had defeated Germany at the cost of ruining the French economy and could not start another big war. And when Béla Kun established a communist regime in Budapest in March 1919 the limits of Allied power were made manifest. American officials in Paris suggested to Marshal Foch that the Hungarians should not be left to their fate at Kun's hands. Foch's reply killed off any illusion about France's preparedness to intervene. He said that he would need a minimum of 350,000 troops to invade and occupy—and he could no longer muster so many soldiers.[42]

Captain T. C. C. Gregory of the American Relief Administration scoffed that 'a battalion and a bugle under the Stars and Stripes' would be quite enough to do the job.[43] Whether this was overly optimistic did not matter; Wilson was never going to agree to such an expedition. The President was exhausted and under attack from all quarters. His former admirer William C. Bullitt resigned from the State Department on 17 May 1919. In his letter of resignation, he told the President that the Allied peace settlement could never hold—it was unfair to so many countries. Bullitt went on to say that the President should have 'made your fight in the open' and kept faith with the millions of people who had been willing him to stick by his principles.[44] He wrote to Lansing more respectfully but ended with a plea against both the German peace terms and America's entry into the League of Nations: he could see no good coming from either.[45]

The German treaty was the first to be concluded at the Peace Conference. Clemenceau had worn down Wilson sufficiently to persuade him to accept terms that were deeply shocking for most Germans. Vast reparations were to be paid and war guilt was to be admitted; and Germany and Austria, regardless of what their peoples wanted, were forbidden to merge into a single German state. Wilson had considered lining up with Lloyd George against Clemenceau in order to soften the treaty, but the negotiations behind the scenes proved fruitless. Tired out and drained of practical ideas, Wilson gave up the struggle and, whereas the British and French experts remained active, American influence declined as the President faded.[46] The treaty was solemnly signed in Versailles' Hall of Mirrors on 28 June 1919. The choice of place was deliberate. It had been there in 1871 that the French had been humiliated by the victorious Prussians. Germany had become a pariah power, its only consolation being that German ministers knew exactly what the Allies were demanding of them. Soviet Russia, the other pariah power, still had no idea what the Allied intentions towards it might ultimately be.

19. EUROPEAN REVOLUTION

While the Allied powers had been conferring in Paris, they were troubled by some of the news that reached them from central Europe. Their fear grew that communism might spread across Europe; and although the German government had crushed the Spartacists in Berlin in January 1919, the fact that an insurrection had even been attempted was a worrying sign that the political far left could exploit a situation where unemployment and food shortages were on the rise. Germany was unlikely to be the only country which experienced such disorder. The victor powers felt anxious about the peace.

The Bolshevik leaders in Moscow drew comfort from exactly the same situation. Having made their own revolution by taking advantage of Russia's wartime disintegration, they remained convinced that European sympathizers would soon emulate them—and although they had not wished for the death of Rosa Luxemburg, her untimely removal meant that Lenin and his Politburo could more easily dominate Comintern. Lenin was in buoyant mood, predicting revolutions that would set the continent on fire. Despite all the military difficulties faced by the Bolsheviks in the Urals, he expressed disdain for the Allied expeditionary forces in Russia. He told Arthur Ransome that Lloyd George might just as well send his soldiers to a communist university.[1] He predicted that if the captured conscripts witnessed Bolshevism at work they would quickly turn into Bolsheviks themselves. The Soviet authorities put Boris Reinstein—a former emigrant to America—in charge of propaganda among British POWs who were allowed to stroll around the streets of Moscow.[2] After intercepting a letter from a Private A. J. Fardon who had exchanged captivity for a job in the People's Commissariat of Foreign Affairs, and seemed to be rather taken with the Soviet model, the Directorate of Military Intelligence in London grew worried about the Soviet tactic—and it was irritated with Ransome for facilitating Private Fardon's correspondence with his family.[3]

Ransome had also riled Lenin by saying that, while communism could succeed for the Russians, it had no chance of doing the same in Britain. Lenin replied:

> We have a saying that a man may have typhoid while still on his legs. Twenty, maybe thirty years ago I had abortive typhoid, and was going about with it, had had it some days before it knocked me over. Well, England and France and Italy have caught the disease already. England may seem to you to be untouched, but the microbe is already there.[4]

When Ransome quipped that any British political disturbances were merely the sign of an abortive revolution, Lenin swatted him aside:

> Yes, that is possible. It is, perhaps, an educative period, in which English workmen will come to realize their political needs, and turn from liberalism to socialism. Socialism is certainly weak in England. Your socialist movement, your socialist parties . . . when I was in England I zealously attended everything I could, and for a country with so large an industrial population they were pitiable, pitiable . . . a handful at a street corner . . . a school class . . . pitiable . . . But you must remember one great difference between Russia of 1905 and England of today. Our first Soviet in Russia was made during the revolution. Your shop-stewards committees have been in existence long before. They are without programme, without direction, but the opposition they will meet will force a programme on them.[5]

Lenin stood by his ideas of historical inevitability. Where Russians had gone, the British would surely follow whether Ransome agreed or not.

The Allied governments knew only too well that this was Lenin's objective and could see that he and his comrades had attracted foreign sympathizers in Moscow who might return home and stir up revolution. The French were the first to take preventive action when Jacques Sadoul indicated a desire to assume a role in public life in Paris and only a bout of typhus held him back in the winter of 1918–19. He planned to tell his compatriots what he knew—or thought he knew—about the Soviet order. He also aimed to divulge information about France's actions in Russia. Attacks on him appeared in the French press. Sadoul suspected that ministers had instigated them so as to keep him in Moscow and pre-empt a political scandal.[6] When the French Socialist Party adopted him as a candidate in the national elections in honour of his struggle against Allied armed military intervention in Russia, the government in Paris forestalled him by setting up a court-martial for treason. He was tried *in absentia* and, in November 1919, sentenced to death for treason.[7]

The next attempt at communist revolution occurred not in Paris or London but in Munich. Soldiers had returned from the western front angry and exhausted. Unemployment was growing and food shortages increased. Resentment at the Allies' demands was on the rise. Strikes and demonstrations spread and the Russian idea of workers electing their own councils was copied. Kurt Eisner, Bavaria's Prime Minister, tried to dampen the fire. His moderating influence was not widely appreciated. Indeed, he was hated at both extremes of the political spectrum, and on 21 February 1919 a fiery young aristocrat gunned him down. The assassination encouraged Max Levien, a leader of the Munich Workers' Council, to think that there would never be a better or more necessary time to seize power. Born and raised in Russia, Levien had come to Germany to take a degree in zoology and unlike other political emigrants he stayed in central Europe after the fall of the Romanovs. His political partner was Eugen Leviné, who hailed from St Petersburg and had studied in Heidelberg after being exiled to Siberia. Their German associates were heavily represented in the liberal professions. They were fervent admirers of the October Revolution, and Levien and Leviné put themselves forward as the Lenin and Trotsky of the political far left in southern Germany.

On 7 April 1919 they proclaimed the Bavarian Council Republic. Factories and large commercial enterprises were expropriated. Church, aristocracy and bourgeoisie were threatened. Patrols were instituted around the city's central districts. Telegrams of victory were sent to Moscow. Lenin replied congratulating the insurrectionaries; yet again he thought he had the proof that communism would spread quickly and easily to the rest of Europe.

The fact that Levien and Leviné were of Jewish parentage and were Russian passport-holders did not go unremarked in Munich. In the eyes of Eugenio Pacelli, the papal nuncio who in 1939 would become Pope Pius XII,

Levien was 'a young man, about thirty or thirty-five, also Russian and a Jew. Pale, dirty, with vacant eyes, hoarse voice, vulgar, repulsive, with a face that is both intelligent and sly.'[8] The nuncio described the female communists as filthy sluts and he associated Levien and Leviné with dirt, slipperiness and even bestiality. Pacelli's prejudices were shared by many Christians in those years, and the Council Republic was widely regarded as a foreign disease. But the leaders of the Council Republic, by mixing exclusively with people who shared their political extremism, failed to detect the revulsion that millions of Germans felt for their creed. Nor did they appreciate how the disruption of social and economic stability that had enabled their seizure of power was only a temporary phenomenon. Retaliation was inevitable. But Levien and his comrades underestimated their enemies' capacity to do them damage—and at a time when Kolchak was threatening Moscow, there was no chance of armed support from the Red Army.

The Bavarian Council Republic lasted only as long as it took for the national government in Berlin to organize an attack. Levien and Leviné were breathtakingly naive. Believing that common criminals were simply victims of the old Imperial order, they released all convicts from prison. (Neither Lenin nor Trotsky was ever tempted into such silliness.) The subsequent wave of robberies and murders in Munich made it a terrible place to live. The economic emergency intensified as businesses closed down. Levien and Leviné had no idea how to restore employment, and their period in power was characterized by a collapse of industry and commerce.

In May 1919 the Freikorps assembled in Bamberg 150 miles to the north and moved on Munich alongside regular army units. Known communists were shot in the streets. The official tally was six hundred deaths, but the reality could well have been twice that. The fighting was over within a few hours as workers' militias quickly laid down their arms. Levien escaped to Vienna until he took refuge in Soviet Russia in June 1921. Leviné, a less worldly person, saw it as his duty to remain with his comrades in Munich. Arrested with the writer Ernst Toller, he was tried for sedition. He was resigned to his fate: 'We communists are all dead men on leave.'[9] He was executed after being found guilty of complicity in the shooting of hostages. The lamps of communism had failed to illumine central Europe. Although Soviet leaders were disappointed, they observed that German politics remained volatile and that the national government could not deal with its enemies on the political far left without bringing in the army and paramilitary forces. The economy was in tatters. Even if the Munich experiment had proved unsuccessful, this did not mean that workers in Germany and elsewhere in central Europe would not eventually find the ingredients to produce a revolutionary order.

Hungarian communists gave grounds for optimism from 21 March 1919, when they swept to power in Budapest with a communist-dominated coalition. The revolution was quickly spread to the entire country—or at least to those parts of Hungary left to the Hungarians by the Allies. Lenin and Trotsky greeted it with the same warmth as they had shown to the Bavarian Council Republic. Béla Kun, the Hungarian revolutionary leader, was a zealot for the Soviet order. He had spent time in Russia after being captured with the armies of Austria-Hungary on the eastern front. As an ex-POW he formed a Hungarian communist group in Moscow in March 1918, returning to Budapest as soon as the Great War was over. Kun had worked as a journalist and wrote lively pamphlets against the Western Allies and the prospect of a humiliating peace. He now found he had a talent for oratory, too. The unstable government that was striving to moderate the Allied terms threw him into prison. But when the social-democrats entered the cabinet they liberated Kun as a comrade on the political left. He walked straight from the cells into a ministerial post. He had been badly beaten while incarcerated and his face showed the wounds that he had received and fully intended to avenge.[10]

Like his friend and fellow communist Tibor Szamuely, Kun was a fanatic. Solidarity with Soviet Russia was proclaimed and reports of Bolshevik achievements were carried in the Budapest newspapers. The Red flag was hoisted on public buildings. Trade unions received a generous quota of free tickets to the theatres. The banks, mines and big textile factories were nationalized. Kun established a security police that soon gained notoriety for its terror against 'class enemies'. Szamuely assembled the 'Lenin Boys' whom he sent into the villages to seize the harvest and impose a system of collective farms. (The same thing was happening in the Ukrainian countryside; but whereas in Ukraine it was against the instructions of Moscow, in Hungary it was on Kun's orders.) Churches were desecrated and priests and landlords were arrested or murdered. When peasants objected to the violence, the Lenin Boys turned on them too. The communization of Hungarian society was undertaken at a faster pace even than in Russia after the October Revolution. Blood flowed copiously.

Such popularity as Kun retained lay in his unequivocal rejection of the Allies' schemes for Hungary. The Western Allies planned to reward Poland,

Romania and Czechoslovakia with territory that until then had been part of Hungary. Hungary would become a third of its previous size. As a result even Hungarians who were wary of Kun's communist internationalist doctrines lent him their support. The communist leadership were willing to act rather than merely grumble.

Recruiting left-of-centre commanders from the Imperial armed forces, Kun mobilized the troops to fight for every patch of 'Hungarian' soil. He vowed to repel the growing incursions by Romanian and Czechoslovak troops. He paraded foreign POWs through the streets of Budapest. Hungary's interests, he implied, were safe in his hands. Although he disliked the Hungarian national flag, he yielded when Ferenc Julier, Chief of the General Staff, told him that without it there might be trouble in getting an army into the field against the Romanians.[11] Kun was cunning in his interviews for the foreign press, pretending to be much more moderate than he really was and claiming that it would be years before any truly communist policies would be applied. For a while he was successful and the communist regime threw back the Romanian and Czech invaders in April 1919.[12] Its Red Army invaded Czechoslovakia, taking several towns before meeting effective resistance. It closed the Danube to shipping, and Austrian attempts to break the river blockade were disrupted 'by the Hungarian Bolshevists who would fire on boats'.[13] The Orient Express continued to run across Hungary from Romania, but Red Guards with their fixed bayonets and grenade belts made crossing the border an unpleasant experience.[14]

The Allies reacted with an economic blockade designed to bring Kun and Szamuely to their knees.[15] Food supplies were depleted. The only solution according to Kun was to expropriate more grain, vegetables and meat from the villages. Clashes with the peasantry intensified as civil war broke out.

Kun and Szamuely had always seen their ultimate salvation in international revolution. They begged Lenin and Trotsky to send a contingent of the Red Army from newly conquered Ukraine.[16] Little did the communist leaders in Moscow and Budapest know that American forces were intercepting Hungarian wireless traffic.[17] So nothing that Kun wrote in his telegrams was truly confidential.[18] It was no secret, of course, that the Soviet leaders, if the opportunity arose, were intent on helping to spread communist revolution westwards. The Bolshevik party's entire foreign policy had been built on this foundation. Just occasionally there were surprises for the Allied powers, such as when the Austrian security agency claimed to have discovered a secret plan of Kun's for a communist seizure of power in Vienna. This may have been a case of counter-intelligence officers trying to prove their usefulness to Austria's new social-democratic government.[19] It would seem that the Americans later used their intercepted information to prevent Kun from heading to Switzerland as an envoy of Lenin and Trotsky.[20] Old 'Austria-Hungary' was boiling up with political conflicts that could spill over the new national borders. It appeared that anything might happen, and it frequently did.

Lenin and Trotsky did not dismiss Kun's requests out of hand, and their Red Army high command began to examine how it might lend assistance to Hungary. It quickly became obvious that a campaign across the Ukrainian frontier would put the Red Army in danger from Kolchak and Denikin. If Russians marched westwards, they might find there was no Soviet homeland to return to. With regret they turned down Kun's request.[21]

By late summer, the Hungarian Red Army faced rebellion throughout Hungary and threats on the northern borders. Desertions grew in number. The last slim hope of the Kun government vanished on 4 August when Romanian forces, after weeks of fighting in the north of the country, stormed into Budapest. Although they were delighted that a power in the region had overthrown communism, the Western Allies did not approve of what happened next. The Romanian military force was a law unto itself and the Bucharest authorities exercised no restraint over it. Red Hungarian terror was replaced with a White Romanian one, and Hungarian groups emerged seeking revenge on the communists who had tormented them for months. Chaos ensued when the Romanians reduced the police service to six hundred policemen. Attacks on Jews in the streets and in their houses became frequent. The economy fell apart entirely and food became scarce in the capital even for those who had possessions to barter.[22] The Romanians stripped the occupied territories of their flour, sugar, medicine and even its railway locomotives.[23] Famine spread across the country.[24]

US officials were aware that communism remained a threat in central Europe—and not only in Hungary. Herbert Hoover, director of the American Relief Administration, wrote to Woodrow Wilson on 28 March 1919:

> Politically the Bolsheviki most certainly represent a minority in every country where they are in control. The Bolsheviki . . . [have] resorted to terror, bloodshed and murder to a degree long since abandoned even among reactionary tyrannies . . . [They have] em-

braced a large degree of emotionalism and . . . thereby given an impulse to [their] propaganda comparable only to the impulse of large spiritual movements.[25]

Hoover's remedy was to counteract Marxism's appeal by shipping American food relief to central Europe. Europe had depended on grain exports from Russia before the Great War. Hoover argued that American farmers would benefit from filling the gap.[26] America had an over-abundance of agricultural produce. Credits should be advanced so that European countries could buy stocks.[27]

Hoover argued that no better way existed to demonstrate capitalist superiority over communism than to bring the bread of life from the world's healthiest market economy and help industry and agriculture to recover. He saw that wherever food was short there was a danger of cities toppling into communist hands. American philanthropy, however, came with strings. Hoover stipulated that the recipient governments should maintain order and keep the political far left out of power. Revolutionary disturbances in Vienna were enough for him to suspend aid to Austria temporarily; and he held back supplies from Hungary under Kun.[28] Meanwhile his American Relief Administration transported cereals, medicines, sugar, tinned meat and fish to Germany, Poland and Czechoslovakia. His efforts in central Europe after the Great War were extraordinary in the face of much obstruction from the French and British, who continued to blockade Germany at the risk of outright mass starvation in 1919. When he learned that American grain cargoes were held up at European ports, Hoover angrily intervened by stressing that he had President Wilson's full support. Undoubtedly the strain took a toll on him—J. M. Keynes described him admiringly as 'a weary Titan' and 'an exhausted prize-fighter'.[29] But Hoover got his way and the French and British stopped being obstructive—and the blockade of Germany was lifted.

Food aid for Germany might help the Allies to avert communist revolutionary advances but it was by no means sufficient in itself. Even incarcerated in Berlin's Moabit prison, Karl Radek refused to believe that capitalism had a long-term future. From August 1919 he was allowed visitors; he held what he called a salon in his cell as politicians and reporters queued to meet the exotic Bolshevik.[30] Another rather unexpected visitor was one of Germany's leading industrialists, Walter Rathenau, who agreed that any return to the old capitalist order in Europe was impossible. Rathenau spoiled this for Radek by adding that his published oeuvre refuted Marx's theories as well as Lenin's prediction of a German proletarian revolution. Radek was also visited by the journalist Maximilien Harden, who came and asked Radek to write a piece for his weekly *Die Zukunft*. General von Reibnitz, an aristocratic member of the officer corps, arrived with his proposal for a Soviet–German rapprochement and even a German revolution on the Soviet model; and the British reporter Morgan Philips Price, the friend he had made in Petrograd, paid a visit to update him on events in the United Kingdom.[31]

At the same time, Radek was keeping up a secret correspondence with the German communist movement. Ruth Fischer, an Austrian Marxist, was a fount of information for him on her visits to the prison. Not all her news was cheering. Germany's communist leaders were heading for a split at their party congress in Heidelberg. Austrian communists were discussing how to organize a seizure of power in Vienna, but they had not got far in their preparations.[32] Radek wrote a critical pamphlet on the German Communist Party and replied to Karl Kautsky's attack on Bolshevik rule in Russia. Both works were published by a friendly press in Berlin.[33] Despite having heard of the difficulties for the revolutionary cause in central Europe, he remained confident that the continent was on the brink of revolutionary transformation.

The activities of the Italian political far left also helped to keep his spirits up. Unlike Hungary and Germany, Italy was one of the victorious powers. Prime Minister Vittorio Orlando had attended the Paris Peace Conference just long enough to secure the cession of the Trentino to Italy before returning to Rome. The big cities of the north, Milan and Turin, were shaken by strikes in the large industrial factories. Appeals for quiet negotiation in the national interest fell on deaf ears. Workers elected factory councils that in summer 1919 began to seize control of whole enterprises. The Italian Socialist Party was divided over how to deal with the crisis, and a split was in the making as the radicals expressed solidarity with the October Revolution in Russia. Comintern sent Nikolai Lyubarski as an agent to hasten this outcome with finance and advice.[34] The young Sardinian militant Antonio Gramsci saw the factory councils as the embryo of a revolutionary administration that could assume power throughout the country. As editor of *L'Ordine Nuovo* ('The New Order') in Turin, he urged Italian workers to overturn capitalism and move towards self-rule. Orlando's government positioned troops into the factories before Gramsci and his comrades could realize their objective—and the embers of revolt were put out in the course of the following year.

At the time nobody could yet be sure that communism had been finally cauterized in Europe. Attempt after attempt had been made at launching a revolution that would join hands with the Soviet political experiment. Each time—in Berlin, in Munich, in Budapest and in Turin and Milan—it had been thwarted. But the conditions that provided communist organizations with an opportunity to challenge their governments had still to be eliminated. In many European countries the discontent with living and working conditions remained deep and wide, and far-left militants turned increasingly to Comintern for their guidance and inspiration. What had happened in Petrograd in 1917 might still take place elsewhere. This was one thing about which there was agreement between the Bolsheviks and the leaders of the Western Allies.

20. THE ALLIES
AND THE WHITES

As the Paris Peace Conference moved to its close, the need for the Allies to define their Russian policy became urgent. They at last did this on 27 May 1919, when Georges Clemenceau, David Lloyd George, Vittorio Orlando and the leader of the Japanese delegation Saionji Kinmochi conferred in Woodrow Wilson's residence to draft a message to Kolchak—wherever east of the Urals he was to be found. None of the Allied leaders thought any good could come from negotiating with Sovnarkom. But they also wanted to assure themselves that the Whites were a tolerable alternative worthy of support.

They told Kolchak that it had 'always been a cardinal axiom of the Allied and Associated Powers to avoid interference in the internal affairs of Russia'. They stressed that Allied intervention had always been limited to assisting those Russians who 'wanted to continue the struggle against German autocracy and to free their country from German rule' and to rescue the legion of Czech troops. Now that the war was over they remained willing to do what they could for Russia and help it towards 'liberty, self-government and peace'. The terms on which they would offer this help were clearly set out. If Kolchak wanted assistance from the Western Allies, he had to promise to call elections to a Constituent Assembly or reconvene the old one. He had to guarantee universal civic freedoms and reaffirm his recognition of Russia's foreign debts. He had to accept the independence of Poland and Finland. Other borderlands of the former Russian Empire—Estonia, Latvia, Lithuania, the Caucasus and central Asia—were to be promised autonomy. Any disputes over territory would have to be referred for adjudication to the League of Nations.[1]

Kolchak replied through the French diplomats attached to his headquarters. He assented to Constituent Assembly elections and added that he would step down from power after military victory if this would help. He declared that he was willing to recognize Russian state debts. While accepting that Poland should be free, however, he limited himself to a vague readiness to discuss other international questions at a later date. Although this lay short of wholehearted compliance it satisfied the Western Allies, who wrote back sympathetically on 12 June.[2] They wanted democracy in Russia, but their greater wish was to bring down Bolshevism; to do so they were more than willing to work with White Russian commanders who had little genuine democratic inclination.

By then, however, the White cause was in terrible straits. Kolchak's advance was halted at Ufa and the Red counter-offensive broke up his forces in June. Just weeks earlier he had appointed Yevgeni Miller to lead White forces in northern Russia; but Miller, based in Archangel with few troops, could do little more than wait on events. Kolchak's situation worsened through the summer, and he retreated stage by stage along the Trans-Siberian railway, taking a vast gold reserve with him. He was pushed steadily eastwards, with no realistic hope of recovery, while his troops were attacked en route by the region's peasants. Meanwhile Denikin had decided that he at last had adequate forces to make his thrust northwards from southern Ukraine. He divided his Volunteer Army into two groups—while one fought its way along the River Volga, the other attacked through central Ukraine. Like Kolchak, Denikin had the simple basic objective of reaching and occupying Moscow with all possible speed. The Red Army, relieved of the threat from the Urals, redeployed its main strength against him and in October 1919, fighting alongside Ukrainian peasant irregulars, decisively defeated Denikin outside Orël, in the border area between Russia and Ukraine, and steadily withdrew to the Ukrainian south.

All this time the Whites pleaded with the Allies to strengthen their military presence in north Russia, southern Ukraine and mid-Siberia. But French commanders in Ukraine fretted about the worsening situation for their troops. General Philippe Henri d'Anselme had never had confidence in France's expedition and in April decided that evacuation was the only option. His troops were demoralized: few wanted to fight the Red Army and military discipline was breaking down.[3] He sent a telegram to Clemenceau saying that it no longer made sense to talk of France's 'army of the East'. The longer the troops stayed by the Black Sea, the graver the discontent among them. D'Anselme proposed instead that the French should train and equip the Romanian army, lending it an officer cadre. The Allies should also send food to Romania so that the Romanian people would be sufficiently well fed to provide useful soldiers.[4] Clemenceau, who was equally anti-Soviet and anti-German, was not pleased, but he was unable to act against the advice from generals on the spot. French military withdrawal was only a matter of time.

Lloyd George was also contemplating the withdrawal of the British expedition from northern Russia. Never having been an enthusiastic interventionist, he had concluded that the time had come to evacuate Archangel and Murmansk. The British labour movement was united against sending troops there and the Hands Off Russia campaign gathered strength on the political left.[5] The troops themselves yearned to be demobbed; any orders for eastward deployment would almost certainly lead to mutinies. And many businessmen wanted to re-enter Russian markets.

Churchill, however, stood out from the national consensus and continued to favour increased support for the Whites and to oppose any resumption of trade with the areas of Russia under Soviet rule. When he made a fuss in the cabinet, Lloyd George wrote a gentle reprimand:

> I wonder whether it is any use my making one last effort to induce you to throw off this obsession which, if you forgive me for saying so, is upsetting your balance. I again ask you to let Russia be, at any rate for a few days, and to concentrate on the quite unjustifiable expenditure in France, at home and in the East, incurred by both the War Office and the Air Department.[6]

The Prime Minister's mind was on British economic recovery since he saw that the country's finances could not withstand another war. But he left the expedition where it was for some months. Apart from anything else, the outcome of the Civil War in Russia was in the balance and Lloyd George had no wish to undermine the chances of the Whites. Most Liberal and nearly all Conservative MPs supported the presence of the United Kingdom's troops in Russia as did the two great newspaper proprietors, Lord Northcliffe and Lord Rothermere.

A sprinkling of parliamentarians challenged this orthodoxy. Labour MPs, many of them having been elected for the first time and not yet experienced in the ways of the House, were quiet on the Russian question; but a small group of independent voices—Colonel Josiah Wedgwood, Commander J. M. Kenworthy and Cecil Malone (who chose not to use his rank after leaving the forces)—criticized the government's policy; they were favourably reported in the *Manchester Guardian*, the new Labour *Daily Herald* and Lord Beaverbrook's *Daily Express*.[7] Churchill ignored the press criticisms of him until the *Daily Express* printed a letter from Lieutenant Colonel Sherwood Kelly on 6 September 1919 alleging that the Secretary for War had misled the country about British army operations in Russia.[8] Kelly, a holder of the Victoria Cross, had returned from service in Archangel disgusted by what he saw as governmental duplicity. The expedition had been told that its purpose was limited to protecting British military stores. Kelly accused Churchill and fellow ministers of deceitfully organizing a covert offensive to overthrow Sovnarkom. Obliged to defend both himself and the cabinet against charges of deceit, Churchill denied pursuing a policy of invasion.[9]

The Americans, like Lloyd George, wanted to help the Whites without actually sending their troops to fight alongside them. This had to be undertaken with discretion. The American labour movement was agitating for official recognition of Soviet Russia and a growing business lobby wanted the US to penetrate the Russian market while foreign affairs were moving towards isolationism. Senator Hiram Johnson from California asked why American boys were being shot in Russia. President Wilson and Secretary Lansing let the British and French take any blame for action against Soviet Russia while licensing their own confidential assistance to anti-Bolshevik forces. In Siberia the Cossack 'strongman' Semënov, whose army was notorious for its arbitrary violence, nonetheless received US finance and supplies. And when Semënov was defeated by the Reds, the Americans turned to Admiral Kolchak, whose officers were only a little less brutal. After Kolchak went the way of Semënov, Wilson rose from his sick bed to approve help for the White general Nikolai Yudenich, who in autumn 1919 led his North-Western Army in an offensive against Petrograd.[10] The Whites had to agree to pay for the supplies they needed. They could not very well object. They understood that if they wanted to have their country back, they had to meet the going price.

Yet Kolchak was exceptional among the White commanders in possessing a large supply of gold bullion; and even he could hardly carry out physical transactions from the middle of Siberia. The Whites found a way round the problem by drawing on funds registered abroad in the Provisional Government's name. They had the blessing of the unofficial Russian Foreign Delegation which formed itself in Paris to press for support against the Bolsheviks and included ex-Minister of Foreign Affairs Sergei Sazonov and ex-Ambassador Vasili Maklakov. Boris Savinkov, who had left Russia after the suppression of his July revolt, joined them at the end of 1918; he was followed from Archangel a year later by Nikolai Chaikovski.[11] The former diplomats in the Allied countries—Sergei Sazonov, Boris Bakhmetev and Vasili Maklakov—made the Provisional Government's accounts available to the White armies, holding their noses as they did so. Sazonov and his friends had no illusions about the reactionary inclinations of the White officer corps, and they complained frequently about the political ineptitude of its commanders. But the Whites embodied Russia's sole chance of eliminating Bolshevism and the diplomats could not risk letting them lose the Civil War because nobody would disburse the money to pay for arms.

The Allied governments favoured this financial solution knowing that Russian accounts held in western Europe and the US were in healthy balance. Predictably there was some reluctance about this in France, but Clemenceau restricted himself to a strong public reminder that French loans to previous Russian governments should be honoured; he also refrained from any raid on the funds controlled by former Ambassador Maklakov after he received them from the Germans at the end of the Great War.[12] The situation was still easier for former Ambassador Bakhmetev in America, where in December 1918 he had $8,000 million at his disposal.[13] He also exercised authority over the military supplies bought by Nicholas II's administration which were still awaiting dispatch from the US.[14] Bakhmetev began to make fresh purchases, informing General Yudenich that three thousand rifles had been bought from the US War Ministry for his use.[15] Yudenich had realized that if he ever succeeded in occupying Petrograd, its citizens were likely to be suffering from starvation; he therefore pressed for food as well as guns and consented to Herbert Hoover commissioning six ships to sail to Tallinn with food supplies. Hoover made Yudenich sign a financial guarantee; and he suggested that, if Yudenich could not hand over the funds, he should apply to Sazonov for funding from the Russian governmental accounts held in Paris.[16]

The Allies were not acting out of altruism. While hoping for a White victory, they looked forward to the restoration of a private-enterprise economy in Russia that would benefit their nations—and they aimed to get first bite of the Russian economic cherry. With this in mind, the British set up a Department of Overseas Trade in the Foreign Office, and made John Picton Bagge their commercial secretary in Odessa.[17]

The Allied powers set about facilitating international commerce in the areas under White control. The trading conditions were not of the easiest kind. The economy of the former Russian Empire had been terribly disrupted in 1917–18. Although business deals continued to be conducted outside the Soviet-occupied territory, corruption and fraud were widespread. Entrepreneurs in Russia and Ukraine lacked financial credit and Western banks were understandably wary of underwriting projects to trade with them.[18] But many businessmen from Russia who were currently based abroad were willing to take chances by re-entering Russian and Ukrainian markets. Vladimir Bashkirov in Paris was one of them. Seeing that he would make no progress in France, he liaised with Bakhmetev's embassy in Washington with a view to restarting the Pacific trade with Vladivostok. The Siberian Creameries Co-operative Union welcomed such initiative and planned to send its products across the ocean to the US ports of Seattle and San Francisco.[19] Western Siberia had exported huge quantities of yoghurt and butter to Germany before 1914; and the Union now looked east for new markets in America, at least until Kolchak started his headlong retreat in summer 1919. The difficulties were immense. It was hard to find shipping companies willing to sail for Vladivostok even though the arms and equipment for the Whites had been assembled in Seattle for transit.[20] Civilian categories of goods were still more difficult to move to and from Siberia. But there were glimmerings of a future very different from the one which Lenin and Trotsky intended for Russia.

Yudenich did not rely entirely on Paris for his funds. Before starting the North-Western Army's offensive, he created a financial consultative committee to help until money reached him from the ambassadors. Emil Nobel was a leading committee member who, together with other oil company owners, put up a loan to tide Yudenich over the campaign. It was a scheme of mutual advantage. If the companies were ever to reclaim their assets in Baku, they needed the White armies to be properly financed to do the fighting.[21]

Appreciation of the difficulties facing the Whites earned them a degree of sympathy—and a blind eye was turned to the evidence that White commanders aimed to conquer all the territories once ruled by the Romanovs. This is what the slogan of 'Russia One and Indivisible' meant to them. The

Whites played along with Allied demands to the extent of expressing semi-compliance with their commitment to make concessions to the peoples of the borderlands of the former Russian Empire. But they failed to follow this up with action. When General Gustaf Mannerheim, the Finnish army leader, came to Paris to propose an alliance against Sovnarkom and the Red Army, he was sent packing. The Whites flatly refused to recognize Finland's independence. Sazonov's reaction was characteristic: 'We shall get along without them, because Denikin will be in Moscow in two weeks.'[22] Denikin himself was furious with the Allies for recognizing the Finnish government and said that war would come of it.[23] The White armies preferred to fight alone rather than compromise their objective of reconstituting Russia complete with all its territorial appendages. Allied governments reinforced this recalcitrance of the Whites by refusing to give official recognition to Estonia, Latvia and Lithuania; and in the Estonian case they put pressure on Tallinn to provide Yudenich with freedom for his military preparations on Estonian soil.

At the British War Office, Churchill energetically removed impediments to the Whites' procurement of supplies. Eighteen aeroplanes were shipped to the North-West Army.[24] Tanks were also made available. Yudenich, though, faced a different kind of shortage as a commander. Operating from newly independent Estonia rather than Russia itself, he had a problem in recruiting Russian troops. Conscription being impossible, he asked the Allies to enable volunteers to leave the POW camps in Germany; he badly needed experienced officers, and again Churchill was helpful.[25] E. L. Spears, who had headed intelligence operations for a while in northern Russia, put him in touch with Boris Savinkov when he came over from Paris for discussions.[26] Churchill and Savinkov took to each other. Savinkov also had a meeting with Lloyd George but immediately sensed the Prime Minister's ambivalence about increasing the assistance to the Whites. Churchill was obviously the best hope of the Whites, although Savinkov complained that he had an alarming tendency to regard the Russians as British subjects. When pointing to a map of Russia with Denikin's regiments marked with flags, Churchill declared: 'Here, this is my army.'[27] This was not a good way to win the respect of a Russian patriot, but Savinkov restrained himself. Churchill's delusions of grandeur did not matter so long as he continued to support the White cause.

The labour movements in Europe remained an obstacle to such efforts since dockers were militantly opposed to British and French assistance to the anti-Bolshevik armies. Germany was another potential source of supplies for the Whites; its military equipment was cheap after the Great War and there was plenty of it on sale. But German workers persistently held up such exports to Russia and Ukraine.[28] As it happened, this mattered less to Denikin than to other White armies because he could buy material channelled clandestinely through Salonika and Alexandria where no trade union was likely to hold things up.[29]

One crucial piece of assistance came free of charge: Western intelligence reports. After the Allies withdrew their diplomatic corps from Russia they usually relocated their espionage networks to wherever the White military headquarters were operating at the time, whether in southern Russia, mid-Siberia or Estonia. The British with their immense empire had established the world's most comprehensive cable system and could tap into almost any message whenever they wanted.[30] Allied and White networks shared a lot of the information they were gathering. Denikin could rely on being told what the French and British military missions learned from their capitals and from their own secret agencies in Russia and Ukraine.[31] Yudenich too obtained material from ministries in Paris and London.[32] He received information of high quality about the political and social situation in Russia and Ukraine,[33] and he usually got the data he needed on the latest deployments and appointments in the Red Army.[34] And although the commanders of the Whites—Kolchak, Denikin, Yudenich and Miller—had their disputes, they did not let them escalate to the point of disrupting each other's military operations. Each White army used its team of radio telegraphists to keep the others informed of their plans, and Sazonov in Paris was also included in the exchange of telegrams.[35]

The Whites conducted a deep surveillance of planning and conditions in the Red Army. Denikin's agency was called Azbuka (or ABC). Its operatives received a wide licence from him for its spying activity—they even kept an informant inside the National Centre despite the fact that it was firmly allied to his Volunteer Army. Azbuka's penetration of Ukraine had been deep ever since 1918;[36] and as the Volunteer Army grew in strength, the agency increased its geographical range and reported in detail on what Russia's workers thought about the Bolsheviks and on how the peasants were reacting to Soviet rule.[37] In 1918, the technical specialists working for Azbuka had often even succeeded in intercepting conversations between Bolshevik leaders on the Hughes telegraph apparatus;[38] they had also been well informed about exchanges between the Germans and the Soviet authorities.[39]

In 1919 they regularly picked up Moscow's confidential news broadcasts
to local Bolshevik administrations across Russia and caught Soviet messages going to and from European radio stations.[40]

Nonetheless these advantages in intelligence and equipment did Yudenich no good when he started his offensive in October 1919. Kolchak
was fleeing eastwards through Siberia with his beaten army; Denikin was
hastily withdrawing to the Ukrainian south. The Red Army was free to concentrate on the military threat emerging from Estonia. And even though
Zinoviev, the Bolshevik leader in Petrograd, began to panic, the Politburo
in Moscow reacted swiftly. Trotsky and Stalin were dispatched to head the
political co-ordination of defence. Stern measures were taken against the
middle classes across the city. A preventive terror was organized. Stalin ordered that formerly wealthy citizens should be paraded in a line in front of
the Red defences so that they would be the first to be hit by the artillery
fire of the North-Western Army. Trotsky travelled away from the city outskirts and saw military action while stiffening the resolve of his troops and
commanders.[41] As the Whites advanced from Estonia into Russia, they gave
a good account of themselves and for a few days the battle for Petrograd lay
in the balance. But the Red Army had the resources and experience it
needed. Yudenich's offensive collapsed and he was quickly forced into retreat with his men and equipment.

A young Russian observed them as they streamed back towards Estonian
territory:

> We saw a vast column on the move. They had arrived by the same
> branch line as us and disembarked at the same place. There were at
> least 2000 of them, wearing British greatcoats and accompanied by
> light artillery and machine guns. Obviously something was wrong
> at the front, and either the Reds had broken through it or outflanked
> it at Luga. The rumour was that Pskov too was about to surrender.[42]

The rumour was all too true; and although the Civil War was not yet over in
the old borderlands, Russia itself was firmly in the hands of the communists.
Bolshevik celebrations in Petrograd and Moscow were long and vigorous.

1. Lenin in deep thought.

2. Trotsky in his Red Army uniform.

3. An encounter between German and Russian troops in the neutral zone.

4. Living quarters of the peace talks delegations at Brest-Litovsk.

5. The peace talks at Brest-Litovsk before Trotsky joined them. The Russian delegation,
led by Adolf Ioffe (seated second on the right) and Kamenev (to his left).
Karakhan stands second on the right.

6. Sir George Buchanan, elegant and weary.

7. David Francis, impatient and determined.

8. Joseph Noulens, gloomy and fearing the worst.

9. Cheka leaders Felix Dzerzhinski (on the right) and Yakov Peters.

10. Leaders of the People's Commissariat of Foreign Affairs abroad in Berlin in 1922: Chicherin in top hat and carrying an umbrella, Radek in uncharacteristic homburg, and Litvinov in the lightest headwear.

11. Bukharin.

12. John Reed. Note the collarless tunic fashionable among wartime communists.

13. Louise Bryant poses in Russian fur hat and American cowboy boots.

14. Sylvia Pankhurst.

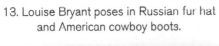

15. A 1919 anti-Spartacist and anti-Bolshevik German poster depicting a Spartacist murdering a family.

16. A poster offering 10,000 marks for the arrest of Karl Radek who went into hiding in Berlin in January 1919.

17. The Spartacists get themselves organized in January 1919.

18. André Marty, communist and organizer of
the French naval mutiny in Odessa in 1919.

19. Kamenev.

20. Béla Kun.

21. Robert Bruce Lockhart.

22. Moura Budberg.

23. Sidney Reilly.

24. Clare Sheridan and son.

25. A Ukrainian recruitment poster for the Red Cavalry.

26. A White Army regiment operating in Siberia in early 1920.

27. An anti-Bolshevik Cossack unit during the Civil War.

28. General Anton Denikin.

29. Sir Paul Dukes, painted after his
intelligence operations in Russia.

30. Agent ST25, also known as Paul Dukes,
in one of his operational disguises.

31. Food pails being carried for distribution during the Civil War in 1919.

32. Turin workers rise against capitalism in 1920.

33. Leaders and militants of the Communist Party of Great Britain in the early 1920s.

34. The Italian delegation to the Second Comintern Congress in July 1920. Their tourist guide on this occasion was the curly-haired, tie-wearing Zinoviev who stands in the middle of the line.

35. Arthur Ransome.

36. Yevgenia Shelepina.

37. Willie Gallacher.

38. Tanks on the streets of Glasgow during the strikes of early 1919.

39. Red Army POWs in Finnish captivity.

40. Session of the Congress of the Peoples of the East in Baku in September 1920. Zinoviev, seated in front of the bell, presided.

41. Leading delegates to the Third Comintern Congress (June–July 1921) gather under the joint statue of Marx and Engels.

42. The Soviet delegation to the talks at Genoa and Rapallo in April 1922. Chicherin stands smiling, third from the left. Litvinov, his deputy, stands second from the right. Krasin is next to him on the left.

43. Joseph Stalin speaking in mourning for Lenin, January 1924.

21. WESTERN AGENTS

The Allied intelligence agents operating in Russia had worked long and hard to prevent the Red victory. None of them failed to appreciate the shortcomings of the Whites; indeed their reports frequently highlighted the urgent need for the White commanders to improve their military potential by paying greater attention to the political and social concerns of people living in the zones they occupied. Western espionage and subversion were conducted in difficult conditions—and the absence of normal diplomatic relations between Soviet Russia and the Allies meant that they had to be imaginative in their activities.

Agents operated in a wide variety of guises. At one end of it, there was the spy Sidney Reilly, who gathered information illicitly and co-organized a plot to overthrow communist rule. Robert Bruce Lockhart, his superior, had covertly initiated that conspiracy while working openly for the British government and enjoying something like official accreditation from the Kremlin. The Allied powers also sent military missions that secretly paid Russians to gather intelligence and carry out subversion. Jean Lavergne busied himself in this way for the French. But military missions were always suspect to the Bolsheviks, and the Allies had to turn to less formal agents for contact with the communist leadership. Raymond Robins of the American Red Cross was the US embassy's main intermediary. He was an American patriot who sincerely believed that a rapprochement between the US and Lenin's Russia was in the interests of both countries. The British reporter Arthur Ransome, a Secret Intelligence Service informant, shared this conviction; he warmed to the Bolsheviks while rejecting the idea of transplanting their ideas and system to Britain. And the French embassy made similar use of Jacques Sadoul before deciding that he was more trouble than he was worth when he identified himself unconditionally with the Bolshevik cause.

The Lockhart Case was a breaking point for the Western agencies. As even unconventional kinds of diplomacy were made impossible, the Allied embassies packed their bags and left Russia altogether; and the Bolshevik leaders, scarred by the experience of Lockhart's trickery, became warier. Nonetheless Ransome continued to be made welcome on his visits and his reports to the British secret service on Kremlin politics retained their immediacy, whereas Robins never returned to Russia. Sadoul stayed in Moscow, but as a convicted deserter and traitor he lost direct contact with French public life.

The West's intelligence networks quickly restored their operations after the damage done by the Cheka raids of September 1918, but it no longer made sense to keep Moscow or Petrograd as their main bases. Allied agents had already renounced any tendencies towards flamboyance. This came hard for a man like George Hill who liked to mix jollity with danger. On arrival in Russia in late summer 1917 he had spent evenings with young grand dukes in the Gypsy encampment at Strelnaya.[1] He had a chum called Colonel Joe Boyle, a Canadian, who was a former US amateur heavyweight boxing champion and used his fists whenever provoked—or even just when he imagined that someone had tried to provoke him.[2] Hill and Boyle disapproved of the October Revolution. But they offered their services to the Bolsheviks in getting the trains moving again around the Moscow regional network because the Western Allies still hoped to keep Russia in the war. Adolf Ioffe, who worked at that time in the Petrograd Soviet's Military-Revolutionary Committee, gratefully signed personal affidavits for them— he overlooked the carping tone of Boyle's insistence that they should be addressed by their military ranks rather than as Comrade Boyle and Comrade Hill.[3]

Their greatest escapade had involved them in transporting the Romanian gold reserve and crown jewels across Russia and Ukraine to Iasi in eastern Romania at the request of Ambassador Diamandy in December 1917. The Romanians had deposited them in Moscow for safekeeping in time of war. Boyle and Hill travelled down from Petrograd by train no. 451 in the carriage of the former empress.[4] The valuables were held in the Russian state vaults, and permission to move them had to be obtained from Moscow's military commandant Nikolai Muralov. Since it was a time when the Bolsheviks and the Allies were still trying to avoid a rupture, Muralov gave his consent. Boyle and Hill prudently packed the valuables into wicker baskets to avoid untoward attention as they moved the heavy load across Moscow to their waiting train. The next stage of the journey involved a route through the lines of Russian and Ukrainian forces ranged against each other near Bryansk.[5] No sooner had this danger been surmounted than the engine became caught in a snowdrift 120 miles north of Kiev. As if this was not bad enough, the crew was hit by shots fired by a Ukrainian army detachment which decided that they were Russian invaders—this was indeed a time of chaotic uncertainty. Boyle and Hill intervened to keep the train moving onwards to Kiev and some temporary safety before attempting the last stage of the journey to Romania.[6]

They used subterfuge and a degree of compulsion, including holding a gun to their driver's head, as they left for the Ukrainian–Romanian border. Arriving at Iasi on 24 December after a trip of nine days they received the thanks of Prime Minister Ionel Bratianu. The King bestowed the Grand Cross of the Crown of Romania on Boyle and the Order of the Star of Romania on Hill.[7]

Returning to Moscow, Hill lived a double life after the Brest-Litovsk treaty. While helping Trotsky to set up a Soviet air force, he established a secret network of informants and couriers across Russia and Ukraine.[8] He also liaised with Savinkov.[9] In the same weeks he sponsored and led irregular units in night raids on German army camps on Ukrainian territory. Hill blew up gasometers in towns where the Germans were garrisoned—and he supervised the sabotage of coal mines by pouring sand into their pumping systems.[10] When the nature of his activities came to the notice of the German secret service, it dispatched an agent to assassinate him at the Moscow Aviation Park. Hill spotted the danger at the last moment. He fought off the agent in an alleyway, leaving him with a bleeding head and triumphantly stealing his Mauser.[11] The Germans made another attempt by putting a time bomb in his office. Hill's sixth sense of jeopardy helped him and he got rid of the device before it exploded.[12] Not all his couriers were as lucky. Two of them were discovered and executed on their way to Murmansk; a further six perished in another of his operations.[13]

After the Allies had seized Archangel, Hill heard that Trotsky had given the order for his arrest.[14] He went undercover. Until then he had worn uniform but now he burned his English clothes. He had several young women working for him. He appreciated their skill in using ciphers and sewing messages into clothing—the messages were produced with the use of a dictionary and coding card. Hill kept a bottle of petrol within reach in case of a Cheka raid when he would need to destroy evidence.[15] Along with three of his women he rented premises as the supposed owner of a sewing business and assumed the false identity of George Bergmann, pretending to be a Russian of Baltic-German descent.[16] For some days he stayed indoors to let his beard grow and told the neighbours he was recovering from a bout of malaria. Then he found a job at a cinematograph studio as a film developer. With a ginger beard and hands discoloured by chemicals, he could easily walk around Moscow unidentified. Regular employment entitled him to a ration card, which meant that he could get food without flaunting his money and attracting undesirable attention. The hours of work—from six in the evening till eleven at night—enabled him to work as a spy during the hours of daylight.[17] The other bonus of the job was that he was able to view the latest official newsreels before release.[18]

Throughout the summer of 1918, Hill created two chains of informers and couriers: one stretched south to the Black Sea, the other went north to the White Sea.[19] In Moscow, he maintained eight clandestine apartments for his operatives.[20] By the autumn he was running a hundred couriers.[21] For his northern chain he organized a route out to Vyatka from Moscow on the Trans-Siberian railway, then up the branch line to Kotlas and beyond.[22] Although this quickened the delivery of reports, it still took twelve to fifteen days to get a message to the British base in Archangel.[23] Hill also paid acquaintances at the Khodynka radio station north of Moscow to send marconigrams direct to the War Office in London for onward transmission to the Russian north—it was not the Cheka but German counter-intelligence which put an end to this dodge.[24]

In October 1918, Hill left with the Lockhart party for Finland but was ordered to go back into northern Russia to help repair the recent organizational damage instead of returning immediately to the United Kingdom. Mission completed, he reached London on Armistice Day.[25] Despite his tiredness, he received an assignment to go to southern Russia with Sidney Reilly in December. Reilly had been running his own separate operation concurrently with Hill's earlier in the year. Now they joined forces. Their instructions were to make for the Volunteer Army's headquarters at Rostov-on-Don disguised as merchants seeking to restore international trade.[26] Arriving shortly before the New Year, they bridled at the condescension shown them by British military officers.[27] Hill and Reilly had a lengthy discussion with Generals Denikin and Krasnov; but since the telegraph system was in some chaos at the time, Hill went down to Odessa to communicate with London before leaving for England with the written report.[28] He thought poorly of Denikin's political set-up and felt he had a lot to learn about ruling a country. On the military side, Reilly was damning about the Volunteer Army's readiness. The equipment and provisioning left much to be desired, and Reilly predicted a hard struggle ahead for Denikin.[29] Hill's mood fell further in Odessa. The French high command had signalled the city's low point on their global priorities list by garrisoning the city with troops from their Senegalese colony.[30] When he got back to London, Hill conveyed his impressions in person to the Foreign Office and the War Office and to the many MPs who contacted him.[31]

He returned yet again to southern Russia after his stay at the Peace Conference, visiting General Denikin in Yekaterinodar.[32] Reilly went back to tending his business interests while paying attention to the Soviet scene from afar. Seeing a chance of making money if the Whites won the Civil War, he wrote to John Picton Bagge in Odessa claiming that the British were being left behind by the French in preparing for this. He commented on how the French government had helped to set up a Paris agency for future commercial, industrial and financial activity in Russia.[33] Reilly wrote a lengthy memorandum on 'The Russian Problem', arguing the need to bang together the heads of Denikin and the leaders of Finland, Poland and the other 'bordering states' with a view to bringing down Bolshevism in Moscow.[34]

Mansfield Cumming's willingness to gamble in selecting agents for the Secret Intelligence Service was not confined to Maugham, Hill and Reilly. One of his inspired choices was Paul Dukes, who until 1914 had worked as a répétiteur at the Imperial Mariinski Theatre and helped conductor Albert Coates with preparations for Stravinsky's *Nightingale*.[35] Dukes's father was a Congregational minister and staunch anti-Papist who often had to change incumbencies because deacons objected to his authoritarian style of leadership.[36] Paul, a sickly child, showed an early talent for music. The Rev. Dukes had a future in mind for him as a chapel organist, but Paul rebelled in his mid-teens and ran away from home with less than four pounds in his pocket. He worked his way from Holland to Poland by teaching English, and his earnings enabled him to enrol as a student at the St Petersburg Conservatoire.[37] Young Dukes lodged for a while with Sidney Gibbes, tutor to the Imperial family, who sometimes took him to Nicholas II's residence at

Tsarskoe Selo. When war broke out, the British embassy employed him to produce daily wartime summaries of the Russian press for Ambassador Buchanan.[38]

In February 1917, according to his own account, Dukes became 'a fiery revolutionary' and took to the streets against the Romanovs.[39] Evidently his friendship with Gibbes had not turned him into an admirer of Nicholas II. Soon afterwards he returned to London to work for the novelist John Buchan at the Department of Information. One of his assignments was to go to Paris under the alias of Dr Robinson to examine Bolshevik correspondence intercepted by the French secret services.[40]

Steadily the scope of his ambition was widening and Buchan proved an understanding boss, allowing Dukes to return to Russia to report on the general situation under cover of a job with the YMCA in Samara and another with the Boy Scouts on the Siberian border.[41] (The YMCA worked closely with the American authorities and set up facilities for the US military expedition to Siberia.)[42] Dukes discharged his tasks impressively and, when Buchan recommended him for more serious clandestine work, a message was sent calling him back to London.[43] As yet he was unaware of what awaited him at the interview in Mansfield Cumming's office in July 1918.[44] The office was like nothing Dukes had seen before. On his desk Cummings kept a bank of six telephones, numerous model aeroplanes and submarines, various test tubes and a row of coloured bottles.[45] Dukes talked so nervously that Cumming was going to fail him as an effete musician until he expressed an interest in the collection of firearms displayed on the wall. Cumming sat him down again and restarted the interview.[46] The outcome was that Dukes received twenty-four hours to think over the invitation to become an agent.[47] When he accepted, Cumming brightly enjoined him: 'Don't go and get killed.' The Secret Intelligence Service expected its men to learn on the job, and Dukes was disconcerted to find that the training course lasted no longer than three weeks.[48]

His first task was to go to Russia and gather information on 'every section of the community', on the scale of support for the communists, on the adaptability of their policies and on the possibilities for a counter-revolution. No Briton knew the streets of Petrograd better and he was raring to go. Cumming let his new agent ST25 decide for himself the best way of getting back on to Russian soil.[49] He started his journey on 3 January 1918 by boarding an American troopship bound for northern Russia. Trying to make his way on foot to Petrograd, he found that the Soviet authorities were guarding the roads to the south. So instead he went to Helsinki, from where he took a train across the Russian border. Having visited Moscow, he moved to Smolensk and Dvinsk near the German front. In February he went to Samara, where the Socialist-Revolutionary leadership had established their anti-Bolshevik government. In his diary he mentioned Arthur Ransome, Yevgenia Shelepina and Harold Williams as being among his acquaintances—a politically broad bunch of people. By the end of June he was in Vologda for a few days before going up to Archangel, Kandalaksha and Pechenga and making his way back to London on 15 July.[50]

Dukes did not stay for long. On 12 August he left again for Archangel on a Russian trip that lasted till early October, when he made for Britain's intelligence base in Stockholm. After a brief respite it was back into Russia for another assignment until early December. A trip to Helsinki followed before he went on yet another Russian mission.[51] One of his jobs was to support the National Centre in Moscow. Its leaders were at first reluctant to accept British money since they wanted their efforts to stay strictly in Russian hands, but the financial assistance from Kolchak had broken down and they agreed to take Dukes's cash. Dukes also met with the Tactical Centre, a clandestine political body which had formed itself to challenge Bolshevik rule throughout Russia, and made contact with Yudenich's North-Western Army. Although none of these organizations was effective in its subversive activity, each supplied him with valuable intelligence about conditions in Soviet Russia. This partnership came to an end when the Cheka penetrated the National Centre and the Tactical Centre and arrested many of the leaders.[52] His informants obtained illicit material for him from the offices of Sovnarkom.[53]

Dukes showed physical courage and, doubtless helped by his theatrical experience, a talent for disguise. Piecing together the stories he told her, his widow later called him the Scarlet Pimpernel of the October Revolution. He even enlisted in the Red Army. By volunteering, he knew he could join a regiment led by a commander who was a secret anti-Bolshevik.[54] This was not the quixotic move it might seem:

> Apart from greater freedom of movement and preference over civilians in application for lodging, amusement, or travelling tickets, the Red soldier received rations greatly superior both in quantity and quality to those of the civilian population. Previous to this time I had received only half a pound of bread daily and had had to take

my scanty dinner at a filthy communal eating house, but as a Red
soldier I received, besides a dinner and other odds and ends not
worth mentioning, a pound and sometimes a pound and a half of
tolerably good black bread, which alone was sufficient, accustomed
as I am to a crude diet, to subsist on with relative comfort.[55]

Dukes travelled about Russia under the alias of artillery commander V. Pi-
otrovski.[56] The runaway pianist became a Red Army officer who filed regular reports to London from whatever place he was moved to.

He had just as many adventures as Hill. Whereas Dukes was modest and
discreet in his memoirs, it would seem that he personally rescued two of
the former emperor's nieces, making himself into a human bridge across a
dyke at one point. A couple of Englishwomen also owed their lives to him,
as did a merchant called Solatin who had tumbled from wealth and influence to destitution after 1917. Dukes and his couriers ran fearful risks—at
least one of them was trapped and shot by the Cheka. He was once pursued
so hotly that he hid in a tomb in a graveyard. The sight of him emerging
from it next morning terrified a passer-by.[57] But he was not just the Pimpernel. His couriers helped him finance counter-revolutionary enterprises
and gather information that was urgently needed in London—and one of
his subordinates fondly recorded him as having been a person of great de-
cency.[58] The reports that Dukes relayed to the Secret Intelligence Service
were concise and vivid. He treasured the spectacle of striking workers who
sang the Marseillaise while carrying a banner that read: 'Down with Lenin
and horse meat, up with the Tsar and pork!'[59]

Whatever may explain the disarray of Western policy and activity in Russia, it was not the absence of efficient spying networks. In 1918 the British
were already picking up Soviet cable traffic to Europe—and when in June
they came across a message from Trotsky to Litvinov, they kept it for their
own information and prevented it from reaching Litvinov.[60] In the following
year a Government Code and Cypher School was created on Lord Curzon's
recommendation and quickly proved its worth. Among its employees was
the leading former Russian Imperial cryptanalyst Ernst Fetterlein, who provided his services after escaping Soviet Russia. Fetterlein was the first director of the School and scarcely any wireless traffic from Moscow was
invulnerable to his attention and that of his Russian colleagues.[61]

Although it had been the American spy network that suffered worst in
the Cheka raids of September 1918, the US never let up in its activity in

wireless interception. Chicherin conducted a lively traffic with Baron Rosen in Berlin seeking a rapprochement between Germany and Soviet Russia; he had no inkling that the Americans were regularly scrutinizing these exchanges.[62] The German Foreign Office was divided into two factions, one supporting an alliance and the other wanting to postpone any decision. The first faction saw the communist governments of Russia and Hungary as offering good trading opportunities for Germany; its advocates supposed that this was achievable on the agreed basis that communism would not be exported into German cities and that Lenin would come to terms with a 'social-democratic or democratic government'. At a time when Denikin's forces were trampling Red resistance in southern Russia and Ukraine it was not implausible to think that Sovnarkom might come to such an accommodation. Against this proposal for foreign policy stood the second faction, which contended that Germany's future interest lay in supporting the Whites and earning their permanent gratitude for making life difficult for the Bolsheviks.[63]

Western intelligence agencies generally offered a sound analysis of conditions in Soviet Russia. They reported that the Red Army, weak in its early months, was getting stronger. This came through the reports of all the British agents. It was also the opinion of people in French intelligence like the wonderfully named Charles Adolphe Faux-Pas Bidet who had helped to expel Trotsky from France in 1916. He was therefore a marked man when undertaking a mission to Russia in 1918 and was swiftly arrested. Trotsky enjoyed the opportunity of interrogating him, using sarcasm rather than threats against his former tormentor. When released on 17 January 1919, Faux-Pas Bidet at his debriefing duly emphasized the growing strength of Soviet rule.[64]

While most agents agreed on this burgeoning strength, Arthur Ransome went further and insisted that the Bolsheviks were nowhere near as bloody as they were painted. This caused controversy in British governing circles, and Bruce Lockhart wrote in the *London Morning Post* that he should keep quiet because he had been out of Russia for half a year.[65] Lockhart went round claiming to be a diplomat pure and simple and Ransome—agent S76—affected to be just a journalist: neither disclosed their work for the Secret Intelligence Service. As it happened, the Secret Intelligence Service shared Lockhart's reservations about Ransome but concluded, on balance, that he did 'quite good work for us'. Ransome was therefore sanctioned to return on the pretext of collecting Bolshevik pamphlets for the British Museum.

His British handlers assumed they could filter out the pro-Soviet bias from his reports and obtain something useful for themselves since no one else could get as close to the Kremlin leaders.[66] Ransome, resourceful as ever, made the best of a bad job by using Lockhart's criticism as a sort of passport to secure interviews with the supreme party leadership. He had missed the October Revolution, but no correspondent after 1917 shuttled quite so easily between Russia and the West.[67]

The results of Western intelligence activity were mixed, through no fault of the agents themselves. There is in fact no evidence that Churchill or Curzon took up the anti-Soviet cause because they were decisively influenced by the secret reports of Dukes, Reilly and Hill or by the *Times* articles of Harold Williams. Churchill and Curzon were political militants against the Bolsheviks from the moment they heard of the October Revolution, and their belligerence was only reinforced by material forwarded to them as ministers. Similarly it is impossible to show that Lloyd George softened his treatment of Russia as the result of Ransome's purrings. Undoubtedly the energetic secret agents and decryption experts of the Allied powers supplied their political masters with information of high quality. In trying to influence politics, they were motivated by patriotism and a sense of adventure (and, in Reilly's case, by financial greed). All of them but Ransome detested communism—and even Ransome did not want it for Britain. But although they often tried to be backseat drivers, the holders of supreme public office—Wilson, Lloyd George and Clemenceau—took little notice unless the received advice conformed to what they themselves wanted.

22. COMMUNISM IN AMERICA

Europe's radical socialists, enthused by the October Revolution and the founding of Comintern, broke away from the old parties of the left. In Italy the Socialist Party burst apart over questions of war, international solidarity and revolutionary struggle. The same happened in France as the socialists lost their far-left wing to communism. Out of these ruptures came the French Communist Party and the Italian Communist Party, which were immediately admitted to Comintern.

Communist organizations also began to sprout across the Atlantic. The US political scene was a peculiar one. No country in the world had more refugees from the Russian Empire. Most of them had no intention of making the long trip back to Russia or its borderlands, but their interest in what happened there was intense. On the east coast, especially in New York, many Russian Jews warmed to a government promising to build a society without social or national discrimination. They were not the only immigrants whose communities provided fertile ground for communist evangelism. Finns, Serbs and Poles too were responding to the appeal to make America a better place for the poor who lived and worked in the industrial cities. The US melting pot had not yet rendered them deaf to militants who suggested that far-left political policies would improve their lives. Although those who joined groups dedicated to communism were a small minority, they made a lot of noise with increasing confidence. The American authorities grew concerned about the possibility that Soviet-style ideas might take root. Conditions in the manufacturing and mining districts could be gruelling. The Socialist Party of Eugene Debs had for years shown the potential that existed to challenge the political establishment, and in June 1918 Debs himself was arrested for campaigning against America's entry into the Great

War. Now that a communist state existed in Russia, there was reason to worry that communists would cause still greater trouble.

The first steps in American communist organization were taken in August 1919 when the Communist Labor Party was formed after a split in the Socialist Party. A few days later the rival Communist Party of America was set up. Despite alarming the US authorities, the two creations failed to gain Moscow's complete approval since Comintern liked to be able to deal with a single communist party in each country. The Bolsheviks themselves had been notorious splitters before 1917, but now they put all this behind them and called for centralism and discipline. The American disarray annoyed them. The Communist Party of America and the Communist Labor Party engaged in ceaseless polemics. At the same time they shared an admiration for Lenin and Trotsky, the October Revolution and Soviet Russia. They praised industrial and agrarian reforms under Sovnarkom's rule. They depicted Lenin's foreign policy as being oriented towards peace; they believed that only communists could put a permanent end to war. They showered plaudits on Trotsky and the Red Army and represented the Bolsheviks as innocent victims of reactionary internal and external forces. The American communists regarded dictatorship and terror as a necessity forced on Russian communists by the military situation. They esteemed the way the Soviet authorities had pulled Russia together with centralism, discipline and order.

Yet from their inception they were consumed by hostility to each other. Charles Ruthenberg, leader of the Communist Party of America, proclaimed: 'We affirm our opposition to unity with the Communist Labor Party.'[1] The two organizations fought a bitter struggle as each carried banners and pasted up posters in defence of Soviet Russia in separation from the other. They celebrated May Day as an occasion to gain support for the Russian communist cause. They sold booklets by Lenin, Trotsky and other Bolshevik leaders. They turned up to hear John Reed and Louise Bryant speaking at Madison Square Garden about their experiences in Petrograd and Moscow. They rejoiced at living in an age which they thought would give birth to a world communist society. But they never considered uniting to help bring that about.

While the two American communist organizations expended energy on their rivalry, the Finnish Information Bureau in New York led by Ludwig Martens and Santeri Nuorteva since 1918 retained some usefulness for the

Soviet government—and in the following year Martens and Nuorteva received instructions from Chicherin to run a Bureau of Information on Soviet Russia from the same offices.[2] In truth the Finnish and Soviet Russian Bureaux were a single operation. On 27 May 1919 Maxim Litvinov wrote to Martens: 'The aim of rapprochement with America has run like a red thread through all our foreign policy this last year.' The Soviet leadership by then were aiming their economic concessions policy at the US in preference to other countries. Martens and Nuorteva were turning into political salesmen. They even contended that if the Americans were to assume responsibility for Russian state debts, the Kremlin was willing to turn over vast territories to them.[3] Obviously this was an initial bargaining ploy: if President Wilson showed the slightest interest, full negotiations could begin. At the same time the Information Bureau maintained its pressure on Boris Bakhmetev to vacate the Russian embassy building in Washington and hand over the funds under its control.[4] Things seemed to be looking brighter for the communists when the espionage case against John Reed was abandoned.[5] The charges had been linked to his anti-war activity in 1917 and although he remained an irritant for the US authorities he would have brought any court into ridicule if proceedings were instituted against him so long after the end of the war. The better option seemed to be to pull him in when he attempted anything directly subversive on behalf of the American communist movement.

On 12 June 1919 the Information Bureau suffered a police raid which yielded compromising material on Martens and Nuorteva. Cash had flowed into the Bureau from an unidentified source thought to be the Soviet government—and Martens had been able to replenish the Bureau's account as expenditure continued, keeping the balance between $5,000 and $9,000. Nuorteva had regular contact with subversive organizations; he also accepted invitations to give public speeches. The Information Bureau sought contact with groups in favour of revolution throughout North America, including Mexico. Martens and Nuorteva simultaneously campaigned for the resumption of full diplomatic and commercial relations between Russia and the US.[6]

The police leaked their findings to the press and the *New York Times* led the attack on the Bureau by reporting that Martens had been registered in England as a 'Hohenzollern subject'.[7] This kind of comment was meant to identify him as a German alien. In fact Martens was a Russian of German descent, born and brought up in the Russian Empire. The same newspaper claimed that the Bureau had compiled a list of Americans to be arrested in Russia. There was also a report that the Bureau had received a letter promising $10,000 for spreading revolutionary propaganda across the Mexican border. As was admitted by the *New York Times*, the Bureau resisted the offer, suspecting that it came from an agent provocateur. But this did not persuade the newspaper to let up in its campaign and its editorials continued to lambast the Bureau.[8] Yekaterina Breshkovskaya, a veteran Socialist-Revolutionary refugee widely known abroad as the 'grandmother of the Russian Revolution', received space to assert that Lenin and Trotsky were Germany's stooges and that the German officer corps was running the Red Army.[9] This was complete nonsense, but the editor was hoping to play on the prejudices of those Americans who might have a sneaking sympathy for Russian communists but had become hostile to the Germans since the war.

The Bureau hit back by beginning court proceedings for the return of its papers—an option that would have been denied them under Bolshevik rule.[10] Martens and Nuorteva had lived for years in the US, making considerable careers for themselves as émigrés. Martens had been vice-president of the Weinberg and Posner engineering company; Nuorteva had been a successful journalist and in 1907 had been elected to the Finnish Sejm. They knew the ways of the American establishment and had funds for suitable legal advice in pursuit of Soviet ends.

Martens and Nuorteva also made commercial approaches to big American firms and were in correspondence with Henry Ford, J. P. Morgan Jr and Frank A. Vanderlip. They promised ready finance, to the value of $200 million, if a deal could be quickly sealed.[11] By spring 1919 the Information Bureau had produced its shopping list of Russia's requirements, presumably on instructions from Moscow, stating that Sovnarkom wanted to enter the US market and purchase railway equipment, agricultural and factory machinery, mining and electrical equipment, cars and lorries, printing presses, tools, typewriters, textile goods, chemicals, shoes, clothing, medicines, canned meats and fats. The only large industrial item missing from their list was military supplies—this must have been thought too likely to provoke a response that would damage the chances of procuring the other items at a time when American troops remained on active service in northern Russia and Siberia. Martens and Nuorteva simultaneously dangled Rus-

sian natural and agricultural products before the eyes of American manufacturers. The Soviet authorities, they claimed, had grain, flax, hemp, timber, minerals, furs, hides and bristles for immediate sale. This was an
implausible idea in a year of growing food shortages in Russia, and wheat
and rye exports in particular would have been hard to organize in the face
of peasant revolts. At any rate the Bureau publicized Soviet official willingness to deposit $200 million in gold in European and American banks to
cover the initial deals.[12]

Its determination was rewarded in September 1919 when a contract was
drawn up with the Antaeus Export and Import Company which wanted to
buy furs from Petrograd. Another deal was put together for Soviet Russia
to import pork and corned beef via the National Storage Company.[13] While
the British and French governments continued to ban trade with the territory under Soviet rule, a small breach in the Allied economic barriers was
achieved in America.

This phenomenon inevitably made the US authorities edgy about the
spread of communist influence from Russia. With President Wilson ailing,
Attorney General Alexander Mitchell Palmer sprang into action—had the
President been in better health he might have asked him to be more cautious. On 8 November 1919 the Department of Justice arranged for two
hundred 'Russian Bolsheviki' to be taken into custody and an official announcement was made: 'This is the first big step to rid the country of these
foreign trouble makers.'[14] All were alleged to belong to the Union of Russian
Workers as irreconcilable subversives. Bomb-making materials were said
to have been found as well as Red flags, revolvers, printing presses and bank-
notes ready for circulation. A further sequence of raids was organized in
New York, Chicago, Pittsburgh, Philadelphia, Cleveland, Detroit and Buf-
falo. The Union of Russian Workers, which had been founded by Bill Shatov
(though in 1917 he left to join the Bolsheviks in Petrograd), was among the
organizations targeted. The most prominent detainees were the anarchist
leaders Emma Goldman and Alexander Berkman, who were accused of having invalid immigration and naturalization papers—and it was emphasized
that they were hostile to political elections and the market economy.[15]

Palmer revelled in the publicity stirred up by his raids; it was widely believed that he had fixed his sights on standing for the Presidency in the near
future. His officials indicated that a further search was under way to lay
hands on five hundred leading 'Red sympathizers' across the country.[16] On

1 December 1919 Charles Ruthenberg, secretary of the Communist Party of America, was arrested in Chicago.[17]

Although a mass deportation of 'Russian Reds' was in the offing, Nuorteva and Martens were spared arrest—an omission which did not go without adverse comment.[18] An editorial in the *New York Times* was headed 'The Plot against America':

> The testimony of Ludwig Martens before the Lusk committee puts an end to his pretensions as an Ambassador from Soviet Russia. He is not even in the status of an unrecognized Ambassador. His errand here is not diplomatic in any sense. He is here as an enemy of the United States, as the agent of conspirators in Russia who are planning to bring about a bloody revolution in this country and destroy its Government by force.[19]

Nuorteva spoke up for his comrade with the odd claim that Martens had no objection to being deported. Just as bizarrely, Nuorteva added: 'But if he goes he will take a million residents in this country of Russian origin with him. The Soviet Russia Republic [*sic*] has eighty-seven vessels ready to bring them back as soon as the way is open. All they want is to be landed in some safe place where the Soviet Government is in control. Petrograd would suit us.'[20] The press campaign intensified as William C. Bullitt was reported as having had contact with Nuorteva and Martens. The newspapers, at least those not under socialist ownership, aimed to demonstrate that an international conspiracy was at work; and the fact that Bullitt had worked for the State Department and the White House gave a piquant menace to the media assault.[21]

Martens claimed that the Soviet leaders generally limited themselves to 'affirmative propaganda'; but when pressed, he admitted that the Bolsheviks had employed terror. The *New York Times* pointed out that Lenin and Trotsky believed in violent revolution everywhere. One of its editorials went further by levelling the charge that the October 1917 seizure of power was effected 'largely by men from America who went to Russia'.[22] With the exception of Trotsky and Bukharin, it was a fantastic exaggeration to assert that ex-residents of New York had supplied the vanguard of the October Revolution. But the newspaper did not feel the need to stick to provable facts. Wild claims were the norm.

Although Ruthenberg was soon released from prison, 249 communist and anarchist leaders who were held on Ellis Island were loaded on to an old transport ship, the *Buford*, and deported on 21 December 1919. The ship was popularly known as 'The Red Ark'. Their ultimate destination was Soviet Russia and the entire group sang the Internationale before embarkation. They refused to be demoralized, believing that their punishment was yet another sign that the American capitalist class was starting to panic. They elected Berkman as their spokesman, who said that he expected to be greeted by old friends in Moscow. His wife Emma Goldman declared: 'I do not consider it a punishment to be sent to Soviet Russia. On the contrary, I consider it an honor to be the first political agitator deported from the United States.' With her flair for publicity she left nobody in doubt about her confidence: 'Incidentally, I am coming back. The plan we have considered, which I am going to work on particularly, is the immediate organization in Soviet Russia of the Russian Friends of American Freedom. I insist that I am an American. This practice of deportation means the beginning of the end of the United States Government.'[13]

Further deportations followed as Palmer, abetted by a young J. Edgar Hoover in the Bureau of Investigation in the Department of Justice, broke up the early communist groupings, and the organization of support for Comintern became downright dangerous for militants even though they succeeded in producing political literature and holding public meetings, albeit on a smaller scale than before. Nobody could be sure that the authorities would not strengthen the measures against the Communist Party of America and the Communist Labor Party by means of lengthy terms of imprisonment for people who could not easily be deported. The communist Linn A. E. Gale fled to Mexico City and took his *Journal of Revolutionary Communism* with him. He recommended exile as a way of avoiding 'the most savage and brutal penalties' that he predicted would be applied by 'the minions of capitalism'.[24] But somehow the remaining militants reassembled their links and resumed activity; and the Central Executive Committee of the Communist Party of America, cajoled by Moscow, agreed in principle to unification with the Communist Labor Party in mid-March 1920.[25] The number of members was in the tens of thousands and was geographically patchy—in 1920 the Communist Labor Party had only 4,525 members and most of these lived on the eastern side of the country.[26] Discipline, moreover, was shaky. A furore occurred in the same year when Jay Lovestone, a leading young activist, appeared in court as a witness for his friends and forswore any adherence to Leninist principles to save them from a potentially heavy sentence.[27]

The militants recognized the need to bring order into their affairs. If they wanted to join Comintern they would have to demonstrate a capacity to be as dedicated and dynamic as the Bolsheviks. The Communist Party of America laid down its guidelines as follows:

- Don't betray Party work and Party workers under any circumstances.
- Don't carry or keep with you names and addresses, except in good code.
- Don't keep in your rooms openly any incriminating documents or literature.
- Don't take any unnecessary risks in Party work.
- Don't shirk Party work because of the risk connected with it.
- Don't boast of what you have to do or have done for the Party.
- Don't divulge your membership in the Party without necessity.
- Don't let any spies follow you to appointments or meetings.
- Don't lose your nerve in danger.
- Don't answer questions if arrested, either at preliminary hearings or in the court.[28]

Gradually a spirit of conspiratorial comradeship was implanted. Recruits were expected to accept the guidelines or risk being shunned or expelled.

The desirability of such precautions was obvious if the communist revolutionaries were going to make any progress in the US. A 'Red scare' billowed as newspaper editors united against the spread of ideological contagion from the east. Attorney-General Palmer had displayed his combative disposition, and many groups of employers were delighted. Politicians in the Democratic and Republican parties were equally pleased to support him. Industrial strikes were increasingly treated as tantamount to treason and the police used much violence.

In December 1921 a founding Convention was at last held for the united Workers' Party of America, bringing together the Communist Party of America and the Communist Labor Party and placing it under Comintern's authority. Comintern immediately set out its priorities. American communists were to infiltrate and manipulate as many organizations as possible in the US, including associations of farmers and 'Negroes'—indeed the line of recruitment was drawn only at the Ku Klux Klan. Moscow stressed that the Workers' Party had to break out of the confines of the party's immigrant ethnic supporters. Key matters for agitation were to involve a campaign against the current legal restrictions on organizing strikes. Illegal activity was not to be abandoned by the Workers' Party—in fact the undercover leaders and militants were to be regarded as 'the real Communist Party' and were to have permanent precedence over the broad open party. No duty was to be regarded as superior to the calls for support for Soviet Russia. While revolution in the US remained the dream for American communists, their primary obligation was to do whatever was required to sustain the October Revolution in Moscow.[29] Although factionalism continued to plague the Workers' Party of America, this served only to strengthen the Russian hold on its affairs. Whenever a dispute arose it was Comintern headquarters which gave the decisive ruling.

The Soviet leaders were not as wise about America as they thought they were; ideas that worked for communism in Russia did not always find a suitable environment in New York. Max Eastman, Trotsky's admirer and confidant, prepared a memo for him and Lenin, pointing out that capitalism was not on the verge of collapse in America and American workers were not in 'a revolutionary frame of mind'. He asked for Comintern to take better account of this. Eastman had a number of organizational bugbears. He denied that Comintern's emphasis on conspiratorial methods was a sensible one. He also objected to the national and ethnic associations that were still permitted in the party. The 'Slavic federation' was deeply distasteful for him.[30] He jibbed at the endless celebrations of Lenin, the October Revolution and the Red Army and called for American specificities to be analysed and acted upon. He was not alone in sensing that the Workers' Party of America would get nowhere if it was a 'hip-hip-hurrah society' for the celebration of the good news from Russia.[31] Consequently America had less to fear from American communism than American political leaders thought. It was a paradoxical situation. If he had but known it, Attorney-General Palmer would have been pleased that American communists were doing such an effective job of rendering the Workers' Party ineffectual.

The Soviet communist leaders in Moscow reinforced the phenomenon. They felt sure that they knew what was best for communism in every country, and they sprayed their advice worldwide. American communists seldom rebelled against Moscow for long. If there was discontent, it was ultimately resolved by forced submission or expulsion from the Workers' Party. American communism was swaddled from birth in Russian clothing that constricted its growth.

23. SOVIET AGENTS

As the world communist movement emerged into the light in Europe and North America, the Cheka steadily discovered how to operate from the shadows. This was slow work as the Chekists felt their way. But the Politburo had a crucial need for a network of secret agents in the West if it wanted to achieve its political and economic purposes abroad. The Chekist leadership had to start their operations almost from scratch. And the fact that Soviet Russia was the declared enemy of absolutely every other state in the world meant that its foreign activity was under constant close scrutiny. In such an environment it is impressive how much the Chekists managed to achieve.

Intelligence agencies are predictably shy about releasing the names of their employees. This has often opened the door to speculation, and one of the enduring controversies from the early Soviet years is about whether Sidney Reilly was a Cheka agent.[1] Suspicion enveloped him after the temporary destruction of the Allied intelligence networks in autumn 1918. De-Witt Poole, acting consul-general for the Americans in Moscow, had left Russia with the rest of the American diplomatic personnel in those weeks. He had formed a poor opinion of Reilly and sounded an alarm when talking things over with Sir Mansfeldt Findlay at the UK embassy to Norway. Poole recounted the rumours that Reilly was a Cheka agent provocateur. Although the evidence was no more than circumstantial, it worried Findlay enough for him to place it before the Foreign Office and the Secret Intelligence Service. Poole's concerns had sprouted from the discrepancy between what Lockhart had discussed with him and what Reilly had apparently enacted. He wanted the British to investigate the possibility that Reilly had betrayed Lockhart.[2] Kalamatiano, the American secret service leader in Russia, languished in Soviet custody and Poole naturally felt sore about this. Poole had confidence in Lockhart and mistrusted Reilly. It did not cross his mind that Lockhart too might have been less than frank with him in Moscow.

Although Lockhart had private reservations about Reilly's personal integrity,[3] he never queried his political allegiance. Reilly expressed outrage at the insinuations against him and complained to Lockhart, a few weeks after they returned from the Russian capital, about 'those unfortunate libels'.[4] Like Lockhart, he called for a hard line to be taken on Soviet Russia; he described Lloyd George as being soft-headed about Bolshevism and planning to use philanthropy as a 'panacea for all social evils'. He thought the British cabinet failed to understand the menace to civilization that would soon spread abroad if it was not stamped out in Moscow.[5] He rejected the view that the Soviet order was an unworkable or weak one. Having seen it in motion in Russia, he had no doubt that it could be made operational elsewhere.[6]

Was this the play-acting of a double agent? Reilly's patron Mansfield Cumming probed the possibility by asking Commander Ernest Boyce, an old Russia intelligence hand, to conduct an internal enquiry. Boyce's researches revealed a brash man with a chaotic personal life. Reilly did everything to excess; he was abstemious only with drink. He loved women, and it was rare for him to limit himself to a single girlfriend—and on his return to London he went around with a tart who rejoiced in the nickname of Plugger.[7] Reilly was a bigamist, never having divorced his first wife Margaret, who tracked him down and squeezed money out of him in return for her silence. He was a gambler who often risked everything in the casino as in the rest of his life.[8] When he had money he spent it ostentatiously, and high society paid him the attention he craved. He bought a flower for his buttonhole daily at Solomons in St James's Street. He took a suite at the Savoy Hotel and, when this palled, he moved to the Ritz. Reilly seemed the quintessential man about town.[9]

Commander Boyce's enquiry into Reilly extended to having lunch with Robert Bruce Lockhart and his wife Jean at the Langham Hotel in Regent Street in December 1918. He arranged for Jean to arrive earlier than her husband so as to do a bit of judicious questioning. Jean told him that 'Bertie' believed that Reilly would always 'work for the highest bidder'.[10] But even this revelation merely suggested that Reilly was nothing more than a money-grubbing rascal rather than a Chekist, and Cumming felt safe in sending him on yet another Russian mission together with George Hill.[11]

But the whisperings against him continued and it may well have been on his return to London that Cumming called in George Hill and Paul Dukes and set up a separate enquiry.[12] Although Reilly was cleared, Cumming refused to grant him a fixed appointment, offering the excuse that the Foreign Office was the source of the hostility. At any rate the Secret Intelligence Service continued to use Reilly for foreign assignments and throughout his time in London he continued to fire off tirades against Lloyd George's softening of Allied policy on Russia. If he had been a Soviet mole, it is difficult to see why his handlers would have approved of this behaviour at a time when Sovnarkom hoped to turn Western public opinion in favour of diplomatic recognition and commercial acceptance. It is still not impossible that Reilly took money from the Bolsheviks at some other time. But whether he did or not, he could never be a reliable double agent: Reilly's first and last loyalty was to himself and his financial interests.

The Soviet authorities were still finding their way in the activities they promoted abroad. They were juggling two priorities. One was to stir communist parties into life and revolution; the other was to agitate for trade with Russia. At the very time that the Bolsheviks were trying to arrange deals with Western big business they were also sending people and funds to undermine capitalism. This 'contradiction' did not worry the Politburo. Communist leaders assumed that if their best hope was fulfilled—revolution—then it would no longer matter what sums had been given or promised to businessmen in the West. And if things went wrong for communism in Europe, at least Sovnarkom would possess signed contracts to facilitate Russian economic recovery from the years of fighting. Often the same agents were stirring up politics while reassuring businessmen. The Politburo lived comfortably with the paradox. Bolshevik leaders accepted that 'history' was messy and that twists and turns in policy were essential if communism was to triumph. They thrived on the 'contradictions' in world affairs. If Bolsheviks lower down the party did not yet appreciate this situation, surely eventually they would do so—and the prestige and authority of Lenin and his close comrades were deployed to ensure that this came about.

The Soviet agents fostered organizational splits in the parties of the political far left so as to win recruits for Comintern. They sent funds and instructions abroad. They gathered reports on discussions among the great powers. They organized propaganda in translation. As agreements were signed with Western countries, the plenipotentiaries working for People's

Commissariats conducted clandestine activity behind the screen of their legal work. Comintern recruited people from the new communist parties for espionage and subversion on the Kremlin's behalf. In June 1919 the Cheka at last set up an illegal operations department for work abroad.[13] The pace of international activity was steadily being increased. Agents were sent to all continents in the revolutionary cause.

Bolsheviks were expert at spiriting funds across frontiers. They had to be: they had committed themselves to international subversion, and governments and police forces everywhere took them at their word. Russia no longer had diplomatic recognition in any country after the closure of the German, Swiss and Scandinavian missions in the winter of 1918–19.[14] This meant among other things that the Russian plenipotentiaries and couriers lost the facilities associated with diplomatic bags. They carried money on their persons for political purposes at their destinations. This was a hazardous undertaking since countries bordering on Russia teemed with policemen under orders to lay their hands on Kremlin agents, who were marked men and women when passing through customs points. The maintenance of the Allied economic blockade around the territory under Soviet rule aggravated the problem, and trade between Russia and its neighbours fell to a small fraction of what it had been before 1914. (During the Great War there had been a substantial exchange of goods even with Germany via neutral Sweden.) Agents who went on foreign trips to buy goods for Sovnarkom had to bring back what they could pack in suitcases because they could not make wholesale purchases for dispatch as rail freight. They restricted themselves to bringing back medicine, saccharine and other easily carried products.[15]

Alternative options were quickly found. Since 1917 Sovnarkom had confiscated a huge quantity of extremely valuable jewels that were small, light and easily exchangeable for cash—and they were used even before the withdrawal of diplomatic privileges. Louise Bryant was one of the couriers. She agreed to the work after her baggage had been seized in Finland on a journey from Petrograd in the winter of 1917–18. When she asked at the People's Commissariat of Foreign Affairs how to avoid such trouble in future, Ivan Zalkind replied: 'Why, I'll make you a courier for the Soviet government!' The advantage was that she could have her bags sealed with wax and the customs men—at least in Scandinavia—would not touch them. This was how she took official material to 'the Bolshevik minister' Vatslav Vorovski on her next trip to Stockholm. The only drawback was that hoteliers treated her with suspicion as a Soviet agent and she found it hard to get a room for the night.[16] Women were the perfect couriers because they could wear the valuables discreetly round their necks and on their arms. When Yevgenia Shelepina made her final departure from Russia with her future husband Arthur Ransome in 1922 she transported diamonds and pearls worth 1,039,000 rubles by arrangement with Chicherin.[17]

Courier work was not an exclusively female occupation. When Francis Meynell, a director of the London *Daily Herald*, agreed to transport two strings of pearls to the United Kingdom he hid them in a jar of butter; and on one occasion he carried jewels inserted into a box of chocolate creams.[18] Meynell advertised his sympathies so widely that Special Branch asked the Secret Intelligence Service to keep an eye on him.[19] The same authorities were watching over People's Commissar Leonid Krasin when he entered the United Kingdom with jewels in his luggage to the value of over seven million rubles.[20] It was an open secret that many couriers were on assignments that involved more than carrying messages, money or jewellery. Some of them became involved in pro-Soviet organizations; others helped to arrange the circulation of revolutionary literature.[21] The difference between a courier, an agent and an activist was often a blurred one. The Special Branch in London knew what was going on but refrained from arguing for stoppage of the courier facilities. British counter-intelligence found it more convenient to use Soviet emissaries as a way of surveying the political left in the United Kingdom than to block their entry into the country.

In January 1920 John Reed received a million rubles' worth of diamonds for disbursal in the US. His American comrade Krīstap Beika (alias Comintern official John Anderson) received a similar amount. The emergent US communist movement would not lack financial support. The record of such assignments kept by the People's Commissariat of Foreign Affairs in 1919–20 referred to several other countries, including Hungary, Germany, Czechoslovakia, Italy and France.[22] It was not a perfect system, as the heads of Soviet diplomatic missions made clear in their reports to the Kremlin. Yan Berzin in Switzerland in 1918 was disgusted by the quality of couriers sent out to him, claiming that several of them had given speeches in favour of the Mensheviks as they passed through central Europe.[23] Nor was every courier distinguished by basic honesty. Just as they could cross borders in one disguise, so they could abandon their communist errand and run off with the valuables that had been entrusted to them. Lenin huffed and puffed about morality and penalties. But it was difficult at long

range to impose discipline on unruly agents until such time as communist
parties were able to act as enforcers, and even then the system was vulnerable to abuse.

The Soviet missions were also active in translating and publishing communist writings. When Yan Berzin arrived in Berne as Soviet plenipotentiary
in May 1918 he rushed Bolshevik texts into print in German and French. A
group of local translators was employed, and a small publisher was found
outside the city so as to avoid governmental interference. Lenin's *The State
and Revolution* received priority alongside his *The Proletarian Revolution and
the Renegade Kautsky*, and Trotsky's *From the October Revolution to the Brest
Peace Treaty* quickly appeared. Books by Radek, Philips Price and Sadoul
went to press. Profit was not the aim. Moscow was willing to shower whatever finance was required to spread the doctrines of communism.[24]

It was not always necessary to do this through communist agents. When
George Lansbury went to Moscow in February 1920 and mentioned that
his *Daily Herald* was in financial trouble he was offered money to save the
newspaper from falling into the hands of socialists who opposed the Soviet
regime. He addressed the Moscow Soviet and commended communists on
their achievements in economic reconstruction.[25] As part of the deal he
agreed to help publish translated booklets by the Russian communist leadership. The Bolsheviks were people of the printed word. There were marvellous orators among them but their basic premise was that thorough
indoctrination required books to be made available for study—and somehow a flow of revolution would proceed from them. Chicherin told Litvinov
to give the funds to the Swedish communist Fredrik Ström for handing over
to Lansbury. The scheme worked as the newspaper moved leftwards and
advocated direct political action in Britain.[26] The *Daily Herald*'s dependence
on Soviet money became public knowledge after Fetterlein decrypted the
telegrams. Lansbury—an early Soviet dupe—denied trying to hide anything shameful, alleging that he was only counteracting a discreet boycott
by British paper suppliers.[27] A Christian socialist, he wrote that everything
was fine in Russia because there was no religious persecution. Even the Bolsheviks laughed when they heard about it.[28]

Another urgent task for the Cheka and the People's Commissariat of Foreign Affairs was to make sense of public opinion in the West. Before 1917
Lenin and Trotsky had assumed that politics merely reflected big economic
interests. They had generally thought that the outstanding foreign enemies
of the October Revolution—Churchill, Curzon or Clemenceau—were

mere puppets of industrial and financial lobbies in London and Paris. As soon as they came to power they recognized the need to take personalities seriously in international politics. They courted the good opinion of Woodrow Wilson in 1918–19. Despite considering him a capitalist scoundrel, they did not dismiss the possibility that he might be induced to depart from the line preferred by Clemenceau and Lloyd George. Lenin in particular followed the ages-old tradition of clever rulers in seeking to divide and influence the enemies of his government.

A lot of what the Kremlin needed to know could be plucked from the air either by its agents or by the telegraphists they bribed. The gigantic Nauen radio station, twenty-four miles to the west of Berlin, had two masts 850 feet high. It was the biggest installation in the world and could transmit signals as far as New York. Soviet leaders regarded it as their 'window on Europe'. There were only undulating hills and no mountains between the Russian and German capitals and Soviet telegraphists had no problem in getting hold of news of political and military importance for the Bolsheviks.[29] The People's Commissariat of Foreign Affairs used a more traditional method by scrutinizing the Western press for information.[30] Its diplomats examined the newspapers for important news and sent the material back to Moscow.[31] The practical usefulness of their reports was diminished by the fact that they applied the same ideological filter as Lenin and Trotsky. Although Yan Berzin commented on the disastrous impact on Western opinion of Trotsky's handling of the Czech Corps and warned Soviet leaders to take account of the international perspective before acting so precipitately, he undercut his own sound advice by assuring Moscow that he had the evidence that 'proletarian revolution is uninterruptedly growing in all countries'.[32]

The fact that he wrote in this fashion from the stable Swiss capital shows that information was only as good as the Bolsheviks were willing to let it be. They allowed nothing to interfere with their belief that the West was teetering on the revolutionary brink. They had to keep comforting each other with lines from their credo. Otherwise the world would take on an altogether bleaker appearance in their eyes.

Arthur Ransome reinforced their preconceptions. The Kremlin knew that he was no mere journalist since a Cheka report in March 1921 stated that 'Lloyd George's group' had sent Ransome on his latest mission to Moscow.[33] (Soviet leaders were wrong on one detail: they were under the mistaken impression that this was the first time that Ransome came to them

with the sanction of the British government.) Whether Ransome mentioned to the Kremlin that he was the emissary of a specific group is not
known, but it was anyhow an open secret that several British ministers were
displeased about the moves by Lloyd George for a rapprochement with Soviet Russia. The communist leaders had always given a warm welcome to
Ransome because his books burnished their image. They also saw him as
someone who could explain the British political scene to them. Ransome
duly complied and gave an account of the factions in ruling circles, one
led by Lloyd George and the other by Curzon and Churchill. He added
the names of Paul Dukes and Harold Williams as protagonists on the anti-
Soviet side along with Leslie Urquhart, George Hill and Sir George
Buchanan.[34] This was not a bad summary of the leadership and opinion-
formers on the Russian question in the United Kingdom, providing information beyond what could be gleaned from *The Times* and the *Manchester
Guardian*.

Ransome went outside the boundaries of his brief as a British agent
when disclosing to the Cheka what he knew about those people in Soviet
Russia who were obstructing the progress towards a trade treaty with the
United Kingdom. He mentioned Simon Liberman, a Menshevik expert and
ex-businessman working in the timber industry, in this connection. He also
gave encouragement to the Bolsheviks in their global rivalry with Britain
by suggesting that Muslims in Asia were responding better to Soviet than
to British 'diplomatic influence'.[35] Getting into his stride, he commented
that France might be willing to resort to military measures in the Baltic Sea
if this would help to bring down the Soviet government.[36] Evidently the
gangly, eccentric Englishman had his own bias about Western politics and
readily deployed it. And he could not stop himself pandering to the ideological prejudices of the Soviet leaders he met. In his references to Liberman, he was even putting an innocent Russian economic official in jeopardy
of arrest by spreading unfounded rumours about him. The best that may
be said is that Ransome was perhaps only acting like many newspaper reporters in seeking to butter up a politician so as to get information out of
him or her. At any rate it was not his finest hour.

Liberman had already been out of favour with Dzerzhinski, who questioned his loyalty at the start of his employment in the Soviet administration in November 1918. But they patched up their disagreements at the end
of 1920 and Dzerzhinski supported him.[37] Ransome came near to messing
everything up for Liberman. Truly he could be a dangerous acquaintance

for Russians who were not Bolsheviks. British intelligence in any case constantly monitored his political allegiance even while using his services. The *Manchester Guardian*'s editor C. P. Scott was asked for a guarantee that he would not print anything from Ransome that was detrimental to British national interests. Only then was Ransome allowed to go on his Russian mission.[38] The Secret Intelligence Service never felt it could drop its guard with him, especially after learning that he had told Russians that a particular British official was 'an agent of the British government'.[39] In Britain he continued to talk up the Soviet cause at the drop of a hat.[40] Such was Ransome's intimacy with the Kremlin leadership that Litvinov took the trouble to wire him about how to avoid the latest travel difficulties.[41] But the Secret Intelligence Service persisted with Ransome, finding him useful because of 'his friendship with the Bolchevik [sic] leaders' and his capacity to supply 'a lot of most valuable stuff'.[42] A fellow British intelligence operative put the problem about agent S76 succinctly: 'He will report what he sees, but he does not see quite straight.'[43]

Lenin and Trotsky saw things no straighter. Having seized power in Petrograd in a spirit of millennial optimism, they could not afford to let themselves think that capitalism might survive and flourish around the world. They sieved out information that might deflate their optimism, preferring the news that pointed to trouble for the post-war settlement in Europe. They looked keenly for disturbances in central Europe. Viewed from the Kremlin, Western countries appeared ripe for Soviet-style revolutions.

24. THE ALLIED MILITARY WITHDRAWAL

The Soviet communist leadership may have magnified the prospects of 'European revolution' but it did not invent them out of nothing. Country after country to the west of Russia was experiencing disorder and discontent. Russia itself emerged under Bolshevik rule from years of civil war and foreign armed intervention. The victor powers in the Great War had irresistible force at their disposal if only they could muster the will to deploy it. But they increasingly lacked that will. The Western Allies had not had properly agreed strategic aims since at least 1917, when America joined them.

After the defeat of Yudenich's North-Western Army outside Petrograd in October 1919, Denikin and the Volunteer Army became the last hope for the White cause. Yudenich tried to transfer his men in British vessels to southern Russia. Denikin himself was allowing the Volunteer Army to rest after the forced retreat to Crimea; his troops needed time for recovery and re-equipment. The French expeditionary force had departed Odessa in April 1919; the Americans who had landed in Siberia spent the second half of the year straggling eastwards from Omsk. Lloyd George had then ordered the British withdrawal and in August 1919 General Henry Rawlinson went to northern Russia to discuss evacuation. His plan was for a complete pull-out by mid-October, but he failed to persuade General Yevgeni Miller's small White force to accompany the departing British troops—and even General Poole continued to say that he himself could advance on Kotlas and Vologda if reinforcements were made available to him.[1] While continuing to supply equipment and military advisers to Denikin's beleaguered forces, the United Kingdom now left the fighting entirely to the Russians. Although the Japanese maintained their armed occupation in eastern Siberia, the foreign military intervention against Soviet rule was all but over.[2] The Allied Supreme Council still refused to make peace with the Bolsheviks; instead it resolved in late December to create a cordon sanitaire between Russia and central Europe. Bordering states would be helped to defend themselves and keep Bolshevism in quarantine behind Russian lines.[3]

Lloyd George was rumoured to want to go further and negotiate a peace treaty with the communists regardless of the other Allies.[4] But on 16 January 1920 the Supreme Council limited itself to resolving to lift its economic blockade; and this decision was confirmed at its London meeting on 26 February.[5]

Litvinov delightedly told the Press Association in Copenhagen that the Allied powers would soon have to make 'a formal and unqualified peace' with Soviet Russia.[6] Bolshevik commentators had always said that greed would bring foreign capitalists to press for a resumption of trade. Even so, the ending of the Allies' blockade was only a decision in principle, which was not the same thing as help from the government in facilitating the making of contracts and financial transfers. If Western businessmen dealt with the men of the Kremlin, they would be doing so at their own risk. The Allied powers still worried about Sovnarkom's commitment to revolutionary expansion and about the activities of its agents and supporters in the West; they were equally agitated by the nationalization of foreign property in Russia since the October Revolution. Furthermore, the Bolsheviks hung on to Western prisoners—and their governments demanded their release before any trading could be sanctioned by treaty. The Allies were angry, too, about the Soviet disregard for the rule of law. Western leaders—or most of them—had yet to be convinced that Sovnarkom would allow businesses to operate without political interference. The French, indeed, were incensed by any suggestion that entrepreneurs of the Allied countries should re-enter Russia.

The Estonian government feared a Red Army invasion after Yudenich's crushing defeat. Ministers had no confidence in the Allied Supreme Council and its talk about a regional barrier under Western tutelage. They looked after themselves by beginning talks with Moscow in November.[7] Soviet Russia had its own pragmatic reasons for a Baltic settlement. If Tallinn became an entrepôt for Russian international commerce, Estonia could be its window on to the West. When the world learned of the profits to be made, other foreign states would surely see the advantage of recognizing Sovnarkom.[8] Wanting to appease its powerful neighbour, Estonia ordered the disarming of Yudenich's forces on its territory.[9] Clothes and equipment were taken from the North-Western Army.[10] A Soviet–Estonian truce was agreed while the discussions continued—and there was nothing the Allied missions in Tallinn could do to halt the process: independent Estonia was acting independently.[11] And on 4 February 1920 the Estonian government signed a diplomatic and commercial treaty with Soviet Russia.[12]

The Kremlin advertised its plan to pay for imports with its gold reserves and to sell Russian natural resources to the highest bidders. Western businessmen flocked to Tallinn. Many were not distinguished by their honesty, but all of them were willing to take the gamble of investing in Russia's international trade. In fact the goods traffic to Petrograd outweighed what went in the opposite direction by a factor of ten to one. Urban Russia remained unproductive and the villages were no longer covering the country's requirements. Flax and veneers were practically all that the People's Commissariat of Foreign Trade could lay its hands on for sale abroad.[13] According to the Estonians, a third of Russian imports consisted of agricultural machinery and equipment.[14] Traditionally Russia had exported food, paper and leather to Europe, but now these items had to be bought abroad.[15] The Estonians were happy to oblige. Estonia had barely started to recover from war and revolution and its ministers now judged it in the national interest to enable the Russians to acquire the products they wanted. The transit fees were too valuable to be ignored.

Soviet leaders continued to press for recognition by the Allies. At the end of 1919 Litvinov affected surprise that the Bullitt proposals of earlier months had not been acted upon. This was nonsense: Lenin on his side had never been genuinely committed to ending the Civil War except with a Red victory. Litvinov was really trying to appeal to all those lobbies in the West which might be tempted to trade with Soviet Russia. And a sequence of events appeared to confirm that the ice was beginning to crack. In mid-January 1920 Radek was released from German custody and sent back to Russia across Poland. He had by then decided that the 'European socialist revolution' was not going to happen very quickly, but he thought that his own liberation indicated the growing willingness of German ministers to adopt a gentler line in their Russian policy. The Soviet leadership made its own moves in the same period. On 7 March the Cheka resolved upon a mass release of seventy-four prisoners with English names from its prisons and camps.[16] The purpose was easy to guess. The Bolsheviks had identified the United Kingdom as the likeliest of the great powers to come to an accommodation immediately after the war. A show of goodwill might be useful before negotiations commenced.

But even though Lloyd George was eager for commerce to be resumed, it would take time for him to clear away the political obstacles. The next move for Soviet leaders was therefore to set their caps at Sweden. The Swedes themselves wanted a share of the Russian trade and had industrial products for sale. Lev Krasin, who in 1918 had served in the Soviet mission in Berlin, joined Litvinov in Stockholm on 1 April 1920. While Litvinov handled the diplomacy, Krasin would lead any talks on trade. Krasin himself was viewed favourably in Europe—by some at least. The *Manchester Guardian* had picked him out as a man to be trusted, its Moscow correspondent W. T. Goode offering this warm portrait: 'In the prime of his powers, sparkling with energy, Krassin [*sic*] is a well-set-up man, with black hair and full beard, a dark but bright complexion, and an engaging man. He is supremely competent, and his personality and conversation convey that impression swiftly to those with whom he speaks.'[17] Having worked in Germany and Russia before 1917 as a manager in the Siemens-Schuckert company, Krasin had an intimate experience of industry. His post in 1920 was as People's Commissar of Foreign Trade. His assignment abroad was to help start the Russian economic recovery by selling off manufacturing and mining concessions. Concentrating on the Scandinavians, Krasin now set out to drive a wedge into world 'capitalist imperialism' as Lenin had demanded. The plan was to use foreign capital for the benefit of communism in Russia.

For this to happen, a degree of subterfuge was required. Most countries were still reluctant to hold talks with Bolshevik Russia, so Sovnarkom sent out its envoys in the guise of leaders of the Russian co-operative movement.[18] It was blatant hypocrisy. Bolsheviks in Russia treated co-ops as suspect organizations that sheltered enemies of the October Revolution. But foreigners who spoke to Krasin could now more easily shrug off criticism that they were talking to a communist state official. An atmosphere of friendliness and confidence was fostered in Scandinavia as the negotiations got under way. Swedish and Danish entrepreneurs put pressure on their government to facilitate trade agreements. The race was joined to re-enter the Russian trade. It was won by Denmark, which signed a treaty on 1 May. A copy was forwarded to the Allied embassies in Copenhagen so that political leaders might understand that any slowness in settling with Soviet Russia would lose them a lot of money.[19] Krasin was pleased by how quickly Armstrong Whitworth, one of Britain's largest metallurgical companies, sent people to Scandinavia to open talks with a view to agreeing a contract. And as a queue of Western businessmen lined up to meet him, he was kept very busy.[20]

The next stage of the Soviet leadership's plan was to send a section of their trade delegation to London to negotiate a treaty with Lloyd George. There was a temporary halt in proceedings when the British refused Litvinov a visa on account of his anti-war propaganda activity two years earlier.[21] The Soviet delegation reacted by cancelling all talks with British businessmen and threatened to call off any trip to the United Kingdom.[22] But this was only a bluff since Krasin had never been one of Litvinov's admirers. Having always found Litvinov pedantic and painful to work with, he was more than content to proceed to London without him.[23] In any case, the priority for the Soviet leadership was to start up the talks. And when Theodore Rothstein was refused permission to enter the United Kingdom there was no reaction from Moscow.[24] Moreover, the British for their part wanted to appear flexible and allowed Litvinov's friend Nikolai Klyshko to return to the United Kingdom as Krasin's interpreter and chief of staff. Klyshko had worked for Vickers Ltd before the war, his English was good and he had plenty of British personal contacts.[25]

Sovnarkom had been officially committed to its concessions policy since mid-1918, but it was only now, in peacetime, that it stood any chance of being implemented. Krasin was empowered to put up mines, forests, railways and telephone networks for auction to the highest bidders in the West. The sole stipulation in the Supreme Council of the People's Economy was that no foreign firm should gain a monopoly. Economic necessity called for instant action and Russian industrial recovery would benefit from external assistance.[26] Lenin and Trotsky promoted the initiative, inviting the world's capitalists to make their profits again in Russia so that the communist party might rebuild Russia's shattered economy. Before 1917 they had denounced the Nobel Oil Company as the greedy and ruthless exploiter of the petro-chemical resources of the Baku fields. But oil was almost the only means of industrial employment in Azerbaijan, so Lenin now wanted the Nobel family to come back with their technical expertise and financial resources. He was also ready to welcome Krupp, a company reviled by communists as a supporter of German militarism, to southern Russia to regenerate agriculture. Having handed the landed estates to the Russian peasantry in the October Revolution, he intended to grab them back so that foreign capitalists could modernize them and make profits for themselves and for the Kremlin.[27]

Trotsky was equally active in this cause and knew how to appeal to foreign businesses. When he gave an interview to the American reporter Lincoln Eyre, he emphasized that Russia aimed to re-enter the world economy and buy foreign machinery.[28] One of Trotsky's protégés, the dapper Viktor Kopp, was reported as being in Berlin and Copenhagen.[29] Kopp duly did the rounds of Krupp, Voss and other leading industrial companies. The overtures had a tempting logic. The Paris Peace Conference had severely restricted the size of the German armed forces for the foreseeable future. German metallurgical enterprises had expanded immensely in 1914–18 in response to the state's military requirements, and Krupp and its rivals had yet to find a substitute purchaser of its armaments. By treating Soviet Russia as a pariah state, the Allied powers freed it to act entirely as it wished; and there was nothing in the Versailles treaty to stop German industry from signing contracts with the Russian communist leadership: Kopp had the authority to negotiate on this basis. Moscow had not abandoned its ultimate revolutionary goals. But until such time as the German Communist Party seized power in Berlin, Trotsky was happy to use Germany's capitalism to enhance Soviet military security.

Lloyd George had no intention of letting the Germans overtake the British, but his ideas were opposed by Churchill, who wrote to him on 24 March 1920: 'Since the Armistice my policy would have been "Peace with the German people, war on the Bolshevik tyranny." Willingly or unavoidably, you have followed something very near the reverse.'[30] While eschewing Churchill's combative rhetoric, the other Western governments bridled at Lloyd George's softness towards communist Russia. French ministers were the first to express doubts about any accommodation with Soviet commercial requests. They continued to draw attention to the losses incurred by France's private bondholders as the result of Lenin's unilateral annulment of Russian state debts. In America opinion was divided and the political situation was unstable. Woodrow Wilson was chronically ill and no longer handled the main diplomatic levers, and no clear policy emerged from the State Department.

The British cabinet proceeded with caution. Lloyd George wanted to keep a good bargaining position and could see that over-eagerness would be counter-productive. The Kremlin leaders were to be made to appreciate that they would get no treaty unless they complied with his demands. Lloyd George also needed to avoid unduly annoying the French government or alarming Washington—and he hoped to placate the Conservative MPs in his governing coalition. Nonetheless he remained confident that trade with Russia was in Britain's best interests. He was being strenuously lobbied by influential business sectors as well as by the moderate political left in favour of a treaty. The Prime Minister believed that Russia's reincorporation into the world community of nations would enhance peace, employment and prosperity in Britain and the rest of Europe. He also thought that the Russian people would drop any lingering preference for communism once there was a resumption of trade. When goods flowed into Soviet territory it would quickly become obvious that capitalism was better at producing a decent standard of living. Communism would shrivel in the Russian ground as Soviet rule collapsed. Although Lloyd George did not predict how this outcome would be achieved, he was confident that capitalism would introduce a fatal infection into Lenin's regime. The Bolsheviks, he considered, would ultimately pay dearly for his fanaticism and the globe would be rid of the pestilence of the October Revolution.

Krasin arrived in London on 27 May 1920.[31] Among the sticking points was the Soviet government's desire to make its purchases in gold. The British government continued to contest the Bolshevik seizure of foreign assets in Russian bank vaults; the bullion stocks in Red hands were widely considered to be tainted and it was going to be tricky for Lloyd George to get round the problem without public controversy. Krasin also had to answer questions about Russia's outstanding state loans, which had been unilaterally annulled by Sovnarkom on 3 February 1918. The *New York Times* characterized the emerging British policy as 'buying off a dangerous enemy'.[32] French newspapers also complained that the Soviet delegation's decision to make for London and avoid Paris showed that Lloyd George was betraying the joint responsibilities of the Allies.[33] Yet public opinion in France was no more hopeful about the Americans. The suspicion was that if the British decided to withdraw from the Russian talks, Washington might step in quickly and sign a commercial treaty with Moscow.[34]

It was not just politicians in Britain and abroad who had doubts about Krasin; many businessmen too were not happy to welcome him. Krasin learned this directly when he was harangued in his hotel by an entrepreneur who been arrested by the Cheka and forced to hand over his English pounds for rubles, a currency without exchange value abroad.[35] A court case was also brought against Krasin for trying to sell Russian timber to a British firm. The plaintiff claimed that his own stocks of timber had been seized without compensation in 1918 and the communist authorities were making illicit profit from them. Although the case moved sluggishly through the judicial system, no one was in any doubt about the possible consequences. If judgement went against the Soviet government, a torrent of such cases might be let loose as disgruntled owners and investors sought financial redress.[36] Krasin's travails continued when the British industrialist Leslie Urquhart began to pester him. Urquhart had advocated the maintenance of business links with Russia after October 1917; but in mid-1918, on a trip to Moscow, he was threatened with imprisonment as a spy. If he had not been fluent in Russian, he might not have been able to extricate himself and repair to safety in northern Russia, from where he departed for the United Kingdom. He was less fortunate with his property because the communists had expropriated his large Russian mining and smelting company—and Urquhart did not intend to let Krasin forget this.[37]

Lloyd George's life would have been easier if the influential business lobby in favour of resuming trade had been willing to come into the open. But no company chairman wanted to push the case too hard in public. Sovnarkom's record in ripping up property rights, persecuting religion and conducting a Red terror was notorious. The men of business were using the Prime Minister as their battering ram without putting their shoulders to the charge. As for the British labour movement, its sympathies with all or some of Lenin's and Trotsky's policies made it less than helpful in persuading the doubters. If an Anglo-Soviet commercial treaty was going to be realized the impetus had to come from the government. Lloyd George was willing to give this a try—and Soviet leaders were hoping that he would succeed.

PART FOUR

◆

STALEMATE

25. BOLSHEVISM: FOR AND AGAINST

From November 1919 a group of leading British anti-Bolsheviks met together in the Savoy Hotel and the Café Royal for 'Bolo Liquidation Lunches'. Bolo was the slang term for Bolshevik used by British and American officials at that time. Those seated around the table included Stephen Alley, Paul Dukes (who signed the menu in Cyrillic script), George Hill, Rex Leeper, John Picton Bagge and Sidney Reilly. All were old Russia hands and were connected with the Foreign Office or the Secret Intelligence Service. As ardent foes of communism, they organized the lunches to discuss how to toughen British policy and bring down Lenin and the Soviet order.[1]

Paul Dukes, when his cover was blown in Russia, began to write articles for the London *Times*. He recounted the terrible food shortages and blamed them on Soviet economic policies rather than war or the weather.[2] He ridiculed the idea that the workers and peasants were on the side of the Bolshevik party and said that the public displays of joy on May Day were an artificial confection. He pointed out that Bolsheviks treated their critics, including factory labourers, as counter-revolutionaries. He hailed the spread of peasant rebellions against communist rule and wished the Greens well in their struggle with the Reds.[3] (The Greens were peasant partisans who fought the Reds and Whites with equal ferocity.) The final article in his series depicted the intimidation, fraud and lying propaganda involved in a local soviet election he had witnessed.[4] He called on the Western political left to shed its illusions: 'Bitterly as they revile the *bourgeoisie*, the Bolshevist leaders reserve their fiercest hatred and their last resources of invective and derision for all other Socialists—Russian, English, German, and American alike. They are never spoken of otherwise than as "social-traitors".[5] Dukes bragged that he had visited Russia not as an accredited journalist but as a private traveller who had conversed with every section of the Russian people—he of course omitted to mention his employment by the Secret Intelligence Service.[6]

According to Dukes, the 'National Centre Party' enjoyed support across the whole political spectrum, apart from monarchists and communists. The National Centre, however, was not a party but a combination of public figures of diverse political opinions. Dukes was deliberately misleading his readers to win their sympathies. He also made the unfounded claim that 'the large majority of socialists have joined [the party]' and were in productive contact with General Denikin.[7] Although Dukes did admit that the so-called National Centre Party aimed to install a temporary dictatorship, he declared that democracy was its ultimate aim. The peasants would be left in possession of the land. The Soviet separation of Church and state would endure and the universal educational provision introduced by the Bolsheviks would be maintained. The National Centre Party would hold elections to a National Assembly and had no desire to restore the survivors of the Romanov dynasty to power. By focusing on the National Centre Party and exaggerating its status as a rallying point for anti-Soviet opinion in Russia, Dukes downplayed the extremism of the officers in Denikin's forces. If anything united the Whites, in fact, it was Russian nationalism and anti-Semitism. They despised all liberals and socialists; they believed that democratic institutions had been tried and found wanting between February and October 1917. The political future they wanted would have little space for politicians, and Russia's fate would have been grim and chaotic under their rule.

Dukes reminded his readers that the leadership in the Kremlin had set up a Communist International with the purpose of subverting governments in Europe and North America.[8] His pronouncements did not go unnoticed by the Bolsheviks. When he joined the Christian Counter-Bolshevist Crusade and began to speak at its meetings, supporters of Soviet Russia attended his appearances to heckle.[9] Dukes responded that since he had served in the Red Army he was speaking from personal knowledge; but in February 1920 his speech at a public meeting in Westminster Hall led to an affray that the police had to quell.[10] When the Soviet government's newspaper *Izvestiya* accused him of subversive machinations he at last admitted to having been in charge of British intelligence operations in Russia, but he still held that he had only been gathering information.[11] Dukes received a knighthood for his services in December 1920—George V had in fact wanted to award the Victoria Cross but was overruled by the army chiefs of staff who insisted that the medal could be received only by members of the armed services.[12]

Conservative and liberal figures such as Professor Bernard Pares at London University's School of Slavonic and East European Studies joined Dukes in signing a letter to *The Times* denouncing Soviet outrages.[13] Dukes also wrote to the *Manchester Guardian* protesting against its indulgent editorial line on Soviet Russia—he was angered by the mild critique of communist rule offered by its reporter W. T. Goode, announcing his own credentials as follows: 'I was at Moscow at the same time as Professor Goode, and I left Russia later than he. I was not, however, a guest of the Bolshevik Government, but, knowing the language thoroughly, lived as a Russian amongst the Russians. My object was to study the effects of Bolshevism on the people.'[14] Although this was another of his misleading descriptions of what he had done in Russia, he efficiently made his point that it was inadequate to find the October Revolution and its leaders merely 'interesting' instead of offering a basic analysis of the revolutionary order. According to Dukes, Goode had praised the new educational system while failing to mention that schools had been compelled to stop teaching morality; he had also overlooked the antipathy of Russians to their Bolshevik rulers and their policies and ideology.

America had few writers on the anti-Soviet side of the debate with the direct experience of Soviet Russia that Dukes could muster. Dukes tried to do something about this by going on an American lecture tour in February 1921.[15] While there he supported the attacks on Bolshevik rule made by Princess Cantacuzène, who before 1917 had belonged to the highest social circles. She printed her reminiscences of the October Revolution in the *Saturday Evening Post*, republishing them in a book. She condemned the daily illegalities in Petrograd, picking out Trotsky for harsh criticism.[16] Her fellow Princess Catherine Radziwill, a best-selling author, concentrated on the secret deals between the Bolsheviks and the German government, but her research methods were less than exemplary since she felt entirely free to invent conversations and incidents involving Lenin and Trotsky.[17]

The Kadet leader Pavel Milyukov produced a steadier work, which appeared on both sides of the Atlantic, about Bolshevism's foreign pretensions. Looking at Soviet efforts to spread revolution abroad, he noted the

Russian linkage to the communist episodes in Budapest and Munich and sounded an alarm about Comintern. Milyukov stressed that 'Mr Lenin' and 'Mr Trotsky' were open about their global ambition; and he argued that the Bolsheviks had planned to use President Wilson's proposal for a Prinkipo peace conference as a way of securing a diplomatic presence in Washington, London and Paris. He mentioned the huge grain fund and military re-sources gathered by Sovnarkom for future use in the revolutionary cause in central Europe.[18] He wanted to depict himself as the constant Russian patriot and therefore omitted any reference to his own less than illustrious record in 1918 when he had sought Germany's military assistance in over-turning the Bolsheviks. He declared that the Hands Off Russia campaign was damaging the interests of his country and the world.[19] He regretted the way the European and American socialist parties, despite deep disagree-ments with Bolshevism, were urging their governments to grant recognition to Sovnarkom.[20] He warned, too, against listening to prominent American and British sympathizers with Bolshevism.[21]

Milyukov's book was all but ignored on both sides of the Atlantic. In frustration he wrote to the London *Times*, repudiating criticism of the White armies and their commanders. He insisted that Alexander Kerenski was wrong to advise against support for Kolchak and Denikin and intimated that if only Kerenski had taken a stronger line in 1917, Russia might have been spared its later torment.[22] This was not the fairest of comments. If it was true that Kerenski had had a genuine chance in summer 1917, Mi-lyukov had been given his own in the spring of that year. Russian political refugees all too frequently subsided into internal polemics. Disputes were bitter as conservative and liberal writers re-examined the events between the fall of the Romanovs and the rise of the Bolsheviks with the same in-tense disputatiousness that had made the émigré socialist colonies notori-ous before the Great War.

Such a reputation had also begun to attach itself to those in the West who were outspoken in their support for the Whites. On 17 July 1919 Win-ston Churchill had given a talk at the British-Russian Club in London and paid tribute to the achievements of the Russian Imperial army on the east-ern front, saying that its valour had saved Paris from the Germans in 1914–15. The Secretary of State for War was on sparkling form: 'Some people are inclined to speak as if I were responsible, as if I was at the bottom of all this trouble in Russia.' When the laughter had subsided Churchill explained that he believed in the 'inherent weakness of Bolshevism'. The Red Army, he declared, was weaker than many supposed. He fulminated against Lenin and Trotsky but did not confine himself to the Russian question. Turning to Hungary, he described the communist leader Béla Kun as 'another fungus, sprung up in the night'. European civilization was under threat. He summarized his standpoint as follows: 'Russia, my lords and gentlemen, is the decisive factor in the history of the world at the present time.'[23] Using extravagant vocabulary as usual, Churchill had a clear understanding of communism's threat to the freedoms fully or partially available in the West; and, ignoring the reproaches of Lloyd George, he gave encouragement to active anti-Bolsheviks in London.[24]

Friends of the Bolsheviks meanwhile queued up to extol what was happening in Russia. Arthur Ransome's *Russia in 1919* was a rapidly written memoir that described the communist leaders in the blandest personal terms, Ransome blithely acknowledging that he was not going to cover the Red terror.[25] And although Morgan Philips Price mentioned the terror in his own account, he claimed that it had lasted only six weeks. He chose instead to stress the sustained awfulness of the White terror while praising the Soviet system of government.[26] Ivy Litvinov, when left behind in London by Maxim, published a booklet in the same spirit. Drawing on Maxim's notes, she asked what worth there could ever be in the Constituent Assembly. She accused the Whites of worse violence than anything done by the Reds, stating: 'As a matter of fact, the Soviet regime has been much less sanguinary than any known in history.'[27]

But of all the books about the new regime, whether favourable or otherwise, the one with the greatest impact was John Reed's *Ten Days that Shook the World*, which appeared in March 1919.[28] His chapters concentrated on the brief period before and after the Bolshevik seizure of power in 1917 and were based on his own notes and memories as well as on his file of *Le Bulletin de la Presse* issued daily by the French Information Bureau.[29] He offered what he called 'intensified history', but he was also providing disguised propaganda. Reed claimed that until the October Revolution Russia had been an 'almost incredibly conservative' country: he entirely overlooked the surge of revolutionary action that had taken place in factories, garrisons and villages long before the Bolsheviks took over. The 'masses' appeared in his pages only when listening to speeches by Lenin and the other communist leaders. Reed wrote about the Mensheviks and

Socialist-Revolutionaries only to indicate how little they understood the scale of the external and internal emergency in Russia. Lenin and Trotsky were his heroes, and Kerenski was depicted as an incompetent fool: no attempt was made to explain the rationale for the Provisional Government's policies. Reed wrote: 'It is still fashionable . . . to speak of the Bolshevik insurrection as an "adventure". Adventure it was, and one of the most marvellous mankind has ever embarked upon, sweeping into history at the head of the toiling masses, and staking everything on their vast and simple desires.'[30] Bolshevism and popular opinion according to Reed were one and the same thing.

He threw himself into the tasks of public speaking and writing for the socialist press; he also prepared a tendentious memorandum for the State Department denying that any parties other than the Bolsheviks had the slightest following. He wrote that the entire social structure in Russia had been transformed because the bourgeoisie had been dispossessed and turned into proletarians. He claimed that the former middle classes could freely 'organize in the Soviets, but only to defend their [new] proletarian interests'. The truth was different. The Soviet Constitution expressly deprived those classes of civic rights. Reed stated that the USA was the foreign partner of choice for Sovnarkom because the British and the French had been unremittingly hostile. He added that it was in the Russian interest for Germany to be defeated in the Great War. The reality was that Lenin and Trotsky hoped for anti-capitalist risings across Europe and North America. Reed dropped his tactful tone just once, when saying of the Russians: 'As for President Wilson, they don't believe a word he says.'[31] Reed wanted the US to recognize Soviet Russia and stop persecuting Bolsheviks in America—and he urged American politicians to get the Japanese to withdraw from eastern Siberia.[32]

Together with Max Eastman, he also produced a booklet that included translated pieces by Lenin and Chicherin. Lenin's contribution was his 'Letter to American Workingmen'. The booklet was distributed in a somewhat abridged edition 'in deference to an extremely literal interpretation of the Espionage Act'. Eastman wrote an imaginary conversation between Lenin and President Wilson. This was wholly to Wilson's disadvantage, with Lenin putting awkward questions to Wilson and exposing him as wealthy, ignorant, insincere and dangerous.[33] Eastman was a communist sympathizer although he did not belong to an organized communist group. He was not alone in taking this position. The outstanding example in France was the novelist Henri Barbusse, who contended that the Bolsheviks had 'attenuated their implacable rigidity' and were adapting to 'the life of an innumerable, young people'.[34] Barbusse implied that France had a superior civilization to Russia: he urged everyone not to expect too much of the Russians. But he insisted that, after a poor start, communism in Russia was changing for the better.

Reed and the other pro-Bolshevik commentators were not the only proponents of conciliation with the Russian communist leaders. A leading American critic of Soviet rule was John Spargo, whose comments were all the more persuasive inasmuch as he was a socialist friend of Georgi Plekhanov.[35] *Russia as an American Problem*, appearing in mid-November 1919, held that Bolshevism was an 'inverted tsarist regime' and an enemy of democracy.[36] But Spargo argued that the Germans remained bent on the economic domination of Russia and that Japanese objectives were not dissimilar.[37] He urged America to get involved before it was too late. US businessmen could help Russia back on its feet by trading in its natural resources. Exports of gold and timber would enable Russians to pay for the capital equipment vital for economic recovery. America should send some of its own experts and make financial credits available.[38] He admitted that there were uncompromising extremists among the Soviet leadership, but suggested that Lenin and a few others were demonstrating a readiness for internal reform. Spargo had vociferously supported the White armies until their defeat in the Civil War; but when the Reds achieved military victory he judged that the resumption of international commerce was the surest way to erode Bolshevism's grip on the country.[39]

In fact the person who gave the most effective succour to Moscow was the economist John Maynard Keynes. In *The Economic Consequences of the Peace*, published late in 1919, Keynes said that Clemenceau had been eaten up with a desire for vengeance on Germany. He thought Wilson was an innocent abroad whose intelligence was overstated, while Lloyd George seemed to lose his political compass when confronted by a Clemenceau on the rampage. Keynes took all Western leaders to task for their treatment of Germany,[40] arguing that the Versailles treaty was a Carthaginian peace which had ruined the chances of recuperation and guaranteed chronic political instability. Territory had been grabbed from the Germans, reparations imposed.[41]

Keynes sombrely predicted that a devastated Russia and an exhausted Germany would draw close; he argued that it could not be excluded that 'Spartacism' would win out in Berlin.[42] But even if the political far left fell short of victory, he wrote, there could still be an alliance between German capitalism and Russian communism—and the British, Americans and French would be the losers unless they changed their policy. Keynes hailed the work of Herbert Hoover and the American Relief Administration— Hoover had condemned the treaty as too harsh while it was being negotiated, and Keynes called him 'the only man who emerged from the ordeal of Paris with an enhanced reputation'.[43] Cheap grain shipments from the US Midwest were currently saving eastern and central Europe from famine. This vital relief, though, would not continue for ever and it behoved the Allies to enable the restoration of Russian cereal exports. Keynes claimed that without them there could be no European economic recovery or political stabilization. He insisted that since the Allies could not yet supply Russia with the agricultural implements needed to regenerate its farming, Germany would be doing everyone a service by trading with Moscow. The world had an interlinked economy and Keynes wanted policy to be adjusted in the light of this.[44]

He wrote his book in a spasm of fervour in autumn 1919 and it came out amid controversy at the end of the year. Few other works by him around that period had quite the same punch. The book was an instant best-seller in many languages, but disparagers quickly appeared in abundance. A London *Times* editorial applauded the Cambridge academic for his cleverness and erudition but denied that the Germans had been treated too severely. Supposedly Keynes was urging a policy that would 'place Germany in effective control of Russia as a recompense for having let loose a war in which one of her principal objects was the economic enslavement of Russia'.[45] The reviewer in the *New York Times* was blunter still, calling the book a 'revolting melodrama'. Keynes had allegedly practised 'the highly perfect art of slurring those who helped to win this war'.[46] The French authorities and press were similarly negative.[47] Only on the left did Keynes experience a warm reception. The *Manchester Guardian* praised him for his 'conspicuous courage'.[48] From donnish obscurity Keynes rose to international fame, leaving no one indifferent regardless of whether they liked or disliked his analysis of the Versailles treaty.

Soviet communist leaders acclaimed the book. Ioffe said it exactly coincided with his own opinions.[49] Even Lenin, who only reluctantly cited authors hostile to Marxism in his writings, welcomed *The Economic Consequences of the Peace*; but if he was flattered by Keynes's reference to his 'subtle mind', he did not say so.[50] Bolsheviks were delighted to witness one of the world's most brilliant economists agreeing that a punitive peace had been inflicted on Germany and a disastrous blockade on Russia. While they waited for revolutions to roll out across Europe, they could at least enjoy watching others spreading their propaganda for them.

26. LEFT ENTRANCE

From late 1919 Sovnarkom denied accreditation to journalists of unfriendly foreign newspapers.[1] Dispatches had to be submitted in advance to the People's Commissariat of Foreign Affairs. Marguerite E. Harrison of the Associated Press noted that the official Soviet reviewer of Western press coverage mysteriously lost or delayed sanctioning the articles he disliked. He confessed: 'Mrs Harrison, your article is perfectly correct in every particular, but I prefer Mr Blank's article. It is more favourable to us. If they both came out in the American press at the same time it might produce a bad impression. I will send his first and hold yours for twenty-four hours.'[2] Meanwhile a Central Bureau for the Service of Foreigners was created in the Russian capital with the idea of arranging evenings of cultural uplift for favoured reporters, and Party Central Committee member Anatoli Lunacharski helped out by compèring a concert by the State Stradivarius Quartet playing Tchaikovsky, Borodin and Debussy.[3]

Such efforts had only patchy success with the anarchists Emma Goldman and Alexander Berkman, who arrived in Russia early in 1920 after being deported from America. In line with the idea of winning friends who could influence international opinion, the Soviet authorities made a fuss of them and gave them rooms in a good Moscow hotel. Goldman had modified her doctrines of anarchism to the point where she no longer advocated non-violence as an absolute principle. But she was never likely to become a Bolshevik and indeed she remarked on the poverty, bureaucracy and fanatical intolerance that prevailed under Soviet rule. Communist functionaries filled their days with meetings with trade union activists and factory workers who would reliably spout the official Bolshevik line; but, as word of her presence got around Moscow, Russian anarchists made contact and told her of the persecution they had suffered since the October Revolution. By December 1921 she and Berkman had had enough and left Russia for good. They decamped to the Latvian capital Riga, where they could write freely about the oppression they had witnessed. Joseph Pulitzer published their work in his *New York World* magazine and Goldman later integrated their articles into her book *My Disillusionment in Russia*.[4]

Soviet leaders hoped for better luck with their efforts to influence the British political left. On 10 December 1919 the Trades Union Congress demanded 'the right to an independent and impartial enquiry into the industrial, economic and political conditions of Russia', aiming to send a joint delegation of the TUC, the Labour Party and the Independent Labour Party to see things for themselves.[5] The Supreme Allied Council decided that no harm would be done, and on 27 April 1920 the delegation left for Scandinavia en route for Petrograd.[6] Lenin remained unconvinced that this was a good idea and called for a press campaign to denounce the projected 'guests' of Soviet Russia as 'social-traitors'. Chicherin pleaded for the trip to happen without any molestation, and Lenin for once gave way.[7]

The British Labour delegation reached Petrograd on 11 May for their six-week trip.[8] Off the train stepped Margaret Bondfield, H. Skinner and A. A. Purcell for the TUC; Ben Turner, Mrs Philip Snowden and Robert Williams for the Labour Party; and Clifford Allen and R. C. Wallhead for the Independent Labour Party. Dr Leslie Haden Guest and C. Roden Buxton travelled as secretaries and interpreters.[9] Bertrand Russell joined them later after undergoing a special interview by British officials in London and overcoming Litvinov's initial reluctance to issue him a visa in Stockholm.[10] The delegates felt they were breaking through to a different world. As Ethel Snowden put it: 'We were behind the "iron curtain" at last!'[11] It is widely assumed that this phrase was coined by Winston Churchill, in his speech at Fulton, Missouri in 1946, as the Cold War started between the USSR and the USA. Nazi propaganda chief Joseph Goebbels had in fact used it a year earlier as the Red Army swept into Romania.[12] But though it was she who had coined it, Mrs Snowden's meaning was quite different from Churchill's. She believed that a curtain of ignorance separated the countries of the West from Soviet Russia. She denied that the Russian communists were a threat to Britain's security—and she opposed any project to renew British armed intervention or giving material assistance to the enemies of Bolshevism.[13]

She and her companions were alert to the risk of being treated like a 'royal family' and manipulated for Bolshevik purposes.[14] Chicherin made a prediction at a banquet of welcome: 'We instructed ourselves whilst the process of creating a new Russia was going on. When you return to England you also will have to learn while building, and then, in the near future, you will be able to greet us as we greet you tonight.'[15] Mrs Snowden tartly noted: 'As propagandists there is surely no race and no class to surpass the Russian Communists.'[16] The repeated singing of the Internationale at the banquet got on her nerves.[17] She also disliked the pomposity of official gatherings. Propaganda was unconvincing on the lips of ill-fed youngsters and she found it 'unspeakably funny tripping from the unaccustomed lips of sober-speeched Britons, anxious not to be outdone in the delivery of explosive perorations'.[18]

John Clarke, travelling with fellow Scot Willie Gallacher in July 1920 to the Comintern Congress, recorded a conversation on the slow train journey south from Murmansk to Petrograd. It was a time when the Red Army and the Polish Army were fighting for supremacy in Ukraine and Poland:

> Gallacher: 'Poles, Poles, are they defeated?'
> Red Army soldier: 'Ne upony mio!' (I don't understand.)
> Gallacher: 'Poles—defeated?'
> Soldier: 'Ne upony mio!'
> Gallacher: 'Poles—beaten—defeated—beaten?' (A little fisticuff display.)
> Soldier (stoically): 'Ne upony mio!'
> Gallacher: 'Poles beaten! y'ken, beaten—washed oot—up the pole?'
> Soldier (with loud guffaw): 'Ne upony mio!'
> And so on, ad infinitum.[19]

Clarke was known for his humour, but he could see that his efforts were lost on an audience of four hundred peasants near Kandalaksha. His political minder had to interpret for them. Although Clarke spoke hardly any Russian, he astutely noticed that the Kandalaksha peasants spoke a dialect so distant from standard Russian that they probably could not understand even the minder.[20] Gallacher and Clarke took over for themselves and simply used 'prehistoric gesture-language'.[21]

Generally the Soviet leadership was keen to keep visiting foreigners away from any Western resident who might puncture their warm illusions about

Soviet Russia. Associated Press correspondent Marguerite Harrison, for example, was told to stay away from H. G. Wells.[22] But Bolshevik connivances were erratic, and Harrison was allowed to consort with Bertrand Russell.[23] She tagged along on the Labour delegation's trip to the Volga region:

> Our tour was a most luxurious one throughout, giving no idea of the ordinary hardships of travel in Russia at the present time. We had a special sleeper, with all the former comforts including spotless linen, and electric lights, a dining car where we had three good meals a day, service and appointments being very nearly up to peace time standards.[24]

The cosseting of body and mind worked with Robert Williams, who declared that the experiences of the delegates would encourage them to argue for the removal of the economic blockade of Russia.[25] In Samara, he stated that the British working class was pleased by every Red military triumph.[26] The delegation's interim report claimed that the ills of Soviet Russia—malnutrition and disease—were all the product of external factors. Policies of blockade or intervention should be put aside and official recognition granted.

Most of the other Britons resisted the blandishments and manipulation. Tom Shaw MP and Ben Turner bridled at the suggestion that the government of the United Kingdom was actively supporting the Polish invasion;[27] and when Mrs Snowden disparaged the Soviet order, the Russian hosts downgraded her from 'Comrade' to 'Madame'.[28] The disappointment of the British delegation was summed up by one of its members who composed an irreverent new stanza for 'The Red Flag' as an antidote to Soviet boastfulness:

> *The people's flag is palest pink,*
> *It's not so red as you may think;*
> *We've been to see, and now we know*
> *They been and changed its colour so.*[29]

Lenin gave up an hour and a half of his time to some of the visitors despite his long-felt contempt for the leaders of British labour. While living in London, he said that George Bernard Shaw was 'a good man fallen among Fabians'.[30] About Sidney Webb he offered the opinion that he had 'more industry than brains'.[31] Lenin predicted that when British workers set up soviets, Ramsay MacDonald would do his utmost to halt the revolution in its tracks.[32] His attitude to Bertrand Russell is unlikely to have been any different. For his part Russell was repelled by Lenin's passion for violence while Ethel Snowden was shocked by his ignorance about Britain; she explained to him that communism in England was constituted by 'only a handful of extremists' who had abandoned the older socialist organizations.[33] Trotsky was too busy with his military duties for the delegates to be granted an interview with him, but he was present when the delegates were treated to a performance of an opera by Borodin. Russell managed a brief chat with him in the interval and formed a poor impression. He never explained the reason for this. But Mrs Snowden revealed that one of the delegates was introduced to Trotsky as a conscientious objector who had spent the Great War in prison. Trotsky commented: 'We can have nobody here who preaches peace and wants to stop the war.'[34] He can only have been talking about Russell. Until that moment Mrs Snowden had envisaged Trotsky as 'the greatest of pacifists' in the Great War. She now knew better.[35]

Yet she, too, stood up and applauded when he resumed his seat in the old Imperial box for the next act of the opera. Conquering her distaste for the Internationale, she sang along with everyone else.[36] But the mood passed, and she was glad to leave Russia with the rest of the delegation at the end of their lengthy trip. Their departure was not uniformly easy. According to H. V. Keeling, some of them were compelled to sign a form promising not to attack the Soviet communists or else they would not be allowed to leave the country.[37] Clifford Allen's case was still more serious since he had fallen ill with pneumonia, exacerbated by the fact that he already suffered from TB, but his exit visa request was refused. Russell and Haden Guest pleaded with Chicherin. There was then a furious row because Chicherin insisted on Allen being examined by two Soviet doctors who would not be available for a couple more days. Russell recalled: 'At the height of the quarrel, on a staircase, I indulged in a shouting match because Chicherin had been a friend of my Uncle Rollo and I had hopes of him. I shouted that I should denounce him as a murderer.' Russell fancifully suspected that the Soviet authorities believed that the anti-Bolsheviks among the delegates wanted Allen to die en route to Britain so that he could not deliver a favourable report on Bolshevik rule.

The dispute resolved, the entire delegation made its way back to Britain where a meeting of welcome was held at the Albert Hall in London and Margaret Bondfield spoke of being impressed by 'the stupendous nature of the drama' of the communist revolution.[38] A brisk discussion ensued over the next few weeks. The Social-Democratic Federation announced disapproval of Soviet tyranny: '[The] realization of Socialism is only possible on the basis of democracy. Every other path leads to ruin.' Mrs Snowden added: 'When you get down to the bottom the dictatorship of the proletariat means the dictatorship of about six men aided by an extraordinary commission.'[39] She rushed a booklet into print:

> Do not, gentle visitor, when you meet the great man, fall victim to this twinkling eye and make the mistake of thinking it betokens a tender spirit. I am sure Lenin is the kindest and gentlest of men in private relationships; but when he mentioned his solution of the peasant problem the merry twinkle had a cruel glint which horrified.[40]

On the other side stood Messrs Purcell, Skinner, Turner, Wallhead and Williams, who appealed to trade unionists to refuse to produce anything for use against Soviet Russia.[41] Purcell called on skilled workers to volunteer for work there.[42] John Clarke declared that Mrs Snowden was too middle class to understand the October Revolution and its greatness; he likened her to an 'abandoned strumpet, harlot, and prostitute of the streets [who] sells her voluptuous merchandise to the very beings who disease her'.[43]

The dispute intrigued H. G. Wells, who made his own journey of exploration in September 1920. As a friend of Maxim Gorki he could count on a warm reception and Gorki lent him his assistant Moura Benckendorff—Lockhart's lover in 1918—as an interpreter. He was fed and watered to his satisfaction;[44] and his speech to the Petrograd Soviet was reported in *Pravda*, presumably because he called for Russia to be left without foreign interference.[45] When Wells interviewed Lenin, they talked about the future of Russian towns, Russian electricity and a little about Russian peasants.[46] Such topics did not unduly threaten the intellectual defences of the 'dreamer in the Kremlin'. Whereas Wells would snipe at Russell for overdramatizing his account, he himself missed a chance to put Lenin under serious scrutiny.

Another Briton, the sculptor Clare Sheridan, was more perceptive when meeting Soviet leaders. She had long felt a penchant for Russia: 'I was insatiably interested, I loved Slavs, Slav music, Slav literature, Slav art and decoration, and had always, since childhood, been drawn to Russia.' She regarded Russians as 'the most mystic, the most barbarous and the most romantic' people in the entire universe. In August 1920, she made the acquaintance of Lev Kamenev in London. Unencumbered by his wife's company on his British trip and amiably fluent in French, he offered to sit for her and they hit it off splendidly.[47] An adventurous widow, she showed him the sights of the capital, taking him to the Tate Gallery and Hampstead Heath. With plenty of free time, Sheridan also escorted him to Hampton Court where they spent the evening on the river. Kamenev invited her to the Café Royal and to the Ritz before suggesting:

'Why don't you come to Russia?'

'How can I?' I asked. And he made the wondrous reply:

'I will take you with me when I go, and I will get Lenin and Trotzki [sic] to sit to you.'[48]

The fact that it would be a paid assignment was an additional attraction for Sheridan, who had debts at the time. She readily agreed, needing only to work out where to deposit her children before departure.[49]

The one person she had to keep this secret from was her cousin Winston Churchill. At a recent lunch with her, he had exclaimed that Bolshevism was a crocodile and that 'either you must shoot it, or else make a detour round it so as not to rouse it'.[50] Sheridan quietly used her personal contacts in the Foreign Office to get visas for Norway and Sweden. Kamenev and the Soviet group—accompanied by Sheridan—made their way by train to the Newcastle ferry.[51] In Norway, Maxim Litvinov held things up, suspecting that she was a spy.[52] Not only was she a close relative of the West's great Red-baiter but she also had no record of involvement in radical politics. But Kamenev would not be put off and when Ivy Litvinov made friends with her and chatted about common friends, Maxim relented.[53]

In Moscow, Sheridan was given rooms in the sumptuous mansion built by the Kharitonenko family on Sophia Embankment on the opposite side of the River Moskva from the Kremlin.[54] (It became the British Embassy in 1931.) It had been sequestrated by the People's Commissariat of Foreign Affairs, and among the other foreigners staying there at the time were H. G. Wells, Washington B. Vanderlip and Theodore Rothstein.[55] Sheridan finished several fine busts—those of Lenin, Zinoviev and Dzerzhinski were outstanding; but it was Trotsky who most appealed to her. She was not the first British woman to succumb to his charisma; even Ethel Snowden had been won over: 'Physically he was a remarkably fine-looking man; a Jew, dark and keen, with penetrating eyes, and a quiet manner suggestive of enormous reserves of strength. He was in an officer's uniform which fitted him extremely well.'[56] At first, though, Trotsky was stand-offish toward Sheridan until Litvinov secured his co-operation.[57] Sheridan had got accustomed to things being cancelled or delayed in Moscow and was consequently surprised when Trotsky's official car arrived to pick her up at the appointed time. She later heard an apocryphal story that Trotsky had shot an unpunctual chauffeur with his own revolver. She was delayed by a punctilious sentry at the entrance to the building, which made her late through no fault of her own. This did not save her from being rebuked, albeit not executed, by the People's Commissar for Military Affairs.

He soon became charm incarnate and obviously liked being sculpted. The fact that the artist was a glamorous, uninhibited woman was a further stimulus:

> He looked up suddenly and stared back, a steady unabashed stare. After a few seconds I said I hoped he did not mind. His *galanterie* was almost French!
>
> 'I do not mind. I have my *revanche* in looking at you *et c'est moi qui gagne!*'
>
> He then pointed out that he was quite asymmetrical, and snapped his teeth to show that his underjaw was crooked. He had a cleft in his chin, nose and brow, as if his face had been moulded and the two halves had not been accurately joined. Full face he was Mephisto, his eyebrows slanted upwards, and the lower part of his face tapered into a pointed and defiant beard. His eyes were much talked of; they had a curious way of lighting up and flashing like an electric spark; he was alert, active, observant, *moqueur*, with a magnetism to which he must have owed his unique position.[58]

And so it went on. "*Vous me caressez avec des instruments d'acier!*" he said as I measured him with the callipers.'[59] At the start of the next sitting, on a cold evening, he 'kissed my frozen hands and placed two chairs for me by the fire, one for me and one for my feet'.[60] When she asked him to loosen his collar, he 'unbuttoned his tunic and the shirt underneath, and laid bare his neck and chest.'[61]

Despite rarely offering a smile, he flirted with her more and more: 'Even when your teeth are clenched and you are fighting with your work, *vous êtes encore femme.*'[62] She replied: 'I had expected you to be most unamiable, and I am surprised to find you otherwise. I wonder how I will describe you to people in England who think you are a monster.' He said: 'Tell them ... tell them that "*lorsque Trotzki embrasse, il ne mord pas!*"' But he added: 'Much as I like you and admire you as a woman, I assure you that if I knew you were an enemy, or a danger to our revolutionary cause, I would not hesitate to shoot you down with my own hand.' Sheridan 'found this vaunted ruthlessness most attractive'.[63] When she showed him pictures of her work, he expressed admiration for her bust of Asquith: 'You have given me an idea— if Asquith comes back into office *soon* (there is a rumour that he might bring in a coalition with labour and recognise Russia) I will hold you as a hostage until England makes peace with us.' Sheridan responded that her cousin Winston was more likely to form any new government; she also told him: 'But if you said you would shoot me, Winston would only say "shoot" ... Winston is the only man in England who is made of the stuff that the Bolsheviks are made of. He has fight, force, and fanaticism.'[64]

Clare Sheridan attracted a lot of attention on her return to Britain, when she published the first of several memoirs of her time in Russia, and during her subsequent book tour of the USA; but she was not taken very seriously, except by the Hands Off Russia people.[65] This was partly her own fault; she had always claimed to be apolitical. But what did irk her was the icy attitude of Cousin Winston, who refused to speak to her. She called him heartless and disloyal, saying that she had been on the same kind of adventure he would have once undertaken. Churchill assured her of his friendship but still reproved her for her dalliance with 'these fiends in human form'.[66] This was conciliatory enough for her to ask him to put in a good word for her to become the UK ambassador to Moscow—she reminded him that he had once said he would vote for her if ever she stood for parliament.[67] Nothing, of course, came of this overture.

Whereas Sheridan's gushing recollections had little impact, the report of the Labour delegation received attentive scrutiny in both Britain and America. But being the product of collective authorship, it was somewhat insipid; and being focused on economic and social policies, it touched on communist politics only indirectly:

> Whether, under such conditions, Russia could be governed in a different way—whether, in particular, the ordinary processes of democracy could be expected to work—is a question on which we do not feel ourselves competent to pronounce. All we know is that no practical alternative, except a virtual return to autocracy, has been suggested to us; that a 'strong' Government is the only type of Government which Russia has yet known; that the opponents of the Soviet Government when they were in power in 1917, exercised repression against the Communists.[68]

Apparently democracy and civic freedoms were all right for the British but not necessarily appropriate for Russians. And the report ended with the comment: 'We cannot forget that the responsibility for these conditions resulting from foreign interference rests not upon the revolutionaries of Russia, but upon the Capitalist Governments of other countries, including our own.'[69]

The individual accounts by visitors were much less bland. H. G. Wells wrote up his thoughts in *Russia in the Shadows*: 'Ruin: that is the primary Russian fact at the present time.'[70] He did not attempt an analysis of Bolshevism, and he could not resist a satirical aside:

> A gnawing desire drew up on me to see Karl Marx shaved. Some day, if I am spared, I will take up shears and a razor against *Das Kapital*; I will write *The Shaving of Karl Marx*.
>
> But Marx is for the Marxists merely an image and a symbol, and it is with Marxists that we now are dealing.[71]

Yet Wells also insisted that the communist order had more support in Russia than any of its Russian opponents, either on Russia's soil or abroad, were ever likely to gather.[72] *The Times* gave his account a backhanded compliment:

> The merit—and it is a real merit—of Mr H. G. Wells's book on Bolshevist Russia is that it tells us nothing new, either about Russia or about himself. It adds the evidence of one more sympathiser with

communist ideals to the testimony of so many other witnesses with similar leanings on the utter and dismal breakdown of the Bolshevist system.[73]

Wells had gone out to Russia with a favourable opinion of communism; his disillusionment carried weight.

Bertrand Russell's book *The Theory and Practice of Bolshevism* described a similar reaction: 'I went to Russia a communist, but contact with those who have no doubts has intensified a thousandfold my own doubts, not as to Communism itself, but as to the wisdom of holding a creed so firmly that for its sake men are willing to inflict widespread misery.'[74] Russell had done his homework and peppered his conversation with Lenin with awkward questions. He interpreted Bolshevism as a secular religion. About Lenin he reported:

> I think if I had met him without knowing who he was, I should not have guessed that he was a great man; he struck me as too opinion-ated and narrowly orthodox. His strength comes, I imagine, from his honesty, courage, and unwavering faith—religious faith in the Marxian gospel, which takes the place of the Christian martyr's hopes of Paradise, except that it is less egotistical. He has as little love of liberty as the Christians who suffered under Diocletian, and retaliated when they acquired power. Perhaps love of liberty is in-compatible with whole-hearted belief in a panacea for all human ills. If so, I cannot but rejoice in the sceptical temper of the Western world.[75]

Russell refused to exercise any toleration of intolerance. He also turned on the Western socialists who suppressed mention of what they saw with their own eyes on trips to Moscow. Communist harshness, he argued, could not be explained away by the military intervention of Britain and France. Al-though war and blockade had undoubtedly made things worse, the funda-mental cause lay in the doctrines of the Bolshevik leaders.

Nonetheless Russell's hostile testimony was inconsistent with some of his private comments. He wrote to his friend Ottoline Morrell from Stockholm:

> I was stifled and oppressed by the weight of the machine as by a cope of lead. Yet I think it the right government for Russia at this moment.

If you ask yourself how Dostoevsky's characters should be governed, you will understand. Yet it is terrible. They are a nation of artists, down to the simplest peasant; the aim of the Bolsheviks is to make them industrial and as Yankee as possible. Imagine yourself governed by a mixture of Sidney Webb and [British Ambassador to Washington] Rufus Isaacs, and you will have a picture of modern Russia.[76]

Whereas *The Theory and Practice of Bolshevism* was a work of lasting value, Russell was tempted into silliness when corresponding with his clever London friends; and his prescription for the 'nation of artists' was condescending at best, callous at worst. His mistress Dora Black, soon to be his second wife, was even sillier. She had always given intellectual approval to the Soviet order and did not modify her ideas when she subsequently made her own trip to Russia—Russell had refused to take her with him. Black enjoyed shocking him by saying that 'she liked Russia just about as much as [he] had hated it'. She scoffed at his opinions as 'bourgeois and senile and sentimental'.[77]

The disagreement between the future spouses was a microcosm of the debates about Soviet Russia on the political left. Quite apart from out-and-out communists, the Bolsheviks had many admirers—and the degrees of approval varied from individual to individual. But there were also plenty of detractors who saw very clearly that the communist revolutionary project could bring the entire labour movement into disrepute. However many delegations went to Moscow, the disagreement was likely to remain.

27. THE SPREADING
OF COMINTERN

The British Labour delegation had been remarkably incurious about global revolution in their talks with Soviet leaders. Whether out of naivety or politeness, they barely mentioned Comintern and its activities abroad. Although Ethel Snowden knew that Lenin had a 'great interest' in insurrections around the globe, she still did not discuss this with him when she had the chance. In Moscow she gained the impression that Comintern was a pretty feeble organization, and she claimed that this was how Russian communist acquaintances felt. They had told her that the policy of excluding weak or wavering groups on the European political far left 'would so restrict [Comintern's] members that it could not become effective as it is'.[1] And with that, Mrs Snowden moved on to topics closer to her heart. Most fellow members of the Labour delegation did not even mention Comintern in their reports. This obviously made it easy for Soviet leaders to sidestep the topic. Whereas they had endlessly asked questions about Bolshevism in Russia, they failed to enquire about Bolshevik ambitions in Europe.

But those ambitions were very real and, since the First Comintern Congress in 1919, Comintern had been the main agency used to realize them. There was indeed no other option while the Red Army and Cheka were tied down in the Civil War. Funds were disbursed to find zealots in every country who would split with the socialists and social-democrats and set up a communist organization. World revolution was an openly stated objective. The Kremlin was in charge from the start and knocked back the objections of Hugo Eberlein, the Spartacist delegate, who did not see why the Russians should boss everyone around. Eberlein objected to the March 1919 gathering calling itself a formally constituted congress. He thought that the cart was being put before the horse, arguing that the global map should be densely dotted with communist parties before any congress could take place.[2] Eberlein got nowhere; Lenin and his comrades simply reverted to tricks they had used before the Great War. They stuffed the 'delegations' with trusted foreigners, including several who were living permanently in Russia—Boris Reinstein was allowed to attend for the American Socialist Party and Khristo Rakovski for the Balkan Revolutionary Social-Democratic Federation. There were thirty-four voting delegates and the Bolsheviks had assured themselves a majority on all matters: Eberlein was the only person even to abstain in the vote for the formal proclamation of Comintern.

Even if Rosa Luxemburg had been present, it is far from certain that she could have successfully counteracted the psychological cunning of the Bolsheviks. The Congress delegates were taken to Petrograd to visit the places of communist glory in 1917. They went to the Finland Station where Lenin and Trotsky had arrived from abroad. They wandered the corridors of the Smolny Institute. They gazed at the Winter Palace. The effect was to dazzle them with the achievements of the Soviet order. The foreign delegates came away with the impression that the Bolsheviks were giants walking the earth. Bright applause greeted Lenin and Trotsky whenever they appeared. Lenin delivered the introductory report and offered 'theses' on bourgeois democracy and proletarian dictatorship. Bukharin supplied a 'platform' and Trotsky a 'manifesto'. Trotsky also gave a spirited speech on the Red Army, praising the achievements of 'socialist militarism'. (This kind of belligerence disconcerted Arthur Ransome but did not put an end to his admiration for Trotsky.) The official drafts and orations won a warm reception. Reports by foreign delegates on revolutionary possibilities abroad invariably supported the line marked out by the Bolshevik leaders, who got the Congress they had planned for.[3]

Lenin and Trotsky performed with a commendable display of modesty and humour, as exemplified by an incident on the last day of the proceedings. After the singing of the Internationale it was time for the official photographs, but Trotsky had stepped down from the stage. The photographer complained loudly till the People's Commissar for Military Affairs returned. There was much merriment when someone joked that Soviet Russia had installed the Dictatorship of the Photographer.[4]

It was ultimately intended that Comintern would be run by its Executive Committee, but until everything was sorted out it was agreed to hand authority to 'comrades of the country where the Executive Committee is'.[5] The natural assumption was that either Trotsky or Lenin would chair the Comintern Executive Committee. But this was impractical since Trotsky needed to travel to the front lines of the Civil War and Lenin had onerous duties in Sovnarkom and the Politburo. It was decided to give the Comintern post to Zinoviev, which was something of a surprise since he had originally opposed the seizure of power in Petrograd in 1917. But Zinoviev had made up for this by showing solidarity with Lenin ever since. Although he ran the Petrograd administration, he was ambitious to prove himself on the international stage and there was no obviously better candidate among the Russians. He set about his new job by demanding lavish funding from the Bolshevik leadership in Moscow. His request was met, and when the Executive Committee met for the first time on 26 March 1919 Zinoviev announced that credit facilities to the value of one million rubles had been opened for Comintern.[6] In May the budget was raised to three million.[7] Despite the size of these sums, much of Comintern's activity was carried out in the traditions of the pre-revolutionary political underground. When Lenin decided that a million pounds sterling had to be transferred to Zinoviev in Petrograd, the Party Central Committee Secretary Yelena Stasova physically took it by train from Moscow.[8]

The founding documents—theses, platform and manifesto—were evasive about Comintern's purposes. One objective alone was clearly set out: world revolution. How Comintern would attain it was left unspecified apart from through the establishment of communist parties and the promotion of revolutionary struggle. The interests of Soviet Russia were to be taken into account in every foreign operation; this did not need to be spelled out since everyone already agreed on it. Comintern refrained from admitting that its purse strings were held by the Bolshevik leadership. Nor was anything said about the requirement to submit all big decisions in advance to the scrutiny of the Bolsheviks. The fact that Zinoviev chaired the Executive Committee was not thought enough by itself: the Russian Communist Party expected to initiate policy, with Zinoviev carrying out whatever the Politburo demanded of him. Comintern was going to send out its agents to distribute money and attract followers. Communist parties had to be created. Newspapers needed to be started and printing presses acquired. The message of communism had to be disseminated to the working classes. Trotsky and the People's Commissariat of Foreign Affairs had begun this work in 1917–18. Comintern was empowered to intensify and expand it.

The set-up had the advantage of deflecting the attention of foreign governments from the People's Commissariat. Chicherin had until then been sending out 'plenipotentiaries' who were already suspected—usually quite reasonably—of subversive activity. Ostensibly Comintern was based on Russian territory by historical accident. The Bolshevik leaders could pretend to have no authority over revolutionary actions designed to bring down capitalism around the globe.

But although Chicherin could now mask Soviet pretensions abroad, he could not make them disappear. The People's Commissariat of Foreign Affairs conducted business for a state that needed to spread the message of revolution to foreign working classes if Sovnarkom was to survive the hostility of world capitalism. At the same time—until fraternal revolutions took place in powerful countries—Chicherin had to conciliate those governments willing to grant diplomatic recognition and open their economies to trade with Russia. Comintern's open espousal of proletarian insurrection and dictatorship inevitably complicated his overtures. The work was made no easier by Zinoviev's poaching of personnel from the People's Commissariat. Even Litvinov and Vorovski were seconded to fulfil tasks for Comintern.[9] This was bound to render them still more suspect in the eyes of states abroad and put obstacles in the path of Soviet diplomacy. Gradually Chicherin achieved agreement that Comintern should publicly be kept separate from the People's Commissariat. Zinoviev saw the sense in this and asked to keep his own couriers rather than share them with Chicherin.[10] In May 1919 the Politburo also ruled that Comintern alone should conduct illegal work abroad, and a ban was introduced on Soviet embassy personnel engaging in efforts that broke local law.[11]

The separation of functions was never as neat in reality, and the Politburo muddled everything again by appointing Litvinov to oversee the Comintern budget.[12] From Litvinov downwards, Soviet diplomats abroad remained in active contact with revolutionaries committed to insurrectionary violence. Chicherin, in fact, had no basic objection. His only stipulation was that embassy officials should carry out their clandestine functions without getting caught. He wanted world revolution no less fervently than Zinoviev.

By July 1920, when the Second Comintern Congress took place, there had been much organizational progress. The Germans already had a communist party and the French and Italians were well on their way to establishing theirs. Advances in America and Britain were slower as the Executive

Committee put militants under pressure to form a single party in each country. The path towards this end was being smoothed by Comintern's money, which always went to communists who toed the Russian line. Comintern leaders picked the British Socialist Party as the likeliest instrument for the Soviet cause in the United Kingdom. Being to the left of the Labour Party, it was a stalwart of the Hands Off Russia movement; and like all groups on the political extreme left, it was experiencing the torments of internal struggle—in this case between factions led by E. C. Fairchild and John Maclean. Their conflict was gradually surmounted through the intervention of Theodore Rothstein acting on Moscow's orders. Rothstein's own influence had risen through his close ties with the Kremlin, and he received a hearing before British militants which began the process that ended in splitting the British Socialist Party and creating the Communist Party of Great Britain in 1920.[13]

The Second Comintern Congress imposed a universal scheme for communist parties to be organized on the Bolshevik model. The parties were to be centralized, hierarchical and disciplined. They had to recognize Comintern as the supreme authority on every matter of importance. 'Internationalism' was to take precedence over national concerns.

Yet Comintern had a long way to go in the cause of creating communist parties everywhere, and delegates came to Moscow devoted to the cause but not yet leading large organizations. Their ways were rough and ready. The communist organization in Mexico chose three comrades, including the American political refugee Linn A. E. Gale, to represent it at the Second Congress. None of them, however, could go. As chance had it, the Japanese communist Keikichi Ishimoto was passing through Mexico City on his way to Moscow via the United States and Norway. Gale, who was himself not Mexican but an American in exile, warmed to Ishimoto as being 'quite young but a fine, sincere fellow'. Gale and his comrades decided to transfer their credentials to him for use in the Congress proceedings.[14] The fact that Mexico's national representation passed so casually into the hands of an obscure Japanese says a lot about the haphazardness of the arrangements. In Brazil it was Comintern which took the initiative. Its agent, a certain Ramison, searched Rio de Janeiro for militants who might found a communist party. He made his first approach to Edgard Leuenroth, who bluntly refused. Pressed to give his reasons, Leuenroth exclaimed: 'Because I'm not a Bolshevist!'[15] Ramison, though, knew that Comintern did not mind who created parties as long as they were created, and he eventually found people who would start the process for him. In Moscow, Zinoviev had confidence that the Executive Committee could cope with any difficulties that might arise. There would be many zigzags on the road to world revolution and the Bolshevik leaders were masters of the art of political manoeuvring.

In July 1921 the Politburo set up a world trade union agency—Profintern—in parallel to Comintern. It was to be an international centre for unions that rejected working inside the capitalist system. Communists would lead and inspire Profintern, challenging the broader labour movement to fortify the resistance to governments and employers. In its first pronouncement Profintern made an open declaration of its hostility to the entire order of capitalism around the world.

The Soviet authorities were not just looking to Europe and America. In September 1920 Zinoviev organized a Congress of the Peoples of the East in Baku. As the capital of Azerbaijan, the new Soviet republic, it appeared the best place for the communist leadership to signal to Muslim peoples that Moscow wanted to befriend national liberation movements. Joint action against the imperial powers was proposed. The treaty of Sèvres in August 1920 subjected the Middle East to British and French control, and the communist leaders in Moscow intended to exploit existing regional resentments as well as those which might arise as the result of the treaty. They also aimed to cause trouble for the United Kingdom in India. If Indians overturned British rule, the entire empire might fall apart—and the French imperial edifice might well collapse soon afterwards. Communism's militant atheism was a barrier to the recruitment of followers since religious belief and affiliation was well-nigh universal in Asia. In Baku, therefore, care had to be taken to avoid giving offence to Muslims, Hindus, Buddhists and other believers; and communist speakers were under orders to avoid showing disrespect for popular traditions. The 'peoples of the East' were instead to be won over by the promise that Comintern could help them to break off the shackles of imperialism and modernize their economies and cultures. Communism would benefit from European and US capitalists losing their grip on the countries of Asia, Africa and Latin America.

Zinoviev, Radek and Kun gave rousing speeches at the ceremonial meeting of welcome. The Azerbaijani communist leader Nariman Narimanov, himself an Azeri, opened the first full session.[16] Although Narimanov was a communist through and through, he argued that the Congress should unite behind a common struggle: 'I say that we are now faced with the task of kindling a real holy war against the British and French capitalists.'[17]

Radek was also fiery, asking: 'How is it that a little handful of British are able to keep under their heels hundreds of millions of Indians?'[18] The speeches were translated instantaneously into Turkish and Persian. Enver Pasha, a prominent figure in the military campaign under Mustafa Kemal to salvage Turkey's independence after the Ottoman defeat in the Great War, sent passionate greetings to the Congress and wished the Red Army well.[19] John Reed, recently returned from the US, denounced American imperialism.[20] A Council for Propaganda and Action was elected with its base in Baku and the audience rose to sing the Internationale.[21] Zinoviev closed the proceedings with a modification of one of Karl Marx's most famous slogans. From Baku onwards, he announced, the words of *The Communist Manifesto* needed to be changed to: 'Workers of all lands and oppressed peoples of the whole world, unite!'[22]

If Comintern was to be effective as the means of bringing millions to the revolutionary cause, however, it had to counteract any assumption that peaceful methods of struggle were sufficient for success. When Lenin learned of objections to violent methods among the British Labour delegation to Russia in 1920, he issued an open letter to the workers of the United Kingdom defending the use of terror and the suppression of press freedom under Soviet rule. Such mechanisms, he argued, constituted 'the defence of the working class against [its] exploiters'. He contended that freedom of the press was merely 'the freedom of the wealthy to conspire against those who laboured'.[23] He also felt it important to note that 'England' and its allies had carried out a 'White terror' in Finland, Hungary, India and Ireland. Somewhat condescendingly, he said he had explained this so frequently over the years that he found it 'not very joyful' to have to repeat himself.[24] This was less than graceful; it was also a wild exaggeration because the British had instigated no killing of communists in Finland or Hungary. But Lenin was a practical revolutionary. It would do no harm if a piece of rhetoric swelled the ranks of support for Comintern.

When a particular national situation was not yet ripe for insurrection it was still possible for communists to render assistance to the Soviet cause. In 1920 Comintern issued a May Day appeal suggesting that peace was impossible under capitalism and calling for the obstruction of troops and supplies going to the anti-Bolshevik forces in Russia. Henriette Roland-Holst, the Secretary of Comintern's Amsterdam Bureau, recommended the resumption of trade with Russia. She admitted that this would involve private business but argued that Russia needed Western manufactures and that the

West needed Russian grain. She suggested that European workers would benefit from the stimulus given to post-war economic recovery.[25]

Lenin, Trotsky and Zinoviev hammered out their message that the Bolsheviks were heroically carrying out the practical objectives of socialism. What Comintern said about capitalist exploitation and imperial oppression was anyway in line with traditional doctrines of socialist, social-democratic and labour parties the world over. There was immense war-weariness after 1918, and most militants thought the biggest danger to peace lay in the temptation for the victor powers to undertake a crusade against the Bolsheviks. Whenever objections were raised against Lenin's policies on terror and dictatorship it was always tempting for radical socialists to argue that the regime in Moscow had been forced to act harshly by the vicious ring of counter-revolutionary armies, Russian and foreign, that was meant to throttle it in 1918–19. The hope was that Bolshevik doctrines and practices would steadily become more moderate if Russia was left alone by foreign armies and permitted to trade with the rest of the world.

Not every Comintern militant was content with the way things were being propelled by Lenin, Trotsky and Zinoviev. Among the critics was John Reed. When talking to friends, he made no secret of his growing distaste for Bolshevik manipulation of the international labour movement. He mixed readily with communist leaders in Russia and witnessed the condescending attitude they had to foreign communists. This attitude was not confined to Lenin and other Politburo members. Yan Berzin, the Soviet plenipotentiary in Switzerland, told Zinoviev that '[Zeth] Höglund and all the other Scandinavian ditherers are people without energy or initiative, but nevertheless it's necessary to operate precisely through them for the moment.'[26]

Reed had come late in his young life to the political far left and brought along with him an idealism about acceptable methods. He looked askance at the discrediting of Sovnarkom's critics. He objected that so many officials were being promoted to high office in Comintern simply because they obeyed Zinoviev. He saw no signs of Bolshevik authoritarianism fading from Russian politics. The Bolshevik leaders knew of Reed's second thoughts about them and were already wondering what to do about him when, on his way back from Baku, he contracted typhus. He and Zinoviev had never got on either personally or politically. Yet when Reed died in October 1920 he received a magnificent funeral and his remains were interred below the walls of the Kremlin. Although his wife Louise Bryant had been shocked by the poor quality of care he received from Russian doctors and nurses, she bore no grudge. The interment, however, rankled. She told fellow reporter Marguerite Harrison: 'John was a real American. I know he would have wanted to be buried on American soil.'[27] In death he was turned into an unquestioning communist hero who remained of use in propaganda for a Comintern which he had come to despise.

Comintern had yet to grow to its mature size and strength, but its dominant features were already clearly delineated. The Russian Communist Party had called it into existence and was exercising parental control. Moscow had the funds, determination and cunning to maintain its dominance. Bolsheviks had made the October Revolution, whereas all the attempts to set up communist regimes elsewhere as yet had failed. The Kremlin planned to maintain its grip in directing communist strategy and operations.

28. TO POLAND AND BEYOND

The Western Allies might have withdrawn their expeditions from Russia and Ukraine but Russian communist leaders had to maintain their vigilance about potential threats from abroad. Foreign powers had intervened in Soviet Russia since 1918 and every Bolshevik thought that they could return on an anti-communist 'crusade'. If the Allied powers did not do this by themselves, they might employ the forces of Russia's bordering states—Finland, Poland or Romania were surely open to being used in this fashion. Travelling around the Baltic in the winter of 1918–19, Adolf Ioffe warned Trotsky that the Poles might soon invade.[1]

From spring 1919 there had been serious clashes between Red forces and the Polish army across the western borderlands of the former Russian Empire. The Bolsheviks had established a joint Lithuanian–Belorussian Soviet Republic in February with its two capitals in Vilnius and Minsk. By its creation, communist leaders disclaimed any association with Russian 'chauvinism' and strove to prove their tolerance of all nations. The Poles saw things differently. Although ostensibly the new republic was independent, it was led by Bolsheviks who remained subject to the discipline of the centralized communist party in Moscow. The 'Litbel' republic, moreover, was a clear and present threat to Poland's security. Józef Piłsudski, the Polish commander-in-chief, ordered military action in April. Vilnius fell immediately, followed by Minsk in August. Since Trotsky's Red Army was then engaged in finishing off the White armies of Kolchak and Denikin, the Lithuanian–Belorussian Soviet Republic was incapable of defending itself. Polish forces in the same months were also involved in heavy fighting with Soviet Ukraine. Thus the entire area of the old western borderlands was under contestation.[2]

The Western Allies appreciated the dangers. The Polish Prime Minister Ignacy Paderewski approached them in September 1919 with an offer to attack Soviet Russia in return for subsidizing his armed forces. Clemenceau had the Allied Supreme Council with him in rejecting any such idea and the British instead proposed the establishment of an eastern Polish frontier short of Grodno, soon to be known as the Curzon Line (even though Lord Curzon, who had recently become Foreign Secretary, played no part in drafting it).[3]

Piłsudski, however, thought the Allies naive in believing that the Bolsheviks would abide by any such settlement, and he continued to work on his strategy of exploiting Moscow's moment of weakness by expanding the territory under Warsaw's control. Aiming to set up a federation with the Ukrainians he agreed a pact with anti-Bolshevik Ukrainian leader Symon Petliura. The coming together of Poland and Ukraine would improve their chances against a resurgent Russia or Germany. Piłsudski rejected any alliance with the Russian Whites because the White commanders believed in 'Russia one and indivisible' and refused to commit themselves to Polish independence. General Yudenich, entirely failing to understand Poland's national sensitivities, expressed annoyance when the Poles refused to cross the River Berezina to render assistance.[4] But while Piłsudski had hopes of Kiev, Lenin's mind was fixed on Berlin. Germany's current government was always going to suffer criticism for having acceded to the treaty of Versailles. Berlin was pulled in all directions by political tension. The far right acted first. On 17 March 1920 a coalition of Freikorps and other paramilitary groups led by Wolfgang Kapp attempted a putsch. Lenin cabled Stalin to speed up the defeat of the Whites in Crimea because he wanted to have the Red Army available to intervene in a German civil war since revolution in Germany was always the communist objective.[5]

But Kapp's putsch quickly fizzled out when the German government mobilized the army and trade unions against him; and the Russian communist leadership shifted its focus back to internal affairs, especially economic recovery. On 23 April Soviet Russia offered a territorial compromise to Poland, proposing a border line which would have handed all Belorussia to the Poles. Piłsudski interpreted this as a sign of weakness and decided that this was the best opportunity to crush Bolshevism in the borderlands and create the federation he desired.[6] Information available to Piłsudski from intercepts of Soviet wireless traffic indicated that the Red Army was being prepared for its own campaign in the west. This made Piłsudski think that he needed to strike before he could be struck,[7] and on 26 April the Polish Army advanced into Ukraine where peasant rebellions against the communist authorities were intensifying. Conscription had been onerous. Grain had been seized without compensation. Bolshevik zealots in some provinces had even forced villagers into collective farms. Piłsudski aimed to pull Ukraine out of the grasp of its Red conquerors and counteract Russia's influence over the entire region. Ukrainian popular opinion was not consulted. Piłsudski and Petliura wanted to accomplish their purposes before the Soviet government had a chance to act.

The Polish army made a lightning advance. By 7 May, to its surprise, it had reached and occupied Kiev. The Reds had been concentrating on finishing off the Volunteer Army in Crimea and Trotsky issued a proclamation declaring the determination of both party and army to drive out the Poles.[8] He called it a war imposed on the Bolsheviks and demanded a resolute effort to defend Russia and Ukraine against the enemy. He appealed for help from Imperial officers who had avoided siding with the Red or White cause in the Civil War. In this he was successful; Poles were the historic national foe and General Alexei Brusilov led the way in volunteering his services in sending Piłsudski packing.

Piłsudski knew that, for Poland to be truly secure, the communist dictatorship in Moscow had to be dislodged. He permitted Boris Savinkov, who respected Poland's right to independence, to base his Russian Political Committee in Warsaw.[9] He also allowed the White general Stanislav Bulak Balakhovich, who had fought for the North-Western Army under Yudenich, to operate on Polish soil.[10] These manoeuvres were kept secret from all but the most consistent anti-communists abroad. In Britain, Winston Churchill was in the know. But Piłsudski was generally hoping to effect territorial and political change before those who—like Lloyd George—sought a commercial treaty with Soviet Russia could do anything to stop him.[11] Soviet leaders as usual assumed that the Allied powers had organized the Polish offensive. They failed to understand the scope for initiative available to Piłsudski as well as his fear that unless he took action the Allies might cage him inside policies that injured Poland's interests. The Polish commanders and politicians were intent on redrawing the map of Europe without delay and eliminating the menace of Bolshevism. Too much consultation with the Western Allies might undermine this purpose.

This did not mean that the Poles lacked Allied assistance—and the People's Commissariat of Foreign Affairs monitored the pages of the Western press for evidence of such a connection.[12] Newspapers from *The Times* through to the Labour-owned *Daily News* were followed with care. Especially alarming was a report in *L'Humanité*, the French communist publication, about the presence of French military cadres in Poland. Already in February 1920 there were 732 French officers, including nine generals, on active service there. *L'Humanité* added that British arms exports had reached Poland in the winter, taking this as proof that 'the West' was engaged in a criminal war against Soviet Russia.[13] Evidence was adduced that an 'American officer' had been conducting sabotage behind the Soviet lines.[14] The monitoring department in the People's Commissariat noted that the *New Statesman* had stated categorically that Lloyd George could have stopped Poland from going to war but instead had chosen to send armaments to Warsaw—his way of getting round the obstacle of 'English' popular opinion, which was hostile to an Anglo-Russian war, even a small one. The People's Commissariat saw Lloyd George as Piłsudski's partner in international villainy.[15] Stalin put it memorably, saying that the invasion of Ukraine was the 'third campaign of the Entente'.[16]

The French officers supplied to help with the training of the Polish Army included the young Charles de Gaulle. Released from German captivity at the end of the Great War, he gave lectures in Poland on military doctrine and methods and joined a Polish combat unit in July 1919. Such links left no doubt in Moscow that France was seeking the demise of Soviet Russia.[17]

Then there was the Kosciuszko Squadron of volunteer US aviators formed by Colonel Cedric Fauntleroy in January 1920 at Prime Minister Paderewski's request. President Wilson gave his consent without putting anything into writing because he wished to maintain the pretence that America had withdrawn from European conflicts.[18] The dozen American airmen were daredevils who swooped over enemy lines on their dangerous missions, developing a new technique of 'low level bombardment with frontal fire power'.[19] The most ebullient of them was Merian Cooper. Shot down in flames and badly wounded in the Great War, he refused to accept his Distinguished Service Cross on the grounds that he did not deserve anything for saving his own life. He then offered himself for work with Hoover's American Relief Administration in Lwów. As fear of Red offensives grew in 1919, he received permission to join the Polish armed forces and joined in their Ukrainian incursions.[20] 'Coop' was shot down on 13 July 1920 and captured by the Reds. The Polish press announced his death but in fact he was held in a Soviet prison until he escaped about ten months later. He was not the only daredevil in the Kosciuszko Squadron. In March 1921 the *Washington Post* was to report the awarding of medals to its members at the Polish legation in Washington.[21]

The British too were involved. Paul Dukes, now under the cover of an assignment for *The Times*, shuttled between Kraków and western Europe liaising with Polish military commanders such as Generals Gustaw Zygadłowicz and Lucjan Zeligowski.[22] Not bothering to disguise his presence, he was photographed with the Polish Women's Death Battalion and was with the Polish army when it retook Grodno at the end of the war.[23] Sidney Reilly joined Dukes on his mission in October 1920, and the two of them met up with Savinkov.[24] Savinkov regarded Reilly as one of the great anti-Bolsheviks and 'a knight without fear or reproach', and this was the beginning of a warm friendship.[25]

But if the Poles failed to hang on to Ukraine, Allied assistance would not be enough in itself. The Politburo now diverted nearly all its forces to fight Piłsudski, and Kiev fell back into Red hands on 13 June 1920. The Polish positions crumbled in central and western Ukraine over the weeks that followed; on 12 July the Red Army reached what Lenin called 'the ethnographic frontier of Poland'. The Bolsheviks exulted. The Party Central Committee aimed at 'the Sovietization of Poland', and on 17 July Trotsky ordered the Red Army Supreme Command to chase the Poles deep behind the Curzon Line.[26] Warsaw was the first big target. Leading Bolsheviks in Latvia and Georgia criticized the decision, not out of respect for Polish independence but from a desire for Trotsky to invade their own countries before he moved into Poland.[27] This discussion was kept secret from the Second Comintern Congress since Lenin thought that many foreign delegates were 'nationalists and pacifists' who could not be trusted with the information. He noted that the 'English' comrades had been aghast at his advice to seek the overthrow of the British government: 'They made the kind of faces that I reckon even the best photograph couldn't capture.'[28] He had no wish to ask what they thought of an offensive using 'bayonets to probe whether the social revolution of the proletariat had matured in Poland'.[29]

On 23 July the Politburo created a Provisional Revolutionary Committee for Poland. Diplomatic duplicity was to be deployed. Britain and France would be assured that the Soviet government was willing to enter peace talks, but this was just a diplomatic manoeuvre to deflect attention from the Red advance on Warsaw. Lithuania was to be told that it had nothing to fear from Russia.[30] This too was insincere because the Bolsheviks wanted to Sovietize the entire Baltic region in due course. But they wanted to limit the number of enemies until the Red Army had dealt with the Poles.

Trotsky told his troops that the objective was not to subjugate Poland but to give power to the 'working Polish people' in their own land. He denied that Russia had started or even wanted the war.[31] The Politburo hoped to attract Polish workers and poor peasants by a series of exemplary measures. Banks and factories would be nationalized in the future area of occupation. A terror would be initiated against landlords, clergy and commanders. Lenin was at his most bloodthirsty when urging Dzerzhinski and the Cheka to send squads into the Polish countryside with a view to seizing and hanging class enemies—the same tactics he had called for in Russia in summer 1918. Communists who had been brought up in Poland were not convinced that the Politburo knew what it was doing; they raised a cry about the strength of Polish national sentiments in all social classes. Stalin added that the Volunteer Army under Pëtr Wrangel in Crimea continued to constitute a serious danger to Soviet rule. But Lenin overrode such pessimism. The opportunity had arisen to spread the revolution westwards and he was going to take it—and Trotsky was only too happy to oblige. The time for 'revolutionary war' had arrived.

Poland was not the only prize in the minds of Soviet leaders. Lenin wrote to Stalin: 'Zinoviev and Bukharin as well as myself think it would be appropriate to stimulate a revolution immediately in Italy. My personal opinion is that this requires the Sovietization of Hungary as well as perhaps Czechia [Czechoslovakia] and Romania.'[32] On 10 August the Politburo approved Trotsky's proposal for Comintern Congress delegates to go home and prepare for revolution. Confident of success, he asked for a hundred German communists to be assigned to the front line to conduct propaganda—he assumed that they would soon be talking to Germans in Germany.[33]

Lenin appreciated that the French and British would not sit on their hands while Berlin ripped up the Versailles treaty. He devised a scheme for a coalition of the far left and the far right in Germany. Although the Freikorps and their sympathizers detested communism and had bloodily crushed the Spartacists, they agreed with Comintern that the Western Allies had reduced their country to slavery. Lenin urged German communist leaders to line up with them to reclaim freedom for their country.[34] The alliance would be strictly provisional. He expected that, once Germany regained its full independence, there would be civil war while the communists and the right-wing paramilitaries fought it out for supremacy.[35] He predicted that a proletarian dictatorship on the Soviet model would emerge from this. He said nothing in public, but Radek referred to the basic idea in *Pravda*. Lenin and Radek had no scruples about exploiting the services of anti-communists so long as the ultimate result might be a communist seizure of power. Strategic flexibility was essential. Lenin had to admit that any alliance with the political far right would be an 'unnatural' one, and communist leftists in Germany justifiably doubted that he would have accepted such a strategy for Russia in 1917. Having joined the communist movement in their country because they despised the compromises favoured by the other socialists, they shunned Lenin's advice to negotiate with the butchers of Liebknecht and Luxemburg.

Soviet leaders anyway accepted the likelihood of a second Great War when the Western Allies crossed the German border in full strength to suppress any government that refused to recognize the treaty of Versailles. But Lenin and his comrades felt they simply had to force a breach in Russia's international quarantine. As the Red Army advanced into Poland there was already a great deal of political unrest in Germany and the government was worried about more than just the German communists. Ministers feared that the Independent Social-Democratic Party might collude in a *coup d'état* in Berlin, especially after Arthur Crispien—one of the leaders of the Independent Social-Democrats—threatened as much in the Reichstag.[36]

Lenin had already discussed with Stalin how best to organize a system of Soviet-style states stretching from the Rhineland to the Pacific. Trotsky stayed out of the debate, having talked throughout the Great War about the achievability of a United States of Europe. But Lenin now wanted a single federation of communist republics linking Europe and Asia. In this way, Soviet Russia and Soviet Ukraine would join up with Soviet Germany and Soviet Poland. Stalin was sceptical, telling Lenin that the German people were unlikely to want membership of a communist federation founded and led by Russians. Lenin had omitted to take the national factor into consideration. Stalin's counter-proposal was to establish not one but two federations, the first being based in Moscow and the other in Berlin. Such federations would of course be headed by parties united under the Communist International, and Stalin implicitly proposed that this was a sufficient safeguard against disunity and strife. He offered the idea in good faith only to receive a furious rebuke from Lenin, who accused him of succumbing to nationalism. Stalin was affronted; he wrote back exclaiming that Soviet leaders had to be intelligent about the challenges that they had to surmount if they were to communize central Europe.[37]

The dispute soon blew over as Lenin focused his attention on the campaign for Warsaw. He and the Politburo turned down Sergo Ordjonikidze's plan for 'a military force to be sent into Persia' in mid-August.[38] Nor did they see any need to recall the Soviet delegation they had sent to London, which from the beginning of August was reinforced by the arrival of Politburo member Kamenev. The idea was that Krasin would continue to lead the talks on trade while Kamenev handled the diplomacy about war and peace in whatever way the changing situation demanded.[39] Lenin and Trotsky were keeping their options open; and Trotsky, while directing the Red Army to break through to Germany, asked the Politburo to use diplomatic means to secure a rail route across Poland for the shipment of arms from German businesses—Central Committee member Alexei Rykov was then given the task of buying the weaponry. The Politburo agreed.[40] The fight was on for supremacy in central Europe. As the Reds hurtled towards Warsaw, Soviet leaders felt no inhibition about simultaneously planning to crush the German capitalist elites and do big business with them.

The British sought to prevent any such outcome by announcing a diplomatic initiative for peace between Russia and Poland. Kamenev and Krasin called at 10 Downing Street for talks with Lloyd George and the Conservative Party leader Andrew Bonar Law on 4 August;[41] but the results were inconclusive, and the next day Kamenev set out Soviet objections in a letter to Lloyd George.[42] A further meeting lasting five hours was held on 6 August. This time Churchill was in attendance for a while as Lloyd George and Bonar Law debated with Kamenev and Krasin, and an agreement was reached which was to be relayed to Moscow. Lloyd George hoped to have Lenin's reply before he met the French Prime Minister Alexandre Millerand in Kent the following day.[43] The British government wanted an immediate armistice. To the French, though, this seemed intolerable as it would lend respectability to a bandit regime, and Lloyd George felt compelled to back down; he also felt that the Poles had to some degree brought the Soviet invasion on themselves by their Ukrainian campaign.[44] He tried to demonstrate his open-mindedness in foreign policy by receiving a Labour Party delegation and listening to their demands for non-interference in Russia. He replied that he could not forget that the Bolsheviks were undemocratic and adduced the latest statements of Bertrand Russell, who had opposed the Great War but then turned against the Soviet leadership. Trade union leader and Labour Party militant Ernie Bevin urged the Prime Minister to ignore French pressure and threatened trouble if military force or supplies were sent to Piłsudski.[45] Lloyd George replied that he had broken with Soviet Russia because Lenin had abandoned the Allies, although he insisted that if Lenin now wanted peace he could have it.[46]

The political temperature in the United Kingdom rose still higher when an influential group in the Independent Labour Party called for Churchill's impeachment as Secretary of State for War.[47] Churchill issued a quick rebuttal:

> It is not the British who are making war, but the Russian Bolshevists. They are at this moment invading Poland and trampling down its freedom. They are doing their best to light the flames of war in Persia, Afghanistan, and, if possible, in India. Their avowed intention is to procure by violence a revolution in every country . . . My sole object has been, and will be, to keep such hateful foreign oppression far from our native land.[48]

While denying he had any wish for a Western crusade against Soviet Russia, he urged that the talks on any commercial treaty be suspended immediately.[49]

Not even Lloyd George was willing to see Poland defeated, and he had already stated that the British would go to war again if the Red Army occupied Warsaw.[50] As a result he was relieved when reports indicated that Piłsudski's headlong retreat had stopped in the Polish capital. Piłsudski declared that Warsaw would be defended to the last man, and he had grounds for confidence. The Reds were exhausted by their hot pursuit of the Polish army; their supply lines were frail and over-stretched and their equipment inadequate. Their commander in the northern sector, Mikhail Tukhachevski, found it hard to co-ordinate his advance as Warsaw came within range. Exposing the naivety and wrong-headedness of Lenin's rationale for the war, Poles of all classes saw the Reds as Russian invaders rather than internationalist liberators. They waited for the enemy on the eastern side of the River Vistula where Piłsudski had time to organize them. He also had the advantage that Stalin, the leading commissar in the southern sector of the Red advance, ignored orders to divert his armies from outside Lwów and reinforce the strategic thrust at the Polish capital. It would probably have made little difference if Stalin had shown greater compliance since Tukhachevski's forces were rapidly torn apart by the resurgent Polish army. By 19 August the Reds were conducting a general retreat from the Vistula. Central Europe was saved from Sovietization.[51]

The scale of the defeat outdid anything suffered by the Reds in the Civil War after Kolchak's initial success at the end of 1918. There was nothing they could do but fall back and sue for a truce. The Politburo convened on 1 September. Trotsky, the People's Commissar for Military Affairs, gave a gloomy account of the campaign and recommended agreeing to a 'compromise peace'—a quaint formulation for acceptance of defeat. Peace talks would be requested with the Poles in Riga.[52] At the next Politburo meeting, five days later, Chicherin pressed for peace to be signed fast with Latvia and Lithuania.[53] It was plain to the leadership that Moscow had to content itself with the territory won in the Civil War or else risk losing everything. Kamenev left for Russia on 11 September.[54] He had had a last meeting with Lloyd George a day earlier and, together with Krasin, had become acquainted with the latest British terms for a trade treaty. On peace, there was no longer anything he could do. Piłsudski and Paderewski were now the men who set the agenda.[55]

When the Party Conference met later in the month, Lenin was frank about the 'gigantic, unprecedented defeat'. He acknowledged that it was the product of a Polish 'patriotic upsurge' rather than action or assistance by the Western Allies. Soviet Russia had to accept that the Poles were unlikely to agree to the frontier proposed earlier by Lord Curzon. Galicia had to be delivered to Poland and the boundaries shifted to the east of the Curzon Line.[56] Lenin added: 'This undoubtedly means that a mistake was committed: you see, we had victory in our hands and we let it slip from our fingers.'[57] He asked forgiveness, admitting that the Politburo should have halted the Red advance in eastern Galicia and been content with gaining a base for a future offensive—'a little push' into Hungary across the Carpathians.[58] Now that peace negotiations were under way the priority had to be the regeneration of the Soviet economy. He expressed doubt that the Bolsheviks could succeed without foreign industrial investment. Communism, he declared, could not be built solely by 'Russian forces'.[59]

29. TRADE TALKS ABROAD

The Polish war punctuated a year of talks on a trade treaty between Soviet Russia and the United Kingdom. The British government played its hand with some caution. Its ministers were determined to prevent foreigners from stirring up revolution and on 16 July 1920 deported Santeri Nuorteva of the Russian Soviet Bureau, as the front organization was known by then—who had landed in Liverpool from New York. Nuorteva was carrying a 'diplomatic passport' stamped by his comrade Ludwig Martens. Back in New York, the Russian Soviet Bureau blustered that Canadian contracts to the value of six million dollars would be cancelled.[1] Martens attended a gathering of 8,000 supporters in Madison Square Garden where he wanted to call on the US government to permit the transport of medical supplies to Russia. He received fifteen minutes of applause before he could start speaking. The Internationale was sung. Martens haltingly read out his speech in English before giving a vivid delivery in Russian: 'There is much talk of Bolshevist propaganda against America. There is no such thing. But there is propaganda against Soviet Russia.'[2] This was of no help to Nuorteva in England, where Lloyd George had to be seen to be standing up to communism to placate the Conservative MPs in the governing coalition. Rejecting pleas on Nuorteva's behalf, he said that his papers were not in order and that normal procedures had been followed.[3]

Yet rather than sending Nuorteva back to America, Lloyd George allowed him to travel on to the Estonian capital, from where he would be able to reach Russia.[4] Nor did Lloyd George object to Kamenev and Krasin coming to London.[5] Things had changed since Kamenev's fruitless visit in 1918. Lloyd George was giving communists a chance to show that they deserved admittance inside the perimeter of formal international relations. Lenin understood this. Worrying that Kamenev and Krasin might get over-excited, he warned them against summoning far-left socialists to get arms for the British working class.[6]

The dominant theme in the talks with Kamenev and Krasin at 10 Downing Street on 4 and 8 August was the Soviet military advance on Warsaw.[7] But after demanding peace and security for Poland, Lloyd George and Bonar Law also took the opportunity to set out their conditions for future trade with Soviet Russia. They insisted that Soviet leaders should cease their political subversion and ideological propaganda in the United Kingdom and its empire. Kamenev affected to understand and agree. But the evidence from telegrams between Moscow and London told a different story, evidence that was eagerly published in *The Times*.[8] Ernst Fetterlein at the Government Code and Cypher School had decrypted the intercepts between Lenin and Kamenev, which were then leaked to the press. Lloyd George disliked what he learned from Fetterlein about the Kremlin's basic intentions and told Kamenev that there was no prospect of resuming Anglo-Russian trade unless Lenin changed his posture.[9] *The Times* also alleged that Kamenev had a hand in Moscow's delivery of the secret subsidy to the *Daily Herald* and was in regular contact with the Council of Action, which the Labour Party and the trade unions had established on 5 August as part of a campaign to prevent Britain from intervening in the Soviet–Polish war. Other newspapers soon took the same line that Kamenev had come as a diplomat and behaved as a subversive. All this angered Lloyd George and he rebuked Krasin and Kamenev for breaking their word that they would not interfere in British politics. He told Kamenev that if he did not quickly leave the United Kingdom, he would be deported.[10]

Lloyd George grew more truculent when news reached London of the Red Army's defeat east of Warsaw. Kamenev accepted that he was no longer *persona grata* in the United Kingdom. Before he departed he sent an open letter to the Prime Minister claiming that the government was exploiting 'paltry and unproved' charges supplied to it by secret police agents; he also deplored the French government's decision to recognize Wrangel rather than Lenin as the leader of Russia. Kamenev worried that the Allies might rediscover their enthusiasm for military intervention, but in fact Lloyd George was being crafty. Nobody in Whitehall really thought Kamenev was worse behaved than Krasin, yet Krasin was allowed to keep his New Bond Street office and continue the trade talks.[11] The truth was that the Prime Minister still desired some kind of commercial treaty with Soviet Russia.

By making a fog of the situation he alleviated the criticism in the press. Lacking the military or political means to eliminate Bolshevism, he was doing what he thought was the next best thing by undermining the Soviet order through a resumption of commercial contacts. Lloyd George saw himself as the mole-catcher who would grub out communism.

Like the other Liberals in his governing coalition, he wanted to avoid giving any impression that ministers were out to provoke an armed clash with Soviet Russia. He also needed to show himself as a friend of the British working man, which would be difficult if he threatened a so-called proletarian government elsewhere in Europe. He was also straining to promote Britain's economic recovery from the post-war recession. Industrialists who had done good business in Russia before 1914 were lobbying him for a resumption of trade with the Russians. National economic self-interest was put forward in justification, and Lloyd George acted with confidence that more people would eventually support him than were writing to *The Times* to denounce him.

Krasin still goaded the British by mentioning the progress being made by the rest of his negotiating team elsewhere in Europe. Among the experts on banking and railways he had left behind in Stockholm was Professor Yuri Lomonosov, once a monarchist but now a supporter of the October Revolution. Lomonosov was involved in Sovnarkom's offer to sell its gold reserves in exchange for locomotives, carriages and rail track, and industrial companies in Sweden competed for the contracts being dangled in front of them.[12] Originally the Soviet intention had been to make such purchases in Germany, but this was scuppered when the Allied powers reaffirmed their ban on deals involving Russian gold of disputed ownership. The Germans, having lost the war, had to comply with what the Allies demanded. Sweden, which had been neutral in the Great War and was therefore unaffected by the Paris peace treaties, was the next best option for the Bolsheviks. An agreement was drafted and, with Krasin's consent, a provisional deal for one thousand locomotives was signed on 22 October 1920. Gold was already in place in Tallinn to complete the agreement. Sovnarkom was delighted at this latest breach in the wall of Russia's economic isolation. It was consequently odd that it should be Krasin who raised an objection. He belatedly expressed the fear that the Allies would compel Sweden to withhold any railway exports under the terms of the contract. He thought there was a risk of depleting Russian gold reserves for the benefit of Swedish business partners but not for Sovnarkom.[13]

There was another snag, and it was a big one. Swedish industry lacked the capacity to manufacture so much railway equipment with any rapidity. The Stockholm deal would depend on Sweden's metallurgical companies quietly buying around eight hundred locomotives from Germany.[14] Business of this surreptitious nature had gone on between Russia and Germany throughout the Great War when German entrepreneurs established 'Swedish' electrical companies to trade with Russian firms in products essential to Russia's military effort. Another wartime dodge had been for German enterprises to stick Scandinavian markings on goods made in Germany. So the Johann Faber works, which had sold pencils in the Russian Empire for decades, simply rebranded its output with Danish insignia; and German razors found their way into Russia emblazoned with the motto: 'To a Brave Russian Soldier for Distinguished Service'.[15]

The ratification of the Swedish contract was scheduled for 18 December, and Krasin had yet to be convinced. The Stockholm members of his negotiating team went to London to plead with him. Krasin was not overly receptive. His talks with the British had never been easy and the Swedish initiative might cause complications. On balance, he thought, a firm, open treaty with Britain was preferable to a dubious set of arrangements in Sweden. He was not being unnecessarily difficult; he bore a huge responsibility. Soviet Russia was economically shattered, and the Politburo would judge his efforts unkindly if he allowed unprofitable deals to be brokered. He was known as pragmatic but on this occasion he spoke to his team like the most ruthless Bolshevik, saying that they should be shot for the deal they were recommending. One of them replied: 'It's fortunate, Leonid Borisovich [Krasin], that you've been saying this to me in London rather than in Moscow. Right now, just listen to me. There will always be time to shoot us later.'[16] Such was the grim humour of communist dictatorship, volunteered by a non-communist seeking to demonstrate his honesty and loyalty. After three hours of discussion Krasin finally gave his approval, admitting that his team had done a good job in Stockholm.[17]

Worries about the Allied reaction had never deterred Lenin and Trotsky; and as the outstanding figures in the Soviet communist leadership, they felt freer to follow their instincts in negotiating with foreigners. Lenin met his first businessmen from abroad in summer 1920 when a certain Washington B. Vanderlip arrived from America. Vanderlip pretended to be a scion of the exceedingly wealthy Frank D. Vanderlip and his business dynasty and also suggested that he could speak on behalf of Senator Warren G. Harding of Ohio who, as the Presidential candidate for the Republican Party, was in favour of resuming trade with Russia. Although Vanderlip had nothing like the wealth or connections he claimed, he knew a bit about Russia since he had prospected for gold in Siberia at the turn of the century.[18] He also had the gift of the gab, and Lenin fell for his blandishments to such a degree that the Soviet authorities signed a provisional deal for him and his backers to take up a vast mining concession in Kamchatka in the Soviet Far East. In November 1920 he fetched up in Stockholm, where he boasted that his company had leased 400,000 square miles in Siberia for sixty years. Vanderlip claimed that he was helping the Soviet government to purchase American goods to the value of $3,000,000,000 which would be paid for with Russian gold and other natural resources.[19]

The *New York Times* immediately warned against Vanderlip's personal credentials and about the dangers and morality of dealing with the communist government;[20] and Senator Harding was not pleased on reading in the press about the ex-prospector's claim to be his business intimate.[21] Lenin incompetently increased American concerns by stating in public that he had granted the Kamchatka concession deliberately so as to play off America and Japan against each other.[22] He naively assumed that no Westerner would read the Russian communist press. He was equally stupid in September when telling H. G. Wells that the Vanderlip deal was the first step towards a US–Russian defensive alliance against Japanese aggression in Siberia. Lenin said that he looked forward to allowing the Americans to build a naval station on the Soviet Pacific coast and signing long-term economic concessions with American companies.[23] Theodore Rothstein, who was doing the interpreting, failed to stop him from blurting out these ideas and pleaded with Wells to keep quiet about what he had heard: 'He is wonderful. But it was an indiscretion . . .' Wells gave his word of honour, only to break it in his book *Russia in the Shadows*: the conversation proved too juicy for him to discard.[24] The world received a lesson that the Soviet rulers could be wily in protecting their interests. Evidently, too, the artful Lenin could be a bungler when his tongue ran away with him.

Vanderlip meanwhile performed like a snake-oil salesman: 'I have joined the frontiers of Russia and America, making a broad band of republicanism around the world from Atlantic to Atlantic.' He called on the US Congress to regularize trade relations without delay.[25] Mining, timber-felling and fur-pelt production had made fortunes for entrepreneurs in Siberia before the

Great War. The region's general potential was famously under-exploited. Vanderlip continued his approaches to west-coast investors asking them to join his scheme and making it seem like a licence to print money; and soon he inveigled the Standard Oil Co. to purchase a quarter of his shares.[26] The impetus towards a commercial treaty with Soviet Russia was gathering strength. On 4 January the *Manchester Guardian* reported that the US authorities were on the point of lifting their restrictions; its source was said to be 'a Moscow wireless message'.[27] The Soviet leadership was probably trying to bounce countries into restoring commercial links.[28] Just as the Kremlin intended, the Republican Party in the US pricked up its ears. Senator Joseph I. France of Maryland led his colleagues in advocating official recognition of Soviet Russia. When the order was given to deport Ludwig Martens in early 1921, Senator France publicly protested and called for an end to the economic blockade.[29] In his eyes simply no American interest was being served by ostracizing the Russian communist regime.

On 26 January his campaign bore fruit in the Senate when Henry Cabot Lodge convened the Committee on Foreign Relations to hold hearings on Russia.[30] Senator France, as a prosperous man of affairs, spoke his mind; but the witnesses were chosen mainly from the American labour movement. This was deliberate. Lodge and France wanted to appear as if they had the interests of working men and women at the forefront of their minds—and they allowed plenty of time for them to argue that trade with Russia would boost industrial production and employment. The trade unionists spoke with admiration for Vanderlip's Kamchatka initiative. They pointed out that a treaty would open the way for the US import of Russian raw materials and export of American manufactured goods. Senators asked briefly about the dictatorship established by the Bolsheviks, then dropped the matter. They were somewhat more persistent in questioning the labour movement's representatives about their attitude to democracy in America. The unionists were ready for this and presented themselves first and foremost as US patriots. Yet this failed to convince several members of the Senate Committee. Under further interrogation, some witnesses declined to repudiate the potential benefits of introducing Bolshevism to the American political scene, and Alexander L. Trachtenberg from the Socialist Party admitted to favouring the 'nationalisation of property'.[31]

This was not what Senators Lodge and France wanted to hear; they knew they would be thwarted in their objective of changing US foreign policy if the idea got around that labour movement leaders were crypto-communists. (They really should have done more research on Trachtenberg, who wanted his Socialist Party to become an affiliate of Comintern.)[32] Lodge and his colleagues were happier when witnesses quoted H. G. Wells and his arguments for a trade treaty. They also liked it when John Spargo was cited as warning that America was falling behind Britain in looking after its economic interests;[33] and under Republican leadership the Committee took the unusual step of including the entire report of the British Labour delegation to Russia in its published proceedings. The thinking behind this was obvious. The Labour delegation argued for the resumption of commercial links, and this was exactly what Lodge and Cabot sought for America.[34] Fortunes could be made in Russia. America should not miss out on the lucrative opportunities.

The divergences among the Allied powers—or rather their governments—were getting wider. The French were resolute in their stand against dealing with Soviet Russia while Lenin refused to recognize obligations for the foreign loans incurred by Russian governments before October 1917. The Americans, through the Senate hearings, were only just beginning to consider whether to change policy. Even in the United Kingdom the situation was fluid. The British were still talking to Krasin, and no one outside the negotiations could yet tell whether they would produce a signed agreement. But the Western Alliance was practically at an end. Indeed Allied leaders took only one big decision jointly about Russia. This was reached on 24 January 1921 when the Allies granted their *de jure* recognition of Estonia and Latvia as independent states.[35] The signal was being given that the Russian Whites were a lost cause. Until then the Allies had avoided contradicting the ambition of Kolchak, Denikin, Yudenich and Wrangel to reconstitute 'Russia One and Indivisible'. They now accepted that at least two new Baltic states deserved official acceptance. As the remnants of Wrangel's forces clambered on boats for Constantinople in November 1920, they left behind the battlefields of defeat and looked to the future without solace. Their paymasters and advisers abandoned them.

The Bolshevik leadership and the Whites were in agreement on one thing: the desirability of gathering back the territories of the Russian Empire. The recent military defeat in Poland ruled out speedy action to the west of Russia, and the Kremlin set about assuring Estonia, Latvia and Lithuania that it had only peaceful intentions towards them. The south

Caucasus was a different matter. Azerbaijan fell to the Red Army in April 1920, Armenia in December that year; like Ukraine, they were quickly turned into Soviet republics. For a while, the Georgians remained under Menshevik rule, but on 26 January 1921 the Party Central Committee decided to correct this anomaly with a plan to provoke a diplomatic breach with Georgia with a view to organizing an invasion.[36]

The same day, the Central Committee examined the latest reports from London. Lloyd George was proving amenable even though the legal status of Russian gold had still presented difficulties as recently as December.[37] But although Krasin had done well with the Prime Minister, the judicial system was another matter. Mr Justice Roche in the same month found in favour of the Briton who had lost his timber in Sovnarkom's nationalizing campaigns of two years earlier and was seeking to impound a Soviet cargo of veneer about to be unloaded in the United Kingdom. Roche's judgment endangered any contract entered into by Krasin, and the *New York Times* warned that this could also have adverse consequences for any American businessmen tempted to trade with communist Russia.[38] The oil of the south Caucasus was another contentious matter. Two British companies, the Baku Consolidated Oilfields and the gloriously named Spies Petroleum Co., had suffered the nationalization of their assets when the Red Army marched into Azerbaijan—some of their staff were thrown into prison. The companies raised a hue and cry when Krasin offered to make these assets available to other British enterprises.[39] The disgruntled Leslie Urquhart also continued to make trouble for Soviet negotiators by denouncing the London talks in *The Times*.[40]

Even so, the Prime Minister was willing to keep the talks going. With a little more compromise on the Soviet side it might soon be possible to conclude a trade treaty. A small working party was created in Moscow to examine questions about Russia's foreign debts in case Krasin needed to give some sort of commitment to recognizing them.[41] Better to sign a half-good treaty than to lose the chance of any treaty at all. But when Lloyd George kept up the pressure on Krasin for the Bolsheviks to refrain from conducting their propaganda and subversion in the British Empire, Krasin affected outrage. If the government in Russia were to accept such a clause, he asked, what was to be done about Secretary for War Winston Churchill's contributions to the Western press?[42] Churchill doubtless caused annoyance to the Kremlin. But his commentary was never published in Moscow, and

Krasin understood full well that Lloyd George simply wanted a reciprocal understanding that the British and the Russian authorities would not interfere in each other's politics. Krasin could easily—if insincerely—give this guarantee. Almost without anyone expecting it, the muddled negotiations began to look as if they might end in a treaty.

30. THE ECONOMICS
OF SURVIVAL

Although the Bolsheviks believed they were close to concluding trade negotiations with Britain and faced no immediate military threat, the domestic situation was far from easy. Until the winter of 1920–1 it looked as if the
Kremlin would indefinitely maintain its wartime economic system which
involved the forcible requisitioning of grain from the peasantry without
compensation. Previous attempts to modify this policy, first by Trotsky and
then by Lenin, met with furious objections from the rest of the leadership.
In February 1920, indeed, Lenin himself had led those who shouted down
Trotsky as a promoter of capitalism. At the end of the same year he received
his own come-uppance when he recommended a milder scheme of his
own.[1]

The party had been distracted by an internal dispute between Lenin and
Trotsky about what limits to place on the freedoms of trade unions in peacetime, but the leadership could not ignore the growing danger of serious insurrection for long. Industrial strikes had broken out in most cities. There
was discontent in every garrison, and mutinies were not unknown. And the
peasants grew ever more hostile to a government that seized their harvests.
On 8 February 1921 the Politburo came to its senses when reports reached
Moscow about the crescendo of rural revolts. Western Siberia and
Ukraine—Russia's bread basket—were ablaze. If their crucial agricultural
contribution was threatened, the cities would starve. The final straw for
the Soviet leaders was a rebellion led by Socialist-Revolutionary A. S.
Antonov throughout Tambov province in the mid-Volga region. Having
won the Civil War, the Bolsheviks were on the point of losing the peace.

The Politburo urgently needed to offer some concessions to the peasants. The solution was obvious: the authorities had to stop seizing the whole agricultural 'surplus' from the villages and introduce a tax-in-kind, allowing them to make a profit from what was left of their harvest after meeting their fiscal obligation. A corner of private trade would be restored to them through this New Economic Policy.

Still troubled by the wrangling over the unions, Lenin was keenly aware that the New Economic Policy would be even more divisive. He and the rest of the Politburo were determined to keep the proposals strictly confidential until all the details had been worked out. The same degree of caution was exercised over the London trade talks, with *Pravda* keeping its reports deliberately vague. Lenin had delayed reopening his campaign on concessions until December 1920 at the Congress of Soviets, where he cited the Kamchatka deal with Vanderlip as the model. But his ideas had met with a stormy reaction from Bolsheviks, and he reverted to discussing the matter behind closed doors; but he had no doubt that the collapse of Soviet oil production made it crucial to attract foreign companies back to Baku.[2] This was deeply uncongenial to Azerbaijani communist leaders who remembered the Nobel Brothers' Petroleum Co. and other enterprises for their careless attitude both to the health of workers and to the environment. Lenin's blandishments to Western petrochemical companies would flood the republic with capitalism. Soviet leaders were naturally nervous about changes in policy that could touch off a split in their fiery party.

The discussions continued long into the New Year, and on 5 February 1921 the Politburo asked Kamenev and Rykov to enquire whether concessions were simply the best way to reverse the decline in Azerbaijani oil output.[3] If Baku industry was to be restored, rapid action was required—and there was no evidence that the communist leaders in Azerbaijan had any idea how they would raise their own capital to begin the process. At a further discussion, nonetheless, the votes in the Politburo were split and the matter was referred to the Party Central Committee rather than risk a dispute throughout the party.[4] This deflected the debate to a wider circle of party leaders as regional officials got to hear about what was being proposed. The Central Committee itself was divided but eventually decided to pronounce concessions acceptable in principle if the 'mortal danger' of the slump in production could be prevented (although it was recognized that foreign companies might not wish to operate again in Baku). Lenin had won the debate, but it was only by a slim majority that he did so; and nobody could be sure that the rest of the party would not raise objections when the decision became public knowledge.[5]

In London, despite reports of continued objections to a trade treaty appearing regularly in *The Times*,[6] there was an air of expectancy. Krasin had signed contracts with British companies in advance of a settlement between the two governments, and Yorkshire textile factories queued to sell cloth to Russia.[7] Businessmen travelled from the United Kingdom to Tallinn to sign their Russian deals using Sweden as the umbrella for their business and readying themselves for what was expected to be an enormous expansion of commerce.[8]

The British government refused to give way on certain of its demands. Soviet Russia had to cease all hostile activities, including propaganda, in the territories of the British Empire. Britons in Russian captivity had to be immediately released; in return the British would repatriate the Russians they had incarcerated. Chicherin, however, told Krasin to resist any pressure because Britain's hold on its empire in the East was no longer as strong as it had been. Lenin was blunter still: 'That swine Lloyd George has no scruples of shame in the way he deceives. Don't believe a word he says and gull him three times as much.'[9] But Chicherin and Lenin soon calmed down since they knew that they would lose the deal if they rejected the British conditions, and Lenin remained pessimistic about Russia's capacity for independent economic recovery without foreign assistance. His sudden explosions were characteristic. When Soviet officials went abroad on missions he frequently accused them of appeasing foreigners and quietly forgot how he had succumbed to the Germans at Brest-Litovsk. At any rate Krasin could show that the British government was willing to overlook the entire question of loans made to Russia's previous governments; and since Lloyd George was not driving the hardest of bargains, Sovnarkom empowered Krasin to strike the deal.

Since the débâcle near Warsaw, the Red Army had stood aside as Estonia, Latvia and Lithuania proclaimed their borders and confirmed their independence. Adolf Ioffe led the Soviet delegation in the peace negotiations with Poland in Riga. The Poles had given up their hope that any Russian force could bring down the Bolsheviks. Wrangel's army felt the full strength of a Red Army which was no longer being asked to fight a campaign on Polish territory. Crammed into Crimea, the Volunteer Army was in a desperate plight by early November 1920 and Wrangel ordered a mass evacuation, along with hundreds of thousands of civilian fugitives, across the Black Sea.

The Russian White cause had gone down to comprehensive defeat. The Polish leadership recognized its incapacity to drive the Reds out of Ukraine and settled for a lot less than Poland's April 1920 war aims. It was no longer convenient for the Poles to host Russian forces, and Piłsudski told Bulak-Balakhovich and his troops to leave the country.[10] The Polish border would stay as it had been established in war by October 1920, hundreds of miles east of the Curzon Line. The Central Committee ordered the People's Commissariat of Foreign Affairs to press for a peace treaty with all speed.[11]

The prospect of peace between Soviet Russia and Poland proved disastrous for Menshevik-ruled Georgia because it freed the Red Army to cross into Georgian territory from Armenia. The campaign began on 15 February 1921. Tiflis fell ten days later and a Georgian Soviet Republic was proclaimed. Almost the entire territory of the Russian Empire south of the Caucasus was drawn back under Moscow's control—just a few slivers of land were ceded to Turkey, which the Kremlin was seeking to placate at a time when it could not contemplate any military initiative abroad.

Hoping to reduce the intensity of all external threats, on 26 February Russia signed a friendship treaty with Persia. The newly appointed Soviet ambassador to Tehran was none other than Theodore Rothstein. Meanwhile Krasin had returned to Moscow to discuss the finalization of the trade agreement with the British. He gave an interview to Louise Bryant, denying that Soviet Russia was in any way a menace to other countries: 'After all, the talk of the Third International is exaggerated and ridiculous. We haven't enough people in Russia to meet our needs. We are not fools enough to send our best people abroad when they are needed here to develop Russia. The best means for the world to get rid of this bogy of Bolshevik propaganda is to begin vigorous trade.'[12] In her report, Bryant stressed that a freshly signed treaty with Afghanistan put aside the 'imperialist' legacy of old Russia. She predicted an end to the 'English' domination of the region and reported that Soviet emissaries in Kabul received an unusual amount of diplomatic freedom.[13] Not long afterwards, Chicherin announced that Turkey too was aspiring to better relations with Soviet Russia.[14] Step by step, the communist leadership were improving their security. None of the world's great powers had yet concluded a treaty with Soviet Russia, but the chances were steadily improving.

But more trouble was brewing off the coast of Petrograd. On 28 February the Soviet naval garrison on the nearby island of Kronstadt assembled to demand an end to communist oppression. Mikhail Kalinin and other Bolshevik leaders held a meeting with them the next day. The list of grievances was a long one. The sailors objected to the Bolshevik political monopoly. They demanded free soviet elections and an end to police terror; they denounced the blocking detachments on city outskirts which stopped the 'sack men' from bringing food supplies from the countryside for illicit sale. Kalinin failed to calm the situation and soon there was open mutiny in Kronstadt. Trotsky, who had spent the winter months polemicizing about the trade unions, lamented the lack of a proper plan to retake Kronstadt and—on 5 March—co-signed a military order with Commander-in-Chief S. S. Kamenev. If the mutineers refused to heed their warnings, the full force of the Red Army would be deployed against them with air support.[15] When Kronstadt held fast to its rebellion, measures were put in hand to suppress it two days later. The symbolism was clear to everyone. The Kronstadters had formed part of the backbone of Bolshevik political and military support in 1917. Now they were turning on Lenin and his party for betraying their hopes. Neither side saw room for compromise.

The Tenth Party Congress opened on 8 March in the shadow of these events. The Politburo by then had clear ideas on the desirable direction of policy and asked Lenin to explain its proposals. The peasantry was to be allowed to sell some of its grain harvest for private profit. The trade unions were to be subjected to greater state control, but not to the degree demanded by Trotsky. Peace was to be ratified with Poland. Foreign concessions were to be encouraged and the draft trade agreement with the United Kingdom confirmed. Lenin stressed the need for the party to deal mercilessly with threats to its power. Peasant revolts and the Kronstadt mutiny alike had to be crushed. Internal party discipline had to be tightened while communists were conducting a retreat from wartime economic policy. Lenin demanded a ban on party factions and denounced the Workers' Opposition, which called for workers and peasants to have decisive influence on economic decision-making, as a 'deviation' from Bolshevik principles. Every single one of these proposals was contentious. But the worse the news about Kronstadt became, the easier it was for Lenin and his group in the leadership to impose their will on the Congress. A consensus developed about the urgent need to fight for the common cause. Even the Workers' Oppositionists overlooked their verbal mauling by Lenin and volunteered for service in the military operation against Kronstadt. A quarter of the 717 full delegates immediately left the Congress in Moscow and travelled north.[16]

Although Trotsky spoke at the Congress at some length about the trade unions and a little about the proposed agrarian reform,[17] he stood shoulder to shoulder with Lenin over Kronstadt and handed the military command to Tukhachevski while warning the Politburo that the mutiny should be liquidated before the spring thaw. Once the ice melted, the rebel sailors would again be able to make contact with foreign countries and the trouble could severely worsen. Tambov province was far from the prying eyes of the Allies, but Kronstadt lay in the Gulf of Finland and was easily approachable from abroad by vessels. Trotsky charged the Central Committee with failing to understand the gravity of the situation.[18]

The Party Congress ended on 16 March with victory for the ascendant group on nearly every big question of policy even though the debates were sometimes fiery. Communists from Azerbaijan repeated their objections to leasing the Baku oilfields to foreigners. But the tightness of the scheduling at the Congress disabled those wishing to express dissent, and the New Economic Policy was raced through to confirmation almost before anyone had time to read the draft decree. The discussion on Anglo-Soviet trade was left until last, and Kamenev barely had time to introduce it before the entire proceedings were brought to a close and everyone stood to sing the Internationale. Lenin had dominated the proceedings and his friends in the leadership gained an easy majority of seats in the election of the Central Committee. And despite banning internal party factions, Lenin behaved as if he headed one both by reducing the number of Trotsky's followers and by clearing them out of the Secretariat. Trotsky in Lenin's opinion needed to suffer for having inflicted an unnecessary dispute about the trade unions on the party. Only then could they again start to work in mutual trust. Lenin regarded this as a priority: the communist leaders faced far too many emergencies for them to fall out.

It was on the very same day in London that the trade talks reached completion with the signing of an agreement by Leonid Krasin and the President of the Board of Trade Robert Horne. While Sovnarkom celebrated, its Russian enemies were justifiably downcast: Lloyd George had rescued the Bolsheviks just at the point when they might have lost everything.[19] The Red Army stormed into Kronstadt on 17 March. The Tambov revolt was in full spate. Other provinces in Ukraine, the Volga region and western Siberia were up in arms against the Bolshevik commissars. If the Allies wanted to undermine the Soviet dictatorship, this was a disastrous moment to choose to come to terms with Sovnarkom and prop up its economy. Anti-

Bolsheviks looked on in dismay and their misfortunes increased when the Poles signed the treaty of Riga on 18 March. The Politburo had weathered the storm. On 19 March its members examined the latest draft of its decree to abolish grain requisitioning and the next day confirmed the manifesto to be issued to the peasants in pursuit of its support.[20] The Bolsheviks had survived a winter of acute emergency by the skin of their teeth—and the British cabinet played not the least part in the denouement.

Lloyd George's insouciance about Soviet revolutionary pretensions was exposed for what it was a few days later, on 24 March, when the German Communist Party called for a general strike with a view to instigating an insurrection in Berlin. Inspiration for this action came from certain communist leaders in Moscow. Chief among them were Zinoviev, Bukharin and Radek. Apparently leaving Lenin and Trotsky in the dark, they dispatched Béla Kun to the German capital as Comintern's plenipotentiary. Kun was still smarting from the collapse of his revolutionary government in Hungary and ardently desired to assist the Berlin comrades in overthrowing Germany's social-democratic government. The thoughtful German communist leader Paul Levi tried to argue against this. He remembered all too clearly what had happened in January 1919 when the Spartacists, lacking popular support, had tried to seize power and had been crushed by government, army and Freikorps. Levi was anxious to avoid a repetition of that disaster.

Kun, however, had come to Berlin invested with the prestige and authority of a Comintern official; he saw to it that Levi was treated as a troublemaker who was breaking party discipline. He relied on the fact that the German communists had joined the party because they thought Germany was ready for communization. They yearned to reproduce the kind of revolution the Bolsheviks had started in Russia in October 1917. Kun drew together Ernst Thalmänn and a group of young leaders with an impulsive desire to take to the streets. Strikes and demonstrations were organized. Proclamations were issued. Rifles were acquired for use when the time came. The German communist leadership rapidly grew in confidence and ordered its supporters to begin what became known as the March Action. It was soon obvious that Kun's plans were based on fantasies. A majority of the working class had no wish to see the elected social-democratic government overturned. At least in Munich in March 1919 there had been a semblance of soviets. There was no equivalent whatsoever in Berlin. Even Kun's failed Hungarian communist republic had attracted support from a large number of workers. In Berlin in early 1921 the social-democrats were more popular than the communists. The communist party was small and inex-perienced and, when it came out on the streets, the Reichswehr and police forced it to withdraw in defeat on 31 March.

In Moscow the Bolsheviks were horrified. If Lenin and Trotsky had been given any advance notice about the March Action they certainly did not admit to it. In fact, they were angry with the bunglers in Russia and Ger-many. Radek and Bukharin had never had a reputation for sagacity, and Zi-noviev was forever trying to make up for his doubts in 1917 about the seizure of power in Petrograd. Although the Politburo refrained from rep-rimanding them, they in return were compelled to accept and endorse Comintern's criticism of the German Communist Party. A scapegoat had to be found. With absolutely no justification—and as a way of bringing Ger-many's communists to heel for the future—Lenin targeted Paul Levi. Levi was the very man who had endeavoured to stop the March Action before it could begin. But he had breached party discipline whereas the bunglers had behaved with perfect loyalty.

The Soviets already had a reputation for oppression at home and sub-version abroad. The March Action, following so soon after the Kronstadt mutiny, forced them to strengthen their propaganda efforts. Louise Bryant faithfully relayed Trotsky's words to the International News Service. He pretended that the revolutionary sailors of 1917 had left Kronstadt long be-fore, adding that the mutiny was largely the work of White naval officers who had taken refuge at Tallinn and then spread their influence to the re-maining garrison.[21] Trotsky insisted, too, that the Mensheviks and Socialist-Revolutionaries were acting like 'the banana peel on which the working class would slip into counter-revolution against the Soviets'.[22] Bryant com-pliantly treated Kronstadt as a minor distraction. In her series of dispatches, she declared that American firms could make huge profits if they started trading with Russia. America's industrial goods would be exchanged for Russian raw materials. It could be a relationship of perfect equilibrium.[23] Bryant probably knew nothing about conditions in the 'disciplinary colony' at Ukhta north of the Arctic Circle where the 'Kronstadt bandit sailors' were sent on Politburo orders after the leaders of their mutiny were exe-cuted.[24] She had also not been in Berlin recently and had no direct acquain-tance with the pointless loss of workers' lives on the streets there. She knew of the concerns of her late husband John Reed about Soviet Russia, and as a foreign journalist she had the opportunity to explore them; but she en-tirely failed to take it.

As winter gave way to spring, the prospects for communist rule were as yet unclear. Economic compromise and political ruthlessness had prevailed over the massive popular resistance. The Bolsheviks had yielded the minimum necessary to maintain their power. They had won the Civil War but did not yet have a lasting plan for the peace. Their policies were not a coherent programme of action, and they had not ironed out the creases in external and internal policy. The Bolsheviks had never been more confused about their general strategy. Their new measures were extricating them from an immediate emergency. But the party had yet to demonstrate that such measures offered a way to realize communism in Russia, far less in the rest of the world.

31. THE SECOND
BREATHING SPACE

The New Economic Policy is usually credited with the regeneration of Russia's economy in 1921, but in fact the enabling legislation for agrarian reform was not passed until April that year. Months were then spent in convincing the peasantry that the authorities were in earnest about permitting private local trade in grain. Three years of forcible expropriation, compulsory labour and endless conscriptions in the Civil War had fostered rural distrust and hatred. It was months into 1922 before the Tambov rural revolt was suppressed. There was famine throughout the Volga region. The Soviet regime had to deploy the Red Army simply to get peasant households to complete the spring sowing.

But the long-awaited Anglo-Soviet trade agreement did indeed foster genuine recovery. Petrograd once again became Russia's chief port. Tallinn lacked enough warehouses for the sudden upsurge in traffic—and after Germany's defeat of course there was no longer any need to rely on Archangel.[1] In April 1921 *Pravda* reported that Soviet officials were already buying rice, jam, salt beef, vegetables and herring from the United Kingdom. With the British trade under way again, the Kremlin hoped that American and Canadian commercial links would soon be in place. Nonetheless, the economic emergency was still acute. Russia had once had more than enough coal to supply the country's needs. Now it had to be imported.[2] The first priority, though, was to lubricate the wheels of exchange between factory and village. Trotsky called for an import strategy that gave precedence to goods that the peasantry needed. In this way he aimed to stimulate agricultural activity and make the New Economic Policy a success, and he was willing to forgo the purchase of big capital goods for a while and requested that the remainder of the gold reserve should be used for such purposes. Timber, oil and grain should be exported to make up for any shortfall—and Trotsky was not deflected from this strategy by the fact that the Volga peasantry was suffering from malnutrition.[3]

Communist hopes of a trade treaty with the US were dispelled by the new administration under President Warren G. Harding, who had won the election in the previous year. On 25 March 1921 Secretary of State Charles Evans Hughes reaffirmed the policy established under Woodrow Wilson that Soviet Russia lacked the necessary conditions for economic co-operation. Litvinov's overtures were brusquely rebuffed.[4] It was Herbert Hoover, recently appointed Secretary of Commerce, who best explained the official standpoint. He denied that Sovnarkom was a legitimate power and predicted that Russian economic recovery would not occur while the communists held capitalism in a vice. The New Economic Policy did nothing to change his mind. He reasoned that the Bolsheviks could not be trusted while they sought financial credits from America despite refusing to guarantee private property as a right under the law.[5] He also doubted that the Soviet regime could export anything much except gold, platinum and jewellery.[6] This did not stop him from welcoming news that American businesses were signing independent deals with the Soviet government. Shoes and farm equipment were being sold in vast quantities to Russia.[7] But if firms conducted business with the communists, they had to do so at their own risk. Hoover was not going to stop American firms trading with Russia, but he was not going to help them either.

Krasin, fresh from his success with the Anglo-Soviet trade agreement, urged that Soviet Russia and the US should agree to disagree about each other's political order. He repeated that America could do itself a favour by supplying the industrial machinery, railway stock and countless spare parts that Russia needed for its economic recovery. Russia had the wherewithal to pay, and Krasin denied that Soviet gold was tainted. Furs, wool, bristles, leather and oil were already available for direct trade, and Sovnarkom was inviting tenders from foreign companies for concessions in timber-felling, fisheries and metal mining. Krasin depicted Russia as an Eldorado waiting to be rediscovered.[8]

Yet while Krasin painted an enticing picture for foreigners, the Soviet leadership hardened their measures against their own rebellious citizens. Strikes were settled by negotiation, but communist officials typically retaliated

against identified troublemakers when things had settled down.[9] The Red
Army was given no rest. Mikhail Tukhachevski was put in charge of sup-
pressing the Tambov peasant revolt. He denied himself no ruthless method
in achieving this objective, deliberately applying terror in those districts
where resistance was stubborn—and the Kremlin was kept fully abreast of
his progress.[10] Other military units were distributed across southern Russia,
Ukraine and western Siberia. Wherever the communist authorities faced
armed resistance, they reacted with force. And following behind the in-
fantry and cavalry were teams of propagandists to explain the merits of the
New Economic Policy to the peasantry. The villagers were told that in return for their political obedience they would receive the freedom to trade
their harvest for their own profit after meeting any fiscal requirements—
and the government promised to hasten the delivery of industrial goods for
peasant households. First the stick, then the promise of carrots.

Nevertheless there remained much unease among Bolsheviks about the
New Economic Policy, and a dispute exploded at the Party Conference in
May 1921. Lenin was left alone to defend the Politburo measures. He was
usually not one to indulge in self-pity—one of his mottoes was: 'Don't
whinge!' Even so, he indicated that the widespread incidence of physical ill
health in the leadership had placed an undue burden on him. Trotsky had
a mysterious chronic ailment and Zinoviev was recovering from two heart
attacks; neither was passed fit enough to go to the Conference. (In fact Zinoviev did attend fleetingly to defend his reputation over the March Action.) Kamenev was also out of action because of a cardiac condition.
Bukharin had been convalescing until a few days before the opening of proceedings and Stalin was laid low by acute appendicitis. It was true that Tom-
ski, Central Committee member and head of the Soviet trade unions, had
been politically active; but Lenin was annoyed with him because he had
given unapproved assurances to trade unions about their freedom from
party control—and Lenin for a while campaigned for his removal from the
Central Committee.[11] Lenin was often described as a dictator and in the
spring 1921 he indeed came close to being the supreme leader of Soviet
Russia; but this was only because so few fellow leaders were available and
willing to work co-operatively.

After getting this off his chest, Lenin led the line in defence of the New
Economic Policy. Had he not done so, it is open to question whether the
official measures would have survived intact.[12] In the Civil War, Bolsheviks

had grown accustomed to thinking that forcible requisitioning of agricultural produce accorded with the communist way of life. The restored markets and the deals with foreign capitalists were anathema to them. Although Lenin had got away with little criticism and short debates at the Congress in March, now at the Conference he had to withstand fierce, sustained assault. But his critics had little to offer as an alternative beyond calling for greater state regulation and planning. In Russia's current circumstances this would be hugely difficult. It would also be risky. The Conference could not bring itself to overturn a leader who had brought them through the October Revolution and the Civil War. Lenin swiftly sensed the mood and cheered everyone up by declaring that private entrepreneurship was only going to be temporary. He assured them that he was still committed to bringing about communism in Russia.

International affairs were easier for him to handle. Ernst Thalmänn, freshly arrived from Berlin, claimed that German workers were turning to the communists in impressive numbers despite the defeat of the March Action.[13] Indeed Béla Kun wanted the Russian Communist Party to applaud the Action. He and Zinoviev infuriated Trotsky by going around hinting that Lenin and the People's Commissar for Military Affairs were divided on this question. Lenin agreed to support Trotsky, issuing a rebuke to those responsible for the débâcle in Germany. Radek was ordered to toe the line in his report on the Comintern. Obediently he explained that the main reason for the defeat was poor leadership. According to Radek, objections to the plan for insurrection by Paul Levi had rendered the German communists ineffective, but other German leaders were also astonishingly inept. Nonetheless Radek also argued that the Comintern had to prepare itself to exploit turbulent situations as they arose, suggesting that the current stabilization of European capitalism would be vulnerable to future shocks. He was following the recent analysis by Trotsky as well as that by the Hungarian communist Jeno Varga; he also cited J. M. Keynes in arguing that the Paris peace settlement was inherently unstable. Radek contended that the US was the only power with reason for confidence. Even victor powers like Britain, France and Italy had difficulties. Rivalries among capitalist states were ineradicable.[14]

This was close to vindicating an early attempt to organize another German insurrection, and Lenin intervened for the sake of clarity, commenting: 'Of course, if revolution arrives in Europe we'll change policy.' But he insisted that no one could make a sensible guess about when this might occur.[15] The Soviet press immediately set about relaying the message that Moscow's international priority was for trade with the big capitalist countries—and articles on revolutionary war disappeared.

Senator Joseph I. France continued to offer hope to the Politburo. In May 1921, convinced that America's interests lay in trading with Russia, he set forth for Moscow to see things for himself. He gave an interview to the *New York Times* before he left in which he sketched out his intentions: 'It is not a matter of personal opinion, political or economic. Approval will be a matter of practical politics. We did not approve of the regime of the late Czar. We do not need to approve of the Soviet. There are many of my colleagues in the Senate of whom I do not have to approve.'[16] Trotsky asked Litvinov to set up a meeting with him.[17] Litvinov had in fact been disinclined to let him into the country, but Krasin had persuaded Lenin and Chicherin that it would be folly to admit Washington B. Vanderlip while closing the frontier to the Senator.[18] Yet Soviet bureaucrats shared a lingering distaste for dealing with prominent 'bourgeois' politicians. On his journey from Riga, Senator France was allotted a crowded, second-class carriage and compelled to obtain his own sleeping bag.[19] He was forbidden to bring his personal assistant or interpreter with him or even to raise questions about the detention of Americans in Russian prisons.[20]

Even so, he obtained his interview with Lenin in Moscow and put a warmer case for US–Soviet relations than he had dared to express publicly in America. Afterwards, Lenin told Chicherin:

> I have just finished a conference with Senator France . . . He told me how he came out *for* Soviet Russia at large public meetings together with Comrade Martens. He is what they call a 'liberal', *for* an alliance of the United States plus Russia plus Germany, in order to save the world from Japan, England, and so on, and so on.[21]

Senator France returned to the US an enthusiast for full diplomatic recognition: 'I found that the Russian Government was handling the situation in a statesmanlike way.'[22] His endorsement of Lenin and Trotsky was unconditional. He even swallowed the official Soviet account of the Kronstadt mutiny, pinning responsibility on Colonel Edward W. Ryan of the American Red Cross for having fomented trouble among the sailors.[23]

One American entrepreneur who followed Vanderlip's example and interested himself in business in Russia was Dr Armand Hammer of the Allied Drug and Chemical Corporation. In November 1921, Hammer signed a deal for an asbestos concession in the Urals. The terms involved him handing over 10 per cent of all output to the Soviet government.[24] The US press quickly published its suspicions. Also involved in the business was Hammer's father Julius, who by then was serving a sentence in New York State's Sing Sing prison for carrying out an abortion. Julius Hammer was also known to have belonged to the Russian Soviet Information Bureau run by Martens and Nuorteva. Then it came out that other directors of Hammer's corporation had no knowledge of any deal with the Soviet government and that the business had no interest in producing asbestos.[25] Armand Hammer was a wily individual and his liaison with the Soviet leadership was to bring him riches in the years ahead. Nor did he confine himself to commerce, carrying out secret political errands for the Kremlin and virtually becoming its intelligence agent. His success in conducting private business in Russia under Bolshevik rule also convinced others that it was safe to sign contracts despite Herbert Hoover's warnings.[26]

Even Leslie Urquhart dropped his campaign against Sovnarkom. When he saw that he might never get his Russian property back under Soviet rule, he approached his old adversary Krasin in June 1921 to examine what kind of deal he too might be able to negotiate.[27] In July he spoke to the annual general meeting of his Russo-Asiatic Consolidated Co. and recommended a change of heart:

> My discussions with Mr Krassin [*sic*] have been of a practical, helpful, and very friendly nature. (Cheers.) I mention this because in ordinary circumstances it would have been very difficult for the representatives of two such antagonistic systems as those of Capitalism and Communism as applied to economics to find a basis of understanding. Capitalism stands for the right of property and economic freedom, while Communism is the absolute negation of both these principles.[28]

Lenin and Krasin hoped that such positive endorsements would have a gold-rush effect on the minds of Western entrepreneurs. The Urquhart question was discussed repeatedly in the Politburo for over a year. Soviet leaders understood that if they could agree an appropriate arrangement with the Scottish mining magnate they could use it as the model for other concessions.[29]

Herbert Hoover did not give up on Russia either. In summer 1921 he responded warmly to an appeal from the Russian novelist Maxim Gorki for famine relief in Russia and Ukraine. The American Relief Administration was closing its offices in Europe. Gorki asked Hoover to divert its activities eastwards rather than back across the Atlantic. Hoover said that he still needed basic assurances from Sovnarkom. American prisoners in Russia had to be released. The relief administrators from America had to be able to travel freely, organize the local committees and have control of the food brought on to Soviet soil.[30]

The fly in the ointment was an allegation that the American Relief Administration had acted dishonestly in its earlier work in Europe. Captain T. C. C. Gregory, one of Hoover's officials in 1919, claimed in the New York magazine *World's Wealth* that the Administration had tried to subvert Béla Kun's government in Hungary. Sovnarkom's sympathizers in the US informed Moscow of the controversy, and Gregory's article was reproduced in Soviet pamphlets.[31] Trotsky feared that Hoover's philanthropic mission might be the first manoeuvre in a campaign of Western military intervention.[32] On a visit to Odessa he declared:

> But here it must be remembered that we are not Hungary. We are not a young Soviet republic. We have been tempered in the struggle against counter-revolution. We have our own special organs, we have the Cheka. The Cheka isn't loved, but we don't love counter-revolution. And we say to Hoover: 'There is risk in your enterprise.'[33]

Trotsky advised vigilance against Americans bearing gifts. Lenin agreed and wrote to Molotov, the Party Central Committee Secretary, that the American Relief Administration was not to be trusted. He recommended that Trotsky, Kamenev and Molotov should monitor the Administration's activities on a daily basis. Indeed, he went further and wanted Hoover 'punished'. In his opinion, Hoover and his subordinates were 'scoundrels and liars' who should be instantly deported or arrested if ever they meddled in Soviet internal affairs.[34]

Hoover cursed Gregory whenever his name came up in conversation.[35] He also issued an order for the strict avoidance of all interference in Russian politics.[36] But this came too late to prevent embarrassment for him in America. Walter W. Liggett of Russian Famine Relief—a pro-Soviet organization—made play with what Gregory had written. Officials in the American Relief Administration had to defend themselves in the press; and George Barr Baker, who directed the operations in Russia, pointed out that Liggett's political accusations brought no succour to the starving people who would die without food shipments from the US.[37]

This had the desired effect and the Soviet leadership anyway soon came round to understanding what a wonderful offer was being made to them. Hoover was proposing to bring food and medicine for free, only asking Sovnarkom to pay for seedcorn.[38] Trotsky told Louise Bryant:

> The ARA organization which has rendered incalculable aid to the hungry masses of Russia was at the same time most naturally a highly skilful feeler projected by the ruling elements of America into the very depths of Russia. More than any other European country [*sic*] America has seen us as we really are; it remains for us to wait till the public opinion of the propertied classes of America will digest the collected data and will draw from it appropriate deductions.[39]

This was hardly an unconditional endorsement; and it indicated that the Politburo had reasons other than humanitarian ones for accepting American assistance. The Politburo in fact failed to prioritize efforts of its own to alleviate the famine. Revenues from exports were being earmarked for industrial investment rather than grain purchases. The Soviet leaders talked as if they cared about the peasantry but the reality was that the Politburo was more interested in restoring Russian industrial and military power. If thousands of peasants died of starvation, so be it.

As the Soviet regime consolidated its rule, efforts by Russians to bring down the Bolsheviks were weakening. The Cheka efficiently liquidated several anti-communist groups it discovered in Petrograd and Moscow. The indefatigable Boris Savinkov had tried to link up with them; he had also tried to raise finance from the industrialist Alexei Putilov. This caused little bother to the Chekists, who imprisoned or executed the activists in Russia.[40] On 13 June 1921 Savinkov as self-styled Chairman of the Russian Evacuation Committee liaised with Sidney Reilly in organizing an Anti-Bolshevik Congress in Warsaw—the meeting was small enough to be held in a private apartment on Marszałkowski Street. The discussion touched

on the general international situation as well as the fate of the White movement, the position of the émigrés and the attitude of the Western Allies.[41]
But in October Savinkov was expelled from Warsaw by the Polish authorities under pressure from Moscow after the treaty of Riga. In this way the
last great enthusiast for a crusade against Soviet Russia with active Russian
participation was compelled to leave for western Europe.[42] The Cheka
prided itself on having eliminated all counter-revolutionary organizations
from Soviet territory. The Kremlin's reach now seemed to extend well beyond that territory.

In capital cities across Europe, Russian political emigrants gathered. In
Paris there was a National Unification congress led by the conservative Pëtr
Struve, the liberal Konstantin Nabokov and the ex-Bolshevik Grigori Alexinski.[43] Paul Dukes continued his public campaigning against the Bolsheviks
and went off on an American lecture tour in February 1921. In November,
on his return, he picked up his links with Sidney Reilly and Boris Savinkov;
he also met up with Harold Williams.[44] But all their efforts were the triumph
of hope over realism. No government in Europe or North America any
longer had the stomach for an anti-Bolshevik military operation.

As the Allied governments stood back, the international race to make
profits in Soviet Russia began in earnest. Since French official policy rendered this next to impossible, the Association Financière, Industrielle et
Commerciale Russe turned its eyes to New York for help, the idea being to
engage with individuals close to 'the outstanding public figure of the United
States, Mr Hoover'. It was believed that the American Relief Administration
might somehow offer cover for Russia's old economic elite to find their way
back into trade with new Russia.[45] Sidney Reilly had been among the first
to notice the Association's ambitions. With an eye for the main course he
was determined to gain a slice of the profits seemingly on offer and was actively engaged in buying up products in Europe on behalf of the British government. Wrangel's intelligence officers noticed that he had some kind of
'link with the Bolshevik delegation in London'. His financial dishonesty in
pre-war Russia was common knowledge by then. Even without access to information about the British Secret Intelligence Service's enquiry about him,
the White officers commented that Reilly was almost certainly an assumed
name; and London's Russian political circles gave him a wide berth despite
the opportunity offered by his connections with the British establishment.[46]

For a while at least, the Soviet leadership resigned themselves to 'peaceful cohabitation' with capitalist countries. Lenin used this term in an inter-

view with the *Christian Science Monitor*. In Soviet Russia itself it was Adolf Ioffe who popularized it and called for 'co-operation' with 'bourgeois re-publics'.[47] But Ioffe laid down a qualification, insisting that this policy would make sense only if it were guaranteed that no military threat would be di-rected at Moscow. The Red Army would show good faith by pulling back from its stations on Russian borders. Capitalists would trade with Russia not out of altruism or even mere greed but because the world economy could not now recover without access to the huge natural resources that lay between Smolensk and Vladivostok. Communists could therefore wait on events. The struggle between Labour and Capital would not cease around the globe, and 'world proletarian revolution' remained the party's objective. But every Bolshevik leader had learned that compromises had to be made if Bolshevik rule was to be sustained.[48]

Soviet rule, as every Russian knew and foreign visitors soon discovered, was chaotic at its lower levels. Official policy was one thing and the reality was frequently very different. Corruption was pervasive. Even transport was never better than uncertain; and when William J. Kelley of the Ameri-can Relief Administration tried to make his way from Riga to Moscow at the end of 1921, he had to bribe the train driver to give him logs to keep himself warm at the lengthy unscheduled stops on the journey.[49] What is more, Bolsheviks often baulked at the party's official encouragement of the purchase of concessions by foreigners. William H. Johnston, president of the International Association of Machinists, was held up in Latvia and could not even get a visa for his trip to Moscow.[50] None of these difficulties caused surprise in the American administration, which had warned its country's entrepreneurs about the dangers of doing business in Russia. They had only themselves to blame if they found that Soviet conditions offered a less than congenial experience. Official US opposition to a trade treaty remained in place; Herbert Hoover was implacable—and he ensured that no American concession, including Vanderlip's well-known Kamchatka venture, could be operated on a grand scale in Siberia unless and until the Washington au-thorities gave their blessing.[51]

There was still a lot for the Soviet leadership to do if economic recovery was to continue, and the growing rivalry between Lenin and Trotsky had the potential to open up yet another damaging controversy. They dis-agreed about the pace and orientation of industrial growth. Trotsky wanted to prioritize investment in heavy industry and introduce mechanisms for central state economic planning. Lenin feared that this would disrupt the reconciliation with the peasantry; his own preference was to grant freedom for private workshops to produce for the rural requirements.[52] For the moment, at least, Lenin had the greater support in the Politburo and Central Committee—and the political situation settled down. The October Revolution survived the first full year of peace.

32. THE UNEXTINGUISHED FIRE

The Bolsheviks had kept their hardness and had kept their faith. Even the pseudonyms they chose for themselves signified unyielding intent. Stalin was a name taken from the Russian word for steel, Molotov was a derivation of hammer. Their generation had been born and brought up in years when armed force was used the world over to expand empires and transform economies. Bolsheviks absorbed this toughness of spirit into their own doctrines and practices. They saw how industrialists, financiers and landowners had become masters of the earth. They learned from the ruthlessness and optimism they witnessed. Like the capitalists they detested, they took chances. The October Revolution had always been a gamble. But it had been successful for them, even though the price was paid by millions of Russians in death, tears and famine. Communists proved themselves flexible. Although they hated compromise, they became adept at scraping off the minimum of skin from their ideology. Bolshevism was founded on the idea that humankind is infinitely plastic, infinitely malleable. The rulers of Soviet Russia aimed to reconstruct the entire edifice of life for the benefit of the working class—and if workers did not yet understand where their best interests lay, the communist party would simply carry out the Revolution on their behalf.

Bolshevik leaders and militants, even if they had not read Lenin's *The State and Revolution* or Trotsky's *Terrorism and Communism*, believed that the October Revolution required the party, the Cheka and the Red Army to exercise a severe dictatorship. The Bolsheviks were known for their dictatorial inclinations long before the experiences of 1917; and although they had looked forward to enabling 'the people' to liberate themselves from capitalism, they had always believed in the need for a framework of authoritarian control to bring this about. By the end of the Civil War, the use of mass ter ror, arbitrary dispensation of justice and political discrimination against groups in society deemed to be inimical had become the norm. The upper and middle classes—the *burzhui*—were treated as 'former people' and stripped of the rights of citizenship along with priests and ex-policemen, and it was a rare ex-businessman who dared to go around town dressed in his pre-revolutionary finery.[1] Although peasants and artisans gained some freedom to sell their goods and services, the communists' ultimate objective had not changed. The entire economy would one day be owned, planned and regulated by powerful agencies of the state. Bolsheviks were engineers of the soul. They intended to manufacture a new collectivist mentality throughout society and were willing to wade through seas of blood to achieve their purposes.

The Bolsheviks still aimed to provide everyone with an abundance of material and cultural well-being. Schooling and health care were already free of charge. Wherever possible, housing was made available to the poor. Trade unions could take up the grievances of individual labourers. Party militants set about promoting working-class youngsters to posts of author ity. The dream was to make the 'proletarian state' ever more proletarian.

The American journalist Anna Louise Strong, arriving in Russia at the outset of the New Economic Policy, bore witness to the preserved ideals. She reported that even entrepreneurs could be found imbued with enthu siasm for Bolshevism. In her account of a trip to the famine-afflicted Volga region she wrote in note form:

> The little East-side Jew whom I met in Samara, the heart of the fam ine, and who went with me as interpreter to organize village kitchens. Speaking English with a vile accent and physically most unattractive. Then I learned that he was manager of two little factories which had just reopened, making doors and windows for the repairing of Samara. He was a machinist; he was so proud of the two or three ma chines he had put together, down in a country where even plain nails were not to be had.[2]

Despite being a communist party member, he was proud of having obtained official permission to put his workers on to piecework. This way they earned the equivalent of fifteen dollars per month. He himself received only rations and lodgings; beyond that point, he worked for free. His wife had to work too, and his offspring had to be fed in a state children's home. But he did not complain. He was 'eager and energetic and happy to be building Russia'.[3]

Strong may well have been, and indeed almost certainly was, one of those many foreigners who fell for a self-serving story. But the situation in Russia was anyway complicated. Its people were emerging from a period of military and political turmoil and trying to come to terms with the often convoluted ways of understanding and practising communism that were being set before them.

Ivy Litvinov directed a questioning gaze at the ambivalent lifestyles of most veteran Bolsheviks. Her scepticism began when she joined Maxim from London in Copenhagen in 1920: 'You see, we lived in grand hotels and he wore fur coats and smoked enormous cigars and things like that. I'd never seen him so plutocratic, and we had cars all the time.'[4] But she also recalled an earlier incident which was in his favour. When he took the train for Moscow from Petrograd the railway officials gave him an empty carriage to himself. Discovering that other passengers had been ejected to accommodate him, he insisted on their reinstatement.[5] Litvinov was far from being the only Soviet leader to undergo a ragged process of *embourgeoisement*. Krasin was a case in point. Attending a private dinner given in his honour by leading bankers at Berlin's Hotel Adlon, he let himself go and said: 'Communism as we have tried it has proved a failure and it must be modified.' Some of the waiters were radical socialists and, overhearing these startling comments, halted work in the kitchen for a while.[6] But the International News Service judged that 'Krasin was just kidding the bankers along for the benefit of [Soviet] business.' Even so, there was an increasing and unmistakable tendency for communist leaders to enjoy the pleasures of the old upper classes. Litvinov and Krasin were sincere communists; but although they were not sybaritic, they were starting to accept privilege as their right.

The American reporter Frank Mason saw Karl Radek as resistant to the sartorial drift of the Soviet elite and noted that he dressed 'like a movie picture Bolshevic [sic]'. Mason commented: 'You could pick him out without hesitation even were he seated in a room filled with stage anarchists.' Radek had a fuzzy brown fringe of a beard, his hair was untroubled by a comb, and curls framed a face that was 'delicate, almost womanly'. He wore a soiled fur-lined jacket and long, black-leather breeches.[7]

Ivy Litvinov resented the communist milieu she found in Moscow. She disliked being introduced to everybody as Maxim's marital adjunct and deposited with the wives of Soviet leaders who only wanted to talk about children or clothing.[8] In the early 1920s the Litvinovs were living in the Kharitonenko House.[9] Ivy's great new friend was Alexandra Kollontai, a prominent Bolshevik whom she loved for her kindness and vivacity.[10] This was not all that helpful for her husband's career since Kollontai had emerged as a harsh critic of the Politburo and an advocate of the Workers' Opposition. But the two women also came together for other reasons. Ivy was a devotee of D. H. Lawrence and, believing in free love, discovered a fellow spirit in Alexandra who scandalized most Russian communists with her uninhibited sexual liaisons. Ivy and Alexandra got on splendidly. They confided in each other about their disillusionment with communist leaders; and Ivy, despite admiring Lenin in many ways, came to believe he was 'a wrong-headed saint'.[11]

Her distaste for the Kharitonenko House surprised Maxim, who had written enticingly to her in London: 'If you ever come here, your eyes will bulge.'[12] Ivy thought the antique furniture hideous, although she herself shopped in expensive stores and hired governesses for her children;[13] but she was shocked by the disparity between the conditions of the Moscow poor and the comfortable life of the elite: 'I saw a woman in Red Square, sort of, just fall down. People just went like that round her, nobody stopped. Oh, of course . . . I thought everyone was a peasant because all the women wore shawls, you see, I was quite sure everybody was peasants, which was sort of not so untrue.'[14] Although Ivy was no communist, she had expected more of communists:

> I thought I was going to the land of Socialism. You see I thought these thoughts so often, I remember exactly. And one thing I thought: how lovely—you see things have always had me in their power. I can't cope with them. And it's so lovely to throw them away every now and then. Get rid of them. And I somehow thought for some unknown reason: now I'm going to a land where 'things'—I suppose I meant property— won't mean so much . . . I very soon discovered that there never had been a place where they mattered so much.

The collapse of manufacturing output made people cling to whatever they possessed and few families could afford what they saw in shop windows.[15]

The Bolsheviks had spent the year 1917 denouncing the Socialist-Revolutionaries and Mensheviks for their denial of the immediate achievability of Russian socialism. Now Bolsheviks presided over the return of markets, and it was their New Economic Policy which had led to the emergence of both fur-coated urban spivs in the cities and well-off peasants—often known as 'kulaks'—in the villages. Although open political opposition was no longer possible, the anti-Bolshevik militants spread their message in other ways. Satirical song was one of these. A Socialist-Revolutionary ditty went as follows:

> I am in a low dive eating
> Kasha from a bowl,
> Trotsky and Lenin are boasting:
> 'We've swallowed Russia whole!'
> In a low dive drinking tea,
> Nothing more to fear,
> My man is a Bolshevik
> And I'm a profiteer![16]

Denied the freedom to stand against the Bolsheviks in elections, Sovnarkom's enemies faced constant adversity if they continued the political struggle. Eventually, in 1922, the patience of the Soviet authorities would be exhausted when the surviving Socialist-Revolutionaries were put on show-trial in 1922; and Lenin wanted to do the same to the Mensheviks.[17]

Yet the communist elite never lost their basic unease about the New Economic Policy. They feared that the reintroduction of capitalism, albeit with severe restrictions, might be the start of counter-revolution by stealth. Ivy Litvinov recalled how badly her husband Maxim had reacted to Lenin's policy: '[He] was terribly depressed. Afterwards I supposed he knew it had to be, but how depressed he was; he felt everything had been sold, you know . . . he was so terribly, terribly depressed.'[18] Bolshevik wives thought and wrote as Bolsheviks and it did not usually occur to them to depict personal moods in their accounts: the bigger revolutionary cause was everything. But Ivy Litvinov was not typical. She was British, possessed little interest in politics and had the eyes and ears of a novelist; and the depression her husband experienced was almost certainly widely shared.

Some Russians nonetheless dreamed that the scope for profit-making might eventually benefit Russia. For them, the New Economic Policy was a first and very desirable breach in the wall of doctrinaire communism. They hoped that the remaining restrictions on the operation of a private market economy would eventually be removed. They were carried away in their speculation. Perhaps the Bolshevik party was undergoing a permanent internal change, dropping its fanatical ideology for a more realistic appreciation of what could be accomplished. In Harbin, across the Siberian frontier in Manchuria, émigré Russian intellectuals became convinced that the Bolsheviks were turning into nationalists. And it is true that Bolshevism as it emerged from the Civil War was committed to gathering back the lands of the Russian Empire under central control. The Bolsheviks unquestionably wanted Russia to be a great military power once more. They also wanted to create an advanced industrial society and spread universal education. They were the most ambitious modernizers the country had known since Peter the Great. Some people regarded them, beneath their red banners, as national champions who were capable of succeeding where tsars, conservatives, liberals and socialists had failed.

Undoubtedly there were leanings in this direction in the Bolshevik leadership, and the émigrés in Harbin were right that the Soviet state was far from being immune to pressures to move away from its violent, oppressive zealotry. Ex-Ambassador Vasili Maklakov in Paris agreed. He could not see how the Bolsheviks could survive without making allowance for the nationally minded elements in the Red Army that had enabled victory in the Civil War.[19] In Russia too it was murmured that the October Revolution was gradually being 'straightened out' and 'moderated' and 'civilized'. Across the professions there were people who welcomed communism's modernizing zeal for Russia without being communists. Teachers felt free to experiment with fresh pedagogical ideas. Economists were attracted by opportunities to plan and regulate production and supply. Scientists welcomed the promise of abundant resources as and when they became available. It was common knowledge that Soviet Russia was a ruthless police state that boasted of its ruthlessness. Russian émigré and Western optimists took Lloyd George's line, believing that it was better to shake hands and do business with Lenin and Trotsky than to face them across military fronts.

The German government had reasons of its own to go further than Lloyd George when the European powers met in Genoa in April 1922 to settle Europe's outstanding international questions. Chicherin attended instead of Lenin, who was thought likely to be assassinated. Trotsky stayed away for the same reason. The Soviet delegation got nowhere with the Western Allies because France refused to deal with Russia until such time as it recognized its obligations to those whose property and investments had been seized by Sovnarkom. The Russians and Germans drew the obvious conclusion: they were both pariah states. Having found plenty of points of mutual advantage, they travelled further down the Italian coast to Santa Margherita and Rapallo where the discussions were fast and fruitful; and a treaty was signed that gave full diplomatic recognition to Russia and opened avenues to the import and export business. Sovnarkom saw its chance to entice German companies to sign big commercial contracts. Secret arrangements were also made for the Germans to evade the military restrictions imposed by the treaty of Versailles by organizing and training their armed forces on Soviet soil, where the Red Army would benefit by seeing and copying up-to-date techniques.

The Bolsheviks had vanquished their enemies at home and begun to neutralize the threats from abroad, and Lenin's firm leadership had been crucial to the survival of the Soviet order. The economy was recovering and society was beginning to recuperate from years of war and disruption. But in January 1924 Lenin died and in the ensuing power struggle it was Stalin who emerged victorious. In his own rough way he introduced radical changes, beginning with a programme of economic deprivatization. Forced-rate industrialization was instigated. State ownership, state regulation and state planning were spread to every corner of production and distribution. The old 'specialists' were replaced by newly trained and promoted Red operatives. The few outlets for cultural criticism were abolished. Compromise with the national aspirations of the many non-Russian peoples of the USSR was ended. Open-ended educational initiatives were replaced by rote learning. Factional dissent was banished from the party not just by decree but also in practice. Trials were organized of prominent figures thought likely to obstruct or undermine Stalin's programme and the penal network of labour camps sucked in victims who never numbered fewer than a million. The Cheka, which was subsumed in the People's Commissariat of Internal Affairs (or NKVD), acquired at least the same importance as the Bolshevik party.

This not only took the world by surprise—it was also widely thought to be an internal phenomenon, safely quarantined from other countries. Yet Soviet foreign policy had not lost its potential to destabilize politics in Europe. As ex-Ambassador Boris Bakhmetev observed, Bolshevism ultimately had to expand westwards or risk withering away. Militarism was inherent in its situation whether it liked it or not.[20] The Kremlin's rulers needed foreign revolutions for their own security since the treaties with capitalist governments could bring only temporary relief—and the possibility of an anti-Soviet crusade was a permanent one. The Bolsheviks were anyway convinced that global capitalism was vulnerable to profound inner instabilities, inevitably leading to world wars and economic depression that would offer opportunities for communist political expansion. Comintern continued to send agents, advice and finance around the globe. Under its guidance dozens of new communist parties promoted the cause of socialist revolution. There had been another, equally disastrous attempt at insurrection in Germany in 1923. Apart from an initial objection by Stalin, it had been supported by the entire Politburo. There were also attempts at urban risings in Estonia and Bulgaria. Despite such disappointments, the communist leaders in Moscow did not give up hope of foreign revolutions— and Germany remained the great target.

Publicly they continued to pretend that the German Communist Party would have to make revolution without external assistance. This was just as misleading as the notion that the Comintern was independent of Moscow. Behind closed doors the Soviet leadership accepted that they would have to send in the Red Army to support any German revolution that might break out. The Western Allies would never tolerate the existence of a communist state in the heart of Europe and would oppose any attempt to contravene the treaty of Versailles. There was unlikely to be a 'European socialist revolution' without yet another great European war.[21] Revolution in Berlin would be the first step towards a continental bloodbath. Bolshevik leaders thought this a price worth paying in the Marxist revolutionary cause. Small wonder that the peoples of eastern and east-central Europe refused to take a casual approach to the possibility that communism might soon be on the march again. Owners of businesses worried for their property; priests and their congregations fretted that spiritual freedom might be crushed. Millions of people yearned simply for peace. The Bolsheviks had no intention of giving them rest.

So a first Cold War took place between the USSR and the Allies even before 1945. Obviously the Iron Curtain that Ethel Snowden had in mind in 1920 was not the same as the one that stretched down the middle of Europe after 1945. What she mainly meant was Russia's isolation from the world rather than a political, ideological and military stand-off between two global military and political coalitions. Yet the potential for the first Cold War to turn into an even bigger and more dangerous one was already present— and it became a reality when the Soviet Union became a great power by dint of the country's industrialization in the 1930s and its victory on the eastern front against the Third Reich in 1944–5.

The October Revolution had lasted longer than most observers had thought possible back in 1917. After breaking the spine of the Wehrmacht in the battles of Stalingrad and Kursk, the Red Army was the first armed force into Berlin in 1945. The spread of communism that had been the dream of Lenin and Trotsky was fulfilled as Stalin communized the entire eastern half of Europe. Immediately he directed the USSR's new industrial might at achieving military parity with the US. The two great military coalitions of NATO and the Warsaw Pact avoided all-out war with each other. Instead there was a second Cold War involving intensified political, economic and ideological competition—and by the 1970s a quarter of the globe's land area was governed by communist states. The tensions between the USSR and the US frequently came close to military clashes, but mercifully the two sides held themselves back from the brink. When deep structural reforms were undertaken in the Soviet Union in the 1980s, the Cold War began to fade in ferocity, and on the very last day of 1991, seventy years after Lenin and Trotsky had seized power in Petrograd, the USSR collapsed under the pressures of its own internal transformation.

From 1917 through to 1991 the West had dealt with Soviet Russia in a confused fashion. There was endless controversy. Some foreigners became communists and worked for revolutionary change in their countries; others aimed at a peaceful coexistence with Russia and hoped that trade and cultural contacts would steadily erode Bolshevik extremism. Another trend of thought regretted that any such compromise was made. There were few advocates of an anti-Soviet crusade in the 1920s, but many argued for the reimposition of an economic quarantine.

The history of the USSR proceeded by sharp twists and turns that nobody could predict in the early years of the Soviet communist dictatorship, and the temptation must be avoided to judge the naivety of contemporaries with the privilege of hindsight. They faced a difficult situation. The war between the Allies and the Central Powers demanded the full attention of the combatant countries. No Allied government was willing to recognize the Soviet revolutionary state, and normal diplomatic relations were suspended. The obvious weaknesses of Bolshevik rule, however, made it sensible for foreign powers to query the capacity of the Bolsheviks to survive. Nor was it easy to adopt genuinely effective methods to bring down the Soviet government or counteract its external menace. All Western leaders

wanting a tougher line to be taken on Bolshevism had to cope with obstruction by their labour movements and with pressures from political and commercial lobbies. In any case, their military expeditions were constantly too
small to overturn communism. The Whites, even with Allied assistance,
were ultimately no match for the Reds; and Western attempts at outright
subversion failed. But this does not mean that the Soviet victory was pre-
ordained. Not at all: the Bolsheviks came close to being overturned by their
own peasants, sailors and workers in early 1921; and Russian and Western
critics of Lloyd George had some justification in complaining that he chose
that precise moment to sign a trade treaty, helping to bail out the Soviet
economy.

After all the excuses are made for them, however, Western political leaders undeniably had abundant information about the purposes and potential
of Soviet communism—and if Winston Churchill could always see Soviet
Russia for what it was, other politicians could have done the same. The
West's diplomats and intelligence officers served them well. And when the
diplomats left Russian soil, the spies and telegraphists as well as the journalists filled most of the gaps in international reportage: communism was
never obscured from view for the leaders who took the big decisions. It is
true that the information was often patchy and even contradictory, but it
was good enough for judgements to be made. Yet the politicians acted on
reports only when the content suited them. They behaved largely on the
basis of instinct and preconception. Policy was quickly decided and intellectual self-doubt was suppressed.

Soviet leaders, too, trusted their intuition and accepted only such counsel as fitted their prejudices. There was still heavier pressure on them than
on Western leaders to act quickly and decisively. The Revolution was ceaselessly threatened. Every Bolshevik knew that inactivity in foreign and security matters was not a safe option. Even a treaty with one or more of the
Western Allies could bring only temporary relief. Soviet Russia, they
thought, would remain vulnerable until such time as a Soviet Germany existed. Communists interpreted everything that happened to them after
1917 through the prism of their long-held suppositions. They saw the
maleficent hand of the West in every setback for the October Revolution.
Lenin, Trotsky and Stalin agreed at least about this. Victory in the Great
War placed the Allies in dominion over the world, and it was their Allied
businessmen who reaped the advantage. Soviet Russia had to be on its
guard against a crusade to bring down the communist order. The Kremlin

was alert to any opportunity to manoeuvre among the victor powers; but at a time when the world seemed to spin on a revolutionary axis, the ideological core of communist thinking remained a fixed one.

Looking out on the world in the early 1920s, the communist leaders breathed more easily than they had done a few months earlier. Western leaders for a while turned their faces away from the Russian question. They had failed to supplant communism in 1917–21 and now they had many other dilemmas of their own to resolve. They hoped that Russia's tumult would stay within Russian borders. For many years it did. But when the Red Army crossed Poland into Germany in 1945, it came with even greater menace to its neighbours and the rest of the world.

POSTSCRIPT

Many of the men and women who have populated this history of early Soviet Russia continued to influence public affairs long after the extraordinary events of 1917–21. There were also some who settled down to lives of quiet seclusion. The October Revolution of 1917 had briefly brought them all together—either in solidarity or else in collision. It was an intense experience; indeed it was the most intense that most of them ever had. But soon after the revolutionary whirlwind had swept them into its vortex, it forcefully scattered them to every point of the compass where they encountered a variety of fates. Although some survived into old age, others came to an abrupt, untimely end.

Lenin could never have imagined what awaited him in death. The body of this militant atheist was embalmed and laid out for worshipful display under a glass canopy in a mausoleum specially erected on Red Square, where it remains to this day. Communists in the USSR and other countries saluted his memory as he was turned into the object of quasi-religious devotion. After the Second World War, 'Marxism-Leninism' became the official ideology of states in Europe, Asia and elsewhere. Even today, decades after the dissolution of the USSR, Lenin is treated with reverence in Russia. The same is not true of Trotsky. In 1929, after losing his struggle with Stalin for political supremacy, Trotsky was deported from the Soviet Union and then sentenced to death *in absentia* in one of the notorious show-trials of the late 1930s. Despite founding an international communist organization to rival Comintern, he never recovered the level of influence he had enjoyed in his period in government. After exile in Turkey, France and Norway, Trotsky eventually found sanctuary in Mexico where in 1940 he was murdered by an assassin sent by the Kremlin; and although his followers still venerate him, their imprint on current politics is small and getting smaller.

Felix Dzerzhinski, who became disenchanted with the official leadership after Lenin's death, succumbed to chronic ill health and died in 1926. Adolf Ioffe joined Trotsky in political opposition but in 1927 fell into despair and committed suicide, leaving Trotsky a note in which he urged him to keep up the fight against Stalin. Georgi Chicherin retired in 1930, worn down by illness and by Stalin's growing disregard for his advice on policy; his funeral in 1934 was a quiet one. Lev Karakhan and Karl Radek disappeared in the Great Terror of the late 1930s. That Karakhan had stayed aloof from the oppositionist activity failed to save him. Radek by contrast had openly supported Trotsky. Although he tried to save his career by doing a political somersault and attacking Trotsky, he was dragged out for a show-trial and shunted into the labour-camp system where he perished in 1939. Maxim Litvinov died a free man in 1951. He had served Stalin punctiliously while privately telling Ivy about his objections,[1] and lived for years in dread of arrest. Ivy Litvinov somehow found the strength to endure. In 1972 she gained permission to leave for England, where she devoted herself to her writing until her death five years later.[2]

The anti-Bolshevik army commanders had mixed fortunes after leaving Soviet-held territory. Pëtr Wrangel ended up in Serbia. His sudden death in 1928 gave rise to suspicion that his butler's brother had poisoned him for some unexplained reason. Nikolai Yudenich retired to the French Riviera and shunned émigré affairs through to his peaceful end in 1933. Anton Denikin lived on fairly quietly until 1947 in France and the US. Symon Petliura also went to France where, in 1926, he was assassinated on a Paris street. This was also the year when Józef Piłsudski, the most effective of the commanders who fought the Reds, organized a *coup d'état* in Warsaw. Despite refusing to become President, he held the real power in Poland and dominated its foreign and military policy until his death in 1935.

The leaders of the Western Allies retained some influence after the Great War. Woodrow Wilson achieved his goal of establishing a League of Nations even though he failed to secure America's entry. Physical debilitation prevented him from standing for a third Presidency and he died in 1924. Herbert Hoover, one of his main associates in developing policy to deal with Soviet Russia, became US President in 1929 only to lose power at the next election as the effects of the Great Depression were registered; but in Europe, country after country saluted his pioneering humanitarian efforts that had saved them from famine at the end of the Great War. Georges Poincaré became French premier a further four times after the Versailles treaty and sent the army into the Rhineland in 1923 to enforce Germany's payment of reparations; he died in 1934. Georges Clemenceau retired soon after Versailles, widely celebrated as the 'Tiger' who had defeated the mighty Germans. He died in 1929. Although David Lloyd George outlived all of these leaders, his own coalition ministry of 1918 turned out to be his last and he lost power in 1922, never to regain it. Among his follies in the 1930s was his advocacy of accommodation with Hitler and the Third Reich. Lloyd George died in 1945, by which time his friend and rival Winston Churchill had supplanted him in national esteem. The anti-Soviet warmonger of 1918 became the ally of Stalin and the USSR in 1941. After the Second World War, Churchill resumed his hostility towards Soviet communism; and although he was defeated in the 1945 elections, he returned to the office of Prime Minister in 1951. At his funeral in 1965, he was mourned as the wartime saviour of his country.

The Western ambassadors of 1917–18 behaved with the discretion associated with their profession. Joseph Noulens returned to French national politics, becoming a senator in 1920 and going to his grave in 1944. Sir George Buchanan remained fitfully active in public debates about Russia; but his health was never good and he passed away in 1924. David Francis followed him in 1927. As things turned out, William C. Bullitt was the diplomat who went on to capture most attention in later years. His criticisms of the Paris Peace Conference had commended him to President Franklin D. Roosevelt as the best person to open the US embassy in Moscow in 1933. Although the new ambassador had shed his early illusions about communist Russia, Soviet leaders welcomed him as someone who might get them a sympathetic hearing in Washington.

In 1924 Bullitt had married none other than John Reed's widow Louise Bryant. But he divorced her in 1930 after finding she had been unfaithful. Had Bryant died of typhoid with her first husband, she might have joined him in his resting place beneath the Kremlin Wall. Instead she was consigned to the footnotes of history along with the other cheerleaders of the early years of Russian communism. Albert Rhys Williams consistently avoided criticism of the USSR even though he was well aware of the oppressive conditions there. In the Second World War he gave speeches across America drumming up support for Stalin. In Britain, Morgan Philips Price was elected as a Labour MP in 1929 and entered Ramsay MacDonald's national government in 1931. This rightward movement in Philips Price's politics did not stop him writing fondly of the times he had spent close to Lenin; he died in 1973.[3] Bessie Beatty switched careers from news reporting to writing film scripts for MGM Studios; she also served as the American Secretary of the International PEN Club, a writers' defence organization, and worked as a radio show presenter in New York until her death in 1947.

Although John Reed had died in 1920 his book lived on and was published in the world's main languages. In 1922 a Russian famine relief edition came out in America, complete with a preface by Lenin.[4] Reed was an admired figure in Comintern and the book was published in Russian translation in Moscow with a frontispiece photo of his monument outside the Kremlin.[5] American communists founded John Reed Clubs in his honour. Reed's chronicle made no mention of Stalin, however, and indeed he had expressed a lively appreciation of communist leaders such as Trotsky, Bukharin, Kamenev and Zinoviev. By the end of 1940 every single one of them was dead, killed as an enemy of the people. The book was withdrawn from Soviet libraries and further foreign editions were blocked by Comintern, which held some of the translation copyrights. After Stalin's death in 1953 his successor Nikita Khrushchëv relicensed publication even though Trotsky, Bukharin, Kamenev and Zinoviev were still refused posthumous rehabilitation in the USSR. Khrushchëv's scribes handled this situation by annotating the text with 'explanatory' footnotes.[6] The world communist movement fell into lock-step with this compromise and Reed's book went into fresh editions around the world—Fidel Castro said how much it had meant to him as a young man.[7]

Most of the Western witnesses of the October Revolution had already departed Russia by the early 1920s. But there were a few exceptions. Jacques Sadoul, having been sentenced to death in France *in absentia*, could not safely set foot on French soil. But he cut a dash in Moscow, as an American reporter noticed: 'He struck me as being thoroughly happy, absolutely at ease in his strange surroundings. He was dressed, when I saw him, in a knickerbocker suit of English tweeds, with woollen golf stockings, and smart brown shoes that betokened a rather fastidious care of appearances.'[8] After various assignments for Comintern, Sadoul in 1924 returned to France and surrendered to arrest and trial. Fifteen sessions of the Council of War were needed before, to the surprise of many at the time, he was acquitted and had his military rank restored to him. He subsequently became the Paris correspondent of the Soviet newspaper *Izvestiya* and spoke up for

Stalin's foreign policy before and during the pact between Hitler and Stalin.[9] When the USSR entered the war against the Third Reich, Sadoul with relief began working against the German occupation of France. He died in 1956, the year that Khrushchëv denounced Stalin in Moscow.

Another Frenchman, René Marchand, stayed on for a while in Soviet Russia after acting as an informer for the Cheka in 1918. He was by no means as content as Sadoul. Despite living comfortably in the Hotel Metropol with his wife and children, he appeared to be under constant nervous strain, which gave rise to speculation that he regretted throwing his lot in with the Bolsheviks.[10] Eventually Marchand left for Turkey where he renounced his ties with Soviet Russia and died in obscurity after years of pamphleteering in support of the Turkish government.[11]

Arthur Ransome and Yevgenia Shelepina married in 1924 and they later moved to the Lake District, as far as was possible from the spotlights of English public life. It is unlikely that she ever again worked for the Soviet authorities. For a long time, though, Ransome could not shrug off the suspicions that were directed at him. Surveillance of his activities continued until 1937, when the Passport Office was finally told that 'this man's name need no longer be retained on the black list'.[12] Although he continued to travel abroad, he had lost interest in Russian affairs and devoted his energies to writing novels for children. Even during the Second World War he refrained from commenting on the USSR. The *Swallows and Amazons* series brought pleasure to millions of readers who had no idea that the venerable story-teller had shuttled between Lenin and Lloyd George and served as agent S76. The marriage endured but was not entirely harmonious. Trotsky's ex-secretary grew intolerant of her husband's eccentricities and tried to make him into a more orderly person than he was ever capable of becoming. He died at the height of his fame in 1967; she survived him until 1975, three years after she had paid a trip to meet her long-lost sisters in Moscow.[13]

Other leading British agents of the early Soviet period maintained their links with the intelligence agencies. Sir Paul Dukes served on various missions and Sidney Reilly badgered him to stand for parliament and speak out against communist rule.[14] Unusually for a secret agent, he acquired an aura of celebrity. Enjoying the high life, he entered a short but disastrous marriage to a wealthy American socialite. Though he continued to write about contemporary Russia,[15] his heart lay in spiritual quest and he steadily felt drawn towards a different way of life. Before the Great War he had read voraciously about Eastern religion and this eventually led him to take up yoga. In his later years, after marrying for a second time, he explored the villages of the Himalayas and studied their religious traditions. He wrote copiously and, returning to his musical interests, composed melodies to accompany his favourite yogic exercises and corresponded with the Dalai Lama. In 1967 Dukes suffered a broken leg when a guest accidentally drove her car into him in snowy conditions outside his house. Although he bore this injury with bravery, there was also irreversible damage to his brain and he died some days later.[16]

Like Dukes, George Hill wrote accounts of his intelligence career. He helped some of the 'girls' who worked for him to escape Soviet Russia and briefly took one of them, Evelyn, as his second wife.[17] But his books involved a breach of the rules of public service, and he was made aware that Mansfield Cumming's successor Sir Stewart Menzies was displeased with him.[18] Nonetheless he was sent back into the USSR in the Second World War as Britain's liaison officer with the NKVD. He later claimed to have co-written the Soviet training manual on sabotage for partisans.[19] This did not discourage the Soviet political police from planting one of his old couriers in the same hotel with mischievous intent; but Hill was too clever for them and wrote a formal complaint to his Soviet counterparts which he copied to London.[20] The NKVD under Lavrenti Beria dropped its trickery and soon Hill was meeting Beria himself to discuss how to improve Anglo-Soviet cooperation. Apparently Beria showed keen interest in what Hill could tell him about undetectable poisons and automatic-weapon silencers.[21]

The Grand Alliance of the USSR, Britain and the US crumbled soon after the war, and Hill set himself up in business in West Germany.[22] One of his money-making plans was to write the biography of Sidney Reilly. In the end it was Robert Bruce Lockhart's son Robin who did the job using Hill's detailed notes, and the book became a best-seller. Its closing chapters told a wretched tale. Although Reilly had not divorced his first wife Margaret, who was still alive, he entered into a bigamous marriage with Nadine Zalessky in 1915.[23] After abandoning Nadine in 1920, he arranged a wedding (again bigamous) to the blonde Chilean actress Mrs Pepita Haddon-Chambers in 1923. When Reilly disappeared on a trip to Russia in 1925, Pepita wrote up his life story on the basis of a colourful draft he had left behind him.[24] By the time the book appeared, Reilly was dead. The Cheka had lured him back to Russia only to arrest, interrogate and execute him in secret. The books by his widow and Robin Bruce Lockhart brought his name to public attention.[25] A Thames Television series glamorized him as 'the Ace of Spies'.[26] Although he was often talked of as having been a model for Ian Fleming's agent 007, truly any one out of that trio of Reilly, Dukes and Hill could have supplied inspiration for James Bond.

Robert Bruce Lockhart was certainly the model for the hero of the 1934 Hollywood movie *British Agent*, which starred Leslie Howard as 'Stephen Locke' and Kay Francis as 'Elena Moura'.[27] In the 1920s he had worked at the Prague embassy where he became close to President Tomáš Masaryk. But despite adoring the night clubs, champagne and beautiful women in Czechoslovakia, he longed to go back to the high life in London and resume an affair with his latest mistress. After switching careers and moving into journalism, he achieved success through his friendship with the *Daily Express* owner Lord Beaverbrook. Lockhart was as profligate as Reilly. To supplement his income, he wrote an autobiography, taking him through to the end of his Russian period. *Memoirs of a British Agent*, on which the film was loosely based, earned vast royalties for him but predictably irritated Soviet spokesmen. Although the Moscow chapters centred on his purely diplomatic functions, the title of the book lent weight to the official Soviet claim that he had been involved in activities inappropriate for a diplomat. Lockhart lamented his notoriety in the USSR,[28] though it was nobody's fault but his own: as a master of the written word he had surely calculated that the resonances of the word 'agent' would increase his sales.

Lockhart had tried the patience of everyone in Whitehall by selling the film rights of his memoirs to Warner Brothers. Before the movie was released, his friends in Hollywood were alarmed by the depiction of him as the leader of an armed conspiracy against Lenin while Moura appeared as a fanatical Leninist who betrayed him. They sent Lockhart a telegram advising him that the script was 'libellous and burlesque'.[29] In 1918, of course, Lockhart really had been engaged in subverting Soviet rule whereas Moura at that time had been a fanatic only in the cause of love. Lockhart prudently let the matter rest and did not sue. When war broke out with Germany, he was appointed Director of Political Warfare and knighted in 1943.[30] From 1945 he found himself without a regular income and wrote frantically about everything from European international affairs to fishing and malt whisky to keep himself in the grand style. He died in 1970 at the age of eighty-two.

After Lockhart left her in Moscow, Moura worked as Maxim Gorki's personal assistant.[31] When in 1921 Gorki left for Italy she returned to her family in Estonia and, after the shortest of courtships, married Baron Nikolai Budberg. The marriage ended in divorce in 1926.[32] As Moura Budberg she lived for a while again with Gorki and then with H. G. Wells in London.[33] But she and Lockhart had never lost their mutual attraction. She was displeased that his memoirs gave prominence to their affair, but she acknowledged that this had the benefit of making her name known in the West; and Lockhart interceded with officials for a successful result when she applied for a British residence permit. Always attracted by a life of glamour, she found work on the production side in the UK film industry. She had never been conventionally good-looking; it was her zest for life that made her so appealing, and this quality remained with her into her retirement when she continued to turn men's heads. Yet no one was absolutely sure where her political loyalties lay and it was often mooted that she might be a Soviet agent. Lockhart defended her gallantly against such aspersions.[34] But he was wrong. An investigation of the Soviet archives revealed that she indeed became an NKVD informer and almost certainly reported on both Gorki and Wells.[35]

The aviator Merian Cooper—'Coop'—had an even more extraordinary career in cinema than Moura. After Poland he went into the American movie business and in 1933 co-wrote and co-directed one of the most famous films of all time, *King Kong*. Cooper gave himself a role in the last scene as he piloted the plane that finished off the monster Kong at the end of the story. In the Second World War, despite being too old for conscription, he volunteered for the US air force; he rose to Chief of Staff in the China Air Task Force and witnessed the final surrender of the Japanese on USS *Missouri*.[36] In 1951 he received an Academy Award nomination as the producer of John Ford's *The Quiet Man*. He died in 1973.

Others had a less fortunate experience after their time in Russia. Xenophon Kalamatiano languished in Soviet confinement until 1921 when Herbert Hoover obtained the release of all American detainees as a condition of the dispatch of food aid. Until then the US authorities had done little on their leading intelligence officer's behalf. Some said that the Cheka released him from prison long before he was repatriated because he had agreed to become a double agent. The Department of State itself seems to have wondered about his allegiance. It gave him a less than warm welcome in Washington, refusing to give him a job commensurate with his experience. A mysterious ailment killed Kalamatiano in 1923.[37] Boris Savinkov, who perished two years later, had an even grislier end. His volatile temperament had often led him into errors of judgement and none of these was greater than when, in 1925, he felt so demoralized about his ruined political career that he went back to Moscow and gave himself up to the Soviet authorities. He told nobody but Dukes about his decision—and Dukes never explained why he did not try to stop him.[38] The Cheka immediately took him into custody. It exploited him for its own propaganda purposes, getting him to write to Reilly about the stability of the Soviet regime.[39] As soon as Savinkov had exhausted his usefulness, he was given a show-trial and executed.[40]

All the people mentioned in this book are now dead and few of them are remembered outside the pages of monographs. Among the obvious exceptions are Lenin, Trotsky, Churchill and Wilson. Lenin and Trotsky remain a benchmark for communist doctrines and practices around the world. Churchill is remembered for his leadership in the war against Nazi Germany. Wilson's creation of the League of Nations is seen as the forerunner of today's institutions of global governance. Yet the other men and women who analysed and reported and fought over the October Revolution also made their contribution to the history of their times. Each could see that something big and unprecedented had happened in Russia in 1917. As through a glass darkly, they glimpsed the October Revolution's potential for good or evil in their world. They were excited, appalled or enraptured. Regardless of their attitude to communism, they appreciated that huge, important questions had arisen from the Soviet revolutionary experiment, questions that have not lost their importance today. Although the USSR has been consigned to the waste-paper basket of history, many of the disputes about the year 1917 are still with us.

The disputes range from the peaks of politics and philosophy to the lowly fates of individuals. An unexpected example of the Revolution's lasting capacity to impinge on our current affairs was given in September 2005, when the General Procuracy of the Russian Federation reopened the posthumous case of Robert Bruce Lockhart. Ever since his trial *in absentia* in 1918, Lockhart had been a demonic figure in Soviet history textbooks— and the popular Soviet movie *Hostile Whirlwinds*, which was released in 1953, reinforced this image. At the turn of the millennium, the General

Procuracy in Moscow was still busy reviewing historic cases of possible miscarriages of justice over the seven decades of Soviet communist dictatorship. Its verdict on Lockhart was flinty but fair: the British agent was found to have engaged in active subversion. He had therefore been guilty as charged at the time and did not qualify for posthumous rehabilitation.[41]

NOTES

1. TROUBLING JOURNEYS

1. *The Times*, 19 March 1917; *Manchester Guardian*, 19 March 1917.

2. I. Maisky, *Journey into the Past*, p. 241.

3. I. Litvinov, 'Letters to Viola', autobiographical fragment, p. 32: St Antony's RESC Archive; I. Litvinov, autobiographical fragment on 1917–1918: Ivy Litvinov Papers (HIA), box 11, folder 7.

4. M. Litvinov, 'From the Diary of a Russian Political Emigre, March 17th, London' (typescript, apparently dictated to Ivy Litvinov): *ibid.*, box 10, folder 5, p. 1.

5. I. Litvinov, 'Letters to Viola', autobiographical fragment, p. 33: St Antony's RESC Archive.

6. D. Marquand, *Ramsay MacDonald*, p. 208.

7. I. Litvinov, 'Letters to Viola', autobiographical fragment, p. 33: St Antony's RESC Archive.

8. *Ibid.*

9. C. Nabokoff, *The Ordeal of a Diplomat*, pp. 83–4.

10. I. Maisky, *Journey into the Past*, p. 245.

11. On the Archangel route see H. Shukman, *War or Revolution: Russian Jews and Conscription in Britain, 1917*, pp. 88–9.

12. C. Nabokoff, *The Ordeal of a Diplomat*, pp. 94–5.

13. *New York Times*, 16 March 1917.

14. *Ibid.*, 17 March 1917.

15. I. Maisky, *Journey into the Past*, p. 255.

16. C. Nabokoff, *The Ordeal of a Diplomat*, pp. 95–7.

17. I. Maisky, *Journey into the Past*, pp. 257–8.

18. *Ibid.*, p. 261.

19. I. Litvinov, 'Letters to Viola', autobiographical fragment, p. 36: St Antony's RESC Archive.

20. HO 144/2158/322428. My thanks to Harry Shukman for sharing the documents in this and the next endnote.

21. HO 144/2158/322428/6 and 9; see also H. Shukman, *War or Revolution: Russian Jews and Conscription in Britain, 1917*, p. 59.

22. J. McHugh and B. J. Ripley, 'Russian Political Internees in First World War Britain: The Cases of George Chicherin and Peter Petroff', *Historical Journal*, no. 3 (1985), pp. 733–4.

23. A. E. Senn, *The Russian Revolution in Switzerland, 1914–1917*, pp. 224 and 228.

24. *Ibid.*, p. 228.

25. See below, p. 331.

26. G. A. Hill, *Go Spy the Land*, pp. 81–2.

27. N. Sukhanov, *Zapiski o revolyutsii*, vol. 2, book 3, p. 6.

28. I. Getzler, *Martov: A Political Biography of a Russian Social Democrat*, p. 150.

29. Sir G. Buchanan, *My Mission to Russia and Other Diplomatic Memories*, pp. 120–1.

2. RUSSIA ON ITS KNEES

1. L. Bryant, *Six Red Months in Russia*, p. 44; J. Reed, *Ten Days that Shook the World* (1960), pp. 13, 219 and 331; G. A. Hill, *Go Spy the Land*, p. 84.

2. J. Reed, *Ten Days that Shook the World* (1960), p. 14.

3. See R. Service, *The Russian Revolution, 1900–1927*, p. 63.

4. See R. Service, *The Bolshevik Party in Revolution: A Study in Organisational Change*, pp. 53–4 and 57.

5. See K. Rose, *King George V*, pp. 211–15.

6. Interview of A. F. Kerenski, N. A. Sokolov investigation (Paris, 14–20 August 1920), pp. 105–9: GARF item (unspecified as to catalogue reference), Volkogonov Papers, reel 15.

7. *Protokoly Tsentral'nogo Komiteta*, p. 87.

8. L. de Robien, *The Diary of a Diplomat in Russia*, pp. 127–8.

9. *Ibid.*, p. 121.

10. *Ibid.*, p. 122.

11. *Ibid.*

3. THE ALLIED AGENDA

1. G. A. Hill, *Go Spy the Land*, p. 77.

2. *Ibid.*, pp. 78–9.

3. L. de Robien, *The Diary of a Diplomat in Russia*, p. 33.

4. *Ibid.*, p. 41.

5. *New York Times*, 21 June 1917.

6. D. Marquand, *Ramsay MacDonald*, pp. 213 and 215.

7. B. Beatty, *The Red Heart of Russia*, p. 37.

8. *New York Times*, 17 May 1917.

9. *Ibid.*, 15 June 1917.

10. B. Beatty, *The Red Heart of Russia*, pp. 37, 41 and 44.

11. *New York Times*, 16 August 1917.

12. *Ibid.*, 18 August 1917.

13. US Consulate—Leningrad [*sic*]: Dispatches to the Secretary of State (HIA), dispatches 274, 293, 330 and 339.

14. R. H. Bruce Lockhart, *Memoirs of a British Agent, Being an Account of the Author's Early Life in Many Lands and of his Official Mission to Moscow in 1918*, pp. 153–4.

15. J. Noulens, *Mon ambassade en Russie Soviétique, 1917–1919*, vol. 1, p. 89.

16. *Ibid.*, vol. 2, p. 243.

17. *Ibid.*

18. *Ibid.*, p. 242.

19. *Ibid.*, pp. 243–4.

20. *Ibid.*, vol. 1, pp. 9 and 21.

21. D. S. Foglesong, *America's Secret War against Bolshevism: U.S. Intervention in the Russian Civil War, 1917–1920*, pp. 108–9.

22. C. Andrew, *For the President's Eyes Only*, pp. 38–9.

23. *Ibid.*, pp. 46–7.

24. *Ibid.*, p. 47.

25. G. R. Swain, 'Maugham, Masaryk and the "Mensheviks"', *Revolutionary Russia*, no. 1 (1994), pp. 83–5.

26. J. Noulens, *Mon ambassade en Russie Soviétique, 1917–1919*, vol. 1, p. 177.

27. L. Bryant, *Six Red Months in Russia*, p. 65.

28. D. S. Foglesong, *America's Secret War against Bolshevism*, pp. 108–9.

29. *Bolshevik Propaganda: Hearings before a Subcommittee on the Judiciary, United States Senate, Sixty-Fifth Congress, Third Session and Thereafter Pursuant to Senate Resolutions 439 and 469—February 11, 1919 to March 10, 1919*, p. 779 (Robins).

30. *Ibid.*

31. C. Nabokoff, *The Ordeal of a Diplomat*, p. 64.

32. Sir George Buchanan, *My Mission to Russia and Other Diplomatic Memories*, pp. 192–3; J. Noulens, *Mon ambassade en Russie Soviétique, 1917–1919*, vol. 1, pp. 89–91.

33. W. Hard, *Raymond Robins' Own Story*, pp. 49–50.

34. *Bolshevik Propaganda: Hearings before a Subcommittee on the Judiciary, United States Senate*, p. 790.

35. W. Hard, *Raymond Robins' Own Story*, p. 52.

4. CHEERING FOR THE SOVIETS

1. R. Chambers, *The Last Englishman: The Double Life of Arthur Ransome*, pp. 72–82.

2. MI5g1: S.F. 39/9/150[?]: Extract from A. Ransome's letter to his wife Ivy, 1 July 1917.

3. *Ibid.*

4. R. Chambers, *The Last Englishman*, p. 166.

5. 'Svidetel'stvo', 7 August 1917: Robert Hamilton Bruce Lockhart Papers (HIA), folder: Robin Bruce Lockhart, '2 Reilly: Documentary Material', folder 2.

6. R. H. Bruce Lockhart, *Memoirs of a British Agent, Being an Account of the Author's Early Life in Many Lands and of his Official Mission to Moscow in 1918*, p. 122.

7. W. F. Ryan, 'The Great Beast in Russia: Aleister Crowley's Theatrical Tour in 1913 and his Beastly Writings on Russia', in A. McMillin (ed.), *Symbolism and After: Essays on Russian Poetry in Honour of Georgette Donchin*, p. 155.

8. 'Svidetel'stvo', 7 August 1917: Robert Hamilton Bruce Lockhart Papers (HIA), folder: Robin Bruce Lockhart, '2 Reilly: Documentary Material', folder 2.

9. J. Noulens, *Mon ambassade en Russie Soviétique, 1917–1919*, vol. 2, p. 115.

10. M. Philips Price (ed.), *The Diplomatic History of the War*, p. 46.

11. J. Reed, 'Almost Thirty', *New Republic*, April 1936, pp. 267–70.

12. *Washington Post*, 4 July 1917.

13. *Ibid.*, 13 April 1917.

14. *Bolshevik Propaganda: Hearings before a Subcommittee on the Judiciary, United States Senate, Sixty-Fifth Congress, Third Session and Thereafter Pursuant to Senate Resolutions 439 and 469—February 11, 1919 to March 10, 1919*, p. 467.

15. L. Bryant, *Six Red Months in Russia*, pp. 19–20.

16. *Ibid.*, pp. 24–5.

17. *Bolshevik Propaganda: Hearings before a Subcommittee on the Judiciary, United States Senate*, p. 563.

18. *Ibid.*, p. 476.

19. *Ibid.*, p. 604.

20. B. Beatty, *The Red Heart of Russia*, p. 132.

21. *Ibid.*, pp. 693–4.

22. J. S. Clarke, *Pen Portraits of Russia under the 'Red Terror'*, pp. 165–6.

23. J. Sadoul, *Notes sur la révolution bolchévique, octobre 1917–janvier 1919*, pp. 37–41: letter to A. Thomas, 2/15 October 1917; J. Noulens, *Mon ambassade en Russie Soviétique, 1917–1919*, vol. 1, p. 83; A. Dunois, draft introduction to an edition of J. Sadoul's correspondence, dated May 1941, p. 2: Jacques Sadoul Papers (HIA).

24. J. Sadoul, 'La Condition des agents consulaires at diplomatiques au point de vue fiscal: thèse pour le doctorat' (Librairie Générale de Droit et de Jurisprudence: Paris, 1908).

25. A. Dunois, draft introduction to an edition of J. Sadoul's correspondence, dated May 1941, p. 1: Jacques Sadoul Papers (HIA).

26. J. Reed, *Red Russia*, book 1, p. 10. See also J. Reed, *Ten Days that Shook the World* (1960), pp. 78–9.

27. B. Beatty, *The Red Heart of Russia*, pp. 201 and 203.

28. *Ibid.*, pp. 13, 196 and 244.

29. J. Reed, *Red Russia*, book 2, p. 12.

30. *Bolshevik Propaganda: Hearings before a Subcommittee on the Judiciary, United States Senate*, p. 542.

31. *Ibid.*, p. 721.

32. J. Reed, *Ten Days that Shook the World* (1960), p. 332.

33. B. Beatty, *The Red Heart of Russia*, p. 134.

34. A. Rhys Williams, *Lenin: The Man and his Work*, p. 79.

35. *Ibid.*, pp. 79–80.

36. *Ibid.*, p. 73.

37. *Ibid.*, p. 80.

5. REVOLUTION AND THE WORLD

1. E. H. Carr, *The Bolshevik Revolution*, vol. 3, pp. 9–14.

2. See R. Service, *Lenin: A Political Life*, vol. 2, p. 273.

3. *Bolshevik Propaganda: Hearings before a Subcommittee on the Judiciary, United States Senate, Sixty-Fifth Congress, Third Session and Thereafter Pursuant to Senate Resolutions 439 and 469—February 11, 1919 to March 10, 1919*, p. 494.

4. See for example J. Reed, *Ten Days that Shook the World* (1960), pp. 220 and 336.

5. *Ibid.*, pp. 240 and 298.

6. B. Beatty, *The Red Heart of Russia*, pp. 193 and 195.

7. L. Bryant, *Six Red Months in Russia*, p. 145.

8. *Ibid.*, pp. 145–6.

9. L. Bryant, *Mirrors of Moscow*, p. 140.

10. J. Sadoul, *Notes sur la révolution bolchévique, octobre 1917–janvier 1919*, p. 68: letter to A. Thomas, 28 October/10 November 1917.

11. *Ibid.*, pp. 55–6: letter to A. Thomas, 25 October/7 November 1917.

12. Letters to A. Thomas, 26 October/8 November 1917, *ibid.*, pp. 58–60, and 27 October/9 November 1917, p. 65.

13. *Ibid.*, p. 83: letter to A. Thomas, 2/15 November 1917.

14. See R. Service, *Lenin: A Political Life*, vol. 2, pp. 183–90.

15. L. Trotskii, *Moya zhizn'*, vol. 2, p. 64.

16. J. Reed, *Ten Days that Shook the World* (1960), p. 347.

17. L. Trotskii, *Sochineniya*, vol. 3, book 2, pp. 164–6.

18. H. Hoover, *The Ordeal of Woodrow Wilson*, pp. 78–81.

19. General Max Hoffman, *War Diaries and Other Papers*, vol. 2, p. 190.

6. IN THE LIGHT OF THE FIRE

1. N. Bukharin, *Vseobshchaya delëzhka ili kommunisticheskoe proizvodstvo* (Izd. V'TsIK R., S., K. i K. Deputatov: Moscow, 1918), p. 8.

2. R. Vaucher, *L'Enfer bolchévik à Petrograd sous la commune et la terreur rouge*, pp. 2–3.

3. N. Bukharin, *Vseobshchaya delëzhka ili kommunisticheskoe proizvodstvo*, p. 8.

4. A. Kovrov, *Domashnyaya prisluga* (Kniga: Petrograd, 1917).

5. L. Trotskii, *Chto zhe dal'she? (Itogi i perspektivy)* (Priboi: Petersburg [sic], 1917), p. 6.

6. *Ibid.*, p. 26.

7. *Ibid.*, p. 28.

8. I. I. Kutuzov, *V strane 'ego velichestva'. Pis'ma i zametki ob Anglii russkogo rabochego diplomata*, pp. 8–10.

9. L. Trotskii, *Chto zhe dal'she?*, p. 6.

10. M. Lur'e (Yu. Larin), *Prodovol'stvie v Germanii i Rossii* (Kniga: Petrograd, 1918), pp. 7–11.

11. *Ibid.*, pp. 14–15.

12. *Ibid.*, pp. 15 and 21.

13. Yu. Larin, *Voina i zemel'naya programma* (Kniga: Petrograd, 1917), pp. 8 and 10.

14. *Ibid.*, pp. 8 and 11.

15. N. Bukharin, *Vseobshchaya delëzhka ili kommunisticheskoe proizvodstvo*, pp. 4–6.

16. Kii, *Vozmozhna-li otmena chastnoi sobstvennosti* (Kniga: Petrograd, 1917).

17. I. Litvinov, autobiographical fragment, pp. 15–16: St Antony's RESC Archive.

18. R. Bruce Lockhart, 'Last Words on Lenin: An Inaugural Address [as] Honorary President of the Associated Societies, Edinburgh University, 26 October 1960', pp. 15–16.

19. L. Trotskii, *Chto zhe dal'she?*, p. 23.

20. A. Ioffe, *O samoupravlenii* (Kniga: Petrograd, 1917), pp. 8–10.

21. V. A. Mau, *Sochineniya*, vol. 1: *Reformy i dogmy: gosudarstvo i ekonomika v epokhu reform i revolyutsii, 1860–1920-e gody*, pp. 207–26.

7. DIPLOMATIC IMPASSE

1. G. A. Hill, *Go Spy the Land*, p. 155; *Washington Post*, 2 March 1918.

2. C. Anet, *La Révolution russe: la terreur maximaliste; l'armistice—les pourparlers de paix (Novembre 1917–Janvier 1918)*, pp. 127–8.

3. Notes by Ye. P. Shelepina, 18 March 1918: http://arthur-ransome.spb .ru/index/0–8.

4. *Ibid.*

5. L. Bryant, *Six Red Months in Russia*, pp. 145–6.

6. Notes by Ye. P. Shelepina, 18 March 1918: http://arthur-ransome.spb .ru/index/0–8.

7. J. Noulens, *Mon ambassade en Russie Soviétique, 1917–1919*, vol. 1, p. 180.

8. J. Sadoul, *Notes sur la révolution bolchévique, octobre 1917–janvier 1919*, p. 124: letter to A. Thomas, 15/28 November 1917.

9. *Bolshevik Propaganda: Hearings before a Subcommittee on the Judiciary, United States Senate, Sixty-Fifth Congress, Third Session and Thereafter Pursuant to Senate Resolutions 439 and 469—February 11, 1919 to March 10, 1919*, p. 50.

10. C. Anet, *La Révolution russe: la terreur maximaliste; l'armistice—les pour-parlers de paix (Novembre 1917–Janvier 1918)*, pp. 54–5.

11. J. Noulens, *Mon ambassade en Russie Soviétique, 1917–1919*, vol. 1, p. 186.

12. Général Niessel, *Le Triomphe des bolchéviks et la paix de Brest-Litovsk: souvenirs, 1917–1918*, p. 203.

13. R. Vaucher, *L'Enfer bolchévik à Petrograd sous la commune et la terreur rouge*, p. 1; G. A. Hill, *Go Spy the Land*, pp. 145–6.

14. C. Anet, *La Révolution russe: la terreur maximaliste*, p. 128.

15. L. Bryant, *Six Months in Red Russia*, pp. 201–2; *Bolshevik Propaganda: Hearings before a Subcommittee on the Judiciary, United States Senate*, p. 564.

16. *Bolshevik Propaganda: Hearings before a Subcommittee on the Judiciary, United States Senate*, pp. 473 (Bryant) and 682 (Rhys Williams).

17. *Ibid.*, p. 566.

18. *Ibid.*, p. 565.

19. B. Beatty, *The Red Heart of Russia*, pp. 222–3; *Bolshevik Propaganda: Hearings before a Subcommittee on the Judiciary, United States Senate*, p. 564.

20. D. R. Francis, *Russia from the American Embassy, April 1916–November 1918*, pp. 173–4.

21. *Ibid.*, pp. 176–7.

22. Sir G. Buchanan, *My Mission to Russia and Other Diplomatic Memories*, pp. 225–6.

23. *Ibid.*, p. 220 (diary).

24. L. de Robien, *The Diary of a Diplomat in Russia*, p. 222.

25. IIO 144/2158/322428/16, 22 and 29. My thanks to Harry Shukman for sharing this document with me as well as the documents in the next three endnotes.

26. HO 144/2158/322428/33.

27. HO 144/2158/322428/85.

28. IIO 144/2158/322428: Assistant Commissioner of Police, 25 October 1917.

29. Sir G. Buchanan, *My Mission to Russia and Other Diplomatic Memories*, pp. 226–7 (diary); see also J. McHugh and B. J. Ripley, 'Russian Political Internees in First World War Britain: The Cases of George Chicherin and Peter Petroff', *Historical Journal*, no. 3 (1985), p. 736.

30. J. Noulens, *Mon ambassade en Russie Soviétique, 1917–1919*, vol. 1, pp. 170–1.

31. C. Anet, *La Révolution russe: la terreur maximaliste*, pp. 162–3.

32. J. Noulens, *Mon ambassade en Russie Soviétique, 1917–1919*, vol. 1, p. 179.

33. Sir G. Buchanan, *My Mission to Russia and Other Diplomatic Memories*, p. 243.

34. *Ibid.*, pp. 239 and 247.

35. D. Lloyd George, *War Memoirs*, vol. 2, pp. 1550–1.

36. *Ibid.*, p. 1551.

37. *Bolshevik Propaganda: Hearings before a Subcommittee on the Judiciary, United States Senate*, pp. 963–4.

38. W. Hard, *Raymond Robins' Own Story*, pp. 97–9.

39. *Ibid.*, pp. 57–8, 64–5 and 70.

40. L. Bryant, *Six Red Months in Russia*, ch. 24.

41. G. Buchanan (*en clair* report to London), pp. i–ii, 2 January 1918: Milner Papers.

42. C. Anet, *La Révolution russe: la terreur maximaliste*, p. 201; Général Niessel, *Le Triomphe des bolchéviks et la paix de Brest-Litovsk: souvenirs, 1917–1918*, p. 187.

43. J. Sadoul, *Notes sur la révolution bolchévique, octobre 1917–janvier 1919*, p. 140: letter to A. Thomas, 25 November/8 December 1917.

44. L. Bryant, *Six Red Months in Russia*, ch. 24.

45. Général Niessel, *Le Triomphe des bolchéviks et la paix de Brest-Litovsk: souvenirs, 1917–1918*, p. 186.

46. L. de Robien, *The Diary of a Diplomat in Russia*, p. 186; *Bolshevik Propaganda: Hearings before a Subcommittee on the Judiciary, United States Senate*, p. 942.

47. *Bolshevik Propaganda: Hearings before a Subcommittee on the Judiciary, United States Senate*, p. 961.

48. D. R. Francis, *Russia from the American Embassy, April 1916–November 1918*, pp. 168–9.

49. *Bolshevik Propaganda: Hearings before a Subcommittee on the Judiciary, United States Senate*, pp. 962–3; D. R. Francis, *Russia from the American Embassy, April 1916–November 1918*, pp. 210–11.

50. G. A. Hill, *Go Spy the Land*, pp. 152–3; G. A. Hill, *Dreaded Hour*, pp. 133–4.

51. J. Noulens, *Mon ambassade en Russie Soviétique, 1917–1919*, vol. 1, pp. 183–4.

52. L. de Robien, *The Diary of a Diplomat in Russia*, p. 190.

53. Sovnarkom meeting, 1(14) January 1918: GARF, f. R-130, op. 2, d. 1, item 1.

54. J. Noulens, *Mon ambassade en Russie Soviétique, 1917–1919*, vol. 1, pp. 186–7.

55. *Ibid.*, pp. 185–9; D. R. Francis, *Russia from the American Embassy, April 1916–November 1918*, pp. 216–17.

56. J. Noulens, *Mon ambassade en Russie Soviétique, 1917–1919*, vol. 1, pp. 190–1; *Bolshevik Propaganda: Hearings before a Subcommittee on the Judiciary, United States Senate*, pp. 963–4.

57. D. R. Francis, *Russia from the American Embassy, April 1916–November 1918*, pp. 219–20.

8. THE OTHER WEST

1. Russia. Posol'stvo (HIA), box 1: Russian ambassador in France to the embassy in Washington, 24, 26 and 29 December 1917 (Old Style).

2. D. S. Foglesong, *America's Secret War against Bolshevism: U.S. Intervention in the Russian Civil War, 1917–1920*, p. 57.

3. National Archives, FO 371/3295/6933.

4. A. E. Senn, *Diplomacy and Revolution: The Soviet Mission to Switzerland, 1918*, pp. 43–53.

5. I. Litvinov, untitled autobiographical fragment: Ivy Litvinov Papers (HIA), box 10, folder 5, p. 27.

6. *Ibid.*

7. D. Lloyd George, *War Memoirs*, vol. 2, pp. 1552–3.

8. *Ibid.*, p. 1553.

9. Russia. Posol'stvo (HIA), box 1: Nabokov's telegram to the US embassy, 3(16) January 1918.

10. *Ibid.*: Paris ambassador to all Russian embassies, 6(19) January 1918.

11. *Ibid.*: Nabokov's telegram to the US embassy, 4(17) January 1918.

12. I. Maisky, *Journey into the Past*, p. 78; *Protokoly Tsentral'nogo Komiteta RSDRP(b): avgust 1917–fevral' 1918* (Gosizdat: Moscow, 1958), p. 165.

13. Maisky's notes on Litvinov's conversational memoir, *Journey into the Past*, pp. 62–5; Russia. Posol'stvo (HIA), box 1: Nabokov's telegram to the US embassy, 4(17) January 1918.

14. Maisky's notes on Litvinov's conversational memoir, *Journey into the Past*, pp. 62–5.

15. Russia. Posol'stvo (HIA), box 1: Nabokov's telegram to the US embassy, 21 January (8 February) 1918.

16. *Daily News and Leader*, 19 February 1918.

17. *Labour Leader*, 24 January 1918.

18. *http://gdl.cdlr.strath.ac.uk/redclyde/redclyo74.htm*; V. V. Aldoshin, Yu. V. Ivanov, V. M. Semënov and V. A. Tarasov (eds), *Sovetsko-amerikanskie otnosheniya: gody nepriznaniya, 1918–1926*, p. 12.

19. Extracts of report by Basil Thomson on Litvinov, 20 February 1918: Milner Papers, dep. 364, fols 49–51.

20. *House of Commons Debates*, 19 February 1918, vol. 103, col. 607.

21. I. Litvinov, autobiographical fragment, 'Letters to Viola', p. 28: St Antony's RESC Archive.

22. *Ibid.*

23. *Ibid.*, pp. 28a–30.

24. I. Litvinov, untitled autobiographical fragment: Ivy Litvinov Papers (HIA), box 9, folder 10, p. 28a.

25. *Ibid.*, p. 37: St Antony's RESC Archive.

26. *Ibid.*

27. M. Litvinoff, *The Bolshevik Revolution: Its Rise and Meaning*, especially pp. 43–6.

28. *Manchester Guardian*, 23 January 1918.

29. Harold Kellock (Finnish Information Bureau, New York) to Lincoln Steffens, 22 April 1918, p. 1: Russian Subject Collection (HIA).

30. *New York Times*, 31 January 1918.

31. *Ibid.*, 2 February 1918.

32. *Ibid.*, 19 February 1918.

33. *Washington Post*, 29 February 1918.

34. *Ibid.*, 1 June 1918.

35. *New York Times*, 11 May 1918.

36. R. Chambers, *The Last Englishman: The Double Life of Arthur Ransome*, p. 177.

37. M. Budberg to R. Bruce Lockhart, n.d.: Robert Hamilton Bruce Lockhart Papers (HIA), box 2, folder 2.

38. A. Rhys Williams, *Lenin: The Man and his Work*, p. 74.

39. G. A. Hill, *Go Spy the Land*, p. 192.

40. *Ibid.*, pp. 192–3.

41. Report from Stockholm, 12 September 1918: CX 050167. My thanks to Andrew Cook for sharing this document with me.

42. G. A. Hill, *Go Spy the Land*, p. 191.

43. *Bolshevik Propaganda: Hearings before a Subcommittee on the Judiciary, United States Senate, Sixty-Fifth Congress, Third Session and Thereafter Pursuant to Senate Resolutions 439 and 469—February 11, 1919 to March 10, 1919*, p. 553.

44. M. Philips Price, *The Soviet, the Terror and Intervention*, pp. 1–14.

45. *Radek and Ransome on Russia* (The Socialist Publication Society: Brooklyn, NY, 1918), pp. 5–7, 10–11, 19–20 and 24.

46. R. H. Bruce Lockhart, *Memoirs of a British Agent, Being an Account of the Author's Early Life in Many Lands and of his Official Mission to Moscow in 1918*, pp. 200–1.

47. *The Diaries of Robert Bruce Lockhart, 1915–1938*, p. 31.

48. R. Bruce Lockhart, 'Last Words on Lenin: An Inaugural Address [as] Honorary President of the Associated Societies, Edinburgh University, 26 October 1960', p. 6.

49. *Ibid.*, p. 7.

50. *Bolshevik Propaganda: Hearings before a Subcommittee on the Judiciary, United States Senate*, p. 801.

51. T. Alexander, *An Estonian Childhood*, p. 41.

52. *The Diaries of Robert Bruce Lockhart, 1915–1938*, pp. 32–3.

53. *Ibid.*, p. 33.

54. *Bolshevik Propaganda: Hearings before a Subcommittee on the Judiciary, United States Senate*, pp. 802–3.

55. *Ibid.*, p. 803.

56. 'Udostoverenie', 5 August 1918: Robert Hamilton Bruce Lockhart Papers (HIA), folder: Robin Bruce Lockhart, '2 Reilly: Documentary Material', folder 2.

57. J. Sadoul, *Notes sur la révolution bolchévique, octobre 1917–janvier 1919*, p. 264: letter to A. Thomas, 15 March 1918; J. Noulens, *Mon ambassade en Russie Soviétique, 1917–1919*, vol. 2, pp. 74–5 and 115.

58. National Archives, FO 371/3290/51340, cited in B. Pearce, *How Haig Saved Lenin*, p. 22.

59. H. Wilson to the War Cabinet, 18 March 1918: Milner Papers, dep. 364, fol. 127.

60. J. Noulens, *Mon ambassade en Russie Soviétique, 1917–1919*, vol. 2, pp. 74–5 and 115.

9. TALKS AT BREST-LITOVSK

1. G. A. Hill, *Go Spy the Land*, p. 115.

2. B. Pearce, *How Haig Saved Lenin*, p. 7.

3. Arthur M. Free Papers, folder Mb (HIA).

4. N. A. Ioffe, 'O moëm ottse': N. A. Ioffe Papers (HIA).

5. J. Sadoul, *Notes sur la révolution bolchévique, octobre 1917–janvier 1919*, p. 140: letter to A. Thomas, 25 November/8 December 1917.

6. O. von Czernin's diary reproduced from the 1923 Russian translation in N. Ioffe, *Moi otets Adol'f Abramovich Ioffe*, p. 135.

7. J. Sadoul, *Notes sur la révolution bolchévique, octobre 1917–janvier 1919*, p. 140: letter to A. Thomas, 25 November/8 December 1917.

8. *Mirnye peregovory v Brest-Litovske*, vol. 1: *Plenarnye zasedaniya. Zasedaniya Politicheskoi Komissii*, pp. 67–8 and 72.

9. *Ibid.*, pp. 52–3.

10. J. Sadoul, *Notes sur la révolution bolchévique, octobre 1917–janvier 1919*, p. 176: letter to A. Thomas, 22 December 1917/4 January 1918.

11. Ye. P. Shelepina, 'Journey to Brest' (notes written in March 1918): Notes by Ye. P. Shelepina, 18 March 1918: http://arthur-ransome.spb.ru/index/o-8.

12. *Ibid.*

13. V. I. Lenin, *Polnoe sobranie sochinenii*, vol. 35, pp. 179–80.

14. *Mirnye peregovory v Brest-Litovske*, vol. 1, p. 208.

15. *Ibid.*, pp. 209–10.

16. *Protokoly Tsentral'nogo Komiteta RSDRP(b): avgust 1917–fevral' 1918*, pp. 194–5.

17. R. H. Bruce Lockhart (Petrograd), 2 February 1918: Milner Papers, dep. 364, fols 66–7.

18. R. H. Bruce Lockhart (Petrograd, via Lindley), 16 February 1918: *ibid.*, fols 34–8; R. H. Bruce Lockhart (Moscow), 21 February 1918: *ibid.*, fol. 143.

19. R. Vaucher, *L'Enfer bolchévik à Petrograd sous la commune et la terreur rouge*, pp. 4–5.

20. *House of Commons Debates*, 18 February 1918, vol. 103, col. 462.

21. *Manchester Guardian*, 26 February 1918.

22. *House of Commons Debates*, vol. 103: 27 February 1918, col. 1478; 28 February 1918, col. 1605.

23. R. Vaucher, *L'Enfer bolchévik à Petrograd sous la commune et la terreur rouge*, pp. 7–10.

24. *Protokoly Tsentral'nogo Komiteta RSDRP(b): avgust 1917–fevral' 1918*, p. 199.

25. *Ibid.*, p. 200.

26. _Ibid._, pp. 204–5.

27. Undated memorandum on 1917–18 by Stephen Alley. I am grateful to Andrew Cook for giving me a copy of this document.

28. J. Sadoul, _Notes sur la révolution bolchévique, octobre 1917–janvier 1919_, p. 243: letter to A. Thomas, 21 February 1918.

29. _Ibid._, p. 244: letter to A. Thomas, 22 February 1918.

30. A. A. Ioffe, 'N. Lenin i nasha vneshnyaya politika' (dated 20 October 1927), APRF, f. 31, op. 1, d. 4, pp. 212–13.

31. _Protokoly Tsentral'nogo Komiteta RSDRP(b): avgust 1917–fevral' 1918_, pp. 206–8.

32. _Ibid._, p. 215.

33. O. M. Sayler, _Russia White or Red_, pp. 160–1; J. Noulens, _Mon ambassade en Russie Soviétique, 1917–1919_, vol. 1, p. 231, and vol. 2, pp. 29, 36 and 38; L. de Robien, _The Diary of a Diplomat in Russia_, p. 237.

34. B. Pearce, _How Haig Saved Lenin_, p. 15.

10. BREATHING DANGEROUSLY

1. B. Pearce, _How Haig Saved Lenin_, p. 9.

2. A. A. Ioffe to V. I. Lenin, 11 March 1918, reproduced in V. Krasnov and V. Daines (eds), _Neizvestnyi Trotskii. Krasnyi Bonapart: Dokumenty, mneniya, razmyshleniya_, p. 40.

3. Sovnarkom formally made Chicherin the 'Acting Deputy' on 13 March 1918: RGASPI, f. 2, op. 1, d. 5483. See also RGASPI, f. 17, op. 2, d. 104, p. 43b (Central Committee and Central Control Commission meeting, 26 October 1923).

4. V. I. Lenin, _Polnoe sobranie sochinenii_, vol. 36, p. 324.

5. W. Hard, _Raymond Robins' Own Story_, pp. 138–9.

6. _Ibid._, p. 141.

7. O. Wardrop to A. J. Balfour, 16 April 1918: National Archives, FO 371/3331 /9741.

8. W. Hard, _Raymond Robins' Own Story_, pp. 140–5. On Francis's links to the American railway engineers in Siberia see B. O. Johnson, 'American Railway Engineers in Siberia', _American Engineer_, no. 81, May–June 1923, pp. 187–91.

9. Letter (in French, on Crédit Lyonnais notepaper) by unknown person to unknown addressee, summer 1918(?), p. 2: Robert Hamilton Bruce Lockhart Papers (HIA), folder: Robin Bruce Lockhart, 'Reilly: Russian Revolution, Etc.: Sources: Sir Edward Spears'.

10. W. Hard, _Raymond Robins' Own Story_, pp. 148–9 and 151–2.

11. V. I. Lenin, _Polnoe sobranie sochinenii_, vol. 36, p. 105.

12. _Ibid._, p. 250.

13. _Ibid._, p. 323.

14. R. H. Bruce Lockhart to A. J. Balfour, 7 November 1918, pp. 1–2: Robert Hamilton Bruce Lockhart Papers (HIA), box 12; R. H. Bruce Lockhart, _Friends, Foes and Foreigners_, p. 273.

15. R. H. Bruce Lockhart, *Friends, Foes and Foreigners*, p. 275.

16. J. Sadoul, *Notes sur la révolution bolchévique, octobre 1917–janvier 1919*, pp. 262–3: letter to A. Thomas, 13 March 1918.

17. *Ibid.* See also N. V. Salzman, *Reform and Revolution: The Life and Times of Raymond Robins*, p. 141.

18. A. Rhys Williams, *Lenin: The Man and his Work*, p. 97.

19. R. H. Bruce Lockhart (Moscow report to London), 18 March 1918: Milner Papers, dep. 364, fol. 126.

20. A. J. Balfour to R. H. Bruce Lockhart, 13 March 1918: *ibid.*, fols 88–9.

21. Col. A. Knox, 'The Delay in the East', 18 March 1918: *ibid.*, fols 131–2 and 134.

22. M. J. Carley, *Revolution and Intervention: The French Government and the Russian Civil War, 1917–1919*, p. 57.

23. P. N. Vrangel Collection (HIA), box 33, folder 5.

24. D. S. Foglesong, *America's Secret War against Bolshevism: U.S. Intervention in the Russian Civil War, 1917–1920*, pp. 194–5.

25. 'President Wilson's Views on Allied Intervention in Russia', circulated to King and War Cabinet, 10 May 1918: Milner Papers, dep. 141, fols 2–4.

26. R. H. Bruce Lockhart, *Memoirs of a British Agent, Being an Account of the Author's Early Life in Many Lands and of his Official Mission to Moscow in 1918*, pp. 248–9.

27. *Ibid.*, pp. 249–50. Lockhart's estimate of Francis's age was out by a decade.

28. C. Kinvig, *Churchill's Crusade: The British Invasion of Russia, 1918–1920*, p. 24.

29. J. Sadoul, *Notes sur la révolution bolchévique, octobre 1917–janvier 1919*, pp. 294–5: letter to A. Thomas, 7 April 1918.

30. C. Kinvig, *Churchill's Crusade*, pp. 23–4.

31. I. N. Steinberg, 'The Events of July 1918': typescript (HIA), p. 3.

32. Ukrainian Ministry of Foreign Affairs to Ukrainian Peace Delegation, 23 September 1918: P. N. Vrangel Collection (HIA), box 35, folder 10.

33. Sovnarkom meeting, 2 April 1918: GARF, f. R-130, op. 2, d. 1.

34. Central Committee meeting, 10 May 1918: *Izvestiya Tsentral'nogo Komiteta KPSS*, no. 4 (1989), pp. 143–4.

35. *Pravda*, 24 May 1918.

36. J. Noulens, *Mon ambassade en Russie Soviétique, 1917–1919*, vol. 2, pp. 27–8 and 55.

37. J. Sadoul, *Notes sur la révolution bolchévique, octobre 1917–janvier 1919*, p. 271: letter to A. Thomas, 18 March 1918; J. Noulens, *Mon ambassade en Russie Soviétique, 1917–1919*, vol. 2, pp. 26–7.

38. Général Niessel, *Le Triomphe des bolchéviks et la paix de Brest-Litovsk: souvenirs, 1917–1918*, p. 326.

39. G. A. Hill, *Go Spy the Land*, p. 190.

40. W. Hard, *Raymond Robins' Own Story*, pp. 197–9.

41. *Ibid.*, pp. 202–3.

42. R. H. Bruce Lockhart report (Moscow), 5 June 1918: Milner Papers, dep. 365, fol. 78.

43. J. Noulens, *Mon ambassade en Russie Soviétique, 1917–1919*, vol. 1, p. 178; J. Sadoul, *Notes sur la révolution bolchévique, octobre 1917–janvier 1919*, p. 367: letter to A. Thomas, 28 May 1918; V. Fić, *The Bolsheviks and the Czechoslovak Legion*, pp. 5–8, 10–13 and 41–3.

44. W. Hard, *Raymond Robins' Own Story*, pp. 202–3.

45. G. Swain, '"An Interesting and Plausible Proposal": Bruce Lockhart, Sidney Reilly and the Latvian Riflemen, Russia 1918', *Intelligence and National Security*, no. 3 (1999), p. 83.

46. C. Kinvig, *Churchill's Crusade*, p. 13.

47. Sovnarkom meeting, 20 July 1918: GARF, f. R-130, op. 2, d. 2.

48. Sovnarkom meeting, 22 January 1918 (NS): *ibid.*, d. 1.

49. V. I. Lenin, *Polnoe sobranie sochinenii*, vol. 36, p. 324.

50. *The Times*, 8 March 1918.

51. L. de Robien, *The Diary of a Diplomat in Russia*, p. 252.

52. R. Vaucher, *L'Enfer bolchévik à Petrograd sous la commune et la terreur rouge*, pp. 208–9.

53. J. Sadoul, *Notes sur la révolution bolchévique, octobre 1917–janvier 1919*, p. 319: letter to A. Thomas, 26 April 1918.

54. R. Vaucher, *L'Enfer bolchévik à Petrograd sous la commune et la terreur rouge*, p. 209.

55. J. Sadoul, *Notes sur la révolution bolchévique, octobre 1917–janvier 1919*, p. 319: letter to A. Thomas, 26 April 1918.

56. *Ibid.*, p. 322: letter to A. Thomas, 27 April 1918.

57. *Ibid.*, p. 365: letter to A. Thomas, 27 May 1918.

58. Sovnarkom meeting, 25 June 1918: GARF, f. R-130, op. 2, d. 2.

59. *Pravda*, 27 April 1918.

60. Sovnarkom meeting, 4 April 1918: GARF, f. R-130, op. 2, d. 1.

61. R. Vaucher, *L'Enfer bolchévik à Petrograd sous la commune et la terreur rouge*, p. 273; G. V. Chicherin, *Vneshnyaya politika Sovetskoi Rossii za dva goda*, pp. 18–19; *New York Times*, 6 July 1918.

62. J. Sadoul, *Notes sur la révolution bolchévique, octobre 1917–janvier 1919*, p. 313: letter to A. Thomas, 16 April 1918.

63. *Ibid.*

64. *Ibid.*, p. 325: letter to A. Thomas, 28 April 1918.

65. R. Vaucher, *L'Enfer bolchévik à Petrograd sous la commune et la terreur rouge*, p. 35.

66. *Ibid.*, p. 157.

11. REVOLTS AND MURDERS

1. *Krasnaya kniga VChK*, vol. 2, pp. 38–9.

2. W. G. Rosenberg, *Liberals in the Russian Revolution: The Constitutional Democratic Party, 1917–1921*, pp. 316–20.

3. R. H. Bruce Lockhart to A. J. Balfour, 1 November 1918: National Archives, FO 371/3337/9828, pp. 8–9.

4. J. Noulens, *Mon ambassade en Russie Soviétique, 1917–1919*, vol. 1, p. 178; J. Sadoul, *Notes sur la révolution bolchévique, octobre 1917–janvier 1919*, p. 367: letter to A. Thomas, 28 May 1918.

5. V. Fić, *The Bolsheviks and the Czechoslovak Legion*, pp. 206, 242, 262, 307–8 and 313.

6. National Archvies, FO 371/3324/107587, cited in B. Pearce, *How Haig Saved Lenin*, p. 44.

7. R. H. Bruce Lockhart to A. J. Balfour, 7 November 1918: Robert Hamilton Bruce Lockhart Papers (HIA), box 12.

8. Z. A. Zeman, *Germany and the Revolution in Russia, 1915–1918: Documents from the Archives of the German Foreign Ministry*, pp. 130 and 137; M. Occleshaw, *Dances in Deep Shadows: The Clandestine War in Russia, 1917–20*, pp. 130–3.

9. J. Noulens, *Mon ambassade en Russie Soviétique, 1917–1919*, vol. 1, pp. 132–3, and vol. 2, pp. 120–1.

10. Sovnarkom meeting, 11 February 1918 (NS): GARF, f. R-130, op. 2, d. 1.

11. Sovnarkom meeting, 9 March 1918: *ibid.*

12. *Ibid.*

13. Sovnarkom meeting, 2 May 1918: *ibid.*

14. Trotsky's 1935 diary in L. Trotskii, *Dnevniki i pis'ma*, p. 102.

15. Sovnarkom meeting, 17 July 1918: GARF, f. R-130, op. 2, d. 2.

16. A. A. Ioffe, 'N. Lenin i nasha vneshnyaya politika' (dated 20 October 1927), APRF, f. 31, op. 1, d. 4, p. 216.

17. *Ibid.*

18. Enquiries to Lenin at the Eighth Party Congress, March 1919: RGASPI, f. 5, op. 2, d. 2, p. 5.

19. G. V. Chicherin, *Vneshnyaya politika Sovetskoi Rossii za dva goda*, pp. 18 19.

20. M. Ustinov, 'Svoevremennye mysli', in S. Rudakov (ed.), *Vokrug moskovskikh sobytii*, p. 10.

21. G. A. Hill, *Go Spy the Land*, pp. 202–3.

22. R. H. Bruce Lockhart (Moscow), 10 and 26 May: Milner Papers, dep. 364, fol. 288, and dep. 365, fol. 47.

23. R. H. Bruce Lockhart (Moscow), 16 May 1918: *ibid.*, dep. 364; R. Bruce Lockhart and A. Kerensky, 'Ordeal by Oratory' (draft; n.d.), p. 5: Robert Hamilton Bruce Lockhart Papers (HIA), box 5, folder 7.

24. Notes taken by Robin Bruce Lockhart from George Hill's account, p. 5: *ibid.*, box 11, folder 1.

25. George Hill's answer to Robin Bruce Lockhart's questionnaire, p. 6: *ibid.*, box 11, folder 1; Ya. Peters, 'Protokol pokazanii Ksenofontova Kalamatiano, on zhe Serpovskii', in *Arkhiv VChK. Sbornik dokumentov*, p. 512.

26. Savinkov's testimony in 'Sudebnoe razbiratel'stvo', *Pravda*, 30 August 1924, pp. 4–5.

27. R. H. Bruce Lockhart (Moscow) 17 May 1918: Milner Papers, dep. 142, fol. 4; see also dep. 365, fols 171–2.

28. Lockhart's telegram, 26 May 1918: National Archives, FO 371/3332/9748.

29. Savinkov's testimony in 'Sudebnoe razbiratel'stvo', *Pravda*, 30 August 1924, pp. 4–5.

30. F. Grenard, *La Révolution russe*, p. 322.

31. *Krasnaya kniga VChK*, vol. 1, pp. 166–7.

32. Savinkov's testimony in 'Sudebnoe razbiratel'stvo', *Pravda*, 30 August 1924, pp. 4–5.

33. G. A. Hill, *Go Spy the Land*, p. 207.

34. F. Grenard, *La Révolution russe*, p. 321.

35. J. Sadoul, *Notes sur la révolution bolchévique, octobre 1917–janvier 1919*, p. 405: letter to A. Thomas, 10 July 1918.

36. A. A. Ioffe to the People's Commissariat for Foreign Affairs, copied to Lenin, Trotsky, Sverdlov and Zinoviev, June 1918: N. Ioffe, *Moi otets Adol'f Abramovich Ioffe*, pp. 65–6.

37. Sovnarkom, 15 July 1918: GARF, f. R-130, op. 2, d. 2.

38. J. Sadoul, *Notes sur la révolution bolchévique, octobre 1917–janvier 1919*, p. 405: letter to A. Thomas, 10 July 1918.

39. G. A. Hill, *Go Spy the Land*, pp. 210–11.

40. V. I. Lenin, *Neizvestnye dokumenty, 1891–1922*, p. 229.

41. *Bolshevik Propaganda: Hearings before a Subcommittee on the Judiciary, United States Senate, Sixty-Fifth Congress, Third Session and Thereafter Pursuant to Senate Resolutions 439 and 469—February 11, 1919 to March 10, 1919*, p. 947; J. Noulens, *Mon ambassade en Russie Soviétique, 1917–1919*, vol. 2, p. 146.

42. J. Noulens, *Mon ambassade en Russie Soviétique, 1917–1919*, vol. 2, p. 148.

43. *Ibid.*, p. 149.

44. D. R. Francis, *Russia from the American Embassy, April 1916–November 1918*, pp. 248 and 250.

45. *Bolshevik Propaganda: Hearings before a Subcommittee on the Judiciary, United States Senate*, pp. 949–50.

46. *Ibid.*, p. 948.

47. W. Hard, *Raymond Robins' Own Story*, p. 191; R. H. Bruce Lockhart report (Moscow), 13 May 1918: Milner Papers, dep. 365, fol. 2.

12. SUBVERTING THE ALLIES

1. Most notably in *The State and Revolution*: see *Polnoe sobranie sochinenii*, vol. 33.

2. I. S. Rozental', *Provokator. Roman Malinovskii: sud'ba i vremya*, pp. 198–207.

3. M. Occleshaw, *Dances in Deep Shadows: The Clandestine War in Russia, 1917–20*, pp. 93–4; C. Andrew, *Secret Service: The Making of the British Intelligence Community*, pp. 261–2.

4. G. Nowik, *Zanim złamano =„Enigme". Polski radiowywiad podczas wojny z bolszewicka Rosja 1918–1920*, pp. 866–9.

5. Kh. Rakovskii and K. Radek, 29 October 1918: P. N. Vrangel Collection (HIA), box 35, folder 10.

6. R. Blobaum, *Feliks Dzierzynski and the SDKPiL: A Study of the Origins of Polish Communism*, p. 30.

7. C. Sheridan, *From Mayfair to Moscow: Clare Sheridan's Diary*, p. 95.

8. *Ibid.*

9. *Bolshevik Propaganda: Hearings before a Subcommittee on the Judiciary, United States Senate, Sixty-Fifth Congress, Third Session and Thereafter Pursuant to Senate Resolutions 439 and 469—February 11, 1919 to March 10, 1919*, p. 557.

10. G. A. Hill, *Go Spy the Land*, p. 154.

11. Karl Radek interview reported in 'Anarchists as Bandits', *New York Times*, 23 April 1923.

12. *The Diaries of Robert Bruce Lockhart, 1915–1938*, p. 35.

13. N. A. Ioffe, *Moi otets Adol'f Abramovich Ioffe*, p. 38.

14. S. Dzerzhinskaya, *V gody velikikh boëv*, pp. 269–70; N. Zubov, *F. E. Dzerzhinskii*, pp. 219–21; A. E. Senn, *Diplomacy and Revolution: The Soviet Mission to Switzerland, 1918*, p. 100.

15. See below, p. 164.

16. B. Thomson, *Queer People* (Hodder & Stoughton: London, 1922), p. 290.

17. *Call*, September 1918 ('Dictatorship and Democracy') and July 1919 ('Towards a Revolutionary World War').

18. R. H. Bruce Lockhart, *Memoirs of a British Agent, Being an Account of the Author's Early Life in Many Lands and of his Official Mission to Moscow in 1918*, pp. 201–2.

19. B. Thomson, *Queer People*, p. 290.

20. See below, p. 161.

21. C. Andrew and V. Mitrokhin, *The Mitrokhin Archive: The KGB in Europe and the West*, p. 37.

22. Report of the Dutch Legation in Petrograd, 15 September 1918: SF 401/3/2; Report from Stockholm, 12 September 1918: CX 050167; File on Ransome, 11.1.5 (no further indication); political report from 'our representative' in Helsinki, 1 May 1920: CX 3646. I am grateful to Andrew Cook for supplying secret service reports on Ransome.

23. *The Times*, 12 July 1918.

24. R. H. Bruce Lockhart to A. J. Balfour, 7 November 1918, p. 2: Robert Hamilton Bruce Lockhart Papers (HIA), box 12.

13. GERMANY ENTREATED

1. K. Baedeker, *Russia with Teheran, Port Arthur, and Peking: Handbook for Travellers*, pp. 334–5; F. J. Funk, 'Fighting after the War', *Purdue Alumnus* (n.d.), p. 7.

2. R. H. Bruce Lockhart report (Moscow), 18 July 1918: Milner Papers, dep. 365, fol. 147; 'Proposals for Allied Enterprise for Russia (assuming French concurrence): *ibid.*, dep. 364.

3. R. H. Bruce Lockhart report (Moscow), 21 July 1918: *ibid.*, dep. 365, fols 156–7.

4. Lord Reading report (Washington), p. 4, 3 July 1918: *ibid.*, dep. 141; aide-memoire from Acting Secretary of State F. Polk, given to Lord Reading, 18 July 1918: *ibid.*, dep. 365, fol. 154.

5. C. Kinvig, *Churchill's Crusade: The British Invasion of Russia, 1918–1920*, pp. 23 and 28–9.

6. R. H. Ullman, *Anglo-Soviet Relations, 1917–1921*, vol. 1: *Intervention and the War*, p. 236.

7. See V. Barnett, *A History of Russian Economic Thought*, pp. 98–9.

8. Editorial, *The Times*, 13 July 1918.

9. *Ibid.*, 18 July 1918.

10. *Daily Herald*, 14 December 1918.

11. *Bolshevik Propaganda: Hearings before a Subcommittee on the Judiciary, United States Senate, Sixty-Fifth Congress, Third Session and Thereafter Pursuant to Senate Resolutions 439 and 469—February 11, 1919 to March 10, 1919*, p. 950.

12. Director of Naval Intelligence, 14 June 1918, p. 2: FO 371/3331/9741. This memorandum is contained in Robert Bruce Lockhart Papers (HIA), box 11, folder 4.

13. A. A. Ioffe to the People's Commissariat of Foreign Affairs, copied to Lenin, Trotsky, Sverdlov and Zinoviev, June 1918: N. Ioffe, *Moi otets Adol'f Abramovich Ioffe*, p. 66.

14. B. Pearce, *How Haig Saved Lenin*, pp. 66–8.

15. *Ibid.*, pp. 33 and 45.

16. M. J. Larsons, 'Au service des Soviets', pp. 30–2: typescript, M. J. Larsons Papers (HIA), box 1.

17. N. A. Ioffe Papers (HIA), 'Ob ottse', p. 5.

18. *Ibid.*, pp. 5–6.

19. *Ibid.*, p. 6.

20. *Ibid.*

21. N. Ioffe, *Moi otets Adol'f Abramovich Ioffe*, p. 35; V. R. Menzhinskii to V. I. Lenin, 20 May 1918 in *ibid.*, pp. 57–8.

22. A. A. Ioffe to V. I. Lenin, May 1918 in *ibid.*, p. 60; M. J. Larsons, 'Au service des Soviets', p. 28: typescript, M. J. Larsons Papers (HIA), box 1.

23. N. Ioffe, *Moi otets Adol'f Abramovich Ioffe*, p. 35.

24. See below, pp. 300–3.

25. V. R. Menzhinskii to V. I. Lenin, 20 May 1918 in N. Ioffe, *Moi otets Adol'f Abramovich Ioffe*, pp. 57–8.

26. V. I. Lenin to L. B. Krasin, 11 August 1918: V. I. Lenin, *Neizvestnye dokumenty, 1891–1922*, p. 284.

27. N. Ioffe, *Moi otets Adol'f Abramovich Ioffe*, pp. 35–6.

28. A. A. Ioffe to V. I. Lenin, May 1918 in *ibid.*, p. 60.

29. A. A. Ioffe, 'N. Lenin i nasha vneshnyaya politika' (dated 20 October 1927), APRF, f. 31, op. 1, d. 4, p. 212.

30. N. Ioffe, *Moi otets Adol'f Abramovich Ioffe*, p. 38. Ioffe could not resist asking Dzerzhinski why the Cheka had failed to prevent the attempt on Lenin's life.

31. S. McMeekin, *History's Greatest Heist: The Looting of Russia by the Bolsheviks*, pp. 97–101.

32. A. A. Ioffe to V. I. Lenin, May 1918 in N. Ioffe, *Moi otets Adol'f Abramovich Ioffe*, p. 61.

33. A. A. Ioffe to the People's Commissariat of Foreign Affairs, copied to Lenin, Trotsky, Sverdlov and Zinoviev, June 1918 in *ibid.*, p. 67.

34. B. Pearce, *How Haig Saved Lenin*, p. 57.

35. G. V. Chicherin, *Vneshnyaya politika Sovetskoi Rossii za dva goda*, p. 5; B. Pearce, *How Haig Saved Lenin*, p. 71.

36. G. V. Chicherin, *Vneshnyaya politika Sovetskoi Rossii za dva goda*, pp. 18–19.

37. B. Pearce, *How Haig Saved Lenin*, p. 49.

38. *Ibid.*, p. 61.

39. V. I. Lenin, *Polnoe sobranie sochinenii*, vol. 50, p. 108.

40. B. Pearce, *How Haig Saved Lenin*, p. 67.

41. *Pravda*, 17 August 1918.

42. V. I. Lenin, *Polnoe sobranie sochinenii*, vol. 37, p. 75.

43. B. Pearce, *How Haig Saved Lenin*, p. 68.

44. Hughes telegraph conversation between G. V. Chicherin and Kh. G. Rakovskii, 5 October 1918: P. N. Vrangel Collection (HIA), box 35, folder 10.

45. L. D. Trotskii to V. I. Lenin, 17 August 1918: RGVA, f. 33987, op. 1, d. 23.

14. SUBVERTING RUSSIA

1. Robin Bruce Lockhart, 'Notes on Sidney Reilly: Information Provided by George Hill', p. 7: Robert Hamilton Bruce Lockhart Papers (HIA), box 11, folder 1. See also A. Cook, *On His Majesty's Secret Service: Sidney Reilly—Codename ST1*, chs 2–7.

2. Robin Bruce Lockhart, 'Notes on Sidney Reilly: Information Provided by George Hill', p. 5: Robert Hamilton Bruce Lockhart Papers (HIA), box 11, folder 1.

3. G. A. Hill, *Dreaded Hour*, p. 102.

4. A. Cook, *On His Majesty's Secret Service: Sidney Reilly—Codename ST1*, pp. 107–18.

5. *Ibid.*, pp. 107–8, 127–9, 131 and 133.

6. E. L. Spears to R. N. Bruce Lockhart, 2 January 1967: Robert Bruce Lockhart (HIA), box 2, folder 10; J. Alley to Robin Bruce Lockhart, 13 May 1966: Robert Hamilton Bruce Lockhart Papers (HIA), box 2.

7. *Ibid.*; G. A. Hill, *Go Spy the Land*, p. 201.

8. Letter (in French, on Crédit Lyonnais notepaper) by unknown person to unknown addressee, summer 1918(?), p. 2: Robert Hamilton Bruce Lockhart Papers (HIA), folder: Robin Bruce Lockhart, 'Reilly: Russian Revolution, Etc.: Sources: Sir Edward Spears'.

9. *Ibid.* See also G. A. Hill's answers to Robin Bruce Lockhart's questionnaire: *ibid.*, 'Reilly: Russian Revolution, Etc.: Sources: Others: 1921–1997'.

10. R. H. Bruce Lockhart, notebooks (1938–1945): Robert Hamilton Bruce Lockhart Papers (HIA), box 4, folder 3.

11. R. H. Bruce Lockhart (Petrograd), 10 March 1918: Milner Papers, dep. 364, fol. 87.

12. R. H. Bruce Lockhart, notebooks (1938–1945): Robert Hamilton Bruce Lockhart Papers (HIA), box 4, folder 3.

13. T. Alexander, *An Estonian Childhood*, pp. 44–6.

14. R. H. Bruce Lockhart, notebooks (apparently 1938–1945): Robert Hamilton Bruce Lockhart Papers (HIA), box 4, folder 3.

15. *Ibid.*

16. Moura's daughter Tanya made the deduction about the pregnancy from letters written at the time by Moura: T. Alexander, *An Estonian Childhood*, pp. 44–6.

17. See below, p. 348.

18. Ya. Peters, 'Delo Lokkarta', in *Arkhiv VChK. Sbornik dokumentov*, p. 495. On the Sheremetev Lane apartment see R. Polonsky, *Molotov's Magic Lantern: A Journey in Russian History*, pp. 43–9.

19. R. N. Bruce Lockhart, 'Notes on Sidney Reilly. Information Provided by George Hill': Robert Hamilton Bruce Lockhart Papers, box 11, folder 1, p. 1.

20. GARF, f. 102, op. 174, d. 69 (vol. 30: 1914), pp. 37–40. My thanks to Andrew Cook for sharing this with me.

21. Translation of Starzhevskaya petition to the Red Cross for Aid to Political Prisoners, 11 November 1918, GARF R8419, op. 1, d. 356, pp. 355–6: Andrew Cook's papers.

22. Ya. Peters, 'Delo Lokkarta', in *Arkhiv VChK. Sbornik dokumentov*, p. 512.

23. *Ibid.*

24. 'Pokazaniya M. V. Fride', in *Arkhiv VChK. Sbornik dokumentov*, p. 506; translation of Maria Fride's Red Cross questionnaire, 30 December 1918, GARF R8419, op. 1, d. 264, p. 35 (double-sided): thanks again to Andrew Cook.

25. 'Pervoe pokazanie A. V. Fride', in *Arkhiv VChK. Sbornik dokumentov*, p. 502.

26. *Washington Post*, 2 March 1918.

27. V. Kingisepp, 'Dobavochnye pokazaniya ot K. D. Kalamatiano', in *Arkhiv VChK. Sbornik dokumentov*, pp. 517–18.

28. Ya. Peters, 'Delo Lokkarta', in *Arkhiv VChK. Sbornik dokumentov*, p. 517.

29. K. D. Kalamatiano, 'Rabota poslednikh 6–8 mesyatsev', in *Arkhiv VChK. Sbornik dokumentov*, p. 519.

30. *Ibid.*, p. 115.

31. 'Tret'e pokazanie A. V. Fride', in *Arkhiv VChK. Sbornik dokumentov*, p. 504.

32. *Ibid.* (A. V. Fride); 'Pokazaniya M. V. Fride', in *Arkhiv VChK. Sbornik dokumentov*, p. 506; K. D. Kalamatiano, 'Litsa, privlechënnye po delu', in *Arkhiv VChK*.

Sbornik dokumentov, p. 520. See also D. S. Foglesong, *America's Secret War against Bolshevism: U.S. Intervention in the Russian Civil War, 1917–1920*, p. 114.

33. R. H. Bruce Lockhart's deciphered report, 26 May 1918: National Archvies, FO 371/3332/9748, p. 424; B. V. Savinkov's testimony in 'Sudebnoe razbiratel'stvo', *Pravda*, 30 August 1924, pp. 4–5.

34. G. A. Hill, *Go Spy the Land*, pp. 200–1.

35. *New York Evening Post*, 16–18 September 1918; *New York Times*, 22 September 1918 and 22 February 1919.

36. G. Creel (Chairman), *The German–Bolshevik Conspiracy* (The Committee on Public Information: New York, 1918), pp. 29–30.

37. R. H. Bruce Lockhart report (Moscow), 11 April 1918: Milner Papers, dep. 364, fols 200–1.

38. R. H. Bruce Lockhart report (Moscow), 7 May 1918: *ibid.*, fol. 271.

39. R. H. Bruce Lockhart to A. J. Balfour, 1 November 1918: National Archives, FO 371/3337/9829, p. 405.

40. See for example his request to be allowed to subsidize the National Centre in his report of 6 July 1918: Milner Papers, dep. 141, fols 75–7.

41. R. H. Bruce Lockhart report (Moscow), 13 June 1918: *ibid.*, dep. 365, fol. 106.

42. R. H. Bruce Lockhart reports (Moscow), 21 and 23 July: *ibid.*, fols 156–7 and 158.

43. R. H. Bruce Lockhart, 'Secret and Confidential Memorandum on the Alleged "Allied Conspiracy" in Russia', enclosure no. 1 in dispatch of 5 November 1918: Milner Papers, fol. 244.

44. Ya. Peters, 'Delo Lokkarta', in *Arkhiv VChK. Sbornik dokumentov*, p. 491.

45. Robert Bruce Lockhart's account in *The British Agent* attributed the leadership of the plot to Reilly. So too did Robin Bruce Lockhart in *Ace of Spies* despite knowing, as he admitted in a letter to the Foreign and Commonwealth Office in 1967, that it was his father who had headed the planning: Robin Bruce Lockhart to P. R. H. Wright, F.O. [*sic*], 19 February 1967: Robert Hamilton Bruce Lockhart Papers (HIA), folder: Robin Bruce Lockhart, 'Reilly: Russian Revolution, Etc.: Sources: Foreign and Commonwealth, 1957–2002'.

46. National Archives, FO 371/3350, p. 37: quoted by G. Swain, '"An Interesting and Plausible Proposal": Bruce Lockhart, Sidney Reilly and the Latvian Riflemen, Russia 1918', *Intelligence and National Security*, no. 3 (1999), p. 90.

47. R. H. Bruce Lockhart, *The Memoirs of a British Agent, Being an Account of the Author's Early Life in Many Lands and of his Official Mission to Moscow in 1918*, pp. 315–16.

48. Robin Bruce Lockhart to P. R. H. Wright, F.O. [*sic*], 19 February 1967: Robert Hamilton Bruce Lockhart Papers (HIA), folder: Robin Bruce Lockhart, 'Reilly: Russian Revolution, Etc.: Sources: Foreign and Commonwealth, 1957–2002'. See also M. Smith, *Six: A History of Britain's Secret Intelligence Service*, p. 233.

49. Ya. Peters, 'Delo Lokkarta', in *Arkhiv VChK. Sbornik dokumentov*, p. 491.

50. *Ibid.*, p. 492.

51. R. H. Bruce Lockhart, 'Secret and Confidential Memorandum on the Alleged "Allied Conspiracy" in Russia', enclosure no. 1 in dispatch of 5 November 1918: Milner Papers, fols 249–50.

52. G. A. Hill, *Go Spy the Land*, p. 238.

53. Ya. Peters, 'Delo Lokkarta', in *Arkhiv VChK. Sbornik dokumentov*, p. 492.

15. A VERY BRITISH PLOT

1. 'Capt. Hill's Report on his Work in Russia for D.M.I.', 11 December 1918: National Archives, FO 371/3350, cited in R. B. Spence, 'The Tragic Fate of Kalamatiano: America's Man in Moscow', *International Journal of Intelligence and Counterintelligence*, no. 3 (1999), p. 353.

2. S. G. Reilly and Pepita Bobadilla, *The Adventures of Sidney Reilly, Britain's Master Spy*, pp. 30–2.

3. Ya. Peters, 'Delo Lokkarta', in *Arkhiv VChK. Sbornik dokumentov*, p. 494.

4. R. Marchand, *Allied Agents in Russia: Complete Text of the Letter of M. René Marchand, Petrograd Correspondent of 'Le Figaro', to M. Poincaré, President of the French Republic, September 1918*.

5. R. Marchand, *Why I Support Bolshevism* (British Socialist Party: London, 1919), pp. 29, 32, 44–7 and 50.

6. *Arkhiv VChK. Sbornik dokumentov*, pp. 489–91.

7. Ivy Litvinov, untitled autobiographical fragment: Ivy Litvinov Papers (HIA), box 10, folder 3.

8. G. A. Hill, *Go Spy the Land*, p. 239.

9. *The Diaries of Robert Bruce Lockhart, 1915–1938*, p. 40; Ya. Peters, 'Protokol pokazanii Ksenofontova Kalamatiano, on zhe Serpovskii', in *Arkhiv VChK. Sbornik dokumentov*, p. 513.

10. *Ibid.*

11. *Ibid.*, p. 514.

12. *The Diaries of Robert Bruce Lockhart, 1915–1938*, pp. 40–1.

13. Ya. Peters, 'Protokol pokazanii Ksenofontova Kalamatiano, on zhe Serpovskii', in *Arkhiv VChK. Sbornik dokumentov*, p. 514.

14. *Ibid.*

15. R. H. Bruce Lockhart, notebooks (1938–1945): Robert Hamilton Bruce Lockhart Papers (HIA), box 4, folder 3; Freddie Hill to Robin Bruce Lockhart, 4 July 1970: Robert Hamilton Bruce Lockhart Papers (HIA), folder: Robin Bruce Lockhart, 'Reilly: Russian Revolution, Etc.: Sources: Others: 1921–1997'.

16. R. H. Bruce Lockhart, *Friends, Foes and Foreigners*, p. 273; M. E. Harrison, *Marooned in Moscow: The Story of an American Woman Imprisoned in Russia*, p. 59; G. A. Hill, *Go Spy the Land*, p. 100.

17. R. H. Bruce Lockhart, 'Last Words on Lenin: An Inaugural Address [as] Honorary President of the Associated Societies, Edinburgh University, 26 October 1960', p. 16.

18. Speech of 7 November 1918, in *Arkhiv VChK. Sbornik dokumentov*, pp. 92–3.

19. R. H. Bruce Lockhart to A. J. Balfour, 7 November 1918, pp. 2–4: Robert Hamilton Bruce Lockhart Papers (HIA), box 12; Ya. Peters, 'Delo Lokkarta', in *Arkhiv VChK. Sbornik dokumentov*.

20. R. H. Bruce Lockhart to A. J. Balfour, 7 November 1918, pp. 2–4: Robert Hamilton Bruce Lockhart Papers (HIA), box 12.

21. *Ibid.*, p. 3.

22. Ya. Peters, 'Protokol pokazanii Ksenofontova Kalamatiano, on zhe Serpovskii', in *Arkhiv VChK. Sbornik dokumentov*, pp. 513 and 515.

23. G. A. Hill, *Go Spy the Land*, p. 243.

24. *Ibid.*, p. 245.

25. Ya. Peters, 'Delo Lokkarta', in *Arkhiv VChK. Sbornik dokumentov*, p. 510.

26. R. B. Spence, 'The Tragic Fate of Kalamatiano', p. 353.

27. A. Cook, *On His Majesty's Secret Service: Sidney Reilly—Codename ST1*, p. 151.

28. R. B. Spence, 'The Tragic Fate of Kalamatiano', p. 353.

29. Report on conversation with DeWitt Poole by UK ambassador to Norway Sir Mansfeldt Findlay to the UK Foreign Office: in A. Cook, *On His Majesty's Secret Service: Sidney Reilly—Codename ST1*, p. 152.

30. R. B. Spence, 'The Tragic Fate of Kalamatiano', p. 355.

31. J. Noulens, *Mon ambassade en Russie Soviétique, 1917–1919*, vol. 2, p. 216.

32. *Manchester Guardian*, 12 September 1918; M. Findlay report (Christiania), 17 September 1918, based on a Dutch diplomatic dispatch: Milner Papers, dep. 365, fol. 237.

33. M. Findlay report (Christiania), 17 September 1918, based on a Dutch diplomatic dispatch: Milner Papers, dep. 365, fols 226–7 and 230; R. Vaucher, *L'Enfer bolchévik à Petrograd sous la commune et la terreur rouge*, pp. 414–15.

34. P. N. Vrangel Collection (HIA), box 35, folder 10.

35. Maxim Litvinov, untitled memoir fragment on 1920: Ivy Litvinov Papers (HIA), box 9, folder 10, pp. 30–1.

36. *Manchester Guardian*, 6 September 1918.

37. Ml1a: S.F. 401/2/2: Message to British Foreign Office about information received from the Dutch government, 18 September 1918. My thanks to Andrew Cook for sharing this document with me.

38. R. H. Bruce Lockhart, 'Notebooks, 1938–1945': Robert Hamilton Bruce Lockhart Papers, box 4.

39. *The Diaries of Robert Bruce Lockhart, 1915–1938*, p. 46.

40. R. H. Bruce Lockhart, *Friends, Foes and Foreigners*, p. 279.

41. *Ibid.*

42. R. H. Bruce Lockhart, *Memoirs of a British Agent, Being an Account of the Author's Early Life in Many Lands and of his Official Mission to Moscow in 1918*, pp. 339–40.

43. *The Times*, 18 October 1918.

44. R. H. Bruce Lockhart, notes for *Cities and Men*, p. 2: Robert Hamilton Bruce Lockhart Papers (HIA), p. 2; M. Findlay report (Christiania), 17 September 1918, based on a Dutch diplomatic dispatch: Milner Papers, dep. 365, fol. 233.

45. MI1a: S.F. 401/2/2: Message to British Foreign Office about information received from the Dutch, 18 September 1918.

46. I. Litvinov, autobiographical fragment on 1917–1918: Ivy Litvinov Papers (HIA), box 11, folder 7.

47. I. Litvinov, untitled memoir fragment on 1920: *ibid.*, box 9, folder 10, p. 31.

48. *The Times*, 26 September 1918.

49. G. A. Hill, *Go Spy the Land*, pp. 11 and 258.

50. *Ibid.*, p. 25.

51. *The Times*, 18 October 1918; *Le Figaro*, 11 October 1918.

52. L. Naudeau, *En prison sous la terreur russe*, pp. 127–30.

53. Ya. Peters, 'Delo Lokkarta', in *Arkhiv VChK. Sbornik dokumentov*, p. 510.

54. L. Naudeau, *En prison sous la terreur russe*, p. 117.

55. R. H. Bruce Lockhart, *Friends, Foes and Foreigners*, p. 274.

56. M. Benckendorff to R. H. Bruce Lockhart, n.d., p. 2: Robert Hamilton Bruce Lockhart Papers (HIA), box 1, folder 22.

57. R. H. Bruce Lockhart to Moura Benckendorff, 2 November 1918, pp. 1–2: *ibid.*, box 1, folder 22.

58. M. Benckendorff to R. H. Bruce Lockhart, n.d. (late 1918?), pp. 1–2: *ibid.*

59. Moura Benckendorff to R. H. Bruce Lockhart, n.d. (summer 1919?): *ibid.*, folder 20.

60. *Pravda*, 15 November 1918.

61. Handwritten report on the second day of the trial, p. 1; no named author: Robert Hamilton Bruce Lockhart Papers (HIA), box 1, folder 11.

62. *Ibid.*

63. 'Protokol zasedaniya Revolyutsionnogo tribunala pri VTsIK': 25 November 1918, in *Arkhiv VChK. Sbornik dokumentov*, p. 549.

64. 'Protokol zasedaniya Revolyutsionnogo tribunala pri VTsIK': 28 November 1918, *ibid.*, pp. 553–4.

65. Handwritten report on the second day of the trial, pp. 1–2; no named author: Robert Hamilton Bruce Lockhart Papers (HIA), box 1, folder 11. See also *Le Figaro*, 11 February 1919.

66. *Pravda*, 4 December 1918.

67. R. B. Spence, 'The Tragic Fate of Kalamatiano', p. 356.

16. THE GERMAN CAPITULATION

1. Kh. Rakovski, 'Avtobiografiya' (HIA), p. 9; RGASPI, f. 17, op. 84, d. 1, p. 1, reproduced in I. Linder and S. Churkin (eds), *Krasnaya pautina: tainy razvedki Kominterna, 1919–1943*, p. 24.

2. V. I. Lenin, *Polnoe sobranie sochinenii*, vol. 50, p. 186.

3. *Pravda*, 7 September 1918.

4. K. Radek, 'Noyabr'. (Stranichka iz vospominanii)', *Krasnaya nov'*, no. 10 (1926), p. 140.

5. G. V. Chicherin, *Vneshnyaya politika Sovetskoi Rossii za dva goda*, p. 22.

6. M. J. Larsons, 'Dans le labyrinthe des Soviets', p. 39: typescript, M. J. Larsons Papers (HIA).

7. I. Maisky, *Journey into the Past*, p. 37. Maiski saw him at the Communist Club at 107 Charlotte Street, London WC1 in 1913.

8. H. Strachan, *The First World War*, p. 316.

9. J. P. Nettl, *Rosa Luxemburg*, vol. 2, p. 710.

10. K. Radek, 'Noyabr'. (Stranichka iz vospominanii)', p. 139.

11. *Ibid.*, p. 140.

12. M. J. Larsons, 'Au service des Soviets', p. 29: typescript, M. J. Larsons Papers (HIA), box 1.

13. A. E. Senn, *Diplomacy and Revolution: The Soviet Mission to Switzerland, 1918*, p. 161.

14. Kh. Rakovskii, 'Avtobiografiya' (HIA), p. 9; M. J. Larsons, 'Au service des Soviets', p. 29: typescript, M. J. Larsons Papers (HIA), box 1.

15. *Ibid.*, p. 30.

16. K. Radek, 'Noyabr'. (Stranichka iz vospominanii)', p. 141.

17. *Ibid.*, p. 142.

18. *Ibid.*, pp. 142–3.

19. M. J. Larsons, 'Au service des Soviets', p. 33: typescript, M. J. Larsons Papers (HIA), box 1.

20. *Ibid.*, pp. 33–5.

21. K. Radek, 'Noyabr'. (Stranichka iz vospominanii)', p. 143.

22. M. J. Larsons, 'Dans le labyrinthe des Soviets', p. 40: typescript, M. J. Larsons Papers (HIA).

23. *Ibid.*

24. K. Radek, 'Noyabr'. (Stranichka iz vospominanii)', p. 143.

25. V. I. Lenin to A. A. Ioffe, 2 June 1918, *Polnoe sobranie sochinenii*, vol. 50, p. 88.

26. K. Radek, 'Noyabr'. (Stranichka iz vospominanii)', pp. 143–4.

27. *Ibid.*, p. 144.

28. *Ibid.*

29. *Ibid.*, p. 145.

30. Kh. Rakovski, 'Avtobiografiya' (HIA), p. 9.

31. K. Radek, 'Noyabr'. (Stranichka iz vospominanii)', p. 146.

32. *Ibid.*, pp. 148–9.

33. *Ibid.*, p. 149.

34. *Ibid.*, p. 150.

35. P. Levi, 'Gedächtnisrede des Genossen Paul Levi' (typescript: HIA).

17. REVOLVING THE RUSSIAN QUESTION

1. R. Cecil, memorandum of 20 October circulated to King and War Cabinet, fols 149–53: Milner Papers, dep. 136.

2. Sovnarkom meetings, 7, 21 and 30 December 1918: GARF, f. R-130, op. 2, d. 1.

3. Azbuka report, 4 November 1918: P. N. Vrangel Collection (HIA), box 28, folder 30.

4. Meeting of Russian delegation in Iasi with Allied emissaries, 17 November 1918: P. N. Vrangel Collection (HIA), box 36, folders 16 and 18.

5. A. Ransome, *The Truth about Russia* (Workers' Socialist Federation: London, 1918), pp. 3–4.

6. D. Marquand, *Ramsay MacDonald*, pp. 225–6.

7. A. Milner to C. Nabokoff, 22 December 1918: Milner Papers, c. 696, fol. 168.

8. R. H. Ullman, *Anglo-Soviet Relations, 1917–1921*, vol. 2: *Britain and the Russian Civil War, November 1918–February 1920*, pp. 59–64.

9. *House of Commons Debates*, 14 November 1918, cols 3015–17.

10. R. H. B. Lockhart, Memorandum on the Internal Situation in Russia, in *British Documents on Foreign Policy*, Part 2: *The Soviet Union, 1917–1939*, vol. 1: *Soviet Russia and her Neighbours, Jan. 1917–Dec. 1919*, pp. 34–44.

11. R. H. Bruce Lockhart to A. J. Balfour, 7 November 1918: Robert Hamilton Bruce Lockhart Papers (HIA), box 12.

12. *The Diaries of Robert Bruce Lockhart, 1915–1938*, p. 47.

13. *Ibid.*

14. *Ibid.*

15. M. Gilbert, *Winston S. Churchill*, vol. 4: *The World in Torment, 1917–1922*, p. 227.

16. R. Quinault, 'Churchill and Russia', *War and Society*, no. 1 (1991), pp. 102–7.

17. D. R. Francis, *Russia from the American Embassy, April 1916–November 1918*, p. viii.

18. *New York Times*, 15 December 1919: reported testimony of S. Nuorteva to the Lusk Committee.

19. *Ibid.*

20. *Washington Post*, 6 August 1917.

21. *The Bullitt Mission to Russia: Testimony before the Committee on Foreign Relations, United States Senate, of William C. Bullitt*, pp. 1–2.

22. Harold Kellock (Finnish Information Bureau, New York) to Lincoln Steffens, 22 April 1918, p. 2: Russian Subject Collection (HIA).

23. *Bolshevik Propaganda: Hearings before a Subcommittee on the Judiciary, United States Senate, Sixty-Fifth Congress, Third Session and Thereafter Pursuant to Senate Resolutions 439 and 469—February 11, 1919 to March 10, 1919*, pp. 5–6.

24. *Ibid.*, p. 82.

25. *Ibid.*, pp. 19–20, 80–1 and 84.

26. *Ibid.*, pp. 109 and 115.

27. *Ibid.*, pp. 112, 114 and 156.

28. *Ibid.*, pp. 379–82.

29. *Ibid.*, pp. 383–4.

30. *Ibid.*, pp. 468 and 472.

31. *Ibid.*, p. 590.

32. *Ibid.*, pp. 641–2 and 669.

33. *Ibid.*, p. 837.

34. *New York Times*, 22 February 1919.

35. *Ibid.*

36. *Ibid.*, 23 February 1919; V. V. Aldoshin, Yu. V. Ivanov, V. M. Semënov and V. A. Tarasov (eds), *Sovetsko-amerikanskie otnosheniya: gody nepriznaniya, 1918–1926*, p. 19 (Rhys Williams testimonial letter of appointment).

37. See S. White, *Britain and the Bolshevik Revolution*, pp. 175–7, for the general trend.

18. THE PARIS PEACE CONFERENCE

1. R. Lansing, *The Big Four and Others of the Peace Conference*, pp. 38–9.

2. *Ibid.*, p. 41.

3. *Ibid.*, pp. 57–8.

4. J. M. Keynes, *The Economic Consequences of the Peace*, p. 16.

5. *New York Times*, 22 January 1919.

6. Bullitt's notes in *The Bullitt Mission to Russia: Testimony before the Committee on Foreign Relations, United States Senate, of William C. Bullitt*, p. 7.

7. *Ibid.*, pp. 7–9 and 10–11.

8. H. Hoover, *The Ordeal of Woodrow Wilson*, pp. 116–17.

9. *New York Times*, 21 January 1919.

10. *Ibid.*, 22 January 1919; *Manchester Guardian*, 23 December 1918.

11. *The Bullitt Mission to Russia: Testimony before the Committee on Foreign Relations*, pp. 1–2.

12. R. Lansing, diary entry, 22 January 1919: Robert Lansing Papers (HIA).

13. *The Bullitt Mission to Russia: Testimony before the Committee on Foreign Relations*, pp. 21–3.

14. A. Ransome, *Russia in 1919*, pp. 1 and 3; *The Bullitt Mission to Russia: Testimony before the Committee on Foreign Relations*, pp. 5–6.

15. *The Papers of Woodrow Wilson, 1856–1924*, vol. 53, pp. 492–4. See D. S. Foglesong, *America's Secret War against Bolshevism: U.S. Intervention in the Russian Civil War, 1917–1920*, p. 279.

16. *The Bullitt Mission to Russia: Testimony before the Committee on Foreign Relations*, pp. 5–6.

17. (H. Nicolson), *The Harold Nicolson Diaries: 1907–1963*, 24 January 1919.

18. W. S. Churchill, *The World Crisis*, vol. 4: *The Aftermath*, p. 173.

19. *Ibid.*, p. 174.

20. H. Wilson to A. Milner, 12 January 1919: Milner Papers, dep. 46/1, fol. 107.

21. Churchill, *The World Crisis*, vol. 4: *The Aftermath*, p. 173.

22. *Ibid.*, p. 174.

23. *Ibid.*, p. 176.

24. *The Bullitt Mission to Russia: Testimony before the Committee on Foreign Relations*, pp. 3–5.

25. *Ibid.*, pp. 34–6.

26. *Ibid.*, p. 37; P. H. Kerr (Paris) to Sir R. Graham: minute, 11 July 1919, *Documents on British Policy Overseas*, no. 105169/43654/38.

27. *The Bullitt Mission to Russia: Testimony before the Committee on Foreign Relations*, p. 39.

28. *Ibid.*, p. 44.

29. A. Ransome, *Russia in 1919*, p. 231.

30. George Hill's answers to Robin Bruce Lockhart's questionnaire, p. 5: Robert Hamilton Bruce Lockhart Papers (HIA), box 11, folder 1.

31. G. A. Hill, *Dreaded Hour*, pp. 98 and 102–3.

32. 'Peace with Honour': *Daily Mail*, 28 March 1919.

33. *The Bullitt Mission to Russia: Testimony before the Committee on Foreign Relations*, p. 66.

34. Board meeting, n.d. (early 1919?), p. 8: P. N. Vrangel Collection (HIA), box 28, folder 33.

35. D. S. Foglesong, *America's Secret War against Bolshevism*, pp. 69–71.

36. D. R. Francis, *Russia from the American Embassy, April 1916–November 1918*, pp. 310–11.

37. *Ibid.*, pp. 309–10.

38. H. Hoover, *The Ordeal of Woodrow Wilson*, pp. 118–19.

39. *Ibid.*, pp. 121–3.

40. 'Diary of P. V. Vologodsky as Prime Minister of Admiral Kolchak's Cabinet', 17 May 1919: Pëtr Vasil'evich Vologodskii Papers (HIA).

41. W. S. Churchill, *The World Crisis*, vol. 4: *The Aftermath*, pp. 179–80.

42. T. C. C. Gregory, 'Stemming the Red Tide' (typescript, 1919), p. 70: T. C. C. Gregory Papers (HIA), box 1.

43. *Ibid.*

44. W. C. Bullitt to President Wilson, 17 May 1919: Robert Lansing Papers (HIA).

45. R. Lansing, diary entry for 19 May 1919: Robert Lansing Papers (HIA); W. C. Bullitt to R. Lansing, 17 May 1919: *ibid.*

46. H. Hoover, *The Ordeal of Woodrow Wilson*, pp. 245–52.

19. EUROPEAN REVOLUTION

1. A. Ransome, *Russia in 1919*, p. 225. The comment was made in March 1919.

2. *Ibid.*, pp. 35–6.

3. A. J. Fardon to Mrs E. Garratt, 5 March 1919: National Archives, KV/2/1903.

4. A. Ransome, *Russia in 1919*, p. 226.

5. *Ibid.*, p. 227.

6. J. Sadoul, *Notes sur la révolution bolchévique, octobre 1917–janvier 1919*, p. 450: letter to J. Longuet, 17 January 1918.

7. A. Dunois, unpublished typescript introduction (May 1941) to an edition of Sadoul's letters, pp. 3–4: Jacques Sadoul Papers (HIA); L. Naudeau, *En prison sous la terreur russe*, pp. 231.

8. J. Cornwell, *Hitler's Pope: The Secret History of Pius XII*, p. 75.

9. R. Leviné-Meyer, *Leviné the Spartacist: The Life and Times of the Socialist Revolutionary Leader of the German Spartacists and Head of the Ill-Starred Munich Republic of 1919*, p. 153.

10. T. C. C. Gregory Papers (HIA), box 2: Hungarian Political Dossier, vol. 1: Alonzo Taylor to Herbert Hoover, 26 March 1919.

11. Memorandum by Ferenc Julier, former Commander of the General Staff of the Red Army; it was prepared for the Hoover Library in 1933 and translated into English: Hungarian Subject Collection (HIA), pp. 3–4 and 14.

12. Memorandum by Ferenc Julier, p. 3.

13. H. James (Inter-Allied Danube River Commission), 'Report on Trip to German-Austria and Czecho-Slovakia' (n.d.), pp. 1 and 4: Henry James Papers (HIA), folder 1.

14. G. A. Hill, *Dreaded Hour*, p. 89.

15. H. James, 'A Solution of the Hungarian Question' (no date given but some time in 1919 before August): Henry James Papers (HIA), folder 2.

16. Telegrams of 2 February and 19 April 1919: RGASPI, f. 17, op. 109, d. 46, pp. 1–2.

17. T. C. C. Gregory, 'Beating Back Bolshevism' (typescript, possibly 1920), p. 6: T. C. C. Gregory Papers (HIA), box 1; A. Taylor to H. C. Hoover, 26 March 1919.

18. *Ibid.*: Philip Marshall Brown to Archibald Cary Coolidge, 17 April 1919.

19. T. C. C. Gregory to H. C. Hoover, 22 June 1918: T. C. C. Gregory Papers (HIA), box 1.

20. T. C. C. Gregory, 'Beating Back Bolshevism' [n.p., n.d.]: *ibid.*

21. Trotsky's message to Kh. G. Rakovski, N. I. Podvoiski and V. A. Antonov-Ovseenko, 18 April 1919: RGASPI, f. 325, op. 1, d. 404, p. 86; Lenin's telegram to S. I. Aralov and J. Vacietis, 21 April 1919, *ibid.*, p. 92; telegram of J. Vacietis and S. I. Aralov to V. A. Antonov-Ovseenko, 23 April 1919, *ibid.*, op. 109, 46, pp. 3–5.

22. Lt Col. W. B. Causey to H. Hoover, 8 August 1919: Gibbes Lykes Papers (HIA), box 1.

23. [James A.?] Logan to the ARA in Paris, 13 August 1919: *ibid.*

24. Inter-Allied Military Mission (Budapest) to the Supreme Council of the Peace Conference, 19 August 1919: Gibbes Lykes Papers (HIA), box 1.

25. H. Hoover, *The Ordeal of Woodrow Wilson*, p. 118.

26. See his comments in H. Hoover, *Address of Secretary Hoover before the Chamber of Commerce of the United States. Eleventh Annual Meeting. New York, N.Y., May 8 1923*, p. 7.

27. H. Hoover, *The World Economic Situation: Address of Herbert Hoover before the San Francisco Commercial Club, October 9, 1919*, p. 19.

28. T. C. C. Gregory, 'Stemming the Red Tide' (n.p., 1919), pp. 66–7.

29. H. Hoover, *The Ordeal of Woodrow Wilson*, pp. 164–5; J. M. Keynes, *The Economic Consequences of the Peace*, p. 274.

30. K. Radek, 'Noyabr'. (Stranichka iz vospominanii)', *Krasnaya nov'*, no. 10 (1926), pp. 163–4.

31. *Ibid.*, pp. 164–5 and 168.

32. *Ibid.*, pp. 166–8.

33. *Ibid.*, p. 168.

34. A. Venturi, *Rivoluzionari russi in Italia, 1917–1921*, pp. 205–7.

20. THE ALLIES AND THE WHITES

1. Telegram to A. V. Kolchak, 26 May 1919: Aleksandr Vasilevich Kolchak Papers (HIA).

2. Aleksandr Vasilevich Kolchak Papers (HIA).

3. A. Marty, *La Révolte de la Mer Noire*, vol. 2, pp. 114 and 118.

4. *Ibid.*, pp. 140–1.

5. W. Kendall, *The Revolutionary Movement in Britain, 1900–1921: The Origins of British Communism*, pp. 241–2.

6. C. Kinvig, *Churchill's Crusade: The British Invasion of Russia, 1918–1920*, p. xii.

7. *Ibid.*, pp. xviii–xix.

8. *Daily Express*, 6 September 1919.

9. C. Kinvig, *Churchill's Crusade*, p. 192.

10. Ministry of Foreign Affairs (Omsk) to Chargé d'Affaires, 18 March 1919: P. N. Vrangel Collection (HIA), box 57, folder 1; S. Uget to B. A. Bakhmetev, 24 March 1919: *ibid*. See also Russian Military Mission in Berlin to Yudenich, 9 September 1919: Nikolai Yudenich Papers (HIA), box 3, folder 25.

11. Savinkov's testimony in 'Sudebnoe razbiratel'stvo', *Pravda*, 30 August 1924, p. 5.

12. Gulkevich to Ambassador[?], 7 June 1919; American note on finance (Hoover's copy), 15 June 1919: P. N. Vrangel Collection (HIA), box 60, folder 1; V. A. Maklakov to B. A. Bakhmetev, 6 September 1920: 'Sovershenno lichno i doveritel'no!': *B. A. Bakhmetev–V. A. Maklakov: perepiska*, vol. 1, p. 227.

13. 'Sostoyanie schëtov na 1-oe dekabrya 1918 g.': P. N. Vrangel Collection (HIA), box 57, folder 1.

14. 'Spisok predmetov i materialov, prinadlezhashchikh russkoi kazne': *ibid.*

15. Telegram from B. Bakhmetev, 14 November 1919: Nikolai Yudenich Papers, box 3.

16. Gulkevich to unknown Ambassador, 7 June 1919; American note on finance (Hoover's copy), 15 June 1919: P. N. Vrangel Collection (HIA), box 60, folder 1.

17. G. A. Hill, *Go Spy the Land*, p. 77.

18. P. V. Vologodskii, 'Otchët po poezdke v Tomsk na Pervyi Obshchesibirskii s"ezd', p. 30: Pëtr Vasil'evich Vologodskii Papers (HIA).

19. Vladimir N. Bashkirov Papers (HIA), box 3.

20. Financial agent S. Uget to B. A. Bakhmetev, 2/15 February 1919: P. N. Vrangel Collection (HIA), box 57, folder 1.

21. Financial consultative committee meeting, 23 September 1919: Nikolai Yudenich Papers (HIA), box 21, folder 20.

22. Savinkov's testimony in 'Sudebnoe razbiratel'stvo', *Pravda*, 30 August 1924, p. 5.

23. GHQ British Salonika Force (Constantinople) to Directorate of Military Intelligence, 29 December 1918: Milner Papers, dep. 143, fol. 212.

24. Telegram to General Kondyrëv, n.d.: Nikolai Yudenich Papers (HIA), box 3, folder 25.

25. E. O. Scafe to General N. Yermolov, 14 May 1919; unnamed military agent in the United Kingdom, 19 May 1919: General A. A. von Lampe Papers (HIA); General Staff Colonel Brandt to General K. I. Globachëv, 16 August 1919: *ibid*. Brandt was Yudenich's 'military agent in Germany'.

26. J. Alley to Robin Bruce Lockhart, 13 May 1966: Robert Hamilton Bruce Lockhart Papers (HIA), box 2; E. L. Spears to Robin Bruce Lockhart, 2 January 1967: *ibid*.

27. Savinkov's testimony in 'Sudebnoe razbiratel'stvo', *Pravda*, 30 August 1924, p. 5.

28. Russian Military Mission in Berlin to Yudenich, 9 September 1919: Nikolai Yudenich Papers (HIA), box 3, folder 25.

29. *Ibid*.

30. V. Madeira, '"Because I Don't Trust Him, We are Friends": Signals Intelligence and the Reluctant Anglo-Soviet Embrace, 1917–24', *Intelligence and National Security*, no. 1 (2004), p. 29.

31. P. N. Vrangel Collection (HIA), box 39, folder 8.

32. French Mission in Estonia to Col. Kruzenshtern, 25 November 1919: Nikolai Yudenich Papers (HIA), box 3, folder 27; 'Communiqué du Ministère de la Guerre de Paris', 29 August 1919: box 4, folder 28.

33. 'Modifications survenues dans l'ordre de bataille bolchévique', September 1918: Nikolai Yudenich Papers (HIA), box 3, folder 26.

34. Nikolai Yudenich Papers (HIA), box 4, folder 11.

35. See for example, Kolchak's communiqué on strategy and appointments, 7 November 1919, as received by Yudenich: *ibid*., box 3, folder 2; Yudenich's telegram to Sazonov, Kolchak, Denikin and Miller, 3 January 1920: *ibid*., box 4, folder 6.

36. P. N. Vrangel Collection (HIA), box 30, folders 3–19.

37. *Ibid.*, box 28, folders 1, 30 and 33; box 39, folder 1.

38. *Ibid.*, box 35, folder 10 (Chicherin and Radek; Radek and Rakovski).

39. *Ibid.*, box 33, folder 5.

40. Nikolai Yudenich Papers, box 4, folder 29.

41. R. Service, *Trotsky: A Biography*, pp. 287–8.

42. N. Andreyev, *A Moth on a Fence: Memoirs of Russia, Estonia, Czechoslovakia and Western Europe*, p. 43.

21. WESTERN AGENTS

1. G. A. Hill, *Go Spy the Land*, pp. 19 and 84.

2. *Ibid.*, pp. 88–9.

3. *Ibid.*, p. 101.

4. *Ibid.*, pp. 115–17.

5. *Ibid.*, pp. 119–27.

6. *Ibid.*, pp. 127–34.

7. *Ibid.*, pp. 145–8; G. A. Hill, *Dreaded Hour*, p. 88.

8. G. A. Hill, *Go Spy the Land*, p. 193.

9. *Ibid.*, p. 196.

10. *Ibid.*, pp. 203, 230 and 251–2.

11. *Ibid.*, pp. 197–8.

12. *Ibid.*, pp. 204–5.

13. *Ibid.*, pp. 228 and 231.

14. *Ibid.*, p. 213.

15. *Ibid.*, p. 223.

16. *Ibid.*, p. 217.

17. *Ibid.*, pp. 220–6.

18. G. A. Hill, 'Reminiscences of Four Years with the N.K.V.D.', p. 120: draft typescript, George A. Hill Papers (HIA).

19. G. A. Hill, *Go Spy the Land*, p. 231.

20. *Ibid.*, p. 217.

21. *Ibid.*, p. 231.

22. *Ibid.*, p. 232.

23. *Ibid.*, p. 213.

24. *Ibid.*, pp. 234–5.

25. *Ibid.*, p. 58.

26. G. A. Hill, *Dreaded Hour*, pp. 62–4.

27. G. A. Hill, *Go Spy the Land*, p. 63.

28. G. A. Hill, *Dreaded Hour*, p. 71.

29. A. Cook, *On His Majesty's Secret Service: Sidney Reilly—Codename ST1*, pp. 160–1.

30. G. A. Hill, *Go Spy the Land*, p. 78.

31. G. A. Hill, *Dreaded Hour*, p. 93.

32. *Ibid.*, p. 105.

33. S. G. Reilly to J. Picton Bagge, 10 October 1919 in A. Cook, *On His Majesty's Secret Service: Sidney Reilly—Codename ST1*, p. 169.

34. See the excerpts in A. Cook, *On His Majesty's Secret Service: Sidney Reilly—Codename ST1*, pp. 170–1.

35. P. Dukes, handwritten untitled memoir (1966?), pp. 7–8: Paul Dukes Papers (HIA), box 1.

36. C. E. Dukes, 'Family Dukes: Yesterday', pp. 21–5: Paul Dukes Papers (HIA), box 1. Cuthbert Dukes was Paul Dukes's brother.

37. P. Dukes, typed untitled memoir (n.d.), p. 4: Paul Dukes Papers (HIA), box 1.

38. P. Dukes, handwritten untitled memoir (1966?), pp. 4–6: Paul Dukes Papers (HIA), box 1.

39. P. Dukes, *Come Hammer, Come Sickle!*, pp. 25–6.

40. Robin Bruce Lockhart, Notes on Meeting with Sir Paul Dukes, 25 June 1966, p. 1: Robert Hamilton Bruce Lockhart Papers (HIA), box 11, folder: Robin Bruce Lockhart, 'Reilly: Russian Revolution, Etc.: Sources: Paul Dukes, 1922–1990'.

41. *Ibid.*

42. William S. Barrett, 'America in Russia. Or the Diary of a Russian Wolfhound' (typescript: IIIA), p. 17.

43. Robin Bruce Lockhart, Notes on Meeting with Sir Paul Dukes, 25 June 1966, p. 1: Robert Hamilton Bruce Lockhart Papers (HIA), box 11, folder: Robin Bruce Lockhart, 'Reilly: Russian Revolution, Etc.: Sources: Paul Dukes, 1922–1990'.

44. P. Dukes, *Red Dusk and the Morrow* (Doubleday, Page: New York, 1922), pp. 3–6. See also K. Jeffery, *MI6: The History of the Secret Intelligence Service, 1909–1949*, p. 137.

45. P. Dukes, *Red Dusk and the Morrow*, pp. 9–11.

46. Jean MacLean's answers to Robin Bruce Lockhart's questionnaire (question 25): Robert Hamilton Bruce Lockhart Papers (HIA), box 11, folder: Robin Bruce Lockhart, 'Reilly: Russian Revolution, Etc.: Sources: Jean MacLean'. Jean MacLean was Robert Bruce Lockhart's first wife and Robin's mother.

47. Lady Dukes to Robin Bruce Lockhart, 14 September 1967: Paul Dukes Papers, box 1.

48. P. Dukes, *Red Dusk and the Morrow*, pp. 9–11.

49. *Ibid.*, p. 7.

50. P. Dukes, '1918 Kalendar'-Otmetchik': Paul Dukes Papers (HIA), box 1.

51. *Ibid.*

52. *Krasnaya kniga VChK*, vol. 2, pp. 43–5.

53. P. Dukes, 'The Onoto Diary for 1919': Paul Dukes Papers (HIA), box 1; P. Dukes, *Red Dusk and the Morrow*, p. 223.

54. *Ibid.*, p. 220.

55. *Ibid.*, pp. 222–3.

56. Affidavit, 30 August 1919: Paul Dukes Papers (HIA), box 1.

57. Lady Dukes, handwritten memoir (n.d.): Paul Dukes Papers (HIA), box 1.

58. Peter Constantinoff to Lady Dukes, 27 June 1968, stating that he was one of the two: Paul Dukes Papers (HIA), box 1.

59. P. Dukes, *Red Dusk and the Morrow*, p. 267.

60. L. D. Trotskii to M. M. Litvinov, 5 June 1918: Milner Papers, dep. 365, fol. 79.

61. M. Occleshaw, *Dances in Deep Shadows: The Clandestine War in Russia, 1917–20*, pp. 93–4; C. Andrew, *Secret Service: The Making of the British Intelligence Community*, pp. 261–2.

62. American Legation, Copenhagen, dispatch no. 3250, 15 May 1919: US Department of State: Records of the Department of State Relating to Political Relations between Russia (and the Soviet Union) and Other States, 1910–29 (HIA).

63. American Legation, Copenhagen, dispatch no. 3338, 16 June 1919: *ibid.*

64. Passport-Control Bureau Chief (Copenhagen), basing himself on British counter-intelligence information: 10 March 1919: P. N. Vrangel Collection (HIA), box 57, folder 1.

65. A. Ransome, *Russia in 1919*, p. 1.

66. K. Jeffery, *MI6*, p. 174.

67. A. Ransome, *Russia in 1919*, pp. 17–18.

22. COMMUNISM IN AMERICA

1. Central Executive Committee of the CPA, 15 November 1919: Theodore Draper Papers (HIA), box 32.

2. *New York Times*, 22 March and 2 April 1919.

3. M. M. Litvinov to L. K. Martens, 27 May 1918: G. N. Sevast'yanov, J. Haslam and others (eds), *Sovetsko-amerikanskie otnosheniya: gody nepriznaniya, 1918–1926*, pp. 101–2.

4. L. Martens and S. Nuorteva to B. Bakhmetev, 10 April 1919: L. K. Martens Papers (HIA).

5. *Washington Post*, 5 April 1919.

6. *New York Times*, 20 June 1919.

7. *Ibid.*, 14 June 1919.

8. *Ibid.*, 20 June 1919.

9. *Ibid.*, 21 June 1919.

10. *Ibid.*, 18 June 1919.

11. *Ibid.*, 27 June 1919.

12. Memorandum of L. K. Martens and S. Nuorteva (n.d.; March or April 1919?): George Halonen Papers (HIA).

13. Both contracts drafted for 16 September 1919: George Halonen Papers (HIA)

14. *New York Times*, 9 November 1919.

15. *Ibid.*, 17 November 1919.

16. *Ibid.*, 27 November 1919.

17. *Ibid.*, 2 December 1919.

18. *Ibid.*, 9 November 1919.

19. *Ibid.*, 19 November 1919.

20. *Ibid.*

21. *Ibid.*, 13 December 1919.

22. *Ibid.*, 19 November 1919.

23. *Ibid.*, 22 December 1919.

24. L. A. E. Gale to C. Ruthenberg, 23 February 1920, p. 2: Jay Lovestone Papers (HIA), box 195, folder CP-USA General Correspondence, February 1920.

25. CEC CPA to NEC CLP, 19 March 1920: Jay Lovestone Papers (HIA), box 195.

26. Conferences and Conventions, 1920: Jay Lovestone Papers (HIA), box 215.

27. CEC CPA collective protest, 24 March 1920: Jay Lovestone Papers (HIA), box 195.

28. Leaflet about March 1920: RGASPI, f. 515, op. 1, d. 34, p. 22.

29. Bukharin, Radek and Kuusinen, 'Concerning the Next Tasks of the Communist Party of America (n.d., but seized on 22 August 1922): Communist International Instructions (HIA).

30. M. Eastman, 'A Statement of the Problem in America and the First Step to its Solution', 1923: Theodore Draper Papers (HIA), box 31.

31. [Ed Fisher] to C. E. Ruthenberg, 11 April 1920: Jay Lovestone Papers (HIA), box 195, folder 10.

23. SOVIET AGENTS

1. See above, p. 159.

2. Paraphrase of telegram from Sir Mansfeldt Findlay, 30 September 1918: National Archives, FO Registry No. 165188. My thanks to Andrew Cook for sharing this document with me.

3. See below, note 10.

4. S. Reilly to R. H. Bruce Lockhart, 25 November 1918: Robert Hamilton Bruce Lockhart Papers (HIA), folder: Robin Bruce Lockhart, 'Reilly: Russian Revolution, Etc.: Sources: Robert Bruce Lockhart— Reilly'.

5. *Ibid.*

6. S. Reilly to R. H. Bruce Lockhart, 24 November 1918: *ibid.*

7. R. N. Bruce Lockhart, 'Notes on Sidney Reilly. Information Provided by George Hill': Robert Hamilton Bruce Lockhart Papers, box 11, folder 1, p. 3.

8. Notes taken by Robin Bruce Lockhart from George Hill's account, p. 4: Robert Hamilton Bruce Lockhart Papers (HIA), box 11, folder 1.

9. Jean MacLean's answers to Robin Bruce Lockhart's questionnaire (question 42): Robert Hamilton Bruce Lockhart Papers (HIA), box 11, folder: Robin Bruce Lockhart, 'Reilly: Russian Revolution, Etc.: Sources: Jean MacLean';

Notes taken by Robin Bruce Lockhart from George Hill's account, p. 10: Robert Hamilton Bruce Lockhart Papers (HIA), box 11, folder 1.

10. Jean MacLean's answers to Robin Bruce Lockhart's questionnaire (question 25): Robert Hamilton Bruce Lockhart Papers (HIA), box 11, folder: Robin Bruce Lockhart, 'Reilly: Russian Revolution, Etc.: Sources: Jean MacLean'.

11. See above, p. 222.

12. G. A. Hill, draft letter to the London *Evening Standard* (n.d.): Robert Hamilton Bruce Lockhart Papers (HIA), box 11, folder 1.

13. C. Andrew and V. Mitrokhin, *The Mitrokhin Archive: The KGB in Europe and the West*, p. 37.

14. Sovnarkom meeting, 11 November 1918 (NS): GARF, f. R-130, op. 2, d. 2(4).

15. L. B. Krasin, *Vneshtorg i vneshnyaya ekonomicheskaya politika Sovetskogo pravitel'stva*, pp. 3–4.

16. L. Bryant, *Six Months in Red Russia*, pp. 292–3.

17. RGASPI, f. 89, op. 52, d. 4.

18. C. Andrew, *The Defence of the Realm: The Authorized History of MI5*, p. 144.

19. K. Jeffery, *MI6: The History of the Secret Intelligence Service, 1909–1949*, p. 184.

20. RGASPI, f. 89, op. 52, d. 6, pp. 1–2.

21. W. Kendall, *The Revolutionary Movement in Britain, 1900–1921: The Origins of British Communism*, p. 242.

22. RGASPI, f. 89, op. 52, d. 6, pp. 1–2.

23. K. Linder and S. Churkin (eds), *Krasnaya pautina: taina razvedki Kominterna, 1919–1943*, p. 31.

24. A. E. Senn, *Diplomacy and Revolution: The Soviet Mission to Switzerland, 1918*, pp. 116–19.

25. *The Times*, 17 February 1920.

26. *Manchester Guardian*, 19 August 1920.

27. *Ibid.*

28. M. E. Harrison, *Marooned in Moscow: The Story of an American Woman Imprisoned in Russia*, p. 60.

29. 'Nauenskaya radio-stantsiya . . . pod Berlinom', *Ogonëk*, no. 16 (1922).

30. *Byulleten' Narodnogo Komissariata Inostrannykh Del*, no. 28, 15 August 1920.

31. Yan Berzin to Moscow, 24 May 1918: K. Linder and S. Churkin (eds), *Krasnaya pautina: taina razvedki Kominterna, 1919–1943*, p. 30.

32. Jan Berzin to Moscow, 16 August 1918: *ibid.*, p. 34.

33. Report of Special Department of the Cheka, n.d. (late March or April 1921?): S. Tsvigun, *Lenin i VChK*, p. 441.

34. Report of Special Department of the Cheka, n.d. (late March or April 1921?): S. Tsvigun, *Lenin i VChK*, p. 441. The report says that Dukes also men-

tioned a Harry Jelly Brand: I have been unable to work out who this person might have been.

35. *Ibid.*

36. *Ibid.*

37. S. Liberman, *Building Lenin's Russia*, pp. 5, 29, 39–42 and 194–7.

38. E. Blackwell to W. Thwaites, 26 August 1918: National Archives, KV/2/1903.

39. Unsigned report to London from Stockholm, 12 September 1918: CX 050167. My thanks to Andrew Cook for sharing this document with me as well as the documents cited in the next three endnotes.

40. See intercepted letter of Elizabeth Freeman to Mary Freeman, 22 April 1919: Directorate of Military Intelligence, I.P. 1210.

41. Log of reports on Arthur Ransome, ending on 11 October 1919: 'MI5 Ransome'.

42. 'Arthur Ransome, ref. B/02277', 25 September 1918.

43. Memorandum from S.8, 17 March 1919: National Archives, KV/2/1903.

24. THE ALLIED MILITARY WITHDRAWAL

1. *Army: The Evacuation of North Russia*, pp. 17–18; Gen. Poole to War Office, 18 September 1918: Milner Papers, dep. 366, box D, enclosure 3, fol. 434.

2. G. A. Lensen, *Japanese Recognition of the USSR: Soviet–Japanese Relations, 1921–1930*, pp. 19–21.

3. London telegram to N. N. Yudenich, 30 December 1919: Nikolai Yudenich Papers (HIA), box 4, folder 6.

4. N. Yudenich to S. D. Sazonov (Paris), A. V. Kolchak (Omsk) and Denikin (Yekaterinodar), 13 November 1919: Nikolai Yudenich Papers, box 3, folder 26.

5. *Manchester Guardian*, 4 June 1920.

6. A. A. Ioffe, 'N. Lenin i nasha vneshnyaya politika' (dated 20 October 1927), APRF, f. 31, op. 1, d. 4, p. 212.

7. A. A. Ioffe (V. Krymskii), *Mirnoe nastuplenie*, p. 16.

8. L. B. Krasin, *Vneshtorg i vneshnyaya ekonomicheskaya politika Sovetskogo pravitel'stva*, p. 4.

9. City Commandant of Reval (Tallinn), 28 November 1919: Nikolai Yudenich Papers (HIA), box 4, folder 2.

10. List of clothes and equipment made on 6 January 1920: *ibid.*, folder 6.

11. Yudenich to S. D. Sazonov, A. V. Kolchak, A. I. Denikin and Ye. K. Miller, 3 January 1920: *ibid.*

12. N. N. Yudenich to Allied governments, 4 January 1920: *ibid.*, box 21, folder 1.

13. 'Estonskaya tranzitnaya torgovlya s Rossiei v 1920 g. cherez Narvu' (typescript: Statistical Department of the Estonian Ministry of Trade and Industry): Revel'skaya gavan' i bol'sheviki, 21 April 1921, Nicolai Koestner Papers (HIA).

14. *Ibid.*

15. *Ibid.*

16. TsA FSB RF, f. 1 os., op. 4, d. 2 in *Arkhiv VChK. Sbornik dokumentov*, pp. 372–4.

17. *Manchester Guardian*, 10 March 1920.

18. L. B. Krasin, *Vneshtorg i vneshnyaya ekonomicheskaya politika Sovetskogo pravitel'stva*, p. 6.

19. *Washington Post*, 3 May 1920; *New York Times*, 5 May 1920.

20. L. B. Krasin, *Vneshtorg i vneshnyaya ekonomicheskaya politika Sovetskogo pravitel'stva*, p. 11; *Manchester Guardian*, 12 April 1920.

21. *Manchester Guardian*, 12 April 1920.

22. *Ibid.*, 15 April 1920.

23. V. Madeira, "'Because I Don't Trust Him, We are Friends'": Signals Intelligence and the Reluctant Anglo-Soviet Embrace, 1917–24', *Intelligence and National Security*, no. 1 (2004), p. 37.

24. *Manchester Guardian*, 4 December 1920; B. Thomson, *Queer People*, p. 290.

25. Unsigned, undated military intelligence report on Anglo-Soviet relations in London (May or June 1921?): P. N. Vrangel Collection (HIA), box 110, folder 22, pp. 20–1.

26. 'K voprosu o plane kontsessii' (Komitet po vneshnei torgovli pri prezidiume VSNKh): typescript in Russian Subject Collection (HIA), box 13, folder 17.

27. V. I. Lenin, *Polnoe sobranie sochinenii*, vol. 42, pp. 107 and 112.

28. L. Eyre, *Russia Analysed* (New York World: New York, 1920), p. 14: interview with L. D. Trotsky, 25 February 1920.

29. *Manchester Guardian*, 15 April 1920.

30. *Winston S. Churchill: Companion*, vol. 4, p. 1053.

31. *Manchester Guardian*, 28 May 1920.

32. *New York Times*, 18 January 1920.

33. *Le Figaro*, 3 and 8 June 1920.

34. *Manchester Guardian*, 16 April 1920.

35. *The Times*, 11 June 1920.

36. *Ibid.*, 22 December 1920.

37. J. Noulens, *Mon ambassade en Russie Soviétique, 1917–1919*, vol. 2, pp. 163–4.

25. BOLSHEVISM: FOR AND AGAINST

1. Menu copies, 19 November and 3 December 1919: Robert Hamilton Bruce Lockhart Papers (HIA), box 11.

2. *The Times*, 15 and 16 October 1919.

3. *Ibid.*, 17, 21, 30 and 31 October 1919.

4. *Ibid.*, 3, 4 and 11 November 1919.

5. *Ibid.*, 12 November 1919.

6. 'Bolshevism at Close Quarters. An Englishman's Experiences. Why I Went to Russia', *The Times*, 14 October 1919.

7. *The Times*, 12 November 1919.

8. *Ibid.*, 14, 15 and 19 January 1920 and 4 January 1921.

9. *Ibid.*, 14 February 1920.

10. *Ibid.*

11. *Izvestiya*, 6 April 1920; *The Times*, 30 April 1920.

12. P. Dukes, diary for 1920, and Robin Bruce Lockhart's notes on a conversation with Dukes's brother Cuthbert: Paul Dukes Papers (HIA), box 1; *The Times*, 20 December 1920.

13. *The Times*, 22 December 1919.

14. *Manchester Guardian*, 12 November 1919.

15. *The Times*, 23 February 1921.

16. Princess Cantacuzène, *Revolutionary Days: Recollections of Romanoffs and Bolsheviki*, pp. 339–59.

17. Princess Catherine Radziwill, *The Firebrand of Bolshevism: The True Story of the Bolsheviki and the Forces that Directed Them*: for examples see pp. 30, 179–90, 236 and 262–3.

18. P. Miliukov, *Bolshevism: An International Danger, its Doctrine and its Practice through War and Revolution*, pp. 115–17 and 147.

19. *Ibid.*, p. 299.

20. *Ibid.*, pp. 189 and 197–200.

21. *Ibid.*, pp. 273–81.

22. *The Times*, 19 November 1919.

23. Russia. Posol'stvo (HIA), box 9, folder 2.

24. See below, p. 216.

25. A. Ransome, *Russia in 1919* (B. W. Huebsch: New York, 1919).

26. M. Philips Price, *The Soviet, the Terror and Intervention* (The Socialist Publication Society: Brooklyn, NY, 1918), pp. 1–13.

27. M. Litvinoff (with a supplementary chapter by I. Litvinoff), *The Bolshevik Revolution: Its Rise and Meaning* (British Socialist Party: London, 1919), especially p. 50.

28. J. Reed, *Ten Days that Shook the World* (Boni & Liveright: New York, 1919), p. xii.

29. J. Reed, *Ten Days that Shook the World* (1960), p. lxviii.

30. *Ibid.*, p. lii.

31. J. Reed, 'Memorandum. Russia. The Soviet Government' (n.d.), pp. 1–14: George Halonen Papers (HIA).

32. *Ibid.*, pp. 15–16.

33. Nicolai Lenin, Tchicherin, John Reed and Max Eastman, *Russia*, pp. 28 and 53–63.

34. J. Sadoul, *Notes sur la révolution bolchévique, octobre 1917–janvier 1919*, Preface by H. Barbusse (Sirène: Paris, 1920), p. 11.

35. J. Spargo, *Russia as an American Problem*, p. viii.

36. J. Spargo, *Bolshevism: The Enemy of Political and Industrial Democracy*, p. 215.

37. J. Spargo, *Russia as an American Problem*, pp. 40–1.

38. *Ibid.*, pp. 259–99.

39. J. Spargo, *Bolshevism: The Enemy of Political and Industrial Democracy*, p. 215.

40. J. M. Keynes, *The Economic Consequences of the Peace*, pp. 35–6, 44–5, 51.

41. *Ibid.*, chs 4 and 5.

42. *Ibid.*, pp. 288–9.

43. *Ibid.*, p. 274.

44. *Ibid.*, pp. 291–5.

45. *The Times*, 5 January 1920.

46. *New York Times*, 29 February 1920 (reviewer Charles D. Hazen).

47. A. Tardieu, *La Paix* (Payot: London, 1921).

48. *Manchester Guardian*, 24 December 1919.

49. M. E. Harrison, *Marooned in Moscow: The Story of an American Woman Imprisoned in Russia*, p. 189.

50. V. I. Lenin, *Polnoe sobranie sochinenii*, vol. 42, pp. 67 and 69; vol. 44, pp. 294–5; J. M. Keynes, *The Economic Consequences of the Peace*, pp. 236–7.

26. LEFT ENTRANCE

1. M. E. Harrison, *Marooned in Moscow: The Story of an American Woman Imprisoned in Russia*, p. 61.

2. *Ibid.*, pp. 57–8.

3. Tsentral'noe byuro po obsluzhivaniyu inostrantsev v Moskve pri NKInoDel (Byurobin): Russian Subject Collection (HIA), box 13, folder 12.

4. E. Goldman, *My Disillusionment in Russia* (Doubleday, Page: New York, 1923); E. Goldman to B. Russell, 8 July 1922: B. Russell, *The Autobiography of Bertrand Russell, 1914–1944*, p. 174.

5. *British Labour Delegation to Russia, 1920: Report* (Trades Union Congress and Labour Party: London, 1920), p. 3.

6. Mrs P. Snowden, *Through Bolshevik Russia* (Cassell: London, 1920), p. 8; *Manchester Guardian*, 28 April 1920.

7. V. I. Lenin, *Neizvestnye dokumenty, 1891–1922*, pp. 332–3.

8. *Manchester Guardian*, 15 May 1920; Mrs P. Snowden, *Through Bolshevik Russia*, pp. 7–8.

9. *The Times*, 28 April 1920.

10. B. Russell, *The Autobiography of Bertrand Russell, 1914–1944*, p. 141.

11. Mrs P. Snowden, *Through Bolshevik Russia*, p. 32.

12. D. Debrestian, 'On the Origin of the Term "Iron Curtain"', *Washington Post*, 26 September 1991.

13. *Ibid.*, p. 8.

14. *Ibid.*, p. 30.

15. *Manchester Guardian*, 21 May 1920.

16. Mrs P. Snowden, *Through Bolshevik Russia*, p. 50.

17. *Ibid.*, p. 55.

18. *Ibid.*, p. 66.

19. J. S. Clarke, *Pen Portraits of Russia under the 'Red Terror'*, p. 49. Clarke laughed at his friend's Paisley brogue but he himself didn't get right the Russian word for 'I understand' (*ponimayu*).

20. *Ibid.*, pp. 56–7.

21. *Ibid.*, p. 92.

22. M. E. Harrison, *Marooned in Moscow*, p. 223.

23. *Ibid.*, p. 181.

24. *Ibid.*, p. 171.

25. *Manchester Guardian*, 2 June 1920.

26. *Ibid.*, 7 June 1920.

27. V. I. Lenin, *Pis'mo k angliiskim rabochim* in *Polnoe sobranie sochinenii*, vol. 41, p. 125.

28. *New York Times*, 23 July 1920.

29. Mrs P. Snowden, *Through Bolshevik Russia*, p. 180.

30. A. Ransome, 'Lenin in 1919', in A. Rhys Williams, *Lenin: The Man and his Work*, pp. 167–8.

31. *Ibid.*, p. 168.

32. *Ibid.*, p. 173.

33. Mrs P. Snowden, *Through Bolshevik Russia*, p. 117.

34. *Ibid.*, p. 76.

35. *Ibid.*, pp. 75 and 117.

36. *Ibid.*, pp. 76–7.

37. *Manchester Guardian*, 29 July 1920.

38. *Ibid.*, 12 July 1920.

39. *Ibid.*, 1 July 1920.

40. Mrs P. Snowden, *Through Bolshevik Russia*, p. 116.

41. *Manchester Guardian*, 29 July 1920.

42. *Ibid.*

43. Mrs P. Snowden, *Through Bolshevik Russia*, pp. 137–8.

44. T. Alexander, *An Estonian Childhood*, p. 120.

45. H. G. Wells, *Russia in the Shadows*, p. 139.

46. *Ibid.*, p. 158.

47. C. Sheridan, *Naked Truth*, pp. 151–2.

48. *Ibid.*, p. 156.

49. C. Sheridan to W. S. Churchill, 23 January 1921: Churchill Papers, CHAR 1/138.

50. C. Sheridan, *Mayfair to Moscow: Clare Sheridan's Diary*, pp. 12–13.

51. C. Sheridan, *Naked Truth*, pp. 157–9.

52. *Ibid.*, pp. 160–1.

53. 'Woman Sculptor Tells Impression of Soviet Chiefs', *New York Times*, 23 November 1920. This excerpt from Clare Sheridan's 'diary' is not contained in the version published as a book.

54. I. Litvinov, autobiographical fragment, 'Moscow 1921', pp. 5 and 7: St Antony's RESC Archive.

55. C. Sheridan, *From Mayfair to Moscow: Clare Sheridan's Diary*, p. 82.

56. Mrs P. Snowden, *Through Bolshevik Russia*, p. 76.

57. C. Sheridan, *Naked Truth*, p. 192.

58. *Ibid.*, pp. 193–4.

59. *Ibid.*, p. 194.

60. *Ibid.*, p. 195.

61. C. Sheridan, *Mayfair to Moscow: Clare Sheridan's Diary*, p. 156.

62. C. Sheridan, *Naked Truth*, p. 196.

63. *Ibid.*, p. 197.

64. C. Sheridan, *Mayfair to Moscow: Clare Sheridan's Diary*, pp. 142–3.

65. C. Sheridan to W. S. Churchill, 23 January 1921: Churchill Papers, CHAR 1/138.

66. W. S. Churchill to C. Sheridan, 21 April 1921: *ibid.*

67. C. Sheridan to W. S. Churchill, April 1921: Churchill Papers, CHAR 1/138.

68. *British Labour Delegation to Russia, 1920: Report*, p. 27.

69. *Ibid.*

70. H. G. Wells, *Russia in the Shadows*, p. 64.

71. *Ibid.*, pp. 83–4.

72. *Ibid.*, pp. 107–8.

73. *The Times*, 8 December 1920.

74. B. Russell, *The Practice and Theory of Bolshevism*, p. 42.

75. *Ibid.*

76. B. Russell to O. Morrell, 25 June 1920: B. Russell, *The Autobiography of Bertrand Russell, 1914–1944*, p. 172.

77. *Ibid.*, pp. 152–3.

27. THE SPREADING OF COMINTERN

1. Mrs P. Snowden, *Through Bolshevik Russia*, p. 121.

2. *Pervyi Kongress Kominterna. Mart 1919 goda* (Partiinoe izdatel'stvo: Moscow, 1919), p. 131.

3. *Ibid.*, pp. 172–219.

4. A. Ransome, *Russia in 1919*, p. 220.

5. *Pervyi Kongress Kominterna*, p. 219.

6. *Politbyuro TsK RKP(b)—VKP(b) i Komintern, 1918–1943. Dokumenty*, p. 26 (footnote 7).

7. *Ibid.*, p. 28.

8. Yan Berzin to G. E. Zinoviev, 28 August 1919: *ibid.*, p. 31.

9. Politburo, 25 March 1919: *ibid.*, p. 25.

10. *Ibid.*

11. RGASPI, f. 17, op. 3, d. 164, p. 2 in *ibid.*, p. 76.

12. *Ibid.*, d. 194, in *ibid.*, p. 93.

13. W. Kendall, *The Revolutionary Movement in Britain, 1900–1921: The Origins of British Communism*, pp. 182–3.

14. L. A. E. Gale to C. Ruthenberg, 23 February 1920, p. 2: Jay Lovestone Papers (HIA), box 195, folder of CP-USA General Correspondence, February 1920.

15. P. S. Pinheiro, *Estratégias da Ilusão: a Revolução Mundial e o Brasil, 1922–1935*, p. 30.

16. *Congress of the Peoples of the East. Baku, September 1920: Stenographic Report*, pp. 21–3.

17. *Ibid.*, p. 35.

18. *Ibid.*, p. 47.

19. *Ibid.*, pp. 76–8.

20. *Ibid.*, pp. 85–8.

21. *Ibid.*, pp. 145–6.

22. *Ibid.*, p. 161.

23. V. I. Lenin, *Pis'mo k angliiskim rabochim*, in *Polnoe sobranie sochinenii*, vol. 41, p. 127.

24. *Ibid.*

25. 'Announcement of the Provisional Bureau of the Communist International': Jay Lovestone Papers (HIA), box 209.

26. Yan Berzin to G. E. Zinoviev, 28 August 1919: *Politbyuro TsK RKP(b)— VKP(b) i Komintern*, p. 31.

27. M. E. Harrison, *Marooned in Moscow: The Story of an American Woman Imprisoned in Russia*, p. 222.

28. TO POLAND AND BEYOND

1. A. A. Ioffe to L. D. Trotskii, 30 January 1919: RGVA, f. 33987, op. 3, d. 2.

2. I. N. R. Davies, *White Eagle, Red Star*, pp. 47–61.

3. *Ibid.*, pp. 91 and 148.

4. Emil Nobel at Yudenich's financial consultative committee, 21 November 1919: Nikolai Yudenich Papers (HIA), box 21, folder 20.

5. V. I. Lenin to I. V. Stalin, 17 March 1920: V. I. Lenin, *Neizvestnye dokumenty, 1891–1922*, pp. 330–1.

6. V. I. Lenin, political report to the Ninth Party Conference: RGASPI, f. 44, op. 1, d. 5, p. 11.

7. G. Nowik, *Zanim złamano =,Enigme". Polski radiowywiad podczas wojny z bolszewicka Rosja 1918–1920*, p. 587.

8. L. D. Trotskii, 'Sovetskaya i shlyakhetskaya', 6 May 1920: RGVA, f. 33987, op. 2, d. 113, pp. 74–5.

9. Savinkov's testimony in 'Sudebnoe razbiratel'stvo', *Pravda*, 30 August 1924, p. 6.

10. 'Svodka agenturnykh svedenii', 20 December 1919: Nikolai Yudenich Papers (HIA), box 4, folder 8; Savinkov's testimonial letter, *Pravda*, 30 August 1924, p. 2.

11. B. Savinkov to unknown general, 11 June 1920: Robert Hamilton Bruce Lockhart Papers (HIA), folder: Robin Bruce Lockhart, 'Reilly: Russian Revolution, Etc.: Sources: Sir Edward Spears'.

12. *Byulleten' Narodnogo Komissariata Inostrannykh Del*, no. 28, 15 August 1920.

13. *L'Humanité*, 17 June 1920.

14. *Byulleten' Narodnogo Komissariata Inostrannykh Del*, no. 28, 15 August 1920, pp. 10–11.

15. *New Statesman*, 10 July 1920.

16. I. V. Stalin, 'Novyi pokhod Antanty na Rossiyu', *Pravda*, 25–26 May 1920.

17. I. N. R. Davies, *White Eagle, Red Star*, p. 95.

18. M. Cooper to US Adjutant General, 8 August 1941: Merian C. Cooper Papers (HIA).

19. M. Cooper to Chief of Staff, USAF, 12 October 1953, pp. 6–7: *ibid.*

20. Polish embassy (Washington), 5 September 1941: *ibid.*

21. *Washington Post*, 15 March 1921.

22. P. Dukes, diary for 1920: Paul Dukes Papers (HIA), box 1. On the North-cliffe connection see Robin Bruce Lockhart, 'Notes on Meeting with Sir Paul Dukes', 25 June 1966, p. 2: Robert Hamilton Bruce Lockhart Papers (HIA), box 11, folder: Robin Bruce Lockhart, 'Reilly: Russian Revolution, Etc.: Sources: Paul Dukes, 1922–1990'.

23. P. Dukes, *Red Dusk and the Morrow*, opposite pp. 227 and 240.

24. Robin Bruce Lockhart to George Hill (n.d.): Robert Hamilton Bruce Lockhart Papers (HIA), box 11, folder G. A. Hill Correspondence with Robin Bruce Lockhart. On the date of Reilly's trip see A. Cook, *On His Majesty's Secret Service: Sidney Reilly—Codename ST1*, p. 177.

25. S. Savinkova to S. Reilly, 19 December 1922: Robert Hamilton Bruce Lockhart Papers (HIA), box 6, folder 39. S. Savinkova was Boris Savinkov's mother.

26. L. D. Trotsky to S. S. Kamenev, copied to E. M. Sklyanskii, Lenin and the Central Committee, 17 July 1920: V. Krasnov and V. Daines (eds), *Neizvestnyi Trotskii. Krasnyi Bonapart: Dokumenty, mneniya, razmyshleniya*, p. 307.

27. V. I. Lenin, political report to the Ninth Party Conference: RGASPI, f. 44, op. 1, d. 5, pp. 13–14.

28. *Ibid.*, p. 16.

29. *Ibid.*, p. 15.

30. Politburo meeting, 23 July 1920: *ibid.*, f. 17, op. 3, d. 96, items 2, 7 and 8.

31. L. D. Trotskii to M. M. Litvinov, 7 July 1921: RGVA, f. 33987, op. 1, d. 409, p. 724.

32. V. I. Lenin to I. V. Stalin, 23 July 1920: V. I. Lenin, *Neizvestnye dokumenty, 1891–1922*, p. 357.

33. Politburo meeting, 10 August 1920: *ibid.*, f. 17, op. 3, d. 101, items 3 and 4.

34. V. I. Lenin, political report to the Ninth Party Conference: *ibid.*, f. 44, op. 1, d. 5, p. 20.

35. V. I. Lenin, *Polnoe sobranie sochinenii*, vol. 41, p. 458.

36. Dresel in Berlin to Department of State, 10 July 1920: US Department of State, Records of the Department of State Relating to Political Relations between Russia (and the Soviet Union) and Other States, 1910–29 (HIA).

37. *Izvestiya Tsentral'nogo Komiteta KPSS*, no. 4 (1991), p. 171.

38. Politburo meeting, 19 August 1920: RGASPI, f. 17, op. 3, d. 103.

39. *Manchester Guardian*, 2 August 1920. See below, pp. 300–1.

40. Politburo meetings, 13 August 1920: RGASPI, f. 17, op. 3, d. 102, item 3; and 19 August 1920: *ibid.*, f. 17, op. 3, d. 103, item 1.

41. *The Times*, 5 August 1920.

42. *Ibid.*, 6 August 1920.

43. *Ibid.*, 7 August 1920.

44. *Manchester Guardian*, 11 August 1920.

45. *The Times*, 11 August 1920.

46. *Manchester Guardian*, 11 August 1920.

47. *The Times*, 4 August 1920.

48. *Ibid.*, 7 August 1920.

49. *Ibid.*, 10 August 1920.

50. *Manchester Guardian*, 5 August 1920.

51. I. N. R. Davies, *White Eagle, Red Star*, p. 274.

52. Politburo meeting, 1 September 1920: RGASPI, f. 17, op. 3, d. 106, items 7, 9 and 10.

53. Politburo meeting, 6 September 1920: *ibid.*, d. 107, item 2.

54. *Manchester Guardian*, 12 September 1920.

55. Politburo meeting, 1 September 1920: RGASPI, f. 17, op. 3, d. 106.

56. *Ibid.*, p. 34.

57. *Ibid.*, p. 26.

58. *Ibid.*, p. 28.

59. *Ibid.*, pp. 36–7.

29. TRADE TALKS ABROAD

1. *New York Times*, 17 July 1920.

2. *Ibid.*, 3 September 1920.

3. *The Times*, 23 July 1920.

4. *Ibid.*, 27 July 1920.

5. *Ibid.*, 20 and 21 July 1920.

6. Politburo meeting, 19 August 1920: RGASPI, f. 17, op. 3, d. 103.

7. See above, pp. 251–2.

8. *The Times*, 6 August 1920.

9. *Ibid.*, 7 August 1920.

10. *New York Times*, 13 September 1920.

11. *Ibid.*, 14 September 1920; *The Times*, 17 September 1920.

12. M. J. Larsons, 'Au service des Soviets', pp. 42–4: typescript, M. J. Larsons Papers (HIA), box 1.

13. *Ibid.*, pp. 43–6.

14. *Ibid.*, p. 50; see also Krasin's explanation to Dr Freund, 1 December 1947, M. J. Larsons Papers (HIA), box 1.

15. A. J. Sack, *America's Possible Share in the Economic Future of Russia*, p. 24.

16. M. J. Larsons, 'Au service des Soviets', p. 47.

17. *Ibid.*, p. 48.

18. W. B. Vanderlip (with H. B. Hulbert), *In Search of a Siberian Klondike*, pp. 4 and 315; *New York Times*, 27 October 1920.

19. *New York Times*, 19 November 1920.

20. *Ibid.*, 28 October 1920.

21. *Ibid.*, 27 October and 19 November 1920.

22. V. I. Lenin, *Polnoe sobranie sochinenii*, vol. 42, pp. 23 and 62–4.

23. H. G. Wells, *Russia in the Shadows*, pp. 164–5.

24. *Ibid.*, pp. 164 and 167; *The Times*, 8 December 1920.

25. *New York Times*, 1 December 1920.

26. *Ibid.*, 11 January 1922.

27. *Manchester Guardian*, 4 January 1921.

28. *Ibid.*, 15 and 19 December 1920.

29. *New York Times*, 3 January 1921.

30. *Relations with Russia: Hearing before the Committee on Foreign Relations, United States Senate. Sixty-Sixth Congress, Third Session*, p. 5.

31. *Ibid.*, p. 62.

32. D. Lincove, 'Radical Publishing to "Reach the Million Masses": Alexander L. Trachtenberg and International Publishers, 1906–1966', *Left History*, vol. 10.1 (Fall/Winter 2004), p. 91.

33. *Relations with Russia: Hearing before the Committee on Foreign Relations, United States Senate*, pp. 72–3.

34. *Ibid.*, pp. 12–28.

35. 'Comments of the Esthonian Press on the De Jure Recognition of Esthonia': Nicolai Koestner Papers (HIA).

36. Central Committee meeting, 26 January 1921: RGASPI, f. 17, op. 2, d. 56.

37. *Manchester Guardian*, 19 December 1920.

38. *The Times*, 22 December 1920; *New York Times*, 29 December 1920. See above, pp. 251–2.

39. *The Times*, 22 and 23 December 1920.

40. *Ibid.*, 8 January 1921.

41. Central Committee meeting, 26 January 1921: RGASPI, f. 17, op. 2, d. 56, item 12.

42. *Manchester Guardian*, 19 December 1920.

30. THE ECONOMICS OF SURVIVAL

1. *Desyatyi s"ezd RKP(b)*, pp. 349–50.

2. Politburo second meeting, 5 February 1921: RGASPI, f. 17, op. 3, d. 130.

3. Politburo first meeting, 5 February 1921: *ibid.*, d. 129.

4. Politburo meeting, 16 February 1921: *ibid.*, d. 134.

5. Central Committee plenum, 24 February 1921: *ibid.*, op. 2, d. 59, item 2.

6. See above, pp. 254–5.

7. *The Times*, 17 September 1920.

8. *Ibid.*, 3 December 1920.

9. C. Andrew, *Secret Service: The Making of the British Intelligence Community*, p. 262.

10. B. Savinkov to P. N. Wrangel, 15 October 1920: Boris Savinkov Papers (HIA).

11. Central Committee plenum, 25 February 1921: RGASPI, f. 17, op. 2, d. 60.

12. L. Bryant (Moscow) via F. Mason (Berlin), 10 March 1921: Frank E. Mason Papers (HIA), box 3, fol. 1, pp. 68–9.

13. L. Bryant (Moscow) via F. Mason (Berlin), 8 March 1921: *ibid.*, p. 79.

14. *Ibid.*, p. 80.

15. V. Krasnov and V. Daines (eds), *Neizvestnyi Trotskii. Krasnyi Bonapart: Dokumenty, mneniya, razmyshleniya*, pp. 339 and 340–1.

16. *Desyatyi s"ezd RKP(b)*, pp. 716–59 and 765–8.

17. *Ibid.*, pp. 349–50, 354, 391 and 393.

18. L. D. Trotsky to the Politburo, 10 March 1921: V. Krasnov and V. Daines (eds), *Neizvestnyi Trotskii*, p. 346.

19. B. A. Bakhmetev to V. A. Maklakov, 19 March 1921: '*Sovershenno lichno i doveritel'no!*': *B. A. Bakhmetev–V. A. Maklakov: perepiska*, vol. 1, p. 329.

20. Politburo meetings, 18 and 19 March 1921: RGASPI, f. 17, op. 3, dd. 138 and 139.

21. *Washington Times*, 17 March 1921.

22. *Boston American*, 16 March 1921.

23. L. Bryant to F. Mason, 12 March 1921: Frank E. Mason Papers (HIA), box 2, p. 61.

24. Politburo meeting, 17 April 1921: RGASPI, f. 17, op. 3, d. 155, item 155.

31. THE SECOND BREATHING SPACE

1. *Petrogradskie izvestiya*, 12 April 1921; 'Revel'skaya gavan' i bol'sheviki', 21 April 1921, pp. 1 and 5, Nicolai Koestner Papers (HIA).

2. *Pravda*, 14 April 1921.

3. L. D. Trotsky to A. D. Tsyurupa, 21 March 1921: GARF, f. 3316s, op. 2, d. 83, pp. 2–4.

4. B. A. Bakhmetev to V. A. Maklakov, 19 March 1921: '*Sovershenno lichno i doveritel'no!*': *B. A. Bakhmetev–V. A. Maklakov: perepiska*, vol. 1, p. 330.

5. *New York Times*, 22 March 1921.

6. *Ibid.*

7. *Ibid.*, 13 July 1921.

8. *Chicago Tribune,* 27 March 1921.

9. J. Aves, *Workers against Lenin: Labour Protest and the Bolshevik Dictatorship,* pp. 158–85.

10. V. A. Antonov-Ovseenko to V. Lenin, 20 July 1921: *The Trotsky Papers,* vol. 2, p. 536.

11. 'Desyataya partiinaya konferentsiya, 26–28 maya 1921 goda': uncorrected minutes, RGASPI, f. 46, op. 1, d. 2, pp. 1, 16, 18 and 60.

12. See R. Service, *Lenin: A Political Life,* vol. 3, pp. 182–4 and 205–12.

13. 'Desyataya partiinaya konferentsiya, 26–28 maya 1921 goda': uncorrected minutes, RGASPI, f. 46, op. 1, d. 2, pp. 58–9.

14. *Ibid.,* pp. 50–62.

15. *Ibid.,* pp. 125 and 133–4.

16. *New York Times,* 25 May 1921.

17. L. D. Trotskii to M. M. Litvinov, 7 July 1921: RGVA, f. 33987, op. 1, d. 409, p. 555.

18. *New York Times,* 30 June 1921.

19. *Ibid.,* 2 July 1921.

20. *Ibid.,* 30 June 1921.

21. V. I. Lenin to G. V. Chicherin, in V. I. Lenin, *Polnoe sobranie sochinenii,* vol. 53, pp. 34–5.

22. *New York Times,* 31 July 1921.

23. *Ibid.,* 4 August 1921.

24. *Ibid.,* 5 November 1921.

25. *Ibid.,* 6 November 1921.

26. E. J. Epstein, *Dossier: The Secret History of Armand Hammer,* pp. 62–73.

27. L. B. Krasin, *Vneshtorg i vneshnyaya ekonomicheskaya politika Sovetskogo pravitel'stva,* pp. 33–4.

28. *The Times,* 7 July 1921.

29. V. I. Lenin, *Polnoe sobranie sochinenii,* vol. 45, p. 220.

30. H. Hoover, *The Memoirs of Herbert Hoover: The Cabinet and the Presidency, 1920–1923,* p. 23.

31. L. Trotskii, *Petlya vmesto khleba* (Penza Gubkom RKP: Penza, 1921), pp. 15–32.

32. *Ibid.,* pp. 11–12.

33. *Ibid.,* p. 11.

34. V. I. Lenin to V. M. Molotov, 11 August 1921, in V. I. Lenin, *Polnoe sobranie sochinenii,* vol. 53, pp. 110–11.

35. A. Gumberg to K. Durant, 21 June 1922: Ronald Hilton Papers (HIA).

36. 8 September 1921: Herbert Hoover Collection (HIA), box 17, folder 6.

37. *New York Times,* 18 February 1922.

38. B. Patenaude, *The Big Show in Bololand: The American Relief Expedition to Soviet Russia in the Famine of 1921,* pp. 28–48.

39. Extract from Trotsky's interview with L. Bryant-Reed (1922): American Relief Administration Russian Unit (HIA), box 353, folder 19.

40. Report of the VCheka, May–June 1921: 30 June 1921: *Arkhiv VChK. Sbornik dokumentov*, pp. 593–612.

41. B. Savinkov to S. Reilly, 12 June 1921: Robert Hamilton Bruce Lockhart Papers (HIA), box 6, folder 24.

42. Savinkov's testimony in 'Sudebnoe razbiratel'stvo', *Pravda*, 30 August 1924, p. 6.

43. Report of the VCheka, May–June 1921: 30 June 1921: *Arkhiv VChK. Sbornik dokumentov*, pp. 593–612.

44. P. Dukes, diary for 1921: Paul Dukes Papers (HIA), box 1.

45. Association Financière, Industrielle et Commerciale Russe (Paris) to V. N. Bashkirov (New York), 23 June 1921: Vladimir N. Bashkirov Papers (HIA), box 1.

46. Unsigned, undated military intelligence report on Anglo-Soviet relations in London (May or June 1921?): P. N. Vrangel Collection (HIA), box 110, folder 22, p. 7.

47. A. A. Ioffe (V. Krymskii), *Mirnoe nastuplenie*, p. 17.

48. *Ibid.*, pp. 9, 17 and 36–8.

49. William J. Kelley to an unknown addressee, 8 December 1921: William J. Kelley Papers (HIA).

50. *New York Times*, 8 June 1921.

51. *Ibid.*, 11 January 1922.

52. Theses on the NEP: RGASPI, f. 325, op. 1, d. 88, pp. 1–5. See also R. Service, *Trotsky: A Biography*, p. 290.

32. THE UNEXTINGUISHED FIRE

1. A. Poliakoff, *The Silver Samovar: Reminiscences of the Russian Revolution*, p. 40.

2. A. L. Strong, *The First Time in History: Two Years of Russia's New Life (August 1921 to December 1923)*, p. 15.

3. *Ibid.*

4. I. Litvinov, typed transcription of taped conversation in 1960 about settling in Russia, p. 10: Ivy Litvinov Papers (HIA), box 10, folder 3.

5. *Ibid.*, p. 11.

6. Frank E. Mason, dispatch of 31 May 1921: Frank E. Mason Papers (HIA), box 2, pp. 68–9.

7. *Dayton Journal*, 4 July 1920. Mason's articles were widely syndicated in the US.

8. I. Litvinov, untitled autobiographical fragment, p. 5: St Antony's RESC Archive.

9. I. Litvinov, autobiographical fragment, 'Moscow 1921', pp. 5 and 7: St Antony's RESC Archive.

10. I. Litvinov, 'Oral History', p. 1: Ivy Litvinov Papers (HIA), box 1.

11. *Ibid.*

12. I. Litvinov, transcription of taped conversation in 1960 about settling in Russia, p. 5: Ivy Litvinov Papers (HIA), box 10, folder 3.

13. *Ibid.*, pp. 8–9.

14. *Ibid.*, p. 10.

15. *Ibid.*, p. 3.

16. M. E. Harrison, *Marooned in Moscow: The Story of an American Woman Imprisoned in Russia*, p. 247.

17. R. Service, *Lenin: A Political Life*, vol. 3, pp. 247–8.

18. I. Litvinov, 'Mysli o nevozrashchenii iz Ameriki, 1942': Ivy Litvinov Papers (HIA), box 10, folder 3, p. 1.

19. V. A. Maklakov to B. A. Bakhmetev, 7 December 1920: '*Sovershenno lichno i doveritel'no!*': *B. A. Bakhmetev–V. A. Maklakov: perepiska*, vol. 1, p. 300.

20. B. A. Bakhmetev to V. A. Maklakov, 20 January 1920: *ibid.*, p. 152.

21. See the revelation of the leadership's assumptions in Zinoviev's speech (confidential printed version) to the joint plenum of the Central Committee and the Central Control Commission of 29 July–9 August 1927: RGASPI, f. 17, op. 2, d. 317 (V-iii), p. 22.

POSTSCRIPT

1. I. Litvinov, 'Oral History: Ivy Litvinov', pp. 6–10: Ivy Litvinov Papers (HIA), box 1; 'Being English in Moscow', pp. 7–8: box 9, folder 9.

2. J. Carswell, *The Exile: A Life of Ivy Litvinov*, pp. 190 and 203.

3. M. Philips Price, *My Three Revolutions*.

4. J. Reed, *Ten Days that Shook the World* (Boni & Liveright: New York, 1922).

5. Dzh. Rid, *10 dnei, kotorye potryasli mir* (2nd corrected edn; Krasnaya nov': Moscow, 1924).

6. B. D. Wolfe, 'Mr K's Favorite Reporter', *New York Times*, 5 June 1960.

7. RGASPI, f. 89, op. 28, d. 5, p. 8: meeting with Komsomol delegation, 13 January 1961.

8. M. E. Harrison, *Marooned in Moscow: The Story of an American Woman Imprisoned in Russia*, pp. 193–4.

9. A. Dunois, unpublished typescript introduction (May 1941) to an edition of Sadoul's letters, p. 4: Jacques Sadoul Papers (HIA).

10. M. E. Harrison, *Marooned in Moscow*, pp. 194–5.

11. V. Serge, *Memoirs of a Revolutionary, 1901–1941*, p. 145.

12. PFR.301/D.S.10: National Archives, KV/2/1904.

13. R. Chambers, *The Last Englishman: The Double Life of Arthur Ransome*, p. 363.

14. S. G. Reilly to P. Dukes, 23 October 1922: Robert Hamilton Bruce Lockhart Papers (HIA), box 6, folder 22.

15. P. Dukes, *Come Hammer, Come Sickle!* (Cassell: London, 1947).

16. Paul Dukes Papers (HIA), boxes 1 and 2. On the accident, see the letter from Mrs Tina Forbes to Mr Lacy, 16 October 1969, in box 1.

17. G. A. Hill, 'Reminiscences of Four Years with the N.K.V.D.', p. 121: draft typescript, George A. Hill Papers (HIA).

18. *Ibid.*, p. 2.

19. *Ibid.*, p. 158.

20. *Ibid.*, pp. 137–43.

21. *Ibid.*, pp. 156–7.

22. Robert Hamilton Bruce Lockhart Papers (HIA), box 11, folder 'George Hill Legal Documents'.

23. A. Cook, *On His Majesty's Secret Service: Sidney Reilly—Codename ST1*, pp. 96–7.

24. Robin Bruce Lockhart's notes taken from George Hill's account to him, pp. 2–3: Robert Hamilton Bruce Lockhart Papers, box 11, folder 1.

25. S. G. Reilly and Pepita Bobadilla, *The Adventures of Sidney Reilly, Britain's Master Spy* (E. Mathews & Marrot: London, 1931); R. N. Bruce Lockhart, *Ace of Spies.*

26. *Reilly—Ace of Spies* (Thames TV, 1983).

27. *British Agent* (dir. M. Curtiz: Warner Brothers, 1934).

28. R. H. Bruce Lockhart, notebooks (apparently 1938–1945): Robert Hamilton Bruce Lockhart Papers (HIA), box 4, folder 3.

29. Cablegram (n.d.) to R. H. Bruce Lockhart at the *Daily Express*: ibid., box 10.

30. R. H. Bruce Lockhart, *Friends, Foes and Foreigners*, p. 274.

31. R. H. Bruce Lockhart, 'Baroness Budberg' (n.d. but after 1956), pp. 5–6: Robert Hamilton Bruce Lockhart Papers (HIA), box 6, folder 14.

32. T. Alexander, *An Estonian Childhood*, pp. 69–71 and 74.

33. *Ibid.*, p. 122.

34. R. H. Bruce Lockhart, 'Baroness Budberg', pp. 1–13: Robert Hamilton Bruce Lockhart Papers (HIA), box 6, folder 14.

35. D. Collingridge, 'Aunt Moura', *The Times*, 2 May 2010. Dmitri Collingridge is a great-great-nephew of Moura Budberg.

36. Merian C. Cooper Papers (HIA).

37. R. B. Spence, 'The Tragic Fate of Kalamatiano: America's Man in Moscow', *International Journal of Intelligence and Counterintelligence*, no. 3 (1999), pp. 356–63.

38. Robin Bruce Lockhart to G. A. Hill (n.d.), recounting what Paul Dukes had told him: Robert Hamilton Bruce Lockhart Papers (HIA), box 11, folder G. A. Hill Correspondence with Robin Bruce Lockhart.

39. B. V. Savinkov to S. G. Reilly, 7 October 1924: Robert Hamilton Bruce Lockhart Papers (HIA), box 6, folder 24.

40. Savinkov's testimony in 'Sudebnoe razbiratel'stvo', *Pravda*, 30 August 1924, pp. 4–6.

41. *Arkhiv VChK. Sbornik dokumentov*, p. 592.

SELECT BIBLIOGRAPHY

ARCHIVES

Arkhiv Prezidenta Rossiiskoi Federatsii, Moscow [APRF]

Bodleian Library, Oxford
Papers of Alfred Milner, Viscount Milner, 1824–1955

Gosudarstvenny Arkhiv Rossiiskoi Federatsii, Moscow [GARF]

Hoover Institution Archives, Stanford University, Stanford, CA [HIA]
American Relief Administration Russian Unit

Vladimir N. Bashkirov Papers
Communist International Instructions
Merian C. Cooper Papers
Theodore Draper Papers
Paul Dukes Papers
Arthur M. Free Papers
T. C. C. Gregory Papers
George Halonen Papers
George A. Hill Papers
Ronald Hilton Papers
Herbert Hoover Collection
Hungarian Subject Collection
N. A. Ioffe Papers
Henry James Papers
William J. Kelley Papers
Nicolai Koestner Papers
Aleksandr Vasil'evich Kolchak Papers
General A. A. von Lampe Papers
Robert Lansing Papers
M. J. Larsons Papers

Ivy Litvinov Papers
Robert Hamilton Bruce Lockhart Papers
Jay Lovestone Papers
Gibbes Lykes Papers
L. K. Martens Papers
Frank E. Mason Papers
Russia. Posol'stvo
Russian Subject Collection
Jacques Sadoul Papers
Boris Savinkov Papers
US Consulate—Leningrad [*sic*]
US Department of State: Records of the Department of State Relating to Political
    Relations between Russia (and the Soviet Union) and Other States, 1910–29
Pëtr Vasil'evich Vologodskii Papers
P. N. Vrangel Papers
Nikolai Yudenich Papers

National Archives, Kew
    HO = Home Office   FO = Foreign Office   KV = Security Service

**Rossiiskii Gosudarstvennyi Arkhiv Sotsial'no-Politicheskoi Istorii, Moscow
[RSGASPI]**
                    fond 2   fond 17   fond 46   fond 325
                    fond 5   fond 44   fond 89   fond 515

Rossiiskii Gosudarstvennyi Voennyi Arkhiv, Moscow [RGVA]

Russian and Eurasian Studies Centre, St Antony's College, Oxford [RESC]
Ivy Litvinov Papers

Churchill Archives Centre, Churchill College, Cambridge
Churchill Papers

CONTEMPORARY PERIODICALS

Byulleten' Narodnogo Komissariata
    Inostrannykh Del
Daily Express
Daily Herald
Daily Mail
Daily News and Leader
Le Figaro
L'Humanité
Izvestiya
Izvestiya Tsentral'nogo Komiteta
    KPSS
Labour Leader
Manchester Guardian
New York Times
Pravda
The Times
Washington Post

BOOKS AND ARTICLES

A. Agar, *Baltic Episode: A Classic of Secret Service in Russian Waters* (Hodder & Stoughton: London, 1963)

R. Albertson, *Fighting without a War: An Account of Military Intervention in North Russia—Exposing British Atrocities in Murmansk and Archangel* (Harcourt, Brace & Howe: New York, 1920)

V. V. Aldoshin, Yu. V. Ivanov, V. M. Semënov and V. A. Tarasov (eds), *Sovetsko–amerikanskie otnosheniya: gody nepriznaniya, 1918–1926* (Mezhdunarodnyi fond 'Demokratiya': Moscow, 2002)

T. Alexander, *An Estonian Childhood* (Heinemann: London, 1987)

C. Alston, *Russia's Greatest Enemy?: Harold Williams and the Russian Revolutions* (I. B. Tauris: London, 2007)

C. Andrew, *The Defence of the Realm: The Authorized History of MI5* (Allen Lane: London, 2009)

C. Andrew, *For the President's Eyes Only: Secret Intelligence and the American Presidency from Washington to Bush* (HarperCollins: New York, 1995)

C. Andrew, *Secret Service: The Making of the British Intelligence Community* (Heinemann: London, 1985)

C. Andrew and V. Mitrokhin, *The Mitrokhin Archive: The KGB in Europe and the West* (Allen Lane: London, 1999)

N. Andreyev, *A Moth on a Fence: Memoirs of Russia, Estonia, Czechoslovakia and Western Europe* (Hodgson: London, 2009)

C. Anet, *La Révolution russe: la terreur maximaliste; l'armistice—les pour-parlers de paix (Novembre 1917–Janvier 1918)* (Payot: Paris, 1919)

Arkhiv VChK. Sbornik dokumentov, ed. V. Vinogradov, A. Litvin and V. Khristoforov (Kuchkovo Pole: Moscow, 2007)

Army: The Evacuation of North Russia, 1919 (War Office: London, 1920)

J. Aves, *Workers against Lenin: Labour Protest and the Bolshevik Dictatorship* (I. B. Tauris: London, 1996)

K. Baedeker, *Russia with Teheran, Port Arthur, and Peking: Handbook for Travellers* (T. Fisher Unwin: London, 1914)

V. Barnett, *A History of Russian Economic Thought* (Routledge: London, 2005)

B. F. Bears, *Vain Endeavor: Robert Lansing's Attempts to End the American–Japanese Rivalry* (Duke University Press: Durham, NC, 1962)

B. Beatty, *A Political Primer for the New Voter* (Whitaker and Ray-Wiggin Company: San Francisco, 1912)

B. Beatty, *The Red Heart of Russia* (The Century Co.: New York, 1918)

C. Bechhofer, *Through Starving Russia, Being the Record of a Journey to Moscow and the Volga Provinces in August and September 1921* (Methuen: London, 1921)

D. Beer, *Renovating Russia: The Human Sciences and the Fate of Liberal Modernity, 1880–1930* (Cornell University Press: Ithaca, NY, 2008)

A. di Biagio, *Coesistenza e isolazionismo. Mosca, il Comintern e l'Europa di Versailles (1918–1928)* (Carocci: Rome, 2004)

A. di Biagio, *Le origini dell'isolazionismo sovietico* (Franco Angeli: Milan, 1990)

R. Blobaum, *Feliks Dzierzyński and the SDKPiL: A Study of the Origins of Polish Communism* (East European Monographs: Boulder, CO, 1984)

Bolshevik Propaganda: Hearings before a Subcommittee on the Judiciary, United States Senate, Sixty-Fifth Congress, Third Session and Thereafter Pursuant to Senate Resolutions 439 and 469—February 11, 1919 to March 10, 1919 (Government Printing Office: Washington, DC, 1919)

R. Braithwaite, *Across the Moscow River: The World Turned Upside Down* (Yale University Press: London, 2002)

British Documents on Foreign Policy, part 2: *The Soviet Union, 1917–1939*, vol. 1: *Soviet Russia and her Neighbours, Jan. 1917–Dec. 1919* (University Publications of America)

British Labour Delegation to Russia 1920: Report, ed. L. Haden Guest (Trades Union Congress and Labour Party: London, 1920)

H. Brogan, *The Life of Arthur Ransome* (Jonathan Cape: London, 1972)

G. Brook-Shepherd, *The Iron Maze: The Western Secret Services and the Bolsheviks* (Macmillan: London, 1998)

P. Broué, *Révolution en Allemagne* (Minuit: Paris, 1971)

K. Brüggemann, 'Defending National Sovereignty against Two Russias: Estonia in the Russian Civil War, 1918–1920', *Journal of Baltic Studies*, no. 1 (2003)

K. Brüggemann, '"Foreign Rule" during the Estonian War of Independence, 1918–1920: The Bolshevik Experiment of the "Estonian Workers' Commune"', *Journal of Baltic Studies*, no. 2 (2006)

L. Bryant, *Mirrors of Moscow* (T. Selzer: New York, 1923)

L. Bryant, *Six Red Months in Russia: An Observer's Account of Russia before and during the Proletarian Dictatorship* (George H. Doran: New York, 1918)

Sir George Buchanan, *My Mission to Russia and Other Diplomatic Memories* (Cassell: London, 1923)

M. Buchanan, *The City of Trouble*, Foreword by Hugh Walpole (Charles Scribner's Sons: New York, 1919)

R. D. Buhite, *Lives at Risk: Hostages and Victims in American Foreign Policy* (Rowman & Littlefield: Wilmington, DE, 1995)

N. Bukharin, *Vseobshchaya delëzhka ili kommunisticheskoe proizvodstvo* (Izd. VTsIKR., S., K. i K. Deputatov: Moscow, 1918)

The Bullitt Mission to Russia: Testimony before the Committee on Foreign Relations, United States Senate, of William C. Bullitt (B. W. Huebsch: New York, 1919)

D. R. Buxton, *In a Russian Village* (The Labour Publishing Company: London, 1922)

Princess Cantacuzène, *Revolutionary Days: Recollections of Romanoffs and Bolsheviki* (Small, Maynard: Boston, 1919)

M. J. Carley, *Revolution and Intervention: The French Government and the Russian Civil War, 1917–1919* (McGill-Queen's University Press: Kingston and Montreal, 1983)

D. Carlton, *Churchill and the Soviet Union* (Manchester University Press: Manchester, 2000)

E. H. Carr, *The Bolshevik Revolution*, vol. 3 (Macmillan: London, 1953)

J. Carswell, *The Exile: A Life of Ivy Litvinov* (Faber & Faber: London, 1983)

R. Chambers, *The Last Englishman: The Double Life of Arthur Ransome* (Faber & Faber: London, 2009)

Chekisty: sbornik, ed. L. Korneshov (Molodaya gvardiya: Moscow, 1970)

G. V. Chicherin, *Vneshnyaya politika Sovetskoi Rossii za dva goda* (Gosizdat: Moscow, 1920)

W. Churchill, *The World Crisis*, vol. 4: *The Aftermath* (Charles Scribner's Sons: New York, 1929)

J. S. Clarke, *Pen Portraits of Russia under the 'Red Terror'* (National Workers' Committees: Glasgow, 1921)

G. Clemenceau, *France devant l'Allemagne* (Payot: Paris, 1918)

Congress of the Peoples of the East. Baku, September 1920: Stenographic Report, trans. and annotated by B. Pearce (New Park: London, 1978)

A. Cook, *On His Majesty's Secret Service: Sidney Reilly—Codename ST1* (Tempus: Stroud, 2002)

J. Cornwell, *Hitler's Pope: The Secret History of Pius XII* (Viking: London, 1999)

G. Creel (Chairman), *The German–Bolshevik Conspiracy* (The Committee on Public Information: New York, 1918)

N. Davies, *White Eagle, Red Star* (Cambridge University Press: Cambridge, 1972)

R. K. Debo, *Revolution and Survival: The Foreign Policy of Soviet Russia, 1917–18* (Liverpool University Press: Liverpool, 1979)

R. K. Debo, *Survival and Consolidation: The Foreign Policy of Soviet Russia, 1918–1921* (McGill-Queen's University Press: Montreal, 1992)

Desyatyi s"ezd RKP(b). Mart 1921. Stenograficheskii otchët (Gosudarstvennoe izdatel'stvo: Moscow, 1963)

The Diaries of Robert Bruce Lockhart, 1915–1938, ed. K. Young (Macmillan: London, 1973)

F. R. Dickinson, *War and National Reinvention: Japan in the Great War, 1914–1919* (Harvard University Asia Center: Cambridge, MA, 1999)

P. Dukes, *Come Hammer, Come Sickle!* (Cassell: London, 1947)

P. Dukes, *Red Dusk and the Morrow* (Doubleday, Page: New York, 1922)

S. Dzerzhinskaya, *V gody velikikh boëv* (Mysl': Moscow, 1964)

E. J. Epstein, *Dossier: The Secret History of Armand Hammer* (Random House: New York, 1996)

L. Eyre, *Russia Analysed* (New York World: New York, 1920)

V. Fic, *The Bolsheviks and the Czechoslovak Legion* (Abhinav: New Delhi, 1978)

D. S. Foglesong, *America's Secret War against Bolshevism: U.S. Intervention in the Russian Civil War, 1917–1920* (University of North Carolina Press: Chapel Hill, NC, and London, 1995)

D. R. Francis, *Russia from the American Embassy, April 1916–November 1918* (Charles Scribner's Sons: New York, 1921)

F. J. Funk, 'Fighting after the War', *Purdue Alumnus* (n.d.)

I. Getzler, *Martov: A Political Biography of a Russian Social-Democrat* (Cambridge University Press: Cambridge, 1967)

M. Gilbert, *Winston S. Churchill*, vol. 4: *The World in Torment, 1917–1922* (Heinemann: London, 1975)

E. Goldman, *My Disillusionment in Russia* (Doubleday, Page: New York, 1923)

J. M. Goldstein, *America's Opportunities for Trade and Investment in Russia* (Russian Information Bureau: New York, 1919)

S. R. Graubard, *British Labour and the Russian Revolution, 1917–1924* (Harvard University Press: Cambridge, MA, 1956)

T. C. C. Gregory, *Beating Back Bolshevism* (n.p., n.d.)

T. C. C. Gregory, *Stemming the Red Tide* (n.p., 1919)

F. Grenard, *La Révolution russe* (Armand Colin: Paris, 1933)

W. Hard, *Raymond Robins' Own Story* (Harper & Brothers: New York, 1920)

M. E. Harrison, *Marooned in Moscow: The Story of an American Woman Imprisoned in Russia* (George H. Doran: New York, 1921)

S. Hastings, *The Secret Lives of Somerset Maugham* (John Murray: London, 2009)

G. A. Hill, *Dreaded Hour* (Cassell: London, 1936)

G. A. Hill, *Go Spy the Land* (Cassell: London, 1932)

General Max Hoffman, *War Diaries and Other Papers* (M Secker: London, 1929)

W. V. Holzer, *The Ghost in the Little House: A Life of Rose Wilder Lane* (University of Missouri Press: Columbia, MO, 1993)

H. Hoover, *Address of Secretary Hoover before the Chamber of Commerce of the United States. Eleventh Annual Meeting. New York, N.Y., May 8 1923* (?Washington, DC, 1923)

H. Hoover, *The Memoirs of Herbert Hoover: The Cabinet and the Presidency, 1920–1923* (Hollis & Carter: London, 1952)

H. Hoover, *The Ordeal of Woodrow Wilson* (McGraw-Hill: New York, 1958)

H. Hoover, *The World Economic Situation: Address of Herbert Hoover before the San Francisco Commercial Club, October 9, 1919* (San Francisco, 1919)

E. House and C. Seymour (eds), *What Really Happened at Paris: The Story of the Peace Conference, 1918–1919* (Charles Scribner's Sons: New York, 1921)

M. Hughes, *Inside the Enigma: British Officials in Russia, 1900–1939* (Hambledon: London, 1997)

A. A. Ioffe, 'Avtobiografiya', *Entsiklopedicheskii slovar' 'Granat'*, part 1 (Granat: Moscow, 1927)

A. A. Ioffe (V. Krymskii), *Mirnoe nastuplenie* (Gosudarstvennoe izdatel'stvo: Petersburg [*sic*], 1921)

A. Ioffe, *O samoupravlenii* (Kniga: Petrograd, 1917)

N. A. Ioffe, *Moi otets Adol'f Abramovich Ioffe: vospominaniia, dokumenty i materialy* (Vozvrashchenie: Moscow, 1997)

K. Jeffery, *MI6: The History of the Secret Intelligence Service, 1909–1949* (Bloomsbury: London, 2010)

D. Kahn, *The Codebreakers: The Story of Secret Writing* (Scribner's: New York, 1996)

A. Kalpaschnikoff, *A Prisoner of Trotsky's* (Doubleday, Page: New York, 1920)

K. Kautsky, *Terrorism and Communism: A Contribution to the Natural History of Revolution*, trans. W. H. Kerridge (George Allen & Unwin: London, 1920)

W. Kendall, *The Revolutionary Movement in Britain, 1900–1921: The Origins of British Communism* (Weidenfeld & Nicolson: London, 1969)

G. F. Kennan, *Russia and the West under Lenin and Stalin* (Little, Brown: New York, 1961)

G. F. Kennan, *Soviet–American Relations, 1917–1920*, vols 1–2 (Princeton University Press: Princeton, 1956–8)

M. Kettle, *The Allies and the Russian Collapse, March 1917–March 1918* (André Deutsch: London, 1981)

M. Kettle, *Churchill and the Archangel Fiasco, November 1918–July 1919* (Routledge: London, 1992)

M. Kettle, *The Road to Intervention, March–November 1918* (Routledge: London, 1988)

J. M. Keynes, *The Economic Consequences of the Peace* (Macmillan: London, 1919)

J. M. Keynes, *Essays in Biography* (W. W. Norton: New York, 1933)

Kii, *Vozmozhna-li otmena chastnoi sobstvennosti?* (Kniga: Petrograd, 1917)

C. Kinvig, *Churchill's Crusade: The British Invasion of Russia, 1918–1920* (Hambledon: London, 2006)

A. Knox, *With the Russian Army, Being Chiefly the Extracts from a Diary of a Military Attaché* (Hutchinson: London, 1921)

S. Koch, *Stalin, Willi Münzenberg and the Seduction of the Intellectuals* (HarperCollins: London 1995)

Komintern i ideya mirovoi revolyutsii: dokumenty, ed. Ya. S. Drabkin (Nauka: Moscow, 1998)

A. Kovrov, *Domashnyaya prisluga* (Kniga: Petrograd, 1917)

L. B. Krasin, *Vneshtorg i vneshnyaya ekonomicheskaya politika Sovetskogo pravitel'stva* (Gosudarstvennoe izdatel'stvo: Petersburg, 1921)

Krasnaya kniga VChK, vols 1–2 (2nd corrected edn; Izdatel'stvo polititicheskoi literatury: Moscow, 1989)

V. Krasnov and V. Daines (eds), *Neizvestnyi Trotskii. Krasnyi Bonapart: Dokumenty, mneniya, razmyshleniya* (Olma-Press: Moscow, 2000).

I. I. Kutuzov, *V strane 'ego velichestva'. Pis'ma i zametki ob Anglii russkogo rabochego diplomata* (TsK Soyuza Tekstil'shchikov: Moscow, 1924)

G. Lansbury, *What I Saw in Russia* (Leonard Parsons: London, 1920)

R. Lansing, *The Big Four and Others of the Peace Conference* (Houghton Mifflin: Boston, 1921)

Yu. Larin, *Voina i zemel'naya programma* (Kniga: Petrograd, 1917)

S. de Lastours, *La France gagne la guerre des codes secrets* (Tallandier: Paris, 1998)

M. P. Leffler, *The Specter of Communism: The United States and the Origins of the Cold War, 1917–1953* (Hill & Wang: New York, 1994)

V. I. Lenin, *Neizvestnye dokumenty, 1891–1922* (Rosspen: Moscow, 1999)

V. I. Lenin, *Polnoe sobranie sochinenii*, vols 1–55 (Gosizdat: Moscow, 1958–65)

Nicolai Lenin, Tchicherin, John Reed and Max Eastman, *Russia* (Liberator: New York, 1920)

G. A. Lensen, *Japanese Recognition of the USSR: Soviet–Japanese Relations, 1921–1930* (Sophia University: Tokyo, 1970)

R. Leviné-Meyer, *Leviné the Spartacist* (Gordon & Cremonesi: London, 1978)

J. K. Libbey, *Alexander Gumberg and Soviet–American Relations, 1917–1933* (University Press of Kentucky: Lexington, KY, 1977)

S. Liberman, *Building Lenin's Russia* (University of Chicago Press: Chicago, 1945)

D. Lincove, 'Radical Publishing to "Reach the Million Masses": Alexander L. Trachtenberg and International Publishers, 1906–1966', *Left History*, vol. 10.1 (Fall/Winter 2004)

I. Linder and S. Churkin (eds), *Krasnaya pautina: tainy razvedki Kominterna, 1919–1943* (Ripol klassik: Moscow, 2005)

M. Litvinoff, *The Bolshevik Revolution: Its Rise and Meaning* (British Socialist Party: London, 1918)

D. Lloyd George, *War Memoirs*, vol. 2 (2nd edn; Odhams Press: London, 1942)

R. H. Bruce Lockhart, *Friends, Foes and Foreigners* (Putnam: London, 1957)

R. Bruce Lockhart, 'Last Words on Lenin: An Inaugural Address [as] Honorary President of the Associated Societies, Edinburgh University, 26 October 1960' (Edinburgh, 1961)

R. H. Bruce Lockhart, *Memoirs of a British Agent, Being an Account of the Author's Early Life in Many Lands and of his Official Mission to Moscow in 1918* (Putnam: London, 1932)

R. N. Bruce Lockhart, *Ace of Spies* (Hodder: London, 1969)

G. V. Lomonosoff, *Memoirs of the Russian Revolution* (Rand School of Social Science: New York, 1919)

J. W. Long, 'Plot and Counter-Plot in Revolutionary Russia: Chronicling the Bruce Lockhart Conspiracy, 1918', *Intelligence and National Security*, no. 10/1 (Jan. 1995)

J. W. Long, 'Searching for Sidney Reilly: The Lockhart Plot in Revolutionary Russia, 1918', *Europe-Asia Studies*, no. 47/7 (1995)

M. Lur'e (Yu. Larin), *Prodovol'stvennyi opyt nemetskikh gorodov* (Sotsialist: Petrograd, 1917)

M. Lur'e (Yu. Larin), *Prodovol'stvie v Germanii i Rossii* (Kniga: Petrograd, 1918)

I. McBride, *Barbarous Soviet Russia* (Thomas Selzer: New York, 1920)

J. McHugh and B. J. Ripley, 'Russian Political Internees in First World War Britain: The Cases of George Chicherin and Peter Petroff', *Historical Journal*, no. 3 (1985)

S. McMeekin, *History's Greatest Heist: The Looting of Russia by the Bolsheviks* (Yale University Press: New Haven, 2009)

S. McMeekin, *The Red Millionaire: A Political Biography of Willi Münzenburg, Moscow's Secret Propaganda Tsar in the West* (Yale University Press: New Haven, 2003)

M. MacMillan, *Peacemakers: The Paris Conference of 1919 and its Attempt to End War* (John Murray: London, 2001)

V. Madeira, '"Because I Don't Trust Him, We are Friends": Signals Intelligence and the Reluctant Anglo-Soviet Embrace, 1917–24', *Intelligence and National Security*, no. 1 (2004)

I. Maisky, *Journey into the Past* (Hutchinson: London, 1962)

R. Marchand, *Les Agissements des Alliés contre la révolution russe: le témoignage d'un bourgeois français* (n.p., 1918)

R. Marchand, *Allied Agents in Russia: Complete Text of the Letter of M. René Marchand, Petrograd Correspondent of 'Le Figaro' to M. Poincaré, President of the French Republic, September 1918* (The People's Russian Information Bureau: London, c. 1918)

R. Marchand, *Pourquoi je me suis rallié à la formule de la révolution sociale* (Édition de l'Internationale Communiste: Petrograd, 1919)

R. Marchand, *Why I Side with the Social Revolution* (Pub. Office of the Communist International: Petrograd, 1920)

R. Marchand, *Why I Support Bolshevism* (British Socialist Party: London, 1919)

D. Marquand, *Ramsay MacDonald* (Jonathan Cape: London, 1977)

A. Marty, *La Révolte de la Mer Noire*, vol. 2 (F. Maspero: Paris, 1970)

V. A. Mau, *Sochineniya*, vol. 1: *Reformy i dogmy: gosudarstvo i ekonomika v epokhu reform i revolyutsii, 1860–1920-e gody* (Delo: Moscow, 2010)

W. S. Maugham, *Ashenden* (Heinemann: London, 1928)

P. Miliukov, *Bolshevism: An International Danger, its Doctrine and its Practice through War and Revolution* (George Allen & Unwin: London, 1919)

V. P. Milyutin, *Sovremennoe ekonomicheskoe razvitie Rossii i diktatura proletariata (1914–1918 g.g.)* (Izd. VTsIK R., S., K. i K. Deputatov: Moscow, 1918)

Mirnye peregovory v Brest-Litovske, vol. 1: *Plenarnye zasedaniya. Zasedaniya Politicheskoi Komissii*, ed. A. A. Ioffe [V. Krymskii] (Izd. NKID: Moscow, 1920)

C. Nabokoff, *The Ordeal of a Diplomat* (Duckworth: London, 1921)

L. Naudeau, *En prison sous la terreur russe* (Librairie Hachette: Paris, 1920)

J. P. Nettl, *Rosa Luxemburg*, vols 1–2 (Oxford University Press: Oxford, 1966)

(H. Nicolson), *The Harold Nicolson Diaries: 1907–1963* (Weidenfeld & Nicolson: London, 2004)

Général Niessel, *Le Triomphe des bolchéviks et la paix de Brest-Litovsk: souvenirs, 1917–1918* (Librairie Plon: Paris, 1940)

J. Noulens, *Mon ambassade en Russie Soviétique, 1917–1919*, vols 1–2 (Librairie Plon: Paris, 1933)

G. Nowik, *Zanim złamano =,Enigme". Polski radiowywiad podczas wojny z bolszewicka Rosja 1918–1920* (Rytm: Warsaw, 2004)

M. Occleshaw, *Dances in Deep Shadows: The Clandestine War in Russia, 1917–20* (Carroll & Graf: New York, 2006)

The Papers of Woodrow Wilson, 1856–1924, ed. A. S. Link, vols 1–69 (Princeton University Press: Princeton, 1966–94)

B. Pares, *My Russian Memoirs* (Jonathan Cape: London, 1931)

B. Patenaude, *The Big Show in Bololand: The American Relief Expedition to Soviet Russia in the Famine of 1921* (Stanford University Press: Stanford, CA, 2002)

B. Pearce, *How Haig Saved Lenin* (Macmillan: London, 1987)

Pervyi Kongress Kominterna. Mart 1919 godu (Partiinoe izdatel'stvo: Moscow, 1919)

Pervyi Kongress Kominterna. Mart 1919 goda, ed. E. Korotkii, B. Kun and O. Pyatnitskii (Partiinoe izdatel'stvo: Moscow, 1933)

M. Philips Price (ed.), *The Diplomatic History of the War* (George Allen & Unwin: London, 1914)

M. Philips Price, *My Three Revolutions* (George Allen & Unwin: London, 1969)

M. Philips Price, 'Note', *Soviet Studies*, no. 4 (1952)

M. Philips Price, *The Soviet, the Terror and Intervention* (The Socialist Publication Society: Brooklyn, NY, 1918)

P. S. Pinheiro, *Estratégias da Ilusão: a Revolução Mundial e o Brasil, 1922–1935* (Companhia das Letras: São Paulo, 1991)

A. Poliakoff (with D. Sacks), *The Silver Samovar: Reminiscences of the Russian Revolution* (Atlantida Press: Nottingham, 1996)

Politbyuro TsK RKP(b)—VKP(b) i Komintern, 1918–1943. Dokumenty (Rosspen: Moscow, 2004)

R. Polonsky, *Molotov's Magic Lantern: A Journey in Russian History* (Faber & Faber: London, 2010)

H. T. Price, *Boche and Bolshevik: Experiences of an Englishman in the German Army and Russian Prisons* (John Murray: London, 1919)

Protokoly Tsentral'nogo Komiteta RSDRP(b): avgust 1917–fevral' 1918 (Gosizdat: Moscow, 1958)

R. Quinault, 'Churchill and Russia', *War and Society*, no. 1 (1991)

K. Radek, 'Noyabr'. (Stranichka iz vospominanii)', *Krasnaya nov'*, no. 10 (1926)

Radek and Ransome on Russia (The Socialist Publication Society: Brooklyn, NY, 1918)

Princess Catherine Radziwill, *The Firebrand of Bolshevism: The True Story of the Bolsheviki and the Forces that Directed Them* (Small, Maynard: Boston, 1919)

A. Ransome, *The Autobiography of Arthur Ransome*, ed. R. Hart-Davis (Jonathan Cape: London, 1976)

A. Ransome, *The Crisis in Russia* (B. W. Huebsch: New York, 1921)

A. Ransome, *Racundra's First Cruise* (B. W. Huebsch: New York, 1923)

A. Ransome, *Russia in 1919* (B. W. Huebsch: New York, 1919)

A. Ransome, *The Truth about Russia* (Workers' Socialist Federation: London, 1918)

H. Rappaport, *Ekaterinburg: The Last Days of the Romanovs* (Hutchinson: London, 2008)

D. Rayfield, *Stalin and his Hangmen: An Authoritative Portrait of a Tyrant and Those Who Served Him* (Viking: London, 2004)

J. Reed, *Red Russia*, books 1–2 (Workers' Socialist Federation: London, 1919)

J. Reed, *Ten Days that Shook the World* (Boni & Liveright: New York, 1919)

J. Reed, *Ten Days that Shook the World* (Boni & Liveright: New York, 1922)

S. G. Reilly and Pepita Bobadilla, *The Adventures of Sidney Reilly, Britain's Master Spy* (E. Mathews & Marrot: London, 1931)

Relations with Russia: Hearing before the Committee on Foreign Relations, United States Senate. Sixty-Sixth Congress, Third Session (Government Printing Office: Washington, DC, 1921)

Dzh. Rid, *10 dnei, kotorye potryasli mir* (2nd corrected edn; Krasnaya nov': Moscow, 1924)

L. de Robien, *The Diary of a Diplomat in Russia* (Michael Joseph: London, 1969)

K. Rose, *King George V* (Weidenfeld & Nicolson: London, 1983)

W. G. Rosenberg, *Liberals in the Russian Revolution: The Constitutional Democratic Party, 1917–1921* (Princeton University Press: Princeton, 1974)

I. S. Rozental, *Provokator. Roman Malinovskii: sud'ba i vremya* (Rosspen: Moscow, 1996)

B. Russell, *The Autobiography of Bertrand Russell, 1914–1944* (Little, Brown: Boston, 1968)

B. Russell, *The Practice and Theory of Bolshevism* (George Allen & Unwin: London, 1920)

W. F. Ryan, 'The Great Beast in Russia: Aleister Crowley's Theatrical Tour in 1913 and his Beastly Writings on Russia', in A. McMillin (ed.), *Symbolism and After: Essays on Russian Poetry in Honour of Georgette Donchin* (Bristol Classical Press: London, 1992)

A. J. Sack, *America's Possible Share in the Economic Future of Russia* (Russian Information Bureau in the US: New York, 1919)

A. J. Sack, *The Birth of Russian Democracy* (Russian Information Bureau: New York, 1918)

J. Sadoul, 'La Condition des agents consulaires et diplomatiques au point de vue fiscal: thèse pour le doctorat' (Librairie Générale de Droit et de Jurisprudence: Paris, 1908)

J. Sadoul, *Notes sur la révolution bolchévique, octobre 1917–janvier 1919*, Preface by H. Barbusse (Sirène: Paris, 1920)

N. V. Salzman, *Reform and Revolution: The Life and Times of Raymond Robins* (Kent State University Press: Kent, OH, 1991)

N. V. Salzman, *Russia in War and Revolution: General William V. Judson's Accounts from Petrograd, 1917–1918* (Kent State University Press: Kent, OH, 1998)

O. M. Sayler, *Russia White or Red* (Little, Brown: Boston, 1919)

A. E. Senn, *Diplomacy and Revolution: The Soviet Mission to Switzerland, 1918* (University of Notre Dame Press: Notre Dame, IN, 1974)

A. E. Senn, *The Russian Revolution in Switzerland, 1914–1917* (University of Wisconsin Press: London, 1971)

V. Serge, *Memoirs of a Revolutionary, 1901–1941* (Oxford University Press: London, 1967)

R. Service, *The Bolshevik Party in Revolution: A Study in Organisational Change* (Macmillan: London, 1979)

R. Service, *Lenin. A Biography* (Macmillan: London, 2000)

R. Service, *Lenin: A Political Life*, vols 1–3 (Macmillan: London, 1985–95)

R. Service, *The Russian Revolution, 1900–1927* (4th revised edn; Palgrave Macmillan: London, 2009)

R. Service, *Trotsky: A Biography* (Macmillan: London, 2009)

G. N. Sevast'yanov, J. Haslam and others (eds), *Sovetsko-amerikanskie otnosheniya: gody nepriznaniya, 1918–1926* (Mezhdunarodnyi fond Demokratiya: Moscow, 2002)

C. Seymour (ed.), *The Intimate Papers of Colonel House: Into the World War* (Houghton Mifflin: Boston, 1928)

C. Sheridan, *From Mayfair to Moscow: Clare Sheridan's Diary* (Boni & Liveright: New York, 1921)

C. Sheridan, *Naked Truth* (Harper & Brothers: New York, 1928)

H. Shukman, *War or Revolution: Russian Jews and Conscription in Britain, 1917* (Vallentine Mitchell: London, 2006)

E. Sisson, *One Hundred Red Days: A Personal Chronicle of the Bolshevik Revolution* (Yale University Press: New Haven, 1931)

M. Smith, *Six: A History of Britain's Secret Intelligence Service*, part 1: *Murder and Mayhem, 1909–1939* (Dialogue: London, 2010)

Mrs P. Snowden, *A Pilgrim in Europe* (George H. Doran: New York, 1921)

Mrs P. Snowden, *Through Bolshevik Russia* (Cassell: London, 1920)

'*Sovershenno lichno i doveritel'no!*': B. A. Bakhmetev–V. A. Maklakov: perepiska, vol. 1, ed. O. V. Budnitskii (Rosspen: Moscow, and Hoover Institution: Stanford, 2001)

J. Spargo, *Bolshevism: The Enemy of Political and Industrial Democracy* (Harper & Brothers: New York, 1919)

J. Spargo, *The Greatest Failure in History: A Critical Examination of the Actual Workings of Bolshevism in Russia* (Harper & Brothers: New York, 1920)

J. Spargo, *Russia as an American Problem* (Harper & Brothers: New York, 1920)

R. B. Spence, *Secret Agent 666: Aleister Crowley, British Intelligence and the Occult* (Feral House: Port Townsend, WA, 2008)

R. B. Spence, 'The Tragic Fate of Kalamatiano: America's Man in Moscow', *International Journal of Intelligence and Counterintelligence*, no. 3 (1999)

R. B. Spence, *Trust No One: The Secret Life of Sidney Reilly* (Feral House: Port Townsend, WA, 2002)

P. Spriano, *L'occupazione delle fabbriche. Settembre 1920* (Einaudi: Turin, 1964)

Z. Steiner, *The Lights that Failed: European International History, 1919–1933* (Oxford University Press: Oxford, 2005)

H. Strachan, *The First World War: A New Illustrated History* (Simon & Schuster: London, 2003)

A. L. Strong, *The First Time in History: Two Years of Russia's New Life* (Boni & Liveright: New York, 1924)

N. Sukhanov, *Zapiski o revolyutsii. V 3-kh tomakh*, books 1–7 (Politizdat: Moscow, 1991)

G. Swain, 'Before the Fighting Started: A Discussion on the Theme of the "Third Way"', *Revolutionary Russia*, no. 2 (1991)

G. Swain, 'The Disillusioning of the Revolution's Praetorian Guard: The Latvian Riflemen, Summer–Autumn 1918', *Europe-Asia Studies*, no. 4 (1999)

G. Swain, '"An Interesting and Plausible Proposal": Bruce Lockhart, Sidney Reilly and the Latvian Riflemen, Russia 1918', *Intelligence and National Security*, no. 3 (1999)

G. Swain, 'Maugham, Masaryk and the "Mensheviks"', *Revolutionary Russia*, no. 1 (1994)

G. Swain, *The Origins of the Russian Civil War* (Longman: London, 1996)

G. Swain, 'Russia's Garibaldi: The Revolutionary Life of Mikhail Artemevich Muraviev', *Revolutionary Russia*, no. 2 (1998)

G. Swain, 'Vacietis: The Enigma of the Red Army's First Commander', *Revolutionary Russia*, no. 1 (2003)

A. Tardieu, *La Paix* (Payot: London, 1921)

B. Thomson, *Queer People* (Hodder & Stoughton: London, 1922)

L. Trotskii, *Chto zhe dal'she? (Itogi i perspektivy)* (Priboi: Petersburg [*sic*], 1917)

L. Trotskii, *Dnevniki i pis'ma*, ed. Yu. Fel'shtinskii (Ermitazh: Tenafly, NJ, 1986)

L. Trotskii, *Moya zhizn': opyt avtobiografii*, vols 1–2 (Granit: Berlin, 1930)

L. Trotskii, *Petlya vmesto khleba* (Penza Gubkom RKP: Penza, 1921)

L. Trotskii, *Rech' t. Trotskogo na massovom mitinge v gor. Gomele, 10 maya 1920 g.* (Gomel'skii gubernskii komitet: Gomel, 1920)

L. Trotskii, *Sochineniya*, vols 2–21 (Gosizdat: Moscow, 1924–7)

The Trotsky Papers, vols 1–2, ed. J. M. Meijer (Mouton: The Hague, 1964–71)

S. Tsvigun (ed.), *Lenin i VChK* (Gosizdat: Moscow, 1972)

T. Tzouliadis, *The Forsaken: From the Great Depression to the Gulags—Hope and Betrayal in Stalin's Russia* (Penguin Press: New York, 2008)

R. H. Ullman, *Anglo-Soviet Relations, 1917–1921* (Princeton University Press: Princeton, NJ), vol. 1: *Intervention and the War* (1961); vol. 2: *Britain and the Russian Civil War, November 1918–February 1920* (1968); vol. 3: *The Anglo-Soviet Accord* (1972)

M. Ustinov, 'Svoevremennye mysli', in S. Rudakov (ed.), *Vokrug moskovskikh sobytii* (Revolyutsionnyi sotsializm: Moscow, 1918)

W. B. Vanderlip (with H. B. Hulbert), *In Search of a Siberian Klondike* (The Century Co.: New York, 1903)

A. Vatlin, *Komintern: idei, resheniya, sud'by* (Rosspen: Moscow, 2009)

R. Vaucher, *L'Enfer bolchévik à Petrograd sous la commune et la terreur rouge* (Perrin: Paris, 1919)

A. Venturi, *Rivoluzionari russi in Italia, 1917–1921* (Feltrinelli: Milan, 1979)

C. J. Vopicka, *Secrets of the Balkans: Seven Years of a Diplomatist's Life in the Storm Centre of Europe* (Rand McNally: Chicago, 1921)

H. Weber, *La trasformazione del comunismo tedesco: la stalinizzazione della KPD nella Repubblica di Weimar* (Feltrinelli: Milan, 1979)

F. Welch, *The Romanovs and Mr Gibbes* (Short: London, 2002)

H. G. Wells, *Russia in the Shadows* (H. G. Doran: London, 1921)

S. White, *Britain and the Bolshevik Revolution: A Study in the Politics of Diplomacy* (Macmillan: London, 1979)

S. White, 'British Labour in Soviet Russia, 1920', *English Historical Review*, vol. 109 (1994)

G. Williams, *The First Congress of the Red Trade Union International, 1921* (Industrial Workers of the World: Chicago, 1921)

A. Rhys Williams, *Lenin: The Man and his Work* (Scott & Selzer: New York, 1919)

Winston S. Churchill: Companion, ed. M. Gilbert, vol. 4 (Heinemann: London, 1977)

P. Winterton, *A Student in Russia* (The Co-operative Union: Manchester, 1931)

B. D. Wolfe, *Strange Communists I Have Known* (Stein & Day: New York, 1965)

P. Wright, *From Stage to Cold War* (Oxford University Press: Oxford, 2007)

Z. A. Zeman, *Germany and the Revolution in Russia, 1915–1918: Documents from the Archives of the German Foreign Ministry* (Oxford University Press: Oxford, 1958)

N. Zubov, *F. E. Dzerzhinskii: biografiya* (3rd edn; Politizdat: Moscow, 1971)

INDEX

*Page references in **bold** type denote complete chapters.*

Aberdeen, 16, 44, 101
Adler, Alfred, 96
agriculture: and American help for, 207;
    Bolshevik policies for, 310, 321; in
    Germany, 68; Keynes's economic view
    of, 266; and Lenin, 252–3; machinery
    for, imported by Russia, 232–3, 250;
    New Economic Policy, 310; peasant
    hostility to seizure of produce,
    309–10; and peasant reluctance to sell
    produce, 30; and peasant village
    communes, 24; and Trotsky, 318; Yuri
    Larin and 'urbanization' of, 68
Albert Hall, London, 14, 273
Alexandra, Empress, 29, 120, 121
Alexandrinski theatre, Petrograd, 23
Alexandrovich, V. A., 125
Alexeev, Mikhail, 118, 123, 151, 180
Alexinski, Grigori, 16, 326
Allen, Clifford, 269, 272
Alley, Stephen, 103, 146–7, 259
Allied Drug and Chemical Corporation, 323
Allied Supreme Council, *see* Supreme
    Council (of Allies)
All-Russia Congress of POW
    Internationalists, 116
Altvater, Admiral, 96
American Railway Mission to Russia, 78, 107
American Red Cross, 40–1
American Relief Administration, 198,
    206–7, 266, 324–5, 326, 327
Anatolia, 58

Anet, Claude, 73
Anglo-Soviet trade treaty: 4, 7, 255;
    British terms for, 298, 301–2, 307–8,
    311; negotiations, 252, 253–4; timing
    of, 312, 318
Antaeus Export and Import Company, 233
anti-Bolsheviks: anger at liaison between
    Reds and Allies, 109; in Britain, 259,
    263; coalition of politicians in Russia,
    118; Congress in Warsaw, 325;
    diplomatic roles, 123; majority in
    Constituent Assembly, 89; press
    reports, 30; Provisional Government
    and, 28; Socialist-Revolutionary
    government, 275; *see also* Volunteer
    Army; Western Allies; White forces
Antonov, A. S., 309
'April Theses' (Lenin), 19, 26
Archangel: Allied occupation of, 128, 137,
    138–9; Allied occupation of: and
    Lockhart, 151; Bolshevik plan for
    German attack on, 140, 143; British
    plan to overthrow Soviet in, 126;
    evacuation of Allied troops from, 212,
    248; importance as international port,
    137
Armand, Inessa, 19
Armstrong Whitworth, 251–2
Association Financière, Industrielle et
    Commerciale Russe, 326
Austria: and armistice, 168; Army of,
    102–3; and blockade of river Danube,
    205; and Bolshevik propaganda,
    59–60; diplomats of, in Petrograd, 78;
    discontent in, 35; ex-prisoners of war
    of, 117, 170; military and diplomatic

Robert Service is a British historian, academic, and author who has written extensively on the history of Soviet Russia, particularly the era from the October Revolution to Stalin's death. He is currently a professor of Russian history at the University of Oxford, a Fellow of St. Antony's College, Oxford, and a senior fellow at Stanford University's Hoover Institution.

PublicAffairs is a publishing house founded in 1997. It is a tribute to the standards, values, and flair of three persons who have served as mentors to countless reporters, writers, editors, and book people of all kinds, including me.

I. F. STONE, proprietor of *I. F. Stone's Weekly*, combined a commitment to the First Amendment with entrepreneurial zeal and reporting skill and became one of the great independent journalists in American history. At the age of eighty, Izzy published *The Trial of Socrates*, which was a national bestseller. He wrote the book after he taught himself ancient Greek.

BENJAMIN C. BRADLEE was for nearly thirty years the charismatic editorial leader of *The Washington Post*. It was Ben who gave the *Post* the range and courage to pursue such historic issues as Watergate. He supported his reporters with a tenacity that made them fearless and it is no accident that so many became authors of influential, best-selling books.

ROBERT L. BERNSTEIN, the chief executive of Random House for more than a quarter century, guided one of the nation's premier publishing houses. Bob was personally responsible for many books of political dissent and argument that challenged tyranny around the globe. He is also the founder and longtime chair of Human Rights Watch, one of the most respected human rights organizations in the world.

·   ·   ·

For fifty years, the banner of Public Affairs Press was carried by its owner Morris B. Schnapper, who published Gandhi, Nasser, Toynbee, Truman, and about 1,500 other authors. In 1983, Schnapper was described by *The Washington Post* as "a redoubtable gadfly." His legacy will endure in the books to come.

Peter Osnos, *Founder and Editor-at-Large*